Reading Lucan's *Civil War*

Oklahoma Series in Classical Culture

Reading Lucan's *Civil War*
A Critical Guide

Edited by
PAUL ROCHE

UNIVERSITY OF OKLAHOMA PRESS : NORMAN

Library of Congress Cataloging-in-Publication Data

Names: Roche, P. A. (Paul A.), author.
Title: Reading Lucan's Civil war : a critical guide / edited by Paul Roche.
Description: Norman : University of Oklahoma Press, [2021] |
    Series: Oklahoma series in classical culture ; 62 | Includes bibliographical
    references. | Summary: "Critical guide of essays which explore the war
    between Julius Caesar and the forces of the republican senate from
    Lucan's epic poem, The Civil War"—Provided by publisher.
Identifiers: LCCN 2021012570 | ISBN 978-0-8061-6939-2 (paperback ; alk. paper)
Subjects: LCSH: Lucan, 39–65. Pharsalia. | Rome—History—Civil War,
    49–45 B.C.—Literature and the war. | BISAC: FOREIGN LANGUAGE
    STUDY / Latin | HISTORY / Europe / Italy | LCGFT: Literary criticism.
Classification: LCC PA6480 .R63 2021 | DDC 873/.01—dc23
LC record available at https://lccn.loc.gov/2021012570

Reading Lucan's Civil War: *A Critical Guide* is Volume 62 in the Oklahoma Series in
Classical Culture.

Contents

Preface

This volume of essays aims to introduce as wide an audience as possible to Lucan's epic poem, the *Civil War* (in Latin, *Bellum Ciuile* or *De Bello Ciuili*, and occasionally referred to as the *Pharsalia*). Its purpose is to offer a critical guide to the poem, particularly for those who may be reading it in an English translation, and to provide its readers with adaptable frameworks for understanding this remarkable work of literature. Lucan has now definitively emerged from a period of being undervalued in the Anglophone world. Our re-evaluation of him began in the late 1960s and made considerable advances in clusters of seminal studies in the mid-1970s, mid to late 1980s, and early to mid-1990s. Lucan's *Civil War* now enjoys a firmly established reputation among critics as one of the greatest literary achievements of the Roman empire. As a result of this, Lucan now regularly appears on undergraduate and postgraduate curricula in universities throughout the world. Moreover, because of the wide availability of high-quality translations of the poem, Lucan is now taught in translation much more commonly than ever before in courses treating Nero and Neronian culture, the culture of the Roman empire, and ancient literature. I hope, then, that there is a real need for an up-to-date, one-volume, accessible guide to the poem, written by experts and offering stimulating and original readings of the poem in its entirety.

This volume comprises a sequence of essays on each individual book followed by five further chapters on key themes arcing across the whole epic. I hope that it will prove accessible to new readers of Lucan. To this end, all Latin and Greek terms used in the book are translated or explained, and a glossary of important or specialized terms used is included. The model adapted for this volume is that of the highly effective collection of essays edited by Christine Perkell, *Reading Vergil's Aeneid: An Interpretive Guide,* published by the University of Oklahoma Press in 1999. It was this model that also suggested the University of Oklahoma as the ideal press to publish the present volume.

It is a great pleasure to express my deep gratitude to the contributors of this volume for their generosity in agreeing to share their expertise and for their patience as the volume came together. I would like to thank Lindsay Holman of the Ancient World Mapping Center for his help with the map that appears in this volume. Thanks go to Emma Barlow for her editorial assistance and to the two anonymous press readers for their feedback on the draft manuscript. I also want to express my gratitude to Eva Silverfine for her excellent copyediting of the manuscript and to to Stephanie Attia Evans for guiding the volume through the production process. Finally, I am very grateful to Ellen Greene for her encouragement and to Alessandra Tamulevich for her support and advice over the course of this project.

Unless stated otherwise, the Latin text of Lucan used in the chapters of this volume is that of Housman (1926) with the orthography modernized (e.g., consonantal *v* changed to *u*), and all inset quotations from the poem are accompanied by Susanna Braund's very accurate and readable 1992 translation. Unless listed below, author abbreviations follow the conventions of the *Oxford Classical Dictionary.*

Aug. *RGDA*	*The Achievements of the Divine Augustus* (*Res Gestae Diui Augusti*)
OLD	P. G. W. Glare, ed., *Oxford Latin Dictionary* (Oxford, 1982)
Sen. *Pol.*	Seneca, *Consolation to Polybius*
TLL	*Thesaurus Linguae Latinae* (Leipzig, 1900–)
Vita Persi	Probus, *Life of Persius* (in the edition of Rostagni, 1944)

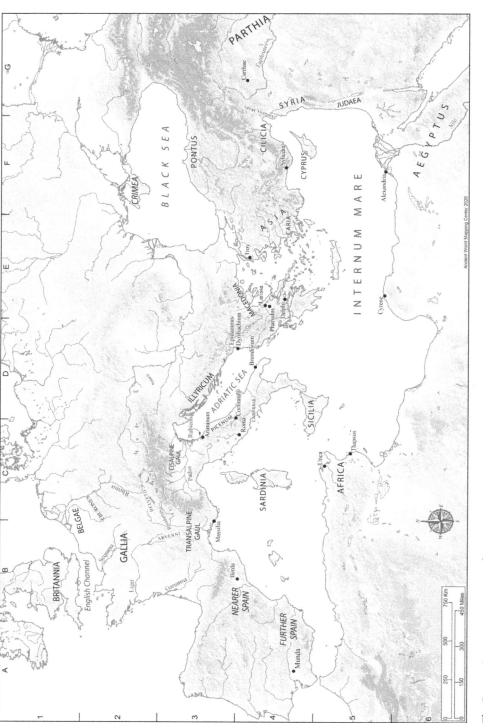

The Roman Empire: Campaigns of Caesar, Crassus, and Pompey, 58–45 B.C.E. Ancient World Mapping Center © 2021 (awmc.unc.edu).

Used by permission.

Introduction

Reading Lucan's Civil War

PAUL ROCHE

> be prepared for rage
> —Robert Frost, *Once by the Pacific*

Life and Death

The poet Lucan committed suicide in the aftermath of a failed conspiracy against the emperor Nero in April 65 C.E.[1] Much of our information on his brief life is preserved in two Latin biographies. One, by Suetonius, was originally written at some point between 107 and 118 and is preserved in the *Commenta Bernensia*.[2] The other is attributed to a certain "Vacca" (of unknown date, perhaps as early as the fifth century) and is preserved in manuscripts dated to between the tenth and twelfth centuries. We should be skeptical about the reliability of the information in this much later biography and aware more generally of the often dubious reliability of ancient poets' lives.[3] These sources tell us that Lucan was born in Cordoba, Spain, on November 3, 39, and was brought as an infant to Rome, where he was taught philosophy and excelled in the highly rhetorical education there on offer to young Roman aristocrats. He began to draw attention for his precocious rhetorical and literary talent in the same period in which his family ascended to political prominence under the patronage of Nero's mother, Agrippina the Younger. Lucan's uncle, Seneca the Younger, had been appointed as Nero's tutor in 49 and enjoyed great influence in the early years of Nero's principate;[4] in 59 Lucan was recalled by the emperor from Athens, where he had gone to further his education (a move typical of his class). At

1

Rome Lucan became an intimate friend of the emperor; he won a prize for his first public performance, a poem in praise of Nero, which he recited at the Neronia in 60. Lucan became a prominent member of the gilded youth of Nero's Rome and one of the brightest literary stars at the emperor's court. He was favored with public roles as well, becoming both quaestor and augur. In the five years from his recall to his death, a prodigious outpouring of literary works is attested, of which only fragments and our ten books of the *Civil War* survive.[5] Lucan's talent soon aroused the emperor's jealousy, and relations between Nero and Lucan declined to the point of the emperor banning him from reciting his work and from speaking in the law courts. We are told in Vacca's life that Lucan had published three books of the epic "such as we now see them" before the ban.[6] In April 65 Lucan joined the Pisonian Conspiracy. Suetonius writes that Lucan was "almost its standard bearer" (*paene signifer*), a phrase that sounds like it attributes a prominent role in the plot to Lucan but most probably indicates that he was the most famous of the conspirators.

The circumstances of Lucan's death resonate so compellingly with the stridently anti-imperial sentiments given voice in the *Civil War* that the poem's invocation of the emperor Nero (1.33–66; quoted and discussed on pages 216–18) has become one of the perennially debated moments in the epic.[7] A number of approaches are available. For some the passage is a positive and sincere remnant of an earlier warm relationship enjoyed between Nero and Lucan. This reading is often joined to Vacca's testimony that Lucan published three books before the ban (the first three are assumed) and takes books one to three as being more positively disposed to Nero or the principate more generally.[8] For others the contrast between the panegyric of Nero and the despairing voice predominating in the narrative has encouraged an ironic reading of the dedication. This interpretation goes back as far as Lucan's late-antique commentators, who read a number of the panegyric's details as lampooning the emperor's physical shortcomings: his squint and his obesity, for example (cf. Suet. *Nero* 51). But the match between Nero's dim sight in Suetonius and the squint seen by some at 1.55 is not exact, and Michael Dewar has shown in an important article how the praise of Nero is completely typical of the extravagant conventions of encomia encountered in imperial culture.[9] If readers are inclined to divest the invocation to Nero of its sincerity, it may be better to take the passage in its totality as magnificently sardonic rather than petulantly humorous: there is certainly nothing in the epic that chimes with Lucan's profession that it was all worth it for Nero (1.37–38).[10] Moreover, Lucan's adoption of Nero rather than the Muses as his poetic inspiration (1.63–66; cf., e.g., Verg. *Aen.* 1.8–11) is shown throughout the poem to be unworkable in traditional terms: Nero is a poor substitute for the real thing because he does not have access to the Muses' memory (the poetic point of invoking them). For this reason, the narrator is not privy to the true causes of events. It is in any case important to be wary of reconstructing Lucan's politics from his biography. The conspiracy in which he died was not one devoted to restoring liberty or the republic but merely to replacing Nero with a more agreeable emperor. Tacitus's account makes clear that Piso was very much a product of the Neronian age (*Ann.* 15.48), that he was himself no champion of liberty, and that the conspirators worked hard to avoid having their momentum usurped by more ideologically driven senators who might actually try to restore the republic (15.52).

Scope and End

The *Civil War* shows every sign of being unfinished. Books 1 to 8 of the poem average 800 lines in length, but book 9 is uncharacteristically long (1,108 lines) and book 10 is uncharacteristically short (546 lines): longer and shorter, respectively, and deviating more from the poem's average book length than does any single book of the *Aeneid* or the *Metamorphoses*. Book 10, moreover, ends abruptly in the middle of an unresolved battle narrative, with Caesar yet to defeat his republican opponents, a major protagonist (Cato) still alive, and an important historical encounter between Caesar and the republicans, the Battle of Thapsus, visible on the horizon. The poem moves to its ending in a way that looks unlike any demonstrably or substantially finished epic, such as the *Aeneid*, the *Metamorphoses*, or Statius's *Thebaid*, and the epilogue itself looks nothing like an ancient sphragis, or "seal," placed at the end of a work of literature (cf. Ov. *Met.* 15.871–79 or Stat. *Theb.* 12.810–19). Moreover, antiquity offered up no model or example of a work of literature cut short deliberately by its author so as to imply an unfinished state.[11]

The question of where or when the poem was designed to end is compelling and important to ask but impossible to answer definitively, although there are more and less probable options. The most common scholarly view is that Lucan intended to end with Cato's suicide after the Battle of Thapsus.[12] This would then become in the poem (as it was in imperial culture) a heavily freighted symbol of the death of liberty. It would also cohere with the rhetoric of both Cato and the narrator throughout the poem regarding his significance as an opponent of Caesar and his association with freedom (e.g., 2.306–19, 9.24–30).[13] It would further work well if the poem were planned as a twelve-book epic on the model of Vergil's *Aeneid*, since Aeneas's killing of Turnus at the end of the *Aeneid* 12 offers an obvious, authoritative model ripe for subversion.[14] Book 10 ends in November 48. If we assume a twelve-book narrative, the Battle of

Thapsus, fought on April 6, 46, would be fairly easy to reach in two and a half books of narrative, and this would also give an overall structure developing in four-book panels ending with increasingly significant deaths (book 4: Curio; book 8: Pompey; book 12: Cato). A number of other possible end points have been suggested: the death of Caesar, the Battle of Philippi, and the Battle of Actium.[15] These are less convincing because they variously assume a disproportionately long epic, an epic with a disproportionate attention to the first twenty months of the civil war (i.e., our surviving poem), the introduction of a new cast of characters, events that come very close to repeating what Lucan has already narrated (the Battle of Philippi, Antony in Egypt with Cleopatra), or a political point of view that is pro-Neronian or pro-imperial. The least commonly expressed view is that the poem is finished as we have it.[16] This view often stresses the coincidence of Caesar's civil war commentaries breaking off at the same moment, it stresses the vulnerability of Lucan's Caesar at the end of the poem, it points to internal models of inconclusive narratives, such as Acoreus's speech to Caesar, and it argues that the ending furthers the poem's theme of the endlessness of civil war. This volume of essays will assume that the poem is unfinished.

The Narrating Voice

Much can be learned about the narrator of the poem from its opening.[17] The *Civil War* begins by haranguing us. A comparison with the opening of the *Aeneid* sets in contrast the highly emotional tone as well as the outwardly turned, "public" (that is, political) orientation of the voice narrating the *Civil War*. Vergil begins by sketching the characteristics of his hero as well as the plot and historical significance of his epic: warfare (*arma*) and a hero (*uirumque*) who originates in Troy and travels to Italy as an exile, afflicted on land, on sea, and in war because of the violence of the gods and the special enmity of Juno. That his suffering has meaning is also made clear: he will establish a city in Latium into which he will transfer his gods, and from there will come the Latin race, the Alban fathers, and the walls of Rome (*Aen.* 1.1–7). Lucan's proem, by contrast, stays elusive on the specific details of his plot, with the exceptions that "wars across Emathian plains" (1.1) points to the Battle of Pharsalus, fought between Caesar and Pompey in Emathia in Greece (and narrated in book 7), and "the pact of tyranny . . . broken" (1.4) alludes to the breakdown of the "triumvirate" between Caesar, Pompey, and Crassus (cited as a cause of the war at 1.84–93). Instead, his proem makes multiple attempts to drum into his audience the moral rather than the historical meaning of the civil war in phrases of varying metaphor and abstraction: legality conferred on crime (1.2), suicide (1.2–4), kin killing (1.4), world war (1.5), universal guilt (1.6), Roman weapons ranged against Roman weapons (1.6–7). The first seven lines favor a superfluity, an excess of expression catching at the true horror of the poem's subject rather than the kind of economy of expression found in earlier epic openings.

Where Vergil turns to the Muses to ask the causes of Aeneas's suffering (*Aen.* 1.8–11), Lucan's narrator turns to the collective citizenry of Rome to censure them. His term of address for them, *Quirites,* suggests him as an orator in the Forum, addressing the people on a subject of public importance. The tone is accusatory and expansive: this is not a narrator aspiring to Vergil's "superbly economical power," as we will surely realize by the end of the poem's enormous introduction, running to 182 lines (cf. Vergil's 11 lines).[18] Blame for the war is laid squarely at their feet: "What madness was this? . . . [D]id it please you to wage wars . . . ? . . . [I]f you had such a love of impious warfare . . . you did not yet lack an enemy" (1.8–23). Later in the proem he attributes the war to the Fates and Fortune (1.33–37, 70, 84, the two are very frequently confounded in our poem); the triumvirate (1.84–97) and the deaths of Crassus and Julia (1.103–6, 119–20); the nature and characteristics of Caesar and Pompey (1.129–57); and to the diminished public morality at Rome in the generations after it acquired its world empire (1.158–82). The angry, accusatory tone, the searching for blame, the struggle to convey the devastating consequences and losses incurred by Rome as a result of the war, the multiple metaphors attempting to capture its true significance (suicide, madness, implosion, cataclysm, inundation) will establish themselves as typical of the voice that narrates the poem. This superfluity of expression sits alongside of, and in some respects tries to compensate for, the obstructed, non-omniscient point of view from which the narrator tells his story.

Lucan's narrator is everywhere present in his poem in a manner that is atypical of epic conventions. Whereas the narrators in Homer and Vergil tend to stay invisible in their narratives, to "show" rather than "tell," Lucan's insists on intervening, on commenting, on expressing disbelief, and on calling down curses on his characters.[19] A significant part of the poem's unique energy comes from the narrator's self-described stance on the wrong side of history: he hates Caesar but commits himself to narrating his irresistible rise to power. On the other hand, he claims that his poem will make its readers favor Pompey while he ruthlessly exposes that man's shortcomings; he venerates Cato while he portrays in him a rigid Stoic orthodoxy that is contravened by his entry into the war and then appears to be both as inhuman as Caesar's ambition and out of touch with the disintegrating world he inhabits.

The very first line of the poem blurs the distinction between paradox and hyperbole and signals the fundamental importance of these two modes of expression for Lucan's narrator. Is it (merely) an exaggeration to say that the wars were "more than civil" (*plus quam ciuilia*), or will the reader's contemplation of the phrase resolve its apparent illogicality that (these) wars can be "more" or "worse" than civil (perhaps especially in light of Cato's declaration that "[c]ivil war is the greatest crime [*summum nefas*]," 2.286)? We may take it, as many have done, as a reference to the relationship by marriage of Pompey and Caesar. Or we may read the phrase as denoting an escalation in intensity and consequences compared with the previous Roman civil wars, as the old man concludes at 2.227–32. Or we may interpret it as the first indication of the poem's overall aesthetic of hyperbole and transgressed boundaries, to be found, for example, in piled corpses damning rivers (2.209–20) and hiding plains (7.794–95), in the hyper-real quality of Scaeva's *aristeia* (6.138–262), or in the plague of snakes afflicting Cato's army in Libya (9.734–838). Throughout the poem Lucan's narrator seeks constantly to elicit the intellectual engagement of his audience in this way.

Caesar

The essential meaning and the basic character of Lucan's Caesar have been more consistently interpreted than those of his Pompey and Cato.[20] This, surely, is because Lucan's characterization of Caesar is at once so extreme and so consistent. We observe him, for example, delighting in the blood, destruction, and the continual warfare of his invasion of Italy (2.439–43). We read of him felling the first tree in an awe-inspiring, sacred grove, dreaded by the local population and by Caesar's soldiers alike;[21] they think they will be killed by their own axes in the attempt, but they follow his lead because Caesar's anger is more fearful to them than that of the gods (3.399–452). We see his contempt for the gods and his own megalomaniacal sense of self amid the sublime terror of a calamitous sea storm (5.560–677; cf. esp., "How mighty is the gods' toil to throw me down, attacking me with sea so great as I sit in a tiny boat!" 5.654–56). We are told he shatters mountains as he raises a siege wall to rival the walls of Troy or Babylon (6.29–63). He rages like Bellona and Mars at Pharsalus, and "sees his gods and fortune" in the carnage strewing the plain on the following day (7.567–70, 7.786–824).

All this chimes with the overreacher introduced in book 1: the never-resting energy; the irresistible, unceasing, amoral, and implacable will to power; the delight in causing destruction; the bolt of lightning that terrifies all, devastating earth and heaven alike (1.143–57). When later authors (in antiquity and beyond) adapt Lucan's Caesar, they offer us a clear view of their own reading of his character. We can see this, for example, in the tyrants of Statius's *Thebaid*, who look repeatedly to Lucan's Caesar as their model,[22] or the ruinous invading forces that threaten the state in Claudian's poetry,[23] or perhaps most evocatively, in the Satan whom we encounter in Milton's *Paradise Lost*. Satan mirrors Caesar as a "titanic actor on a cosmic stage";[24] he similarly captivates the imagination of an audience who should resist his evil and is even made to re-enact Caesar's Lucanian itinerary, such as the sea storm in book 5, a powerful model for Satan's crossing of chaos at *Paradise Lost* 2.910–1055.[25]

Milton's Satan, and the unbalancing effect his charisma has upon the epic in which he appears, may sharpen for us a dynamic in Lucan that was observed by Masters in 1992 and has been very influential since, namely that the poet was essentially conflicted about his creation. He is ideologically opposed to Caesar's victory and so hates his creation and seeks always to delay him, to obstruct or retard his success. At the same time, his claim to fame as a poet is intrinsically bound with Caesar's success, which is the subject matter and plot of the *Civil War*.[26] Lucan's animosity toward Caesar is normative throughout the poem; jarring in its variance and in the picture of their complicity is this apostrophe to Caesar in book 9:

> o sacer et magnus uatum labor! omnia fato
> eripis et populis donas mortalibus aeuum.
> inuidia sacrae, Caesar, ne tangere famae;
> nam, si quid Latiis fas est promittere Musis,
> quantum Zmyrnaei durabunt uatis honores,
> uenturi me teque legent; Pharsalia nostra
> uiuet, et a nullo tenebris damnabimur aeuo.
>   (9.980–86)

> O how sacred and immense the task of bards! You snatch everything
> from death and to mortals you give immortality.
> Caesar, do not be touched by envy of their sacred fame;
> since, if for Latian Muses it is right to promise anything,
> as long as honours of the Smyrnaean bard [i.e., Homer] endure,
> the future ages will read me and you; our Pharsalia
> shall live and we shall be condemned to darkness by no era.

The Caesar we are shown in book 10 shows some variation in character.[27] On the one hand, Caesar seems more vulnerable from the outset. He enters Alexandria "with his face always concealing fear" (10.14). His ceaseless forward energy comes to a standstill in an affair with Cleopatra (10.53–106): he is subject to her alluring power (10.71, passion devours him; cf. 137, her harmful beauty), lets the republican forces gather strength while he indulges in the relationship (10.79–80), and learns to squander riches (10.169). The nadir of his energy comes as he locks himself in the palace at the approach of Achillas's army (10.434–85): the palace is an ignoble hiding place (10.441), his anger is mixed with dread (10.443–44, 453), and he is compared first to a boy or a woman in a captured city, remaining in the safety of the house (10.458–59), and then to Medea waiting for her father (10.464–67). On the other hand, even in book 10 this new side of Caesar is balanced by more characteristic qualities. His intellectual energy has the same overreaching ambition as his military verve (10.181–92, cf. esp. his agonistic comparisons of himself to Plato or the declaration that his calendar will not be defeated by that of Eudoxus). By the time the palace is besieged (10.486–533), Caesar's restless energy is certainly back: "everywhere Caesar is present in defence" (10.488–89); he has such great firmness of mind that he does the work of a besieger (10.490–91); he takes the island of Pharos, "successful always in his use of headlong speed of warfare" (10.507–8).

Whether the picture of Caesar in acute crisis in the last thirteen lines of the poem (10.534–46) should be read as a part of the varied characterization in book 10 and perhaps as marking a shift in Caesar's overall presentation in the *Civil War*, as stressing the magnitude of Caesar's danger as a foil to his eventual escape, or as befitting an improvised conclusion (perhaps hinting at Caesar's assassination) will depend, in part, upon the reader's conception of the poem as finished or unfinished.

Cato

Lucan's Cato occupies the opposite moral extremity to his Caesar, and books 2 and 9 act as a kind of echo chamber, mutually reinforcing our impression of him in word and action.[28] When he first appears, we view him through Brutus's eyes: sleepless with anxiety, ruminating on the fate of the republic and the city's misfortune, fearful for all "but secure in himself" (*securumque sui*), a philosophical phrase denoting equanimity that recurs throughout the poem (2.239–41).[29] Throughout the *Civil War*, Lucan stresses Cato's exceptionalism. We see his unshakable peace of mind, for example, in the midst of the chaos and grief at Rome (described at 1.484–522, 2.16–36), in the face of a mutiny after Pharsalus (9.217–93), and among the terror of his soldiers in Libya (9.734–949).

In a poem of desperate attempts to learn the future—the Roman senate summoning the haruspex Arruns (1.584–638); Appius consulting the Delphic Oracle (5.67–236); Sextus seeking out the witch Erictho (6.413–830)—only Cato resists, refusing to consult the oracle in the Temple of Jupiter Ammon (9.511–86) since he himself is "filled with the god he carried in his silent mind," secure in his creed and in the knowledge that death is the only certainty (9.573–84). The main contours of his characterization—his "customs" (*mores*) and his "way of life" (*secta*, a word evoking the code of the Stoics)—are set before the reader at 2.380–91: moderation (*seruare modum*), tenacity of purpose, life in accordance with nature, selfless patriotism. He is an ascetic sustained by minimal food and shelter; he wears an archaic woolen toga, like a hair shirt; and he is a puritan for whom sex means procreation. Lucan calls him the father and husband of the community, a metaphor that resonates with the simile at 2.21–28 comparing Rome at the beginning of Caesar's invasion to a grief-stricken house recently bereft of a son and with Cato's comparison of himself to a father at the funeral of his son: he will embrace Rome's lifeless body and follow the empty shade of liberty "all the way," that is, to death (2.297–303), a declaration prefiguring his march across the Libyan desert in book 9, which will end historically in his suicide at Utica (outside the narrative of the extent poem).

The qualities described in book 2 compare as well with Sallust's wholly positive estimate of Cato the Younger at *Bellum Catilinae* 54 as they do with Cicero's more critical evaluation of his inflexibility in his speech *Pro Murena* (60–66), and it is at times difficult to judge the tone of Lucan's presentation. Is Cato the answer to the emergent age of Caesarism, "a nasty caricature," or something worse?[30] On the one hand, Lucan's narrator insists upon his virtue. His mind is "invincible" (9.18); his excellence (*uirtus*) is hardened (9.445). His party is wholly that of freedom (9.29–30). The state would have ended with the defeat at Pharsalus but for him (9.253–54). The war becomes "just" when he assumes leadership (9.292–93). The highpoint of the narrator's praise of Cato comes after the description of Cato's selfless generalship, when he declares he would rather follow Cato's "triumphal march" through the desert than accompany the triumphs of Pompey or Marius in Rome: in the narrator's view, Cato should and will be deified if Rome ever casts off its servitude (9.587–604).

On the other hand, inconsistencies both large and small between his creed and his actions as well as the contrast between Cato and the world he inhabits seem to encourage a critical evaluation even of Lucan's "Stoic saint." He can be seen to breach his own Stoic code at a number of points in the poem: he is driven by emotion to enter the war (e.g., 2.297–99: grief) and at various other moments in the narrative (9.509: anger), whereas the Stoic wise man sustains *ataraxia* ("imperturbability"). In his defense we might counter that Cato is not perfect: he accounts for his emotions in his speech to Brutus in book 2—the choice between impassively watching the destruction of the republic and acting in its defense admits only one acceptable response—and, as Fantham observed, an unemotional Cato would be a disaster within epic, a genre that relies upon the emotions for its power.[31] Cato lives in accordance with "nature"—to the Stoics this term could be interchangeable with their god and his providential plan—but he inhabits a narrative in which the gods support Caesar's rise to autocracy (1.128). His lonely moral supremacy sometimes makes Cato behave or sound like his nemesis Caesar: "Cato's excellence not knowing how to linger" (9.371–72; cf. 1.144–45); he wants his soldiers to think it beautiful and Roman to undergo extreme suffering with him as their witness (9.390–92; cf. Caesar as witness to his troops at 7.285–92, esp. 285–87). And they both have or claim a privileged right to knowledge (9.554–55 Labienus speaking about Cato; cf. 10.181–83 Caesar speaking of himself).

Especially troubling to critics is Cato's decision to march across Libya with his army and his behavior during this march. The puritanical, explicitly penitential dimension attributed to the event—for example, "Libya alone with its brood of evils can show that it is honorable for warriors to have fled" (9.405–6), "hard is the path towards legality and love of crashing fatherland" (9.385)—may suggest a dangerous martinet whose vision for his army is a path to moral redemption through an excess of suffering rather than victory or safety ("the one safety . . . to die with necks unconquered," 9.380); note in particular Cato's lip-smacking description of Libya's dangers at 9.401–3. It is clearly designated as their general's march to his own suicide ("a journey not to be retraced," 9.408–10: evoking descents of the soul into the underworld).

The march provides a spectacle of fascinating horror as Cato's troops are decimated by a plague of snakes. To what end? Cato witnesses myriad casualties (9.735–36), and his soldiers acquire from him "strength for death" (9.886) as they learn to suffer and die and are ashamed to groan with him as a witness to their last moments (9.886–87). And yet, Cato has earlier tried but failed to keep his army in ignorance by moving them on from especially unpleasant deaths (9.760–61), and it remains ambiguous whether the main benefit of his soldiers' deaths falls to the soldiers themselves or to Cato: "What power could any pestilence have *against him*? In others' breasts he conquers misfortunes and as a spectator shows that mighty pain is powerless" (9.887–89). His soldiers' agonizing deaths seem to be yet one more endurance event from which Cato emerges with his *uirtus* intact. In the end it is luck (*Fortuna*), not his leadership or providence, that ends their suffering and brings them to safety (9.890–91).

Pompey

Lucan's Pompey is best read as occupying a middle position between the extremities of Cato's virtue and Caesar's ambition.[32] He is an imperfect human being; he has a recognizably human relationship with his wife and sons; he cares what others think about him; and he needs love. He is also in some sense trapped in his own past: as incredible as were the achievements of his earlier career, they cannot now guarantee his position of supremacy within the state with the emergence of Caesar (cf. 1.121–26).

A cluster of characteristics conveyed in his introduction and the oak tree to which he is compared defines him in pointed contrast to Caesar (1.129–43). He is slipping into old age; in fact, Pompey was fifty-seven and Caesar was fifty-one when the war broke out. He has been made *tranquillior* ("milder") by a long period of civilian, as opposed to military, life. Pompey had returned to Rome at the end of 62 B.C.E. after his eastern campaigns, but Caesar had been on campaign in Gaul from 58–50. Lucan claims that Pompey has by now forgotten the art of generalship (1.130–31). He is a populist, rejoicing in the applause of the crowd in his theatre (1.131–33): throughout the poem he is much occupied with his reputation. Finally, he does not renew his strength but trusts in his former fortune. In sum, he is "a shadow of his own name" (1.134–35), a programmatic description alluding to Pompey's honorific cognomen "Magnus" ("The Great") on which Lucan will frequently pun throughout the poem via the adjective *magnus* ("great").[33] The crushing comparison of Pompey to a venerable old oak tree, devoid of strength and unable to stand but for its own weight, vividly conveys both an enervate passivity seen throughout the poem and the inevitability of his fall before Caesar's onslaught (the oak is "ready to fall beneath the first breath of wind," 1.141). Importantly, it also shows the esteem in which Pompey is held by his community (1.143): it is made very clear throughout the poem that Rome and Pompey love each other very passionately (cf., e.g., 7.7–27), and, for example, the peoples of Larisa and Mytilene remain devoted to him even after his defeat (7.712–27, 8.109–46).

Pompey's historical strategy of abandoning Italy and Rome before Caesar's invasion seems only to reinforce the impression in the *Civil War* that he has "unlearnt the general's part." His lack of leadership at Rome leads to a night of panic and confusion in the city that evokes in its details the poetic set-piece descriptions of captured cities and Vergil's account of the destruction of Troy (1.469–522; cf. Verg. *Aen.* 2.250–794). His goals of defending Italy and of levying manpower along the Italian peninsula are failures (2.392–98, 526–27); so too his first speech in which he attempts to rouse the spirits of his forces at 2.531–95. His generalship, or his fortune in war, improves as his defeat draws near:[34] he anticipates Caesar's plan to seize Dyrrachium, moving with more than Caesarian speed to secure that city's defense (6.15–18). Caesar's siege of Pompey, while it has the effect of causing a plague to erupt in Pompey's camp, fails to contain his forces (6.29–137, 263–83), and Pompey has the upper hand in the maneuvering that follows the siege (6.284–99) to such a degree that if Pompey had pressed his advantage at this point, the narrator assures us, Pharsalus would have been averted by Caesar's defeat (6.300–313). At times in book 6 Pompey is described in terms suggesting the same titanic energy as Caesar: he wants to emerge from the siege by widespread destruction, smashing the towers "through all the enemy's swords and on a path made by slaughter" (6.118–24); he breaks the siege with the relentless energy of a raging storm at sea (6.265–67) or the river Po in full spate (6.272–78). When the two armies are in Thessaly, Pompey's strategy of avoiding confrontation and blocking Caesar's supplies is working (7.92–101, 235–36). Through its scale and worldwide repercussions, Pompey's fall is presented as colossal or sublime:[35] his forces are drawn from the whole world, and he is a kind of "king of kings," grander than Cyrus or Xerxes (3.169–70, 284–97). It is drummed into the reader that at Pharsalus the nations (*populi, gentes*), the world (*orbis*), or the universe (*mundus*) was lost (e.g., 7.46, 89, 233–34, 617–18).

Lucan's Pompey has a more complex psychological profile than either Caesar or Cato.[36] We see an example of this in his thinking through the nature of death after Julia's apparition to him (3.38–40) and in his dream at Pharsalus of his own youthful success (7.7–12). Pompey often "senses," "realizes," or "perceives" things that are contrary to his expectations (e.g., 2.598, 7.85, 7.648, 8.327). We are privy to his fear after Pharsalus (8.5–8)—so contrary to the nobility of mind with which he withdraws from battle (7.676–86)—and the vivid description of his humiliation and resentment at his former fame (8.18–23); we are made to feel his love and concern for Cornelia (5.722–815, 7.675–77, 8.40–108), in whose presence he twice weeps (5.734–38, 8.107–8). This vivid psychological portrait reaches its apogee in book 8. We see Pompey's sleepless anxiety about where to turn next: his "hatred of the future" (8.161–66). We hear his desperate and morally misguided flirtation with the idea of seeking Parthia's help (8.211–38, 279–327). In the harbor of Alexandria, he realizes he is betrayed but even so leaves his fleet and enters the vessel where he will be assassinated (8.572–74). He wants his family to witness his final actions (8.579–82). His troops are worried that he may grovel to save his own life (8.592–95), but Pompey's final moments are a triumph of hard-won self-control, achieved by the thinnest of margins ("then he closed his eyes and held his breath to stop himself from breaking into speech and marring his eternal fame with tears," 8.615–17). In Pompey's dying soliloquy, in which he contemplates future audiences "watching" his death scene, he tells himself to think of his own fame, encourages himself to face death bravely, and finally seeks the admiration of his family who witness his death as a measure of their love for him (8.622–35). This is a fitting last look at a complex psychology and adds at the last moment yet more nuances to Lucan's complex portrait of a brilliant and flawed humanity.

Tone and Aesthetics of the *Civil War*

The *Civil War*'s overall tone and aesthetics can be found in its fascination with the grotesque and the macabre, in a hyperrealism that is often rooted in the conventions (e.g., of battle or of prophecy) found in Vergilian or Homeric epic but pushed to new extremes, and in a hyperbole facilitated by the cosmic proportions Lucan attributes to his subject matter. It can be felt in an intellectualism that is often expressed in paradox, and the suggestion or exploration of its implications, and is reflected in the poem's deep interest in magic, religion, and the supernatural. We see it in Lucan's attention to the fragmented and disintegrating body, and we encounter it in the highly rhetorical nature of the poem, which is found both in the narrator's constant interruptions of his own narrative and in speeches made by the poem's characters, which veer from the magnificent to the shocking and overblown.[37] The first-time reader might acquire a feel for these characteristics (and their combination in the one scene) by considering the following moments in the poem:

- The centurion Laelius's oath of loyalty to Caesar, in which he swears that if asked he will massacre his own brother, father, or pregnant wife, plunder and burn down temples, and level the walls of Rome (1.359–86)
- The description of the hideous innards and abnormal liver of the victim during Arruns's extispicy (1.605–29)
- The torture and killing of Marius Gratidianus and the mass executions under Sulla (2.174–220)
- The sea battle at Massilia, which becomes a faux land battle by dint of the closely packed ships and features a cluster of bizarre and paradoxical deaths (3.509–762)
- The speech of Vulteius to his cohort of troops—trapped on a raft and watched by Pompeian soldiers from the shore—to make a spectacle of their mutual slaughter and the description of this event (4.474–581)

- The Delphic priestess Phemonoe's possession and her vision of all time (5.161–224)
- The titanic storm, and Caesar's contempt for it, which threatens to submerge his little skiff in the Adriatic Sea (5.560–702)
- The *aristeia* narrative of Scaeva, who, inter alia, throws corpses as siege weapons, makes mountains of dead, fights a whole army, is "protected" by javelins sticking in his body, and removes and stomps on his own pierced eyeball and who appears to die yet appears still living in the last lines of the poem (6.138–262, cf. 10.543–6)
- The witch Erictho's reanimation of a corpse to prophesy to Sextus Pompeius (6.413–830)
- Caesar's breakfast among the carnage at Pharsalus (7.786–824)
- Pompey's decapitation (8.663–91)
- The plague of snakes inflicting heavy losses and bizarre deaths on Cato's army in Libya (9.734–838)
- Caesar inadvertently trampling on the ruins of Homer's *Iliad* at Troy (9.964–99)
- Acoreus's massive, inconclusive speech to Caesar on the origin of the Nile (10.194–331)

Philosophical Frameworks

The two main schools of thought influencing the *Civil War* (and early imperial intellectual culture) are the Hellenistic philosophies, Stoicism and Epicureanism.[38] Lucan should be read as engaging with these philosophies, especially Stoicism, throughout his epic in the same creative and often combative manner in which he engages with previous literature. The most pertinent aspects of these philosophies for the poem are set out below (but the following does not represent an introduction to the schools or offer even coverage of their respective doctrines).

The Stoics believed in a universe unfolding in accordance with a preordained and benevolent plan—that is, fate—the design of their supreme god who could also be referred to as "the gods," "nature," or "fortune," according to Seneca (*Ben.* 4.8.3). This contrasts strongly with the Epicurean belief in uncaring gods and a universe ruled by chance. These opposing beliefs—in fate and chance respectively—are made the terms of an unresolved dilemma expressed by the narrator at 2.7–13. Throughout the poem the Latin terms for fate (*fatum*) and chance (*fortuna*) are so frequently used in pairs or in close proximity as to be confounded, and while we have seen above that Stoics could refer to the workings of fate as "fortune," this confusion in the *Civil War* also points to the narrator's limited knowledge of his universe as well as his reluctance to accept that Caesar's victory and the loss of republican liberty—as understood by a Stoic—must have happened in accordance with a divine, providential plan. The Stoics thought that the entire universe would periodically dissolve into fire and be regenerated anew, a concept that Lucan uses (stripped of any notion of renewal) in his first programmatic simile in the poem (1.72–80) and one that offers him the imagery and language of cosmic dissolution and universal cataclysm that pervades the *Civil War.*

The Stoics also taught that humans should live in accordance with nature and that virtue or moral excellence is all one needs for happiness. The exploration of the meaning of "moral excellence" or "courage" (*uirtus*) in the *Civil War* offers Lucan some of his most trenchant paradoxes and reaches its most extreme moments in the poem in the mass suicide of Vulteius's men (4.474–581), in Scaeva's misguided *aristeia* ("Unhappy man! With such enormous valor [*uirtus*] you bought a master!" i.e., helped Caesar come to sole power, 6.262), and in Cato's steadfast behavior in extremis in book 9 (9.294–949). For some, Cato's life lived unswervingly "in accordance with nature" (2.382) sits in contrast with the malfunctioning Stoic universe that he inhabits. For Stoics the emotions are always bad, and for both schools the ideal state was *ataraxia*, an impassive freedom from disturbance. This ideal contrasts not only with the emotions that prevail amid the characters in the epic—Caesar's hope and anger, Pompey's fear and anxiety—but with the extreme emotions exhibited by the narrator, who rails against history in the form of his own plot and also with the predicted emotional effect of the poem upon future readers, who will feel hope and fear and pray in vain in their support for Pompey (7.207–13).

Regarding death, the Epicureans taught that the soul is made of atoms and dies with us: that there is no sensation after death. For the Stoics the wise man is able to attain "astral immortality," the return of his soul to the upper regions of the ether from where it came. We can see these conflicting views explored at various points in the poem: in the narrator's curse on Crastinus that he alone suffer "feeling in [his] corpse after death" (7.470–71) and especially in the ascent of Pompey's soul to the abodes of the blessed at the beginning of book 9 (9.1–18), an event that implies his privileged status as a Stoic sage and sits sharply in contrast with the poem's characterization of the living Pompey.

Conclusion

I have sketched here only a few basic coordinates for readers in the hopes that they are equipped as efficiently as possible to turn both to the chapters in this book and—more importantly—to the poem itself. I hope that this first chapter creates an appropriate horizon of expectations for new and first-time readers of the *Civil War*: that they have a sense of what to expect and where to see what is typical, stimulating, and brilliant in the poem and—again, more importantly— that they feel equipped to read and re-read Lucan in the same critical and engaged way that his epic so insistently demands and continuously rewards.

Notes

1. See Tac. *Ann.* 15.49.3, 15.70.1 with Ash 2018, 225–26, 306–8. On Lucan's life, see Ahl 1976, 35–47, 333–57; Fantham 2011; Newlands 2011, 224–25.

2. See Kaster 1995, xxi–xxix.

3. Rostagni 1944, 148, made him a contemporary of Lucan; most scholars place him much later: see, e.g., Ahl 1976, 333–34.

4. On Seneca's influence in securing advancement for others, see Griffin 1984, 78–82.

5. For surviving fragments of his works, see Courtney 1993, 352–66.

6. For scepticism, see Masters 1992, 219–23; contrast, e.g., Fantham 1992a and 2010.

7. For an overview, see Masters 1992, 137n101, and Roche 2009, 129–30, adding Casali 2011, 89–92; Kessler 2011; Nelis 2011; Galli Milić 2016. In this volume, see further the chapters of Galli Milić and Nelis, and Arampapaslis and Augoustakis.

8. Fantham 1992a, 2011. Roche 2009, 1–10, has argued that the political outlook of the poem does not change after book 3.

9. Dewar 1994.

10. Cf. Leigh 1997, 25.

11. For the issue of "closure" in ancient poetry, see Roberts, Dunn, and Fowler 1997; Fowler 2000, 235–307; Grewing, Acosta-Hughes, and Kirichenko 2013.

12. See references at Stover 2008, 571n2.

13. Stover 2008

14. See Stover 2008. For more on Lucan and Vergil's *Aeneid*, see Cowan (chapter 11) in this volume.

15. Surveyed by Ahl 1976, 307–19.

16. Most notably Master 1992, 216–59; Tracy 2011.

17. On Lucan's narrator, see Masters 1992, 5–6, 87–90; Ormond 1994; D'Alessandro Behr 2007; Asso 2008. In this volume, see the chapter of D'Alessandro Behr.

18. I quote Feeney 1991, 130, on Vergil's transition from proem to narrative.

19. See D'Alessandro Behr in this volume.

20. On Lucan's Caesar, see Ahl 1976, 190–230; Henderson 1987, 141–51; Johnson 1987, 101–34; Narducci 2002, 187–278; Sklenář 2003, 128–51; Day 2013, 106–78.

21. Cf. 3.437 "mine is the guilt—believe it!"; cf. 7.269 (Caesar to his troops before Pharsalus) "Rule and let me take the blame."

22. Roche 2015.

23. Roche 2016.

24. Hardie 2011, 492.

25. Blisset 1957; Norbrook 1999, 442–62.

26. Masters 1992.

27. See further my chapter on book 10 and Cowan's chapter on Lucan and Vergil in this volume.

28. On Lucan's Cato, see Ahl 1976, 231–79; Johnson 1987, 35–66; Narducci 2002, 368–429; Sklenář 2003, 59–100; Bexley 2010; Seo 2011; Tipping 2011; Caterine 2015; Galtier 2016b.

29. Cf., e.g., Domitius Ahenobarbus's deluded reasoning for dying "free and secure" (*liber . . . et securus*) at 7.610–15.

30. I quote Sklenář 1999, 281.

31. Fantham 1992a, 134.

32. On Lucan's Pompey, see Ahl 1976, 150–89; Johnson 1987, 67–100; Bartsch 1997, 73–100; Leigh 1997, esp. 110–57; Narducci 2002, 279–367; Sklenář 2003, 106–27; Day 2013, 179–233.

33. Feeney 1986.

34. See Zissos in this volume.

35. Day 2013.

36. Roche 2019, 8–10, focusing on book 7.

37. Although none of the following works are exclusively concerned with the aesthetics of the poem, good orientation can nevertheless be found in Bonner 1966; Martindale 1976; Johnson 1987; Most 1992; Bartsch 1997; Gorman 2001; Malamud 2003; Dinter 2012, 2013.

38. For an introduction to both philosophies, see Long and Sedey 1987; Inwood 2003; Warren 2009; Kenney 2014, 1–5. For discussions of Lucan and philosophy, particularly Stoicism, see Lapidge 1979, 1989, 1405–9; George 1991; Sklenář 1999; D'Alessandro Behr 2007; Roche 2019, 7–8; D'Alessandro Behr in this volume.

1

Book 1

A New Epic Program

LAVINIA GALLI MILIĆ AND DAMIEN NELIS

Lucan's famously sententious style makes it easy to reduce the poem's first book to a few highly memorable phrases: "Wars . . . worse than civil wars"; "He stands, the shadow of a great name"; "there was peace, though not by the leaders' wish"; "a Rome prepared for slavery"; "lying on the river sands, an unsightly headless corpse." These and many other expressions summon up brilliantly vivid and memorable images that highlight key moments and themes. On one level, a list of them could be used to construct a summary of the complete narrative, but the complexities of Lucan's style extend far beyond his flair for epigrammatic expression, and his verbal artistry demands our closest attention. The opening words of the poem, "Of wars," declare the dominant subject. The narrator goes on quickly to reveal that in this poem the war, that most traditional of all epic subjects from Homer's *Iliad* on, will be of a particular kind: this will be a civil war and, indeed, in some way even worse ("Wars . . . worse than civil wars," 1.1). The poet next unleashes a series of striking images reinforcing the particularly horrible nature of such a conflict: it is a criminal act of self-destruction; it is a battle involving people who know each other; it is a form of madness that involves Romans using against Romans the weapons and energies that should be put to ensuring worldwide domination; it is a conflict that has left all Italy desolate (1.24–32). Then, unexpectedly, such horrors are granted a positive aspect. The poet seems to admit that it was worth suffering civil wars, since in the end they brought about the advent of imperial power and Nero himself, whose eventual deification is associated with the onset of universal peace and cosmic order, before Lucan declares him to be already a source of divine inspiration for the poem that is to follow (1.33–66). This passage has mystified many readers, some treating it as an example of a typically Roman form of poetic eulogy, others seeing it as evident mockery of the Emperor.[1] Whatever way we read it, it is clear that this extended opening section of the *Civil War* presents to the reader a number of themes and techniques that will occur throughout the rest of the work. Indeed, the whole of the first book is in obvious ways programmatic.

In standard historiographical mode, one of its aims is to delineate the causes and the outbreak of the conflict. In doing so, it introduces many of the narrative's main characters and their motivations. Caesar is the person who undoubtedly dominates the book, but Pompey, Cato, and the Roman people as a collective are all introduced, and Rome herself appears, as place and space are also shown to be important. Throughout, much in the first book looks forward and prepares for all that is to follow, setting in motion a narrative that is headed inevitably toward disaster and annihilation. Overall, Lucan also imposes a clear sense of unity upon the book by very deliberately bringing it to a close with a scene that replays aspects of the prologue.

In the book's final moments, an unnamed woman pronounces a speech (1.678–94) in which she foresees the Battle of Pharsalus, followed by further conflict in Egypt and Libya, before a return to Rome enables her to allude to the murder of Caesar and the beginning of another cycle of civil strife. When at the beginning of her speech (1.681) she says, "What madness this, O Phoebus," the alert reader instantly recalls the prologue and specifically line 1.8, "What madness was this, O citizens?" The final words she utters are "already have I seen Philippi," 1.694), doing so in such a way as to fuse the sites of the battles at Pharsalus and Philippi into one. After that, she, and with her in some sense the poet too, can only collapse in a state of frenzied exhaustion, at the close of a book full of the powerful emotions and destructive energies that accompany an apparently endless and unstoppable cycle of civil strife.

As a whole, book 1 is arranged in the following main sections:

1–182: extended prologue
183–465: Caesar and the invasion of Italy
466–695: events in Rome

Within this tripartite structure most of the book is taken up by a series of distinctly memorable scenes: the comparison of Pompey and Caesar (1.129–57), the immorality of Roman society (1.158–82), the crossing of the Rubicon (1.183–232), the taking of Ariminum (1.233–391), the catalogue of Gallic tribes (1.392–465), panic in Rome and terrifying prodigies (1.466–583), and the purificatory rites of Arruns, Figulus's astrology, and the climactic vision of the matron (1.584–695). In all of this the reader encounters ten speeches and fourteen similes, as the narrative progresses only fitfully in a discontinuous manner. The action contained within the book, covering just a few days in mid-January 49 B.C.E., is limited to the crossing of the Rubicon, the taking of Ariminum, and events in Rome as fear of Caesar's advance from the north grips the city. Some large-scale events of obvious historical importance are referred to almost in passing, as in lines 1.467–68, which inform us about Caesar's taking of towns across northern Italy. Others are greatly exaggerated, such as when the situation in Rome, as news of Caesar's advance comes in, is described in terms that evoke the actual sacking of a city. Given the ease with which most of the book can be broken down into discrete episodes, it is understandable that scholars have privileged the idea of Lucan as a brilliant composer of individual, set-piece scenes who pays little attention to narrative coherence and large-scale structural and thematic unity.[2] This approach certainly catches a powerful element in Lucan's manner, but if taken to extremes it does scant justice to the intricacies of his narrative technique. All together, these scenes fulfill a number of functions in a carefully planned manner: first comes essential historical causality and contextualization; next the very act of beginning and the characterization of Caesar are highlighted by the crossing of the Rubicon; then the focus turns to two cities, Ariminum and Rome. The former is typical of so many of the places that will be caught up in the mayhem of Roman civil strife in this poem, while the latter will remain at the center of attention throughout, despite the spatial dislocation of the first line, with its "Emathian plains." The city's destiny will be fought out in Greece and elsewhere, but this is essentially a book and a poem about the fate of Rome and the Roman people (see already 1.2, "a mighty people").

While setting the scene and providing so much vital information about the origins of the war, Lucan adapts to his own needs standard features of the epic genre. Many of his artistic choices and stylistic habits quickly catch the eye, such as the absence of a Muse or Muses and of the whole divine machinery of traditional epic. Also present is a particularly complex type of verbal allusion that pulls the reader into close engagement with both the epic tradition as a whole and with specific models that are of particular importance. Lucan uses verbal repetition to help construct thematic patterns and draw our attention to recurring types of imagery as well as the question of epic heroism. One also sees examples of such standard epic features as similes, speeches, dreams, and visions. Finally, we observe the poet's taste for paradox and antithesis, for pointed expression and the accumulation of rhetorical flourish, for the consistently hyperbolic description of the grimly spectacular. A survey of some of these aspects will help to illustrate key features of Lucan's astounding virtuosity in this remarkable book of poetry.

The Divine

The first-person verb "we sing" of line 1.2, echoing the "I sing" of *Aeneid* 1.1, leaves no place for a Muse to inspire or accompany the poet, as Lucan distances himself from Homer and Vergil. The fact that the opening sentence is of seven verses, as in both the *Aeneid* and its direct model, the *Iliad*, helps draw attention to his originality. As we have already seen, at lines 1.63–66, if he has Nero to help him, Lucan will require neither Apollo nor Bacchus, and it is in these lines that we encounter some of the vocabulary traditionally associated with epic openings and moments of poetic inspiration (the bard, his breast as site of inspiration, secrets and song). If we privilege variation on Vergilian precedent as a typical critical move, the absence of a figure like Juno, so prominent at the opening of the *Aeneid*, is equally striking and is perhaps quite deliberately underlined by the question of line 8, "What madness was this, O citizens?" Vergil's Juno is on one level the personification of madness. As the source of much of the madness that pervades Vergil's epic, her absence at the start of Lucan's is felt all the more strongly.

It does not take long, however, for the obvious lack of the standard divine machinery to be problematized on various levels. Juno herself may be absent, but her violent insanity remains. There may be no gods in the opening scenes, but the apparent certainty of Nero's apotheosis is given prominence at 1.45–62; the apparition of *Patria*, his fatherland, at 1.185–92, conforms to standard epic description of a divine vision, even if it ends with Caesar's highly formal renunciation of peace and his declaration that it is Fortune that he follows (1.226); at 1.234 "the will of the gods" is offered as a possible explanation of cloudy darkness on the morning Caesar takes Ariminum, described as the "first day of the tumult of war." When references to Fortune (1.84, 111, 124, 135) and Fate (1.33, 42, 70, 94) begin to pile up, it becomes clear that they are coming to replace the traditional deities of epic action.[3] In the case of Fate in particular, it is hard not to recall Vergil's insistence on the etymological connection of fate (in Latin *fatum*) with what Jupiter says (in Latin *fatur*) in his great prophetic speech at *Aeneid* 1.257–96, the like of which is unthinkable in Lucan. In this poem, there will be no comforting prophecy announcing eventual victory, glory, and peace. Lucan deals in events that are explicitly "not to be told," using repeatedly the Latin word *nefas* (1.6, 21, 37), which means literally "an offence against divine law" but which can also be taken to denote things that should not be spoken of, thereby at a stroke setting this poem in direct opposition to the usual function of a Roman epic, "the narration of *Fata*, the divine plan for the gods of the Roman mission."[4] Despite that his poem is Stoic on so many levels, Lucan sets himself against the standard Stoic doctrine of Providence, its elimination from the poem allowing for the view that the world is ruled by mere chance.[5] This is another way of establishing both the unnatural nature of the story he has to tell and the original and unpredictable ways in which he will recount it. In this poem about collapse and annihilation, as has been well noted, "Lucan is at his best when he has some pattern to follow, adapting, reversing, or negating it."[6] Full appreciation of these negotiations with literary tradition depends to a very great extent on analysis of the poem's allusive strategies.

Intertextuality

As an author dealing with Roman history, Lucan writes in the wake of Julius Caesar, Pollio, and Livy, all of whom had covered the conflict between Caesar and Pompey and the fall of the republic more generally.[7] As someone writing epic poetry in the middle of the first century c.e., Lucan joins a long literary tradition that goes all the way back to Homer, and his highly intertextual writing allows him to situate himself in relation to this epic tradition. In addition, the very subject matter of his poem inevitably entails reckoning with historical and philosophical concerns already addressed by numerous texts in other genres. The first book of the *Civil War* and, especially, its prologue are ideal places for the reader to assess the nature of Lucan's intertextuality, considered not only as a fundamental feature of his literary technique but also as a means of defining himself as a poet of Roman civil war.[8] A programmatic feature of Lucan's allusive strategy is the recurrent meshing and merging of previous texts simultaneously. Extremely dense and interwoven, his intertextuality emerges from a combination of structural, metrical, verbal, and rhetorical strategies, as a detailed look at the poem's opening lines will show:

> Bella per Emathios plus quam ciuilia campos
> iusque datum sceleri canimus, populumque potentem
> in sua uictrici conuersum uiscera dextra
> cognatasque acies, et rupto foedere regni
> certatum totis concussi uiribus orbis
> in commune nefas, infestisque obuia signis
> signa, pares aquilas et pila minantia pilis.
>
> (1.1–7)

Of wars across Emathian plains, worse than civil wars,
and of legality conferred on crime we sing, and of a mighty people
attacking its own guts with victorious sword-hand,
of kin facing kin, and, once the pact of tyranny was broken,

of conflict waged with all the forces of the shaken world
for universal guilt, and of standards ranged in enmity against
standards, of eagles matched and javelins threatening javelins.

It is not surprising to find Homer and Vergil as the main models of this open-ing. Of course, references to them allow the poet to define his poem as *epos*, a genre remarkable both for its essential conservatism and its ability to undergo significant variation and change. In the *Iliad*, Homer explores the heroic and warlike dimensions of the world he depicts, while in the *Odyssey* he handles the themes of travel and identity and offers a wider view of the human condi-tion. As for Vergil, he establishes himself as the Roman national epic poet dur-ing the reign of Octavian/Augustus and composes his *Aeneid* at the intersection between the Greek epic tradition and archaic Latin epic (Livius Andronicus, Naevius, Ennius). And any epic poet after him cannot escape the confrontation with this double inheritance that the *Aeneid* conveys.

In the *Civil War*'s proem, verbal and structural references to Homer, far from stemming from a purely imitative approach, highlight Lucan's original-ity and underline from the very beginning a radical change in his view of the world. The difference between the paratactic and cumulative structure of these lines and the hypotactic structure of *Iliad* 1.1–7 is striking. The main protago-nist of the *Civil War* is not a hero like Achilles or Agamemnon (*Iliad* 1.1, 6–7), but the Roman people as a whole, a body of fellow citizens fighting each other in a frenzy of perverted heroism. In the proem of the *Iliad*, the emphasis is placed on greatness, while Lucan highlights the self-destructive aspect of this war. The anthropomorphic gods have no place in his epic, nor even the Muse, and the distance proper to the Homeric epic narrator (*Iliad* 1.1 "The wrath of Achilles sing, goddess") is annihilated by the use of the first person *canimus* ("we sing"), a poetic plural that depicts the hyperbolic voice of the poet.[9] We have already noted the relationship between Lucan's first seven lines and *Aeneid* 1.1–7, and these Vergilian references again help to bring out the originality of Lucan's epic poem and its status as an anti-*Aeneid*, a traditional and still cur-rent scholarly approach frequently applied to Lucan's poem.[10] The *Civil War* is indeed an *epos* without heroes, without *prouidentia* ("[divine] providence"), and without divine intervention; its subject is anti-Vergilian insofar as it deals with a *nefas*, an inexpressible war, which opposed fellow citizens and which led to the collapse of the republic. From another perspective, the intertextual relation-ship between the two authors might also be assessed in more sophisticated ways: it can be said that the Neronian poet sometimes also teases out the ambigui-ties that are latent in many Vergilian passages, about his vision of the imperial regime, the relation between gods and men, and the definition of heroism.[11]

Besides, some scholars rightly underline the importance of other models and the multiplicity of sources that are also in play. Thus, lines 1.6–7 also contain a reference to Ennius, with Lucan's "javelins threatening javelins" recalling *Annales* 582 (Skutsch), "the javelins facing the oncoming javelins." Ennius and his *Annales*, which unfortunately have come down to us in fragments, represent the starting point of the tradition of Roman historical epic in hexameter form. By establishing this Ennian connection, Lucan presents himself in a fully Roman tradition, but he also draws attention to a key historical shift. Whereas in this fragment Ennius was describing Roman javelins clashing during some war of conquest against an external enemy, in Lucan Romans fight Romans, and the clashing weapons underline the self-destructive insanity of a civil war. Remarkably, in the very same lines, Lucan alludes also to Seneca (if Seneca is not referring to Lucan), who in his *Phoenissae* had pointed out the horror of the fratricidal Theban war with these words: "standards shine near opposing standards" (414–15). The presence of the rhetorical figure of polyptoton (the repetition of a word in various cases) underpins both allusions. That said, the reader has to take into account that the same rhetorical device is used in a myriad of other texts, which could also be meaningful intertextual presences in Lucan's proem. We should think, perhaps, of Dido's curse at *Aeneid* 4.628–29, "may coast with coast face off, sea with sea, I pray, and arms with arms," establishing the etiology of enmity between Romans and Carthaginians.[12]

These passages, taken into account all together, highlight the "genetic predestination" of the Roman people to civil strife and self-destruction, thus undermining from within the ideal of a peaceful imperial era after the destruction of the last years of the republic. Thus, the intertextual connections may have ideological implications: Lucan could use these references to deconstruct some elements of Neronian propaganda, which we find developed, for example, in some *Eclogues* of Calpurnius Siculus.[13] In *Eclogue* 1, the shepherd Ornytus declares prophetically that the Golden Age will come back after the accession to power of a young emperor (1.33–88), which scholars identify with Nero. The Lucanian expression "attacking its own guts" (1.3) is similar, on the one hand, to Calpurnius Siculus's eulogy of the emperor at *Eclogue* 1.48, where the goddess of the war, Bellona, is depicted as consuming herself in a Neronian world of peace ("she will attack with rabid teeth her own guts") and, on the other hand, to *Aeneid* 6.833 ("and do not attack with violent strength on the guts of your fatherland"), where Anchises, meeting his son Aeneas in the underworld, reveals to him Rome's fate and urges Caesar and Pompey to avoid a civil war. It is of course impossible to establish with certainty whether it was Lucan who imitated Calpurnius or vice versa. What is certain is that the two poets both have the Vergilian line in mind and are using his vocabulary and image with different purposes: Lucan draws attention to the Roman people's failure to take the reins of their own destiny and thus they gradually slip into imperial rule, whereas Calpurnius twists the Vergilian line into a pattern of Neronian propaganda.

Nor does all this mark the end of the allusive potential of the passage in question. The opening line of the proem echoes the *Georgics* as well as the *Aeneid*, with "across Emathian plains" recalling *Georgics* 1.592, "Emathia and the wide plains of Haemus," from a passage in which Vergil is describing the horror of the Battle of Philippi (42 B.C.E.) and the fall of the Roman republic.[14]

Moving away from detailed analysis of the opening verses, an impressive list of other models has also been seen as important for Lucan elsewhere in book 1. Lucretian echoes in this book are also meaningful, for example, at 1.72–82, where Lucan compares Rome's fall caused by the civil war to the dissolution of the universe. Here the poet uses images and vocabulary derived from accounts of conflagration in accordance with Stoic philosophy, whereby cosmic annihi-lation is a transitional stage of the regeneration of the universe, but he merges them with Lucretian references to the perishable nature of the cosmos (Lucretius 5.93–96).[15] He even goes so far as to engage also with the ambiguous Manilian rewriting of Lucretius at *Astronomica* 2.67–70 and 804–7.[16] This creates in the reader a sense of uncertainty about the Stoic notion of providence that first seemed to underpin these Lucanian lines. Simultaneously, Lucan activates Ovid-ian memories, as 1.74 ("reverting to primeval chaos") is clearly modeled on *Metamorphoses* 2.299 ("we are caught up in primeval chaos"). Scholars have recognized for a long time the pervasive influence of Ovid on Lucan's poetics and cosmology.[17] As regards book 1, it has a close relationship with *Metamorpho-ses* 1, especially with the proem and Ovid's description of primordial chaos, and also with *Metamorphoses* 15 and its speech of Pythagoras.[18] Allusion to these passages contributes to the definition of the civil war as a process of metamor-phosis, that of republic into empire, but an inverted logic in comparison with the *Metamorphoses* is also at work, with the *Civil War*'s relentless march toward destruction reversing the plot of the Ovidian poem, which, at least on one level, begins from chaos and ends with the order of the Augustan age.[19] Furthermore, this pattern of allusion draws attention to Lucan's understanding of Ovid's *Meta-morphoses* as a reply to or a meditation on the *Aeneid*, another poem that can also be read as a story of the shift from chaos to order.

Yet another Augustan poet influenced Lucan. References to Horace's *Odes* (especially 1.2, 2.1, 3.25) and *Epodes* (especially 7 and 16) enhance the represen-tation of the internal narrator as a contemporary spectator of the events being narrated and ensure his pathetic involvement in the history of the last days of the Roman republic.[20] On the one hand, Lucan refers to Horace in order to strengthen his statements about the causes of civil strife, such as the loss of deeply felt ancestral customs (*mores maiorum*) and also its consequences, through reuse of Horace's adaptations of key Augustan themes (compare 1.158–82 and *Odes* 1.12.41–44 and 2.15.10–16). On the other hand, allusion to Horace can also be contrastive. This holds especially true for the end of book 1 (1.673–95), where the matron seized by Apollo and announcing civil war is compared to a bacchant. The phrasing used by Lucan here refers, as commentators note, to *Odes* 3.25.1–8: compare "Whither are you snatching me away, Bacchus . . . ? Into what groves, into which caves am I being hurried away so swiftly?" and *Civil War* 1.678–83, "O Paean, where are you taking me? You whisk me over the ether; where do you set me down?"[21] The Bacchic possession of the lyric *persona* signifies inspiration and Horace's awareness of his ability to write a poem praising Augustus. The matron, as an *alter ego* of Lucan, can only prophesy Pompey's and Caesar's murders and the twin battles of Pharsalus and Philippi, her ecstatic madness, as book 1 comes to a close, embodying the very essence of the subject of the poem, the madness of civil strife. In conclusion, once one gets to grips with its astonishing complexity, study of Lucan's intertextuality can be a wonderful gateway toward a better understanding of the historical, philosophical, literary historical, and metapoetical concerns of the whole poem.

Intratextuality

As a careful reader of Vergil in particular, Lucan will have noticed how in the *Aeneid* the reuse of certain words and phrases helps to create resonances that build up into discernibly cohesive patterns of imagery.[22] One of the main functions of such repetitions is often to emphasize the importance of certain key ideas or themes in the poem. They also create links between scenes and characters in such a way as to involve the reader in an ongoing process of comparison and contrast. Such repetitions are neither accidental nor otiose but a fundamental aspect of Lucan's style. An early example of such writing comes at 1.67–97, where the third section of the extended prologue, devoted to the causes of the war, both poses as a new beginning even as it picks up quite systematically motifs occurring in the preceding sections, the initial proem and the passage about Nero. The lines in question read thus:

> Fert animus causas tantarum expromere rerum,
> immensumque aperitur opus, quid in arma furentem
> impulerit populum, quid pacem excusserit orbi.

> (1.67–69)

> My spirit leads me to reveal the causes of such great events,
> and an immense task is opened up—to tell what drove
> a maddened people to war, to tell what cast out peace from the world.

At first glance this sentence may not seem particularly complex, but the demands made of the reader are in fact considerable. On top of the combined allusions to the proems of Ovid (cf. "my spirit leads me," *Met.* 1.1) and Vergil (cf. "causes . . . drove," *Aen.* 1.8–11),[23] the phrase "of such great events" here recalls "such great freedom" at 1.8, "such great love" (1.21), and "such great disasters" (1.30). The repeated adjective *tantus* ("so great") in itself may seem banal, but its accumulation contributes to Lucan's pervasive rhetoric of excess (as well as establishing Vergilian precedent for it by recalling the final line of *Aeneid*'s extended prologue, "such great effort it took to found the Roman race," *Aen.* 1.33). Next, the expression "maddened people" combines "mighty people" (1.2) and "What madness" (1.8). By doing so it repeats the idea that the Roman people is an important actor (in book 1 alone the noun "people" [*populus*] occurs twenty-three times), while also reaffirming the theme of civil war as a form of madness.[24] The second half of the sentence sets war and peace (*pacem*) in opposition. The former, expressed by the Latin word for weapons (*arma*), has already appeared at line 1.44 ("citizens' weapons") and 1.60 ("lay down its weapons"), and Lucan uses it eighteen times in book 1. But when referring to the people driven into war and peace driven from the world ("to tell what cast out peace from the world") Lucan is specifically inverting an image from his praise of Nero:

> tum genus humanum positis sibi consular armis
> inque uicem gens omnis amet; pax missa per orbem
> ferrea belligeri compescat limina Iani.
>
> (1.60–62)

> Then may humankind lay down its weapons and care for itself
> and every nation love one another; may Peace be sent throughout
> the world and close the iron temple-gates of warring Janus.

And this repetition helps to make visible another key word. Before its occurrence in lines 1.61 and 69 Lucan has already referred to "the world" (in Latin *orbis*) four times (1.5, 22, 53, 58). He will go on to use it 16 more times in the remainder of the first book and 132 times in the poem as a whole.[25] Lucan is at pains from the outset to establish both the global aspect of Rome's civil war (verbal play on the similarity between the Latin words for city [*urbs*] and world [*orbis*] is in operation already in lines 1.22–27), and to delineate a cosmos-wide epic space for the poem's action to reverberate within. In addition, the repeated references to war and peace provide an example of verbal repetition with thematic inversion that suggests a cyclic view of history, with Rome caught up in an apparently endless cycle of civil strife.[26]

A quick look at a second example will help demonstrate how this kind of intensely intratextual writing is typical of Lucan's style:

> imminet armorum rabies, ferrique potestas
> confundet ius omne manu, scelerique nefando
> nomen erit uirtus, multosque exibit in annos
> hic furor. et superos quid prodest poscere finem?
> cum domino pax ista uenit. duc, Roma, malorum
> continuam seriem clademque in tempora multa
> extrahe ciuili tantum iam libera bello.
>
> (1.666–72)

> Because war's frenzy is upon us: the power of the sword
> shall overthrow legality by might, and impious crime
> shall bear the name of heroism, and this madness shall extend
> for many a year. And what use is it to ask the gods to end it?
> The peace we long for brings a master. Rome, prolong your chain
> of disaster without a break and protract calamity
> for lengthy ages: only now in civil war are you free.

A remarkable number of words and phrases in these lines echo moments earlier in the book: the sword (cf. 1.8, 355), legality (cf. 1.2), crime (cf. 1.2, 37, 326, 334), madness (cf. 1.8, 96, 106, 255, etc.), peace (cf. 1.61, 99, 171, 241, etc.), calamity (cf. 1.30, 470, 649), civil (cf. 1.1, 14, 32, 44, etc.). This is a remarkably dense tissue of verbal reuse, by any standards. Coming near the book's close, it ensures thematic continuity and also draws attention to certain key features both of the war itself and of the poem that recounts it.

Madness, Crime, Destruction, and Narrative Delay

In the lines just considered, the concentration of words suggesting the horror of civil war is striking, and scholars have often drawn attention to Lucan's use of the vocabulary of crime, madness, and destruction as well as to his frequent use of this kind of vocabulary in combination with the desirable features that civil war destroys, such as virtue, respect for tradition, peace, and harmony. As we have already seen, Lucan even goes so far as to draw a parallel between civil war and cosmic disintegration, drawing on the Stoic idea of ekpyrosis, the fiery destruction of the world.[27] This match between the human, historical action and the physical cosmos within which it takes place links the individual, the Roman people, Rome itself, and the whole world in the poem's narrative of inevitable and apparently endless violence and horror. One of the great paradoxes arising early in book 1 is that Lucan describes at the outset his chosen topic in terms of *nefas* ("evil," 1.6). As we have seen, and as many scholars have noted, he thus turns his poem into a telling of things that should not be told. Concomitantly, the reader is caught up in a process of coming face to face with unfathomable horrors. If civil war means the destruction of Rome, what makes readers persist with such a tale, what makes them want to experience and watch such grim suffering?[28] One of the ways in which this dynamic plays out at the level of the narrative as a whole is the gradual realization on the part of readers that as they make their way inevitably toward the victory of Caesar and end of liberty, they get involved in a long process of deferral.[29]

Simply put, once Lucan decided to make the Battle of Pharsalus the climax of the civil war, he could not describe the battle too early in his poem. So after announcing war on the plains of Emathia in the poem's first line ("across Emathian plains"), he goes on to draw things out in such a way that it is only in the seventh book, the beginning of the second half of a poem that was almost certainly planned in twelve books, that the climactic battle takes place.[30] This long process of delay (in Latin *mora*) that continually pushes back the inevitable historical climax of the story begins early in the book. At lines 1.99–100, Crassus is described thus, "the only check to future war was Crassus in between." Lucan's point here is that Caesar and Pompey would have come into conflict even earlier had it not been for the presence of Crassus as one of the triumvirate ("of masters three," 1.85) controlling Rome. And so Lucan can memorably say of the Parthians when they killed Crassus at the Battle of Carrhae, "to the conquered you gave civil war" (1.108). Immediately, Julia, who was Caesar's daughter and Pompey's wife, is introduced, but her sudden death in 54 B.C.E. removes another potential block on war:

> quod si tibi fata dedissent
> maiores in luce moras, tu sola furentem
> inde uirum poteras atque hinc retinere parentem.
>
> (1.114–16)

> But if destiny had granted you
> a longer stay in the light, alone you could have
> here restrained your frenzied husband.

Recalling lines 1.99–100, Lucan insists on what will become a key theme. Crassus delayed the war, but by killing him the Parthians visited war on

Romans; Julia could have stopped the war, but she was not allowed by fate to linger long enough in life to do so. Inexorably events take their course:

> inde moras soluit belli tumidumque per amnem
> signa tulit propere;
>
> (1.204–5)

> Then he broke the barriers of war and through the swollen river
> quickly took his standards.

Here Caesar's crossing of the Rubicon is presented as the removal of another hindrance, and the idea is restated soon after, when dawn breaks at Ariminum:

> noctis gelidas lux soluerat umbras:
> ecce, faces belli dubiaeque in proelia menti
> urguentes addunt stimulos cunctasque pudoris
> rumpunt fata moras:
>
> (1.261–64)

> Day had dissipated night's chill shadows
> and now the Fates put to his undecided mind the torch of war
> and goads which urge to battle, so breaking
> all the barriers of restraint;

And at 1.280, sensing indecision in Caesar's mind, Curio declares "end delay." The importance of the theme of delay is thus obviously established, but there is much more to Lucan's handling of the keyword *mora* than simple repetition. On the level of verbal play, only delay (*mora*) can both save Rome (*Roma*) and preserve love (*amor*) of Rome as long as possible. But on a grander scale, the delaying of the inevitable battle at Pharsalus until the seventh book shows that *mora* plays a key role in Lucan's structural imitation of Vergil, a poet for whom delay was also an important theme.[31] In both the *Aeneid* and the *Civil War* books 1 and 7 are closely interconnected.[32] Events that could theoretically happen right at the outset of the narrative (for Vergil the Trojans' arrival in Italy, for Lucan the confrontation between Caesar and Pompey, which can perhaps be figured in Vergilian terms as the Romans' arrival at the site of Pharsalus) occur only at the start of the second half of the poem, thus structuring the narrative as a whole. On top of this similarity comes another closely related one. Lucan clearly studied carefully the way in which Vergil, after the end of book 7, went on to delay the confrontation between Aeneas and Turnus for six books in order to make it the final scene of his epic. The conclusion of Lucan's poem will probably have been the Battle of Thapsus and the death of Cato, paralleling that of Turnus, as, in the broadest structural terms, Lucan reworks quite closely the design of the *Aeneid*.

Speeches

Book 1 contains ten speeches: the exchange between Rome and Caesar (1.190–92 and 195–203), Caesar at the Rubicon (1.225–27), the inhabitants of Ariminum (1.248–57), Curio's incitement of Caesar to action (1.273–91), Caesar to his troops (1.299–351), the centurion Laelius to Caesar, again urging war (1.359–86), and finally the three speeches by Arruns (1.631–37), Figulus (1.642–72), and the anonymous matron (1.678–94) that together bring events in Rome to a climax of tension and form the final movement of the book. This adds up to 176 lines in all, amounting to almost a quarter of the book. While the highly rhetorical nature of Lucan's speeches has been abundantly commented upon, following on Quintilian's famous remark (10.1.90) that "Lucan is . . . more to be imitated by orators than by poets," it is more revealing to concentrate on other aspects of the poet's technique in this area.[33] Thematically, the speeches contribute to establishing Caesar as the book's main character, since most of the direct discourse either comes from his mouth or is addressed to him. The first words in direct speech are spoken by Rome herself, when she appears to Caesar at the Rubicon:

> quo tenditis ultra?
> quo fertis mea signa, uiri? si iure uenitis,
> si ciues, huc usque licet.
>
> (1.190–92)

> Where further do you march?
> Where do you take my standards, warriors? If lawfully you come,
> if as citizens, this far only is allowed.

The extremely close relationship between these words and the prologue, drawing attention to boundaries and the theme of transgression (the words "lawfully" and "citizens" recall "civil" and "legality" at 1.1–2), suggests that it is necessary to pay close attention to the relationship between narrator and speakers in the narrative. On this occasion the similarity between what Rome herself says and the narrator's opening words establishes the patriotic credentials of the latter. Such a dialogue between narrator and speaker becomes less harmonious when Caesar speaks, his words occupying sixty-five lines over his three speeches. Consider the following lines:

> hic pacem temerataque iura relinquo;
> te, Fortuna, sequor. procul hinc iam foedera sunto;
> credidimus satis <his>, utendum est iudice bello.
>
> (1.225–27)

> here I abandon peace and desecrated law;
> Fortune, it is you I follow. Farewell to treaties from now on;
> I have relied on them for long enough; now war must be our referee.

In prayer-like language, he renounces peace, justice, and treaties in favor of war (in Latin *bello*, a favorite word used by Caesar twenty-nine times in all in the poem), placed in striking proximity to the word "referee." This combination recalls, of course, *war* and *legality* at 1.1–2, but whereas the narrator had presented war as a crime, for Caesar it becomes the arbiter of what is just, as he aligns himself at this crucial moment, as we have already seen, with Fortuna. In a typical combination of antithesis and sententiousness, peace gives way to war, treaties (*foedera*) to Fortune (*Fortuna*). Another notable aspect of Caesar's words in the text is their placing. The exchange of speeches at Ariminum involving Curio, Caesar, and Laelius (1.273–386) occupies a central position in the book. It marks a turning point, as hesitations cede before the power of persuasive speech, lingering doubts are scattered, permitting the focus of attention to move on from Ariminum to Rome. And within this pivotal section Caesar's address to his troops comes as the centerpiece (1.299–351).[34] At crucial moments in the poem's action Lucan often favors speech over straightforward narration, and this is indeed an extremely powerful example of that technique. Caesar brilliantly criticizes Pompey, justifying an attack on Rome that is presented as bringing liberty by driving out tyrants from a servile city. But perhaps surprisingly, with Caesar's troops hesitating to act, it takes the additional words of a centurion named Laelius, a fictitious character created by Lucan for just this moment, to sway the army definitively in favor of war. In an extremely dark and violent speech he declares his readiness to do whatever is necessary once Caesar has given the order, even if it means killing his brother, his father, or his pregnant wife and toppling the very walls of Rome itself.[35] The last traces of *pietas* ("dutiful respect") are scattered and up goes a roar that is as loud as the raging north wind that bends trees in the forests of Mount Ossa (1.388–91).

Similes

Book 1 contains fourteen similes: civil war as cosmic ruin (1.72–80); Crassus as the Isthmus of Corinth (1.100–103); Julia as the Sabine women (1.118); Pompey as an oak tree (1.136–43); Caesar as a lightning bolt (1.151–57); Caesar as a lion (1.205–12); the silence at Ariminum as calm in nature (1.258–61); Caesar as a race horse (1.291–95); Pompey as a tiger (1.327–31); soldiers' shouts as strong winds (1.388–91); Rome as a ship in a storm (1.498–503); a Fury in Rome as a

Fury at Thebes (1.574–77); a Roman matron as a Thracian bacchant (1.674–75).[36] These can all be studied from a number of angles: complex multiple correspondence between simile and narrative, pairings of similes, their contributions to characterization, their epic models, and so on. The first may be taken as a showcase example of Lucan's manner on all these levels:

> sic, cum compage soluta
> saecula tot mundi suprema coegerit hora
> antiquum repetens iterum chaos, [. . .] ignea pontum
> astra petent, tellus extendere litora nolet
> excutietque fretum, fratri contraria Phoebe
> ibit et obliquum bigas agitare per orbem
> indignata diem poscet sibi, totaque discors
> machina divulsi turbabit foedera mundi.
>
> (1.72–80)

> So, when the final hour
> brings to an end the long ages of the universe, its structure dissolved,
> reverting to primeval chaos, then fiery stars will plunge
> into the sea, the earth will be unwilling to stretch flat her shores
> and will shake the water off, Phoebe will confront
> her brother and for herself demand the day, resentful
> of driving her chariot along its slanting orbit, and the whole
> discordant mechanism of universe torn apart will disrupt its own laws.

The main point of comparison here is that between the destruction of Rome and the dissolution of the universe. This simile thus plays a crucial role in Lucan's handling of specifically cosmological and also more generally scientific and Stoic themes in the poem as a whole. The subject matter of the simile helps underscore the cosmic vision that allows the narrator to situate any single historical event in a wider context. The display of scientific knowledge thus shown also aligns heroic epic with didactic epic, as Lucan takes part in a literary game of generic definition and dialogue that places him in the hexameter tradition in Latin poetry that runs from Ennius to the late-Augustan didactic poet Manilius via Lucretius, Vergil, and Ovid. In specifically Vergilian terms, Lucan's inclusion of cosmological themes reveals him to have been an insightful reader of the *Aeneid* as a poem that aligns the story of Roman *imperium* ("authority") with the workings of the cosmos.[37] In a brilliant inversion, however, whereas Vergil can be seen as telling the story of Rome's foundation and the history that culminates in birth of Augustan empire, Lucan chooses to tell the story of Rome's destruction. This simile is thus the linchpin in one of Lucan's crucial poetic strategies, that which has been seen as one of his most brilliant and influential contributions to the history of the Roman epic tradition, his consistent and unwavering focus on violence, death, decline, and annihilation.

Roman History

By bringing the first book of his epic to a close with a vision that culminates, as we have seen, in Pharsalus and Philippi (1.680, 694), Lucan gestures toward formal closure at the level of the individual book, even as he opens the way to the rest of the story that will carry readers on toward his own account of Pharsalus in the climactic book 7. The two battles are at times presented as mirror images, one of the other, but they are also two distinct stages in the wider narrative of Roman history and the history of Rome's dissolution, as Lucan makes clear at 7.847–68, before mixing them up again at 7.872. The *Civil War* as a whole is highly conscious of its generic identity as an historical epic, and throughout book 1 both the narrator and speaking characters have recourse to events in Roman history. The narrator begins the process when at lines 1.30–32 he remarks on the paradox that through civil war Roman citizens have done more damage than foreign enemies such as Pyrrhus and Hannibal. At 1.183, Caesar's crossing of the frozen Alps reinforces the similarity with the latter. When the people of Ariminum bemoan their proximity to Gaul, which meant they were the first to suffer the incursions of the Senones, the Cimbri, the Carthaginians, and the Teutones (1.254–56), they situate the civil war in a long line of Roman wars, with an emphasis on invasion by foreigners that stands in stark contrast with the reality of the civil strife that is now beginning. Caesar's speech at 1.299–351 picks up on this historicizing reference in a number of ways. As leader of an invasion of northern Italy he again adopts the comparison with Hannibal (1.303–5), but this time it is clearly focalized through the eyes of those in Rome who equate Caesar's advance with the Carthaginian invasion, thus emphasizing all the menace of the situation as foreign attack turns into looming civil war. And as we have seen throughout this chapter, the first book of this poem is very much to be read both as the introduction to that imminent war and as a programmatic display of the literary style and techniques that Lucan will adopt to describe it, in a brilliant combination of historical reconstruction and dramatic recreation, rhetorical virtuosity, generic invention, and creative allusion, all put to the service of evoking the almost unimaginable horrors of civil war.

Notes

1. From the large bibliography on this passage, see Dewar 1994; Roche 2009, 8–10, 129–46.

2. See, e.g., Williams 1978, 248; Dinter 2012, 27–29.

3. On the relationship between Fate and Fortune in the poem (in book 1 at 70–94, 264–65, and 392–95 they are clearly distinguished one from the other), see Roche 2009, on 1.33.

4. Feeney 1991, 276.

5. See Quint 1993, 135–36.

6. Bramble 1982, 543.

7. See Lintott 1971; Roche 2009, 36–47.

8. For a detailed discussion of the sources and models of book 1, see Roche 2009, 19–47.

9. Cf. Conte 1966.

10. Thompson and Bruère 1968; Narducci 1979, 2002; Leigh 1997.

11. See, e.g., Esposito 1996; Roche 2009, 20–30; Casali 2011; Galli Milić 2016.

12. And it may not be irrelevant that Livy uses polyptoton to underline the internecine nature of the conflict between Romans and Latins, e.g., 8.8.2 and 14; Leigh 1997, 38n60 notes that this is a "recurring device in Livy." On further use of Livy by Lucan, see Radicke 2004.

13. Despite some uncertainty about when Calpurnius Siculus lived, most scholars place his literary production under Nero, and more precisely in the years 54–59 C.E.; cf. Karakasis 2016, 1–2n1 for discussion and exhaustive bibliography.

14. On Lucan and the *Georgics*, see Kersten 2018.

15. Lapidge 1979.

16. Esposito 1996, 537n52 notes that the intertextual relationship between Lucan and Lucretius is frequently mediated by the reference to another text; see Galli Milić 2016 on Manilius in this role.

17. Wheeler 2002.

18. See in particular the beginning of the second proem at 1.67, comparing "My spirit leads me to reveal the causes of great events" to Ovid's *Metamorphoses* 1.1–2 "My spirit leads me to tell of forms changed into new bodies."

19. Tarrant 2002; cf. also Wheeler 2002.

20. Gross 2013.

21. For other intertextual links in this passage (Vergil's *Aeneid* and Seneca's *Agamemnon*), see Roche 2009, 375–77.

22. See Moskalew 1982.

23. See Roche 2009 on 1.67 for discussion.

24. Roche 2009 on 1.2 states that the "progression of adjectives and participles applied to the *populus Romanus* throughout the *Civil War* is indicative of their dislocation from power to servitude." On the *Civil War* as "an epic of crowds," see Hardie 2013, 231; on collective slaughter and mass suicide, see Day 2013, 191–96.

25. For further discussion of this topic, see Hardie 2008; Pogorzelski 2011; Wills 2011.

26. For some possible further connections and ramifications, see Nelis 2014.

27. See Lapidge 1979.

28. See Leigh 1997.

29. On narrative and *mora*, see Masters 1992; Roche 2019, 3–4.

30. For discussion of the different views on the number of books, see Ahl 1976.

31. On *mora* in the *Aeneid*, see Reed 2016.

32. See Roche 2009, 17–19.

33. See Morford 1967.

34. See Roche 2009, 14.

35. See Roller 1996, 329.

36. On the similes of book 1 and Lucan's similes generally, see Aymard 1951 and Heitland 1887, lxxxiv–lxxxix. On first similes in a number of Latin epics, see Feeney 2014.

37. See Hardie 1986.

2

Book 2

Civil War in Italy: Past, Present, and Future

Annemarie Ambühl

Introduction: Book 2 in Context

After the preparations for war have started in book 1, the full impact of the civil war now strikes home at the city of Rome. The second book exhibits a range of characters, themes, and literary strategies that will be developed further in the course of the epic.[1] Among these are Lucan's intertextuality with Greek and Latin epic and other genres, his religious and philosophical outlook, his interests in geography and the natural world as a mirror of human violence, and his skills in bringing to life the motivations and emotions of individual and collective agents, often through direct speeches.

The plot of Lucan's second book initially focuses on the entire body of Roman citizens, consisting of combatants and noncombatants, and their fears and reminiscences of civil war (2.1–233). Then individual members of the political elite take center stage, as Brutus and his uncle Cato discuss how to react to the outbreak of the civil war (2.234–325). The role of women is highlighted, too, first through the collective mourning of Roman matrons (2.21–42) and then through the exemplary (or perhaps not so exemplary) figure of Marcia, Cato's old and new wife (2.326–91). Moreover, as another quasi-personified player in the civil war, the Italian landscape is introduced in the form of a catalogue of mountains and rivers (2.392–438). And finally, the military confrontation between the protagonists Caesar and Pompey is unleashed, if only in an indirect way: the two civil war leaders are not to meet until the battle at Pharsalus in book 7 and actually never stand face to face (except when Pompey's severed head is presented to Caesar at the end of book 9). As Caesar forces his way through Italy in pursuit of Pompey, at the end of the book, Pompey makes a narrow escape from Brundisium, never to return to his homeland (2.439–736).

Throughout his epic Lucan interacts with his literary models in a highly self-conscious manner. So it is very likely that besides his engagement with his historiographic sources (especially Caesar's own civil war commentaries and Livy's lost books on the civil wars) he invites his audience to compare his second book with other second books in the epic tradition. Unfortunately, the Roman republican epics by Naevius and Ennius have survived only in fragments, so that from the perspective of modern readers the main models are Homer's *Iliad* and Vergil's *Aeneid*. Yet Lucan's epic has close ties not only with historical and mythological but also with didactic epic, and so the geographical description of Italy at the heart of the book (2.396–438; see pages 43–45) recalls and rewrites the praise of Italy (*laudes Italiae*) from the second book of Vergil's *Georgics* (2.136–76).[2] On the level of narrative episodes and characterization, one notable aspect of intertextuality with the *Iliad* in book 2 of the *Civil War* are the links between Lucan's Pompey and the Homeric Agamemnon, both successful leaders who however (partly) fail to accomplish their missions. In *Iliad* 2, encouraged by a deceitful dream that promises him immediate victory, Agamemnon puts the motivation of his troops to the test by ordering them to return home. This test (the so-called *Peira* or *Diapeira*; cf. Hom. *Il.* 2.73) notoriously fails, for the Greeks are all too eager to take Agamemnon's instruction literally and can be stopped only with great difficulty. Pompey's first harangue to his troops in book 2 is announced by Lucan's narrator as a test, too (2.529 *temptandasque ratus moturi militis iras*—"he thought to test the indignation of the soldiers soon to fight").[3] Also in Pompey's case, the lack of enthusiasm on the part of his soldiers and their fear of Caesar (2.596–600; see pages 47–48) bodes ill for the battle to come.

The structural parallels of Lucan's second book with the second book of the *Aeneid* are even closer, for it, too, contains a flashback by a first-person narrator. While Vergil's Aeneas at Dido's court tells of the last night of Troy and the terrible deeds he witnessed during the capture of his native city by the Greeks, in Lucan the recollections by an anonymous old man of the atrocities committed during the earlier civil war between Marius and Sulla in the eighties are both more succinct (although they form the longest direct speech of Lucan's epic) and at the same time more close to home for his Roman audience (cf. pages 38–41). This flashback is built from several layers: the fictive reconstruction of an individual's memories, the collective memory of the civil wars that still haunts the generation of Lucan and his audience, and intertextual references to literary and mythological precedents. Some of the horrible events remembered by the old man seem to be modeled after the fall of Troy;

so, for instance, the aged pontifex Scaevola, who is murdered by Marius's hench-men in the very temple of Vesta (2.126–29), recalls the fate of Troy's old king Priam butchered at the altar in his own palace.[4] The structural links with the *Iliad* and the *Aeneid* underline that the Trojan War has been transformed into a civil war among the Romans themselves; the foreign attacker has become the enemy within.

In addition, the myth of Aeneas as told in Vergil's *Aeneid* is also evoked as an intertextual background for Pompey's flight at the end of the book. Like Aeneas, Pompey is an "exile" accompanied by his wife, his sons, his household gods, and his people (2.728–30). But whereas Aeneas has to leave Troy in order to find a new home in Italy, Pompey leaves Italy for the East.[5] The civil war between father-in-law (Caesar) and son-in-law (Pompey), as it were, reverses the process of history, threatening to annihilate Rome and all its achievements. In an analogous sense, the myth of the Argonauts features in a simile comparing the narrow escape of Pompey's fleet from Caesar's trap to the Argo's nearly unscathed passing through the Clashing Rocks (2.714–19; cf. Ap. Rhod. *Argon.* 2.549–606).[6] Unlike the Argonauts, however, Pompey will not return home again.

Yet epic is not the only point of reference for Lucan's second book. The fall of Troy also forms the subject of Greek and Roman drama, and Lucan's old man shares some illuminating traits with tragic characters such as Hecuba, the for-mer Trojan queen, who laments the fate of Troy and that of her family.[7] Through such precedents expectations are raised that Rome, too, will suffer a similar fate or even worse.

The Burden of the Past: Fears and Reminiscences of Civil War

In the first lines of the second book, Lucan's narrator addresses the role of the gods:

> Iamque irae patuere deum manifestaque belli
> signa dedit mundus legesque et foedera rerum
> praescia monstrifero uertit natura tumultu
> indixitque nefas. cur hanc tibi, rector Olympi,
> sollicitis uisum mortalibus addere curam,
> noscant uenturas ut dira per omina clades?
>
> (2.1–6)

And now the anger of the gods was patent, the universe
gave open signs of war, foreknowing nature

overturned her laws and bonds with turmoil full of portents
and proclaimed civil war. Ruler of Olympus, why did you
decide to impose this anxiety on troubled mortals—to learn of coming
    calamity by hideous omens?

Such a personal appeal to the highest god at the beginning of the book seemingly contradicts the widespread view that Lucan's epic does not represent gods
in action. The presumed absence of the gods, however, is a question of perspective: rather than excluding the gods from his universe, Lucan chooses to focus
on the bottom-up view of mortals who are subjected to hopes and fears, try to
interpret ill omens, accuse the cruel gods, and finally turn to desperation. Such
a puzzling representation of various and sometimes conflicting viewpoints not
only characterizes the (failed) communication between the human and the
divine level but is an innovative feature of Lucan's epic as a whole.[8] Moreover, the
perspective of the narrator, who does not normally comment upon the action
from a higher vantage point but often immerses himself into the events he is
telling, shapes the readers' perspective, too. They experience the narrative as if
they were participating in it themselves and could still change the outcome.[9]
Such a poetics of reception based on hope and fear will explicitly be addressed in
book 7 (7.207–13), but already here it is hinted at, when the narrator pleas with
Jupiter that "the fearful at least be allowed to hope" (2.15 *liceat sperare timenti*).

    In the first part of book 2, such collective bodies, with whom the audience
is apparently invited to sympathize, are given a voice.[10] Following a simile that
likens the city of Rome to a household paralyzed in the face of a sudden death
(2.21–28), first the matrons in mourning garments gather at the temples and
use their shrill laments as reproaches against the gods (2.28–42). They perform
an anticipated mourning ritual, for they foresee that as soon as there will be a
victor in civil war, the people will be ordered to rejoice. Then the men, who are
about to join enemy camps, speak for the last time with one voice (2.43–64).
They represent the community that is going to be torn apart by civil war, as
they have to leave behind their families, not to fight a foreign aggressor, as they
would prefer, but their fellow citizens and even their own kinsmen—and for
what? So that the victorious leader can rule over Rome. After a brief passage
that introduces the fears of the older generation (2.64–66), by far the longest
of the three direct speeches is given to an anonymous old man as their representative (2.67–233). By conjuring up the atrocities committed by both sides
during the civil conflict between Marius and Sulla half a century ago, the
speaker suggests a cyclic model of history repeating itself. In his speech, pain-
ful memories of the past, present grief, and anxiety for the future are combined
to convey a sense of helplessness and despair (2.64–66; 223–24, 232–34).

After recounting a series of "unspeakable" crimes (2.148 *infandum*; cf. 176 *non fanda*, 179 *nefandae*), the old man's tale reaches its emotional climax in the "autobiographical" recollections of this fictive eyewitness:

> cum iam tabe fluunt confusaque tempore multo
> amisere notas, miserorum dextra parentum
> colligit et pauido subducit cognita furto.
> meque ipsum memini, caesi deformia fratris
> ora rogo cupidum uetitisque imponere flammis,
> omnia Sullanae lustrasse cadauera pacis
> perque omnis truncos, cum qua ceruice recisum
> conueniat, quaesisse, caput.
>
> (2.166–73)

Already the corpses, melting with decay and blurred with time's
long passage, have lost their features; only now do miserable parents
gather and steal in fearful theft the parts they recognize.
I recall how I myself, keen to place my slain brother's
disfigured face on the pyre's forbidden flames,
examined all the corpses of Sulla's peace
and searched through all the headless bodies for a neck
to match the severed head.

This short passage condenses several characteristic features of Lucan's style: the "tortured" syntax abounds with gruesome details such as decaying corpses and severed heads.[11] Use of these details, however, does not serve as a manneristic end in itself but helps to render the traumatic experience of civil war tangible for his audience.[12] Paradoxically, the imagery of fragmented body parts binds together the fabric of the epic, as these leitmotifs will return in crucial scenes such as the battles at Massilia (book 3) and at Pharsalus (book 7) or Pompey's decapitation (book 8).[13] Another such leitmotif are brothers; in Lucan's topsy-turvy world of civil war, normally they fight each other, but here, in a rare example of brotherly love, a brother tries to fulfill the last rites for his murdered sibling, defying the victor's prohibitions—perhaps recalling for the reader the tragic figure of Antigone, who buries her brother Polynices in defiance of Creon's ban. Finally, the oxymoronic pun "Sulla's peace" for the bloody proscriptions sarcastically denounces the victor's propaganda.

Although set at such an early stage in the epic, it might seem that the horrors evoked so graphically in this speech could not be outdone, yet they form only the preparation for worse to come. The older generation fears that history will not only repeat but even surpass itself, for the present civil war leaders are much more powerful than their predecessors Marius and Sulla (2.225–32).[14] This time, it is not only Rome that is at stake but the whole world.

An Interlude Pointing to the Future: Cato Joins the Civil War

From the atmosphere of anxiety in Rome the focus now shifts to two extraordinary characters who apparently do not fall prey to the general panic: Brutus and his uncle Cato the Younger, Caesar's adversary in the civil war, who owes his fame to his suicide at Utica. Both men are well-known to Lucan's audience (e.g., from the works of Lucan's uncle Seneca the Younger) and to modern readers familiar with Roman history, indeed perhaps too well-known, for it is precisely their later reception that renders their roles in Lucan's epic problematic—roles playing at a time long before their images have become fixed. At this moment, Cato could still decide not to join the civil war, and young Brutus would perhaps have retreated from politics and thus not become involved in Caesar's murder, had he not been goaded to an excessive desire for civil war by the words of his uncle (2.324–25).[15] In any case, Lucan's Cato (who will return in a major role only in book 9) is not a simple stock figure illustrating Stoic doctrine but a highly complex literary character, and the problems connected with his participation in the civil war are not easy to solve. He is probably the most controversial character of the whole epic, and his interpretations range from an exemplary Stoic wise man to a seriously flawed character (as most of Lucan's protagonists) or even a grotesque caricature.[16] Here is not the place to discuss the philosophical and political implications of this episode in detail; instead, we will focus on its function in the context of, and the poetic leitmotifs linking it with, the rest of the book.

Amidst the terror that paralyzes the city, Brutus pays Cato a nocturnal visit and finds him awake, worrying over all the Romans except himself (2.234–41). Brutus tries to convince him not to choose a side in the civil war and thus lend it legitimacy but to stay aloof of the parties (2.242–84). The night setting of their conversation is reflected in the image of the heavenly stars imperturbably following their course, by which Brutus illustrates the attitude of tranquility and impartiality he expects from Cato (2.266–73). Yet Cato in his reply draws a different image of a cosmos not unaffected by the chaos on earth:

"summum, Brute, nefas ciuilia bella fatemur,
sed quo fata trahunt uirtus secura sequetur.
crimen erit superis et me fecisse nocentem.
sidera quis mundumque uelit spectare cadentem

expers ipse metus? quis, cum ruat arduus aether,
terra labet mixto coeuntis pondere mundi,
compressas tenuisse manus?"

(2.286–92)

"That civil warfare is the greatest crime, I admit, Brutus,
but where the Fates lead, confident will Virtue follow.
To make guilty even me will be the gods' reproach.
Who would wish to watch the stars and universe collapsing,
free from fear himself? to fold his arms and keep them still
when ether rushes from on high and earth shudders
beneath the weight of the condensing universe?"

Already at 1.72–80 the dissolution of the cosmos had served as a metaphor for the civil war. Here Cato refuses to be a mere spectator and the only Roman to live in peace (2.295 *otia solus agam?*). However, his decision to join Pompey's side (2.319–23) is not to be mistaken as a statement of political allegiance, for he realizes that by participating in the civil war he will inevitably become guilty despite his best intentions. Rather his decision amounts to a religious statement, for he idealistically imagines his death in battle to become the ultimate self-sacrifice that will save Rome (2.304–19).[17] In a way, he takes over the matrons' perspective from the beginning of the book when he reproaches the gods for their cruelty (2.288, 304–5; cf. 1.128) and likens himself to a father performing a mourning rite (2.297–303).

At daybreak, with another knock at the door a third figure makes her surprising appearance: Cato's former wife Marcia, freshly widowed (in a rather unusual arrangement, she had been given by Cato to the orator Hortensius, who had requested her as a wife in order to bear his children). Brutus's and Marcia's dramatic entrances mirror each other (2.236–38 *nocte sopora . . . | atria cognati pulsat non ampla Catonis*; 326–27 *interea Phoebo gelidas pellente tenebras | pulsatae sonuere fores*), and the funereal imagery employed in Cato's speech is now turned into an actual scene of mourning. Unlike the other matrons, who lament the imminent civil war casualties in advance (2.28–42), Marcia comes straight from the funeral of her second husband (2.327–37). After fulfilling her duty of bearing offspring for two families, she is now free to remarry her first husband Cato, at whose side she wants to endure the hardships of the civil war, as she tells him herself (2.338–49).[18] The ensuing remarriage is as unusual as the circumstances it takes place in (2.350–80): described in the form of a negative catalogue, the ceremony resembles a funeral more than a wedding and thus continues the simile of the household in mourning from the beginning of the book (2.20–28).

Marcia in a sense is the perfect wife for Lucan's Cato, for she plays the exemplary Roman matron in a rather weird way, too. They both seem to be preoccupied with their public roles and their future reputation, which they keep up at all costs. Marcia while still alive inscribes her own epitaph "Catonis Marcia" (2.343–44), and Cato in his rigorous adherence to the Stoic doctrine of "following nature" (2.382 *naturam . . . sequi*) denies himself even the simplest pleasures (2.380–91). This odd couple may be the last steadfast Romans in a collapsing world, but their relationship at the same time illustrates the emotional precarity characteristic of a civil conflict and the breakdown of all normal social bonds. If Cato is compared to a parent who mourns Rome like his own child (2.297–303), who is father and husband for the city (2.388 *urbi pater est urbique maritus*), his sterile reunion with his wife comes to symbolize the unnatural barrenness of civil war that produces nothing but death.

The Present Disaster Unfolding: The Civil War in Italy

The Italian Landscape Embodying Civil War

After the interlude with Cato and Marcia, the narrator "zooms in" on Pompey, who occupies the town of Capua as his strategic base (2.392–98). The ensuing catalogue (2.399–438) at first looks like a geographical description of the Apennine region from a military or scientific point of view, but soon it turns into an imaginary map of mountains and rivers with hyperbolical and almost surrealistic traits.[19] Their struggle amounts to a battle of the elements, as the sky-high mountain range dividing the Italian peninsula brings forth violent mountain streams that threaten to carry the land into the sea, and the sea in turn attacks the continent. As an example of such a blending of physical, historical, mythological, and allegorical levels, let us select the river Eridanus, which can be identified with the river Po but at the same time represents its mythical counterpart:

> quoque magis nullum tellus se soluit in amnem
> Eridanus fractas deuoluit in aequora siluas
> Hesperiamque exhaurit aquis. hunc fabula primum
> populea fluuium ripas umbrasse corona,
> cumque diem pronum transuerso limite ducens
> succendit Phaethon flagrantibus aethera loris,
> gurgitibus raptis penitus tellure perusta,
> hunc habuisse pares Phoebeis ignibus undas.
>
> (2.408–15)

and Eridanus, who rolls shattered forests into the seas
and drains Hesperia of waters; into no other river
is earth dissolved more. This river was the first,
the story says, to shade its banks with a ring of poplars;
and when Phaethon drove the day downwards on a crossways
path and with blazing reins ignited the ether
and the streams were torn completely from the scorched earth,
this river had waters equal to the fires of Phoebus.

Through the myth of Phaethon, who when driving the sun chariot of his father caused a catastrophic fire that nearly destroyed the whole earth, again an apocalyptic scenario is evoked.[20] By means of such subtle hints the Italian landscape functions as a mirror of the civil war. The global dimension of the conflict is further emphasized through the comparison of the Eridanus with two other major streams, the Nile and the Hister (2.416–20), for the people living in the delta of the Danube (cf. the catalogue of Pompey's troops in 3.200–202) and in Egypt (books 8–10) will become involved in the Roman civil war, too. Moreover, the Nile and its unknown sources form the subject of an extended digression in book 10.

In general, the concept of landscape embodying civil war is a recurrent feature of Lucan's epic. The description of the Apennines looks forward to another extended catalogue of mountains and rivers in book 6 (6.333–412), where the primeval landscape of Thessaly turns out to be the predestined stage for the decisive battle at Pharsalus. But also within the second book, nature and especially bodies of water inform the epic narrative in various ways. In the old man's speech, the countless victims of Sulla's proscriptions jam the river Tiber and dye its water crimson; at its mouth, the bloody torrent divides the blue sea, resulting in a sharp color contrast that underlines the transgressive man-made violence (2.209–20). At the end of the book, the sea turns blood red in the first naval battle of the new civil war (2.713), to be echoed by the bloody rivers at Pharsalus that color the sea red as Pompey sails away (7.789–90 and 8.33–34). The battle of winds in a sea storm simile illustrates the wavering behavior of the people that are torn between their loyalty for Pompey and their fear of Caesar (2.454–60). Finally, rivers and the sea play an important role in the military campaign, too. In order to besiege the Pompeian Domitius at Corfinium (2.478–504), Caesar has to cross another Italian river after the Rubicon:

nam prior e campis ut conspicit amne soluto
rumpi Caesar iter, calida proclamat ab ira
"non satis est muris latebras quaesisse pauori?
obstruitis campos fluuiisque arcere paratis,

ignaui? non, si tumido me gurgite Ganges
summoueat, stabit iam flumine Caesar in ullo
post Rubiconis aquas. equitum properate cateruae,
ite simul pedites, ruiturum ascendite pontem."

(2.492–99)

since Caesar from the plain saw first his passage being barred
by unbridged river, and in hot anger he exclaims:
"Are hiding-places behind walls not enough for your terror?
Are you blocking the plains and trying to keep me off with rivers,
cowards? After the waters of the Rubicon, Caesar
will now halt at no river, not if Ganges prohibit me
with his swollen flood. Make haste, squadrons of the cavalry,
forward, infantry, too: ascend the bridge before it falls."

By having Caesar mention the Rubicon, Lucan self-consciously refers back to
the beginning of the civil war and at the same time to the initial scene of his
epic; moreover, by hyperbolically stating that he would not even be stopped by
the Ganges, Caesar implicitly likens himself to Alexander the Great, who had
abandoned his Eastern campaign at this point, and even claims to surpass him.
At the end of the second book, in another near-hubristic attempt that is likened
to Xerxes's famous bridging of the Hellespont during the Persian Wars (2.672–
77), Caesar almost succeeds in blocking Pompey's fleet in the harbor of Brundisium by constructing a gigantic mole from rocks and trees (2.660–79).[21]

Caesar and Pompey as Antagonists

The characterization of the two opponents elaborates upon their respective portrayals in the first book, notably in the corresponding similes of the oak and
the lightning (1.129–57). Caesar, as demonstrated in the two episodes just mentioned, is the ever-active general who now employs the tactic skills he had
acquired during his campaigns in Gaul against Pompey and whose easy domination of nature lends him a superhuman touch (a trait that will become more
prominent in the course of the epic, especially during the sea storm in book
5).[22] Yet it is precisely his absolute will to win that is highly problematic in a
civil war, as emerges from his first appearance in book 2:

Caesar in arma furens nullas nisi sanguine fuso
gaudet habere uias, quod non terat hoste uacantis
Hesperiae fines uacuosque irrumpat in agros
atque ipsum non perdat iter consertaque bellis

bella gerat. non tam portas intrare patentis
quam fregisse iuuat, nec tam patiente colono
arua premi quam si ferro populetur et igni.
concessa pudet ire uia ciuemque uideri.

(2.439–46)

Caesar, mad for war, rejoices to proceed only by shedding
blood, rejoices that Hesperia's lands he tramples
are not empty of the enemy, that the fields he invades are not deserted,
that his march itself is not for nothing, that non-stop he wages
war after war. He would rather smash the city-gates
than enter them wide open, with sword and fire devastate
the fields than tread them with the farmer unresisting.
He is ashamed to go by paths permitted, like a citizen.

The image of Caesar using the towns of Italy as a training camp for his legions raises the worst expectations concerning his eventual aim, the capital. The fear of a bloody capture of Rome by either of the two civil war leaders has already been expressed in the old man's speech (2.227–32), and the dread that Caesar's legions are even worse than the Gauls was spread in the panic in book 1 (1.466–86). After Caesar has pursued Pompey throughout Italy, the narrator again suggests that the capture of Rome has only been postponed:

sufficerent aliis primo tot moenia cursu
rapta, tot oppressae depulsis hostibus arces,
ipsa, caput mundi, bellorum maxima merces,
Roma capi facilis; sed Caesar in omnia praeceps,
nil actum credens cum quid superesset agendum,
instat atrox et adhuc, quamuis possederit omnem
Italiam, extremo sedeat quod litore Magnus,
communem tamen esse dolet;

(2.653–60)

Others might be satisfied with capture of so many city-walls at first
assault, with sudden conquest of so many citadels, the enemy dislodged,
and with the easy seizure of Rome itself, the capital of the world
and war's greatest prize; but Caesar fiercely presses on,
impetuous in everything and thinking nothing done when there remains
still something more to do: although he occupies all Italy,
yet because Magnus remains on the seashore's edge it rankles
that the country is shared between them still.[23]

Eventually, the expectations that have been built up throughout the second book are not fulfilled in book 3 (3.84–112), as Caesar enters a terrified Rome without bloodshed.

Another controversial scene from book 2, mentioned briefly above, that points forward to a later episode in the epic is Caesar's siege of Corfinium (2.505–25). After the Pompeian commander Domitius has been handed over to Caesar by his own soldiers, the leader grants pardon to his opponent. Lucan's narrator relishes in the paradox of *clementia* ("forgiveness") in a civil war:[24] Caesar uses the positive gift of clemency as a quasi-punishment, for Domitius would have preferred to die in battle or to be put to death by the victor. Domitius gets his revenge at 7.599–616 when he meets Caesar again at Pharsalus, now fatally wounded but still having the last word, whereas in book 2 his concluding self-exhortation was audible only for the external audience: he is glad to be spared a second act of such clemency. Both passages taken together illustrate Lucan's vision of civil war turning all things upside down; words and values lose their meaning as the world to which they refer is collapsing.[25] Another paradox might be seen in that Domitius as Caesar's opponent is at the same time an ancestor of Nero's, who inherited the throne thanks to his adoption into the Julio-Claudian dynasty. The rather ahistorical epic role given to Domitius thus cannot be used as a decisive argument for or against Lucan's alleged republicanism or his relationship with Nero, nor can the political stance of Lucan's narrator be pinned down unambiguously throughout the work.[26]

While Caesar is mainly defined through his actions, Pompey in book 2 is mainly characterized through his speeches. His exhortation speech to his troops (2.528–95) indirectly answers Caesar's speech from 1.299–351.[27] Here Pompey sketches yet another picture of Caesar, one highly colored by civil war propaganda. Caesar is associated with foreign enemies such as the Gauls, whom he did not even manage to defeat (as Pompey spitefully insinuates), and with rebels such as Catiline. On the opposite, Pompey claims the better cause for his own side:

> "o scelerum ultores melioraque signa secuti,
> o uere Romana manus, quibus arma senatus
> non priuata dedit, uotis deposcite pugnam.
> ardent Hesperii saeuis populatibus agri,
> Gallica per gelidas rabies effunditur Alpes,
> iam tetigit sanguis pollutos Caesaris enses.
> di melius, belli tulimus quod damna priores:
> coeperit inde nefas, iam iam me praeside Roma

supplicium poenamque petat. neque enim ista uocari
proelia iusta decet, patriae sed uindicis iram."

(2.531–40)

"O you avengers of crimes and followers of the better standards,
O truly Roman army, given weapons by the Senate
on the State's behalf, pray for battle.
The Hesperian fields are ablaze with savage devastation,
the rabid frenzy of Gaul is pouring over icy Alps,
already there is blood on the defiled swords of Caesar.
It was better that the gods made us the first to bear the injuries of war:
from his side let the guilt begin; now, now, with me as leader,
let Rome seek punishment and penalty. And in fact, those battles ahead
    are not
called rightly real battles, but the wrath of your avenging country."

Through a long enumeration of his conquests and triumphs (2.576–95), Pompey tries to encourage his troops, but ultimately this confirms the image from 1.129–35 that Pompey is too reliant upon his past successes. In the end, Pompey utterly fails to motivate his soldiers, for his army has already been beaten by the mere rumor that Caesar is approaching—or by his fame (2.600 *iam uictum fama non uisi Caesaris agmen*). This impression is only seemingly contradicted by the subsequent simile likening Pompey to a herd-bull, who after being expelled by his rival gathers his strength, soon to return triumphantly (2.601–9). Rather than anticipating the course of action, this simile represents Pompey's self-image.[28] The obvious contrast with his actual situation makes his hopes appear ambivalent, not to say delusional. The more consistent authorial characterization of Pompey and his soldiers as passive, reluctant, and fearful will reappear at the eve of the battle at Pharsalus in book 7, announcing his decisive defeat.

In a second speech, Pompey, who is now cut off from all support, addresses his elder son Gnaeus and dispatches him to stir the East and even the Parthians (2.628–49). The ideas presented in this speech will be developed further in books 8 and 9 with Pompey's aborted plans to seek help from the Parthians and with his testamentary mandate that his sons are to continue the civil war after his death. The list of his triumphs repeated in both of his speeches here almost sounds like an obituary; consequently, at the end of book 2, the narrator states that Fortune has grown weary of Pompey's triumphs (cf. Pompey's dream of his youthful triumph at the beginning of book 7, his address to Fortune at 7.665–66, and the narrator's comment on her treachery at 7.685–86) and that the fate awaiting him is a grave in a foreign land (2.725–36; cf. the imaginary epitaph for his grave on the Egyptian shore in 8.806–15). According to the narrator, who empathizes with the doomed loser by addressing him personally in an extended apostrophe, the only consolation is that the Roman soil will not be stained by Pompey's blood.

Conclusion: Civil War in Book 2

In the second book, many seeds are planted that are to sprout important ramifications in later books. Besides the main antagonists Caesar and Pompey, Cato is introduced as a third major character, who will return only after Pompey's death in order to continue the civil war. Another minor character, the Pompeian commander Domitius, will feature again at the Battle of Pharsalus in book 7, both times engaging in a brief hostile exchange with Caesar. Collective bodies such as matrons, the older generation, and soldiers play an important role, too, sometimes represented by anonymous speakers. These various agents offer different perspectives on the civil war, underlined by the exceptionally high proportion of direct speech in this book (amounting to more than half of the text). Geographical descriptions, too, take up considerable space, notably the catalogue of the mountains and rivers of the Apennine region and the ekphrasis of Brundisium and its harbor; through the natural or man-made interventions and violent transformations taking place there, these landscapes mirror the upheaval caused by the civil war. Conversely, the epic action focusing on the military campaign is pushed somewhat into the background and does not bring about major changes but proceeds mainly along the lines that had already been mapped out in book 1, with Caesar moving forward aggressively (but not yet approaching the city of Rome) and Pompey retreating until there is no place left in Italy for him to hold on to. The second book thus revolves more around the past and the future than around the present, exploring the hopes and fears provoked by the civil war.

Notes

1. Fantham 1992a is a very accessible commentary on book 2. In this chapter, Lucan's text is taken from Shackleton Bailey 1997.

2. On Lucan's reception of the *Georgics* in general (not on this specific passage), see Kersten 2018.

3. In his reworking of Homer, Lucan separates the test from the narrative device of the dream, which he applies to Pompey at the beginnings of books 3 and 7. On Lucan's reception of Homer, see Lausberg 1985, esp. 1575–76 on this episode, and Fantham 1992a, 179 *ad loc.*

4. Cf. Fantham 1992a, 105 *ad loc.*; on the fall of Troy as a model for the old man's speech, see Ambühl 2010.

5. Cf. Fantham 1992a, 220 *ad loc.*; Rossi 2000, esp. 572–75, reads Pompey's journey as an "antiphrastic revisitation of Aeneas's journey."

6. On the connections between the Argonautic myth and Pompey's triumphal self-image (cf. below Caesar and Pompey as Antagonists), see Murray 2011.

7. On tragic reminiscences in Lucan's second book, see Ambühl 2010; cf. the extended version in Ambühl 2015, 304–36.

8. On the complex interactions between gods, supernatural forces, and humans in Lucan, see Feeney 1991, 269–301; cf. also several contributions in Baier 2012. For a more comprehensive treatment of religion in Lucan, see Arampapaslis and Augoustakis's chapter in this volume.

9. On such "alternative futures" in Lucan, see Ambühl 2020.

10. On the crucial role of the speeches of the "masses" in Lucan, see Schmitt 1995; on their interaction with the protagonists, see Gall 2005.

11. On the style of the passage, see Conte 1968 and Day 2013, 82–87, esp. 82 ("tortured hyperbata," "a syntax . . . distorted"), who dubs it "presenting the unpresentable." The graphic descriptions of violence and mutilated bodies in Lucan (especially in book 2) have recently been approached from various perspectives, see Galtier 2018; Nill 2018; Backhaus 2019; McClellan 2019, 115–69, esp. 116–20.

12. For the *Civil War* as a "literature of trauma," see Walde 2011; cf. also Thorne 2016: a comparative reading of Lucan alongside literary representations of the 1994 Rwandan civil war and genocide. On the traumatic memories of Marius and Sulla in Lucan cf. also Schrijvers 1988, Galtier 2016a, and Mebane 2020, and generally on the memory of Sulla's proscriptions as a Roman "cultural trauma," Eckert 2016.

13. On body imagery and dismemberment as stylistic and structural devices of Lucan's epic, see Dinter 2012.

14. At various points in the epic, Marius and Sulla are evoked as role models of Caesar and Pompey. Even more worryingly, the ghosts of Marius and Sulla emerge from their graves at 1.580–83, announcing the outbreak of a new civil war.

15. The age contrast (in reality only ten years) between the grey-haired Cato (cf. 2.375 *canos* "white hair") and his younger nephew (cf. 2.324 *iuuenis* "youth") seems to be exaggerated for dramatic purposes; likewise, Marcia appears considerably older than she would have been in real life, and her husband Hortensius had actually died several months earlier.

16. Widely differing interpretations of Lucan's Cato can be found, among others, in Ahl 1976, 231–79; Johnson 1987, 35–66; Sklenář 2003, 59–100; D'Alessandro Behr 2007, 113–61; Thorne 2010; Seo 2011 (extended version in Seo 2013, 66–93); Tipping 2011; Galtier 2016b (revised version in Galtier 2018, 247–66); Kersten 2018, 186–215. Wildberger 2005 discusses Lucan's allusive use of elements of Stoicism in his portrayal of Cato; cf. now also Kaufman 2020 and D'Alessandro Behr 2020. Graver 2011 points out the destabilizing effects of Lucan's inconsistent engagement with Stoic concepts in staging the marriage between Cato and Marcia.

17. Cf. Fantham 1992a, 30. This ambiguous and ultimately futile idea of self-sacrifice in a civil war will be echoed by Pompey in book 7 (esp. 7.117–20, 356–60, and 647–72).

18. Ironically enough, in contrast to Pompey's wife Cornelia, whom she wants to emulate (2.348–49), Marcia is not to reappear in the *Civil War*; it is Cornelia who claims to be the only matron to accompany her husband to the camp (8.648–49). On Marcia and her connections to other female characters in the poem, see Finiello 2005; Sannicandro 2007, 2010, esp. 83–100; Dangel 2010. Gallia 2020, esp. 183–86, reads Marcia and the mourning matrons as refractions of the trauma of civil war through the lens of family.

19. On the geographical catalogues and the landscape of war, see Bexley 2013; on the polyvalent functions of rivers in Lucan, see Walde 2007. Helzle 1993 gives a stylistic analysis and a symbolic interpretation of Lucan's description of the Apennines. It goes without saying that there are no simple one-to-one correspondences between the landscape and the events and protagonists of the civil war.

20. Cf. Ap. Rhod. *Argon.* 4.596–626 and Ov. *Met.* 2.1–366. The myth had been alluded to already at the beginning of book 1 (1.48–50), where the future god Nero is addressed as an anti-Phaethon who will not set the world on fire.

21. See Masters 1992, esp. 29–34, for an overtly metaliterary reading of Caesar's construction works in the *Civil War*.

22. On "Caesar as a larger-than-life, hyper-kinetic, awe-inspiring source of destruction, a literally superhuman force," see Day 2013, 106–78 (quote from p. 106), who identifies the "Caesarian sublime" in "his association with and response to objects and phenomena of the natural world."

23. The inability to share power is identified as one of the main causes of civil war at 1.84–111. Caesar accuses Pompey of not letting go of his power (1.333; cf. Curio's exhortation in 1.289–91), but for Caesar's part, too, he refuses to share even the tiniest bit of Italian soil with him.

24. The term *clementia* itself does not occur but is paraphrased by *uenia* "pardon" (2.511, 515), *munus* "gift" (2.512, 525), and *ignosci* "obtain forgiveness" (2.521).

25. On such paradoxes that make up the linguistic, rhetorical, and ideological stance of Lucan's epic, see Bartsch 1997, esp. 48–61, and in general Henderson 1987.

26. Ahl 1976, 47–54 interprets Lucan's Domitius as proof of Lucan's hostility to Caesarism and Nero; cf. Leigh 1997, 63–67 on *clementia* as a monarchic concept. Over against such ideological readings, Kimmerle 2015, esp. 232–42 on this episode, has recently made a convincing case against any consistent political message conveyed by Lucan's epic.

27. Cf. Fantham 1992a, 178–96, esp. 181.

28. See Fantham 1992a, 196–98. On Lucan's similes and their uses as a means for characterization, see Blaschka 2015, with further references (esp. 149–54 on this simile); cf. also Kersten 2018, 159–65.

3

Book 3

Crime and Reward

Markus Kersten and Christiane Reitz

Lucan's third book covers events from March to September 49 B.C.E.;[1] it thus comprises the longest span of narrative time in the *Civil War*. Beginning with Pompey's flight from Brundisium to Greece and ending with the Caesarians' victory at Massilia, the narrative alternates between elements of epic poetry and historical account.[2] In the *Civil War*, plot developments and events can occur suddenly, contrary to the conventions of ancient epic where the reader, and even the narrator who is inspired by the Muses, can expect a certain traditional unfolding of such matters. But set against the foil of traditional epic poetry, Lucan's epic poem offers itself to plentiful intertextual interpretations. Rather than to state that Lucan converts, erodes, or parodies fixed literary structures (which to some extent he surely does),[3] we shall look at the manner in which he actually uses and thereby affirms conventional narrative patterns.

The plot of book 3 is as follows. After a final look back from his ship to the shore of Italy, which he is destined never to see again, Pompey falls asleep. In a dream, his dead wife Julia (Caesar's daughter[4]) appears and warns the commander about the change of his proverbial luck (3.1–45). Meanwhile, Caesar marches toward Rome. In quick succession he provides sufficient food supply for the Italian mainland and violently forces his way to the treasury (3.46–168). Pompey's allied forces, mainly from the east, assemble; the narrator describes this with a conventional catalogue of troops, interspersed with ominous hints at the disastrous outcome of the war (3.169–297). Caesar travels to Massilia, a city that in Lucan's version of events remains loyal to its pledged neutrality agreement in the conflict.[5] While the inhabitants try to negotiate peace, Caesar proves inexorable. He gives the command to cut down a holy grove in order to besiege the city (3.298–508). As the siege does not lead to the expected success, the conflict between the Massilians and the Caesarian troops is fought out in a murderous sea battle (3.509–762).

The narrative of book 3 affirms the opening characterization of the protagonists at 1.129–57.[6] Pompey has no idea of the defeat to come and no strategy to prevent it. Unfrightened by the vision in his dream, he stays asleep—and he stays inert, unprepared, and reactive rather than active until the end of book 5, when he brings his wife Cornelia to Lesbos shortly before the Battle of Dyrrachium. Caesar, on the contrary, ruthlessly pursuing his goals, enters, violates, and subdues everything he needs to gain supremacy.

Two powerful frameworks for reading the *Civil War* in general and this book in particular are intertextuality and self-referentiality. In this chapter, we draw attention to the way book 3 consistently displays—and questions—the vanity of (epic) tradition and the power of innovation: we will see that the distance that Lucan (or his poetic characters) keeps from customary thinking, customary writing, and reading functions as a persistent motif throughout the book.

Vain Dreams: Pompey's State of Mind

In Pompey's dream vision (3.8–35), Julia reveals that the underworld is being prepared for the countless dead of the civil war and that punishments are being readied in Tartarus.[7] She concludes by prophesying Pompey's own fate: "civil war will make you mine" (3.33–34). Pompey reacts like the traditional epic hero who encounters the dead: Aeneas who cannot touch the floating image of his wife Creusa, Odysseus who seeks in vain to embrace the shade of his dead mother. But on the other hand, the dreaming leader does not want the vision to affect him and makes no attempt to take any consequences. On the contrary, he reassures himself not to mind the dream, but rather to stay indifferent:

> "quid . . . uani terremur imagine uisus
> aut nihil est sensus animis a morte relictum
> aut mors ipsa nihil"
>
> (3.38–40)

> "Why am I alarmed by the apparition of an empty vision?
> Either no feeling is left to the mind by death
> or death itself is nothing"

This reaction is not typical for an epic hero.[8] It may even hint at a Stoic position, although the unimportance of death is a philosophical position equally in line with Stoicism and Epicureanism. Popular philosophy in the first century C.E. mainly consisted of a simplified code of Stoic conventions. [9]

Unlike his great epic idol, Agamemnon,[10] whom Zeus leads astray with a dream in *Iliad* 2.1–47, Pompey does not believe that the vision has any meaning for him. He seems to accept that he might die in the war, but he is not afraid of death, quite the contrary: we are told that "he rushed more eagerly to arms with a mind made up for calamity" (3.37 *maior in arma ruit certa cum mente malorum*). Adducing a rational twofold explanation, he convinces himself that death is meaningless for men and that, therefore, the furious image of his former wife reminding him of his responsibility is an empty vision (3.38). In particular, he does not consider it as a warning, and readers may imagine Pompey's ship steering to its destination without any change. By not reacting to the dream, Pompey makes a mistake similar to the one made by Agamemnon, who does react: he leads many of his men into defeat. The irony lies in the fact that his own vanity prevents him from changing his plans. Pompey the Great, whom thousands of people have applauded in his theater (1.131–35), is still hoping to regain leadership of Rome. When he pursues his course after the dream, he behaves even "Greater" (3.37 *maior*: one of the narrator's frequent puns on Pompey's title). In the night before the Battle of Pharsalus, Pompey has a second dream: "He dreamt that, as he sat in his own theatre, he saw the innumerable likeness of the Roman plebs, and his name was raised to the stars by joyful voices and the resounding tiers competed in applause" (7.9–12). On this later occasion, Pompey probably does not want the dream to be meaningless. But this time it is the narrator who explicitly states that the general's dream is empty (7.6–7).

Vain Honor: Caesar and the Corrupt Republic

Caesar enters Rome without encountering any resistance. The people are willing to obey him, and he demands even less than Rome is willing to cede to him (3.111–12). However, when Caesar tries to lay his hands on the state's treasury (traditionally kept in the Temple of Saturn), one man opposes him: Metellus, a tribune of the year 49. The narrator somewhat provocatively styles him as "stubborn" (3.114 *pugnax*), and in this he seems to focalize the events through the perspective of Metellus himself: Caesar's assault will be a test case to prove whether *Libertas* will stand up and law will be able to resist power. But Metellus's motivation for barring Caesar's path is not that of an exemplary Roman. He is guided neither by a deep feeling for traditional Roman honor nor by piety toward the gods.[11] His motive is simply greed. The narrator complains that only love of gold remains unmoved through fear of death (3.118–19).[12] Caesar understands Metellus's intent, and instead of making him a martyr of the republic, he mocks his false indignation:

> "uanam spem mortis honestae
> concipis: haud" inquit "iugulo se polluet isto
> nostra, Metelle, manus; dignum te Caesaris ira
> nullus honor faciet. te uindice tuta relicta est
> libertas? non usque adeo permiscuit imis
> longus summa dies ut non, si uoce Metelli
> seruantur leges, malint a Caesare tolli."
>
> (3.134–40)

> "Empty are the hopes of honourable death
> which you conceive: my hand will not pollute itself
> with your slaughter, Metellus; no office you hold will make you
> deserving Caesar's wrath. Are you the champion to whose safe-keeping
> freedom has been left? The length of time has not confused the highest
> and the lowest to this extent, that, if by Metellus's voice
> the laws are saved, they would not rather be destroyed by Caesar."

Caesar is surely wrong to break into the treasury, and it is surely of little value if one villain blames another. Lucan's reader may in fact have knowledge of another incident: before Caesar, the Pompeians themselves had tried to lay their hand on this same treasure.[13] However, what matters here is the frankness by which the author characterizes Caesar. Lucan's Caesar openly takes what he wants without any feigned pretensions. In particular, he scorns Metellus by alluding to the phrase "champion of freedom" (3.137–38 *libertatis uindex*), which in the year 49 usually referred to the republican standards set by exemplary heroes like Brutus[14] but later would be a core feature of Julian self-representation. Augustus, Caesar's heir, claimed that he had avenged and restored republican freedom.[15] By denying Metellus an "honorable death," Caesar once more seems to subvert a traditional literary set piece. In epic poetry, the man who begs for his life is typically put to death. Caesar, however, spares those who want to die (as we have seen at 2.511–15 with Domitius), and he prevents Metellus from claiming Roman exemplarity.[16]

A certain Cotta has the last word in this episode. He finally gets Metellus out of the way by explaining that resistance against a tyrant will do no good. Though the name sounds familiar, even illustrious, it is difficult to identify Cotta as a historical figure. We do not need to read this short scene as yet another example of senatorial cowardice. Cotta's declaration is at least ambiguous: "The freedom of a people coerced by tyranny perishes by freedom" (3.145–46).[17] More-over, when Cotta calls the money robbed by Caesar "the evil seeds of war" (3.150 *mala semina belli*), he echoes the narrator's introductory remarks on the causes of the war (1.158–82). Lucan thus bestows some general authority on him. Although Cotta seemingly accepts Caesar's power and the new role of the sen-ate, he is well aware that the new ruler's actions do not correspond to republican behavior. This might lead him finally to acknowledging the failure and the responsibility of his class. The reader is left in the dark as to whether Cotta explicitly does so.[18] Blaming Caesar with a keen *sententia*, he leaves the scene: "the poverty of slaves is dangerous not to themselves but to their master" (3.152 *non sibi, sed domino grauis est, quae seruit egestas*).[19] Caesar does not reply any more; he collects the money and Rome is, as the narrator remarks, "for the first time poorer than [a] Caesar" (3.168).

Vain Glory: The Catalogue of Pompey's Troops

A catalogue is an essential structural element of epic poetry. Longer cata-logues conventionally begin with an invocation of the Muse or the Muses. The narrator usually applies for divine help since the task of remembering is too much for a human being; moreover, a catalogue of troops usually features the contingents about to enter into battle and focuses upon the names of the mili-tary leaders in particular.[20] Both conventions are contradicted by Lucan. His account is nevertheless deeply rooted in tradition—namely that of "Alexan-drian" allusive didaxis, a technique of combining intertextual allusions with learned detail—which is another feature recognizable in most Roman epic catalogues.[21]

The narrator starts abruptly. The troops from all over the earth assemble in order to share Pompey's downfall (cf. 3.170 "domed to fall"). However, instead of being instructed by a traditional invocation, the reader of the catalogue has to sort out for themselves how this enumeration of troops is organized. The contingents mentioned first come from Amphissa, Cirrha, and Mount Parnas-sus (3.172–73): that is, from Delphi. Mount Parnassus "with its two peaks" is not exactly a densely populated area. On the other hand, it is well-known as the mountain of Apollo and the Muses.[22] That this mountain is now deserted can be read as a metapoetic commentary on the catalogue itself. The position of the catalogue poet is problematic and indeed problematized in the epic tra-dition. Unlike other poets, however, Lucan does not receive the assistance he might require for this task (cf., e.g., Hom. *Il.* 2.484–87, Ap. Rhod. *Argon.* 1.22, Verg. *Aen.* 7.641–46).[23] Since his whole list will have to deal with the entanglement of facts and fiction, his fact-heavy geographical enumeration and the many mythological details he includes might get in each other's way. The reader is pushed from the outset to consider that the catalogue might not be "true" or at least not of "epic" dimension. In fact, it aims at reflecting on the futility of things, rather than recording exactly the numbers of foreign vassals under Pompey's command.[24]

The Greek soldiers come from places associated with oracles (3.174–80) that are either famous but silent or active but unknown (and, therefore, perhaps untrustworthy). Lucan's readers may infer that the men would hardly have come to fight had they been prophesied the truth. Athens sends but three ships, a pale reminder of the times when they defeated Persia ("three vessels ask us to believe that Salamis is true," 3.183). Support comes also from Iolcos, but the narrator adds that from there the Argo, the first ship, has set sail and brought death to many a man (3.196–97). The most significant remark, however, concerns both Pompey and Caesar:

> Iliacae quoque signa manus perituraque castra
> ominibus petiere suis, nec fabula Troiae
> continuit Phrygiique ferens se Caesar Iuli.
>
> (3.211–13)

> Trojan bands too, with their usual bad omens, head for the standards
> and the camp, doomed to perish, not restrained by the story
> of Troy or by Caesar's claim of descent from Phrygian Iulus.

Readers are bound to realize the significance of Troy coming to help despite the bond it has with its offspring Caesar: it strongly suggests the war amongst kin alluded to in the poem's first line (*bella plus quam ciuilia*). From a different point of view, the fact that the Trojans support Caesar's foe undermines the origin myth of the Julio-Claudian dynasty and Rome's foundation legend: the central issue of Vergil's *Aeneid*. The historical Caesar, however, will eventually emerge as the winner and will be able to establish his Trojan self-fashioning. The story of Caesar's adaptation of the dynastic and genealogical background that will become so important for imperial Rome starts in Troy, where he prays to his ancestral gods and promises to rebuild the ancient city at 9.990–99. The idea that a feigned narrative like a pro-Caesarian Trojan myth can be obliterated simply on rational grounds (this is what the narrator conveys by so obviously focalizing the Pompeians' confidence in their own legitimacy) proves entirely wrong.[25] Not only will the tale continue; it will even become *the* grand narrative of Rome. There is no need to suspect anti-Vergilian sentiment here.[26] Indeed, readers will notice repeatedly that Lucan's Caesar could hardly benefit from a profound comparison with *pius Aeneas* ("dutiful Aeneas"). Every kind of propaganda needs a critical mass of truth. Lucan draws attention to this by confirming rather than dismissing the moral authority of the *Aeneid*, often to Caesar's disadvantage.

The implications of fact and fiction for every kind of record as well as the importance of (poetic) transmission is further enhanced by the reference on the Phoenician invention of writing: "they were the first, if rumour is believed, who dared to mark speech to last forever with crude symbols" (3.220–21). We have already argued that the beginning of the catalogue points, through mentioning Mount Parnassus, to its own literariness. That the Muses have withdrawn from their dwelling place can be read as an allusion to the difficulty the catalogue poet encounters. Another metapoetical hint might be deduced from the reference added to the Phoenician contingent (3.220–24). The Phoenicians are characterized as being probably (*famae si creditur*, "if report speaks true," 3.220) the inventors of writing. The written text, the list, is the ancestor of all forms of catalogues, more so than the Egyptian inscriptions that are mentioned next. By introducing this learned detail, the list positions itself firmly in the written catalogue tradition.[27]

Lucan is fond of rivers, lakes, and seas;[28] these often feature as symbolical bearers of memory. Hydrological items form an important element in Pompey's catalogue (Lucan names more than a dozen), where conflict, change, and fading glory are the overarching ideas they symbolize. The poet's remark on the Tigris famously resembles a couple of verses by the emperor Nero:[29]

> at Tigrim subito tellus absorbet hiatu
> occultosque tegit cursus rursusque renatum
> fonte nouo flumen pelagi non abnegat undis.
>
> (3.261–63)

> the earth with a sudden chasm swallows up Tigris
> and covers his secret course, but does not withhold
> from sea's waves the river, which is born again from a new source.

Compare Nero:

> quique pererratam subductus Persida Tigris
> deserit et longo terrarum tractus hiatu
> reddit quaesitas iam non quaerentibus undas
>
> (Nero *frag.* 1 *FPL* Blänsdorf)

And the Tigris, that covertly leaves Persia having wandered through it.
He will disappear; and being drawn through a long cleft beneath many

a land, he gives back his flood to those who have searched for it and
now need not search any longer.

It is not possible to reconstruct what this parallel could have meant for a Neronian audience, nor can we determine which passage actually alludes to the
other. But we can detect a profound difference between the two. Whereas Nero
describes the triumph of the river, Lucan tells of the defeat of the earth
("swallows up . . . covers . . . does not withhold"): a mood that is perfectly in line
with his gloomy catalogue. The narrator then briefly calls the river Halys "fatal
to Croesus" (3.272) and, more elaborately, explains that Hercules's Pillars are
not unique in their significance:

> quaque, fretum torrens, Maeotidos egerit undas
> Pontus, et Herculeis aufertur gloria metis,
> Oceanumque negant solas admittere Gadis;
>
> (3.277–79)

> [People also came from] where Pontus drains off the waters of Maeotis,
>   the torrential
> strait, and steals glory form the Pillars of Hercules,
> and so men say that Ocean does not enter only at Gades.

This is not only a side note by a learned poet, since to deny glory (which itself
hints at the κλέος, "glory," of traditional Greek epic) is precisely one of the functions of this catalogue. In a way, it is not the glory of the pillars that is robbed,
but that of their constructor, Hercules, whom people admire for his eagerness
to overcome or at least to compete with nature.[30] There is no chance for heroism in the *Civil War*, not even for Hercules.[31]

The catalogue ends with the conclusion that Fortune has raised all these
peoples doomed to devastation in order to bestir a worthy funeral procession
for Pompey—and to make it easy for Caesar ("to ensure that lucky Caesar
received everything at one stroke," 3.296). In the end, as the readers know, Pompey's allies cannot prevent his downfall. Interestingly enough, in the *Civil
War*, they do not even count. The narrator mentions hardly any single military
action of the non-Roman allies coming from nearly all over the world to support the Great Pompey.[32] The military deployment Lucan records in this catalogue is useless.

The structural element of the catalogue is used by Lucan, in this case, to
reflect on memory as well as historical and even mythical events that, for the
disordered situation at hand, prove to be irrelevant. By different means, but with
the same effect, the catalogue of Caesar's troops (1.392–465) points to the absur-
dity of civil war instead of emphasizing the prowess of the soldiers and their

leaders.[33] Caesar's troops assemble from all over Gaul, and the catalogue is organized by regions the Roman troops have left. They left the occupied country,
and the inhabitants rejoice about their newly regained freedom, whereas the
occupant is on his way to destroy the freedom and liberty of his own country.
Viewed as an ensemble, the catalogues show a world in turmoil where past
deeds and virtues are to no avail and where even the traditional ways to construct a catalogue are overturned.[34]

Vain Fidelity and Vain Fear: Caesar at Massilia

In our historical sources, the city of Massilia did not take a neutral position in
the civil war. Lucan, by claiming the Massilians' neutrality, is able to accord to
its inhabitants a declaration of deep humanity.[35] After Caesar's arrival, a Massilian embassy—bearing an olive branch, the symbol of peace—brings forward
a petition. The Massilians request that they might not be forced to take sides;
they would rather dare to keep their loyalty to Rome (9.301–2). This means they
want to stay loyal to the Rome they used to know.[36] The core issue of their speech
reads as follows:

> "sit mens ista quidem cunctis, ut uestra recusent
> fata, nec haec alius committat proelia miles.
> cui non conspecto languebit dextra parente
> telaque diuersi prohibebunt spargere fratres?
> finis adest scelerum, si non committitis ullis
> arma quibus fas est . . .[37]
> . . . .
> uel, cum tanta uocent discrimina Martis Hiberi,
> quid rapidum deflectis iter? non pondera rerum
> nec momenta sumus, numquam felicibus armis
> usa manus, patriae primis a sedibus exul,
> et post translatas exustae Phocidos arces
> moenibus exiguis alieno in litore tuti,
> inlustrat quos sola fides."
>
> (3.324–29, 336–42)

"Let everyone indeed share this intent, to refuse a part in your
fate and let no foreign soldier wage these battles:
who will not drop his arm when he sees his father facing him?
  Who will not
be stopped from throwing weapons by brothers on the other side?

The end of the crime is here if you refuse to fight
your lawful enemy . . .

. . . .

Why do you divert your rapid march to us when such great crises
of Iberian warfare summon you? Not weighty in the world are we
nor do we swing the balance; never have we used weapons
prosperously, exiles from our country's first abodes;
and since Phocis's citadels were transferred,
we are protected on a foreign shore by tiny city-walls,
with loyalty our only glory."

Yet if, they add, Caesar still wants to fight them, they will resist bravely: "and this people is not afraid to endure for the sake of freedom the ordeal of Saguntum besieged by Punic warfare" (3.349–50). The Massilians reinforce their message by introducing an unfavorable comparison between Caesar and Hannibal.[38] Caesar's reaction is comparable to his behavior toward Metellus. He tells the envoys that they are speaking in vain: *uana mouet Graios nostri fiducia cursus* (3.358). But there the similarity stops. Caesar might have had a reason for mocking Metellus's obviously unfitting rhetoric. The Massilians, however, are not degenerated aristocrats, but rather—as their remark on exile, low fortifications, and freedom suggests—a people similar to the Romans of a former time.[39] Caesar does not or will not notice this resemblance. Again, as in front of the Roman treasury, his answer is spoken from wrath and aims to taunt (3.356, cf. 142). He deliberately misunderstands the Massilians' claim to trust (3.342 *fides*) with his remark on the futility of their confidence in his speed (3.358 *fiducia cursus*): that is, their trust that he will depart rather sooner than later from their shores. While the Massilians parade their *fides* as a virtue belonging to a former Rome where civil war was not possible, Caesar makes fun of them and of their fidelity. "Credit shaken and war advantageous to many" (1.181 *et concussa fides et multis utile bellum*): that is how the narrator sums up the cause of war in book 1. By laughing at the sheer concept of *fides*, Caesar compromises himself even more than by the spoliation of the Temple of Saturn for purely financial reasons. In Massilia, religion is indeed at issue. Caesar, in the first episode, really needed the money from the treasury, otherwise the Pompeians would have taken it. At Massilia, as the poet painstakingly suggests, the maneuver is unnecessary in terms of strategy and results in a straightforward war crime. Accordingly, Lucan lets his Caesar shout with an obvious feeling of pleasure: "There is time to destroy Massilia. . . . You will suffer for your bid for peace" (3.360, 370). The general even claims a self-invented "natural law" when he compares himself and his maneuvers to nature:

"uentus ut amittit uires, nisi robore densae
occurrunt siluae, spatio diffusus inani,
utque perit magnus nullis obstantibus ignis,
sic hostes mihi desse nocet, damnumque putamus
armorum, nisi qui uinci potuere rebellant."

(3.362–66)

"As the wind loses strength and is dissipated in empty space
unless the forests thick with timber block its path,
and as a great fire dies without fuel,
so lack of enemies hurts me and we think it a loss
of warfare if those who could be defeated do not fight back."[40]

Fittingly enough, he subsequently starts cutting down trees for his siege works. The deforestation of the eerie holy grove (3.399–452), which everybody except Caesar believes to be a sacrilege, dominates the book and is one of the most popular pieces of the whole poem. At first sight, it appears like a "purple passage" *par excellence,* since it contains the topical description of a wood, beginning with a very formulaic phrase *lucus erat* (3.399 "There was a grove . . ."). Presumably, though, Lucan was very much aware that he was using a stock motif of poetry. Horace's critical remark on topics and *topoi* like these was in all probability well known: "one or two purple patches to shine out far and wide, such as when we have a description of Diana's grove and altar" (*Ars P.* 15–16). In Horace, there follows yet a sneering quip about poets who put conspicuous ornaments at every place regardless of plausibility: "and perhaps you know how to portray a cypress: what is the good of this, if you were given money to paint a man swimming for his life from a wrecked ship?" (*Ars P.* 19–21).[41] The trees in Lucan's grove are hewn in a specific order, the cypress forming the climax. However, there is another kind of tree even less fitting the purpose: Caesar orders the alder tree to be cut, though it is more suitable for shipbuilding than for building a rampart (3.441). It rather seems Lucan has accepted Horace's challenge. The rich texture of the passage, including allusions to contemporary history as well as intertextual links to a huge range of poems makes it all too easy to read it as a set piece meant simply to inflate the book with a creepy description of Caesar's adventurousness.

This is not the place to analyze the passage *in extenso* and to deal with the different (and, as often with Lucan, contradicting) interpretations scholars have proposed.[42] A selective overview, though, about the ways of approaching Lucan's grove may be useful. First, we shall have a look at three significant intertextual relations—to the *Metamorphoses,* to the *Aeneid,* and to the *Georgics*—and then we shall discuss two perspectives to evaluate Caesar's deforestation, namely blasphemy and enlightenment.

Intertextuality or (in Wooden Terms): ὕλη and ἐνάργεια

Lucan's grove is an uncanny place; it is old, dark, cold, and, most of all, untouched: "never profaned since time remote" (3.399). Apart from that, however, Lucan's description is remarkably vague. No Roman pastoral gods dwell there (which might be no surprise), but the barbarian gods who receive worship in the grove are actually unknown (3.416–17). All the trees are consecrated with human blood (3.405). Does that really mean that the grove is a place where human sacrifices happen? The narrator is eager to state that nearly everything there—animals being anxious to enter the grove, strange yells from beneath the earth, trees falling down and rising again, snakes twined around trunks—depends on legend ("if antiquity at all deserves credence," 3.406; "now it was rumored," 3.417). An air of uncertainty wavers around the sanctuary's majesty.

For readers, an important effect of that *lucus* depends on its general intertextual relation to the idea of an eerie grove;[43] or, in other terms, the poet could easily have used conventional *topoi* had he wished to give a vivid description instead of vague beliefs and superstitions. The ekphrasis of mythical, holy, or gruesome places is a traditional epic device, and as Horace's sarcastic comment indicates, it is often found in epic as well as in other genres. But since Lucan avoids clearly describing the sanctuary, a detailed comparison with the typical ekphrases of *loca horrida* in Ovid or in Senecan tragedy will not elucidate his dark wood very much.[44] It is rather more important to focus on the narrative embedding of the scene. The actual cutting of the trees is Caesar's achievement, and the act of destroying the traditional epic grove is an emblematic feature of Lucan's narrative. In ancient epic, trees are cut, generally speaking, for two reasons: in order either to fight the gods by destroying a sanctuary or to build a pyre for dead heroes. The first is the exemplary deed of Erysichthon (Ov. *Met.* 8.738–884), the latter that of the Trojans, including Aeneas (Hom. *Il.* 23.114–22; Verg. *Aen.* 6.179–82).

The tale of Erysichthon, who cuts down a tree sacred to Diana and is therefore punished by insatiable hunger, is not only transmitted in Ovid but is already in Callimachus (*Hymn* 6.31–117).[45] We may therefore imagine that Caesar's soldiers have heard of the mythical story and its ethical implications.[46] They shrink back and hesitate to execute Caesar's orders. It was Erysichthon's fate to lacerate his body to eat his own flesh.[47] Accordingly, the soldiers have a reason not to follow orders:[48]

sed fortes tremuere manus, motique uerenda
maiestate loci, si robora sacra ferirent,
in sua credebant redituras membra securis.

(3.429–31)

But courageous hands faltered; and affected by the place's
awesome majesty, they believed the axes would rebound
on their own limbs if they struck the sacred trunks.

Astonishingly, and for the first time in the book, Caesar's reaction to opposition is not anger and wrath. Instead, he takes an axe, but not to truncate the reluctant soldiers—as does Ovid's Erysichthon—but to strike the first blow against an oak himself (3.433–34). Apart from that, however, he behaves as could be expected, by mocking the soldiers' baseless fears: "Now none of you need hesitate to cut down the wood: mine is the guilt (*nefas*)—believe it!" (3.436–37). In particular, it seems as if Caesar wants to attack both the Gauls' primitive cult (by testing whether the gods will punish him) and his legionaries' inappropriate remembrance of a typical epic setting: the evil deed of felling trees (by laughing at the term *nefas*).

The men, however, do not believe him. They obey, just because they have the choice between Caesar's immediate wrath and the god's future revenge: "all the throng obeyed his orders, not free from fear with dread removed, but weighing in the scales the wrath of the gods" (3.437–39). Subsequently, the trees fall, and the readers cannot but notice that they fall in a truly epic manner (emphasis added by authors):

procumbunt orni, nodosa impellitur ilex,
siluaque Dodones et fluctibus aptior alnus
et non plebeios luctus testata cupressus.

(3.440–42)

Down fall the ash-trees, the knotty holm-oak is overthrown;
and Dodona's wood and alder, more fit for the waves,
and cypress, witness to no plebeian grief.

Book 6 of the *Aeneid*, in which Aeneas cuts the trees for Misenus's funeral, forms an obvious model:

procumbunt piceae, sonat icta securibus ilex
fraxineaeque trabes cuneis et fissile robur
scinditur, aduoluunt ingentis montibus ornos.

(Verg. *Aen*. 6.180–82)

Down fall pitch-pines, the holm-oak sounds from the blow of the axe,
ashen timber and the fissile wood of the oak are split
with wedges, and from the high mountains they roll down ash-trees.

Cutting down trees is an ambiguous act, even if executed in preparation of the burial of a hero. In Aeneas's case, it is a necessary step to a still greater, still more virtuous achievement: the search for the golden bough and, eventually, the foundation of Rome. This may be a justification.[49] That Caesar is about to conquer Massilia, while on his way to re-found Rome as capital of the Caesarian empire, may function as a justification as well—as long as one feels inclined to adopt a Caesarian perspective on tradition and innovation. For readers, however, a comparison between Aeneas and Caesar does not automatically lead to an exculpation of the general. The grove, we must not forget, provides the material for the siege of Massilia, which Caesar wants to destroy because he has enough free time to do so and because he does not respect the Massilians' *fides*, their respect for treatises and social relations. Is his violent act against the holy trees really directed against barbarian faith and not rather against civilized religion? Lucan leaves the decision to the readers.[50]

Nevertheless, the poet offers another meaningful allusion to Vergil. In the *Georgics*, in a famously controversial section, the deforestation of old groves is suggested as a means to get new farmland (Verg. *G.* 2.203–11). The readers encounter the same ambiguity: the apparently impious cutting of trees on the one hand and the improvement of (agri-)cultural yield on the other. In Lucan however, the narrator painstakingly hints at the agricultural damage Caesar causes:[51]

utque satis caesi nemoris, quaesita per agros
plaustra ferunt, curuoque soli cessantis aratro
agricolae raptis annum fleuere iuuencis.

(3.450–52)

And when enough of the grove is felled, it is carried on wagons
seized throughout their territory and, their oxen stolen, the farmers
weep for the harvest of the soil untouched by curving plough.

Jamie Masters has pointed out that Lucan's Caesar does not destroy just arbitrary woodlands but a specific holy *lucus* ("grove"):[52]

Topos—*locus*—*lucus* is one avenue; but, more importantly, *silua* ("woods"), like Greek ὕλη ("woods"), is often used as a metaphor with the sense "material, subject-matter." Thus deforestation

becomes a metaphor for the plundering of poetic material from
another source, and inasmuch as this example of deforestation is
itself continually a *topos* that comes from another source, we see that
it enacts on the plane of epic action what it represents on the plane of
literary activity.

It is precisely Lucan's intertextuality that makes things difficult, and the grove
is most emblematic in that direction. Does the author plunder his predecessors' works by allusion to and subversion of their epic projects or does he reflect
on figures of recent history who ignore and destroy the conventions of culture
and literature?[53] There are reasons to see the parallels between the author and
his "hero" Caesar (as Masters does). There is, however, also much evidence that
Lucan damns the murderous activities of the man who revolutionized Rome.

Enlightenment in Gaul versus Darkness at Pharsalus

Caesar brings light into the grove, he shows that there is no reason to fear this
place, and, furthermore, he does not suffer punishment for his desecration. He
is exactly the man to win the civil war. He overcomes the corrupt republic and
its defender, Pompey, just as he abolishes this outdated barbarian sanctuary.
Here again, he becomes the lightning bolt to strike the oak. That Caesar dis-
pels superstition is impressive and has been admired by several scholars just
as his recklessness has been condemned. Indeed, both perspectives are necessary to come to terms with a character that is entirely ambiguous:

> tum primum posuere comas et fronde carentes
> admisere diem, propulsaque robore denso
> sustinuit se silua cadens. gemuere uidentes
> Gallorum populi, muris sed clausa iuuentus
> exultat; quis enim laesos inpune putaret
> esse deos? seruat multos fortuna nocentis
> et tantum miseris irasci numina possunt.
>
> (3.443–49)

[These trees] then for the first time shed their tresses and, robbed
    of foliage,
let in the daylight; and thrown down on its packed timber
the falling grove supports itself. The Gallic people
groaned at the sight, but the soldiers blockaded inside the walls
are jubilant—for who would think that the gods are injured

without revenge? Often their good fortune guards the guilty
and the deities can only be enraged with the unlucky.

Caesar's deforestation is an act that stands in stark contrast to the civilizing
technological projects that formed (especially since Augustus, but also in
Lucan's own time) such an important part of imperial propaganda. Matthew
Leigh, who has offered the most astute analysis of the passage, sums up the
importance of the metaphor of light for cultural development. By comparing
Caesar's deforestation to major Augustan projects of Romanization, like the
transformation of Lake Avernus into a naval base, he stresses the contradictory
appearance of the general:

> The villainous Caesar will therefore be considered in the paradoxical
> guise of culture-hero. As surprising as this role may be, moreover, it
> is also one which Caesar attracts in spite of himself and almost in
> contradiction of his titanic ambitions.[54]

Caesar does not even understand that he could indeed propagate a "modern,"
more philosophical approach toward religion and cult, had he only something
constructive to say and to do at Massilia. In fact, by laughing at the vanity of
tradition he completely fails to notice his own vanity. He himself is not yet
enlightened:

> The hero who reveals the absence or impotence of the gods is one
> who is frustrated in his fundamental desire to perform the truly
> grand and charismatic deed of matching himself against those
> gods.[55]

Moreover, the clearing of the forest does not contribute anything to the eluci-
dation of nature or the education of the Romans who are committing the crime
of civil war. At Pharsalus, in fact, all of them ignore the divine warning. Phoebus withdraws from the sky in order not to have to look at the Roman misdeeds
(7.1–6). The soldiers do not care for this nor for the many other portents that
precede the battle:

> dementibus unum
> hoc solamen erat, quod uoti turba nefandi
> conscia, quae patrum iugulos, quae pectora fratrum
> sperabat, gaudet monstris, mentisque tumultum
> atque omen scelerum subitos putat esse furores.

> (7.180–84)

> The frenzied people had
> this one comfort, that the multitude is conscious of its wicked
> prayer—it hoped for father's throats, for brother's breasts—
> and it rejoices in the portents, and thinks its mental turmoil
> and its sudden madness is an omen of their wickedness.

Finally, we shall briefly mention three issues that may raise further suspicion about Caesar's success and impunity. (1) The wooden construction, for which the timber was actually acquired, proves useless. Unable to overcome the city by these conventional means, Caesar leaves the scene to his admiral Decimus Brutus Albinus (3.453, 761–62). Decimus prevails in the gruesome naval battle, but, as the readers know, will later join the conspiracy against Caesar (3.453, 500–508, 761–62). (2) Several times in the course of the war, the same Caesarians who have cut down holy trees suffer from a virtually "Erysichthonian" pain: they starve (4.93–97, 4.409–14, 5. 450, 6.106–17). (3) Felling trees is a conventional metaphor for killing people.[56] Eventually, when the Pharsalian groves send birds to lacerate the corpses of the dead soldiers, from their claws—as if as a kind of belated punishment for the deforestation—blood and gore drop down on the Caesarian victors (7.836–46) who in their majority can be identified as criminals.[57]

The Naval Battle: Vain Victory?

Lucan hardly needed to remind his readers that two of the most decisive battles in the Roman civil wars—Naulochus and Actium—were fought at sea. This of course contributes to the significance of Lucan's Massilia. As is the case with several other parts of the *Civil War*, this passage can stand for the war as a whole. Forming a coda of the book, it offers a concluding epitome of the crimes and vanities that have happened so far.[58]

Naval battles are rare in ancient epic. How historical epic poetry before Lucan dealt with the military importance of fights at sea (and the increasing popularity of mock sea-battles, *naumachiae*, at the theater) is difficult to reconstruct. However, even taking this uncertainty into account, we may perhaps assume that Lucan's example might have disappointed his readers' expectations at first sight.[59] Of course, readers will compare Vergil's ekphrastic description of Actium, the triumphal fight between good and evil (*Aen.* 8.675–713). Lucan's narrator supports this with the portrayal of the future victor: "loftier than all, the praetorian ship of Brutus" (3.535 *celsior . . . cunctis Bruti praetoria puppis*), a description that recalls Vergil's Augustus at Actium, "standing aloft in his ship"

(*Aen.* 8.680–81 *stans celsa in puppi*). But Lucan's sea battle comprises a relentless sequence of unusual and cruel death scenes. As regards the overall spirit, there are not many similarities with Vergil.[60]

Lucan leaves aside virtually all strategic explanations; rather than telling a certain course of events he elaborates several "static" scenes of individual disaster. The sea itself just forms the decorative setting for the fights, which develop exactly as if the soldiers fought ashore (cf. 3.569–70 "in the naval battle the sword achieves the most").[61] This is, however, what Lucan's Caesarians intended in the first place by prohibiting the Massilians from reaching the open sea: the immovable ships finally form an artificial battlefield. Interestingly, in remaining close to the shore and avoiding the quick motions of the smaller Greek vessels (3.553–66), Lucan's Brutus pursues a strategy opposed to that of Agrippa at Actium.[62] The readers may therefore infer that, in terms of metapoetics, the Romans rightly seem to lack the sublimity of a "real" victory at sea. The final defeat of the Massilians is fortuitous (cf. 3.752–62). The battle in Lucan's description has little importance for the war: readers are informed neither about Massilia's final defeat and destruction nor about the profit that Caesar gains therefrom.

The key issue is not the naval battle itself but a tragic defeat against an overwhelming power and the mutilation and death of the soldiers. There is no individual heroism; the perspective is rather like that of the end of *Iliad* 4, when the two great armies clash for the first time like surges of the sea and with the result that many a man dies (Hom. *Il.* 4.422–544). Lucan's narrative serves the victims (not only, but mostly, Greek) as it bestows glory upon their bravery and once more reveals their old-style Roman exemplarity. There is the Greek twin, injured to death, who saves his brother with his own body (3.603–26), and the father of Argus who commits suicide in order not to outlive his dying son (3.723–51). The most bewildering moment is the death of a certain Lycidas who perishes, cruelly lacerated, by slowly bleeding to death (3.635–46). It has been suggested that this description was the obscure passage that Lucan (according to Tacitus at *Ann.* 15.70) cited when he had his veins opened by command of Nero.[63] This suggestion is attractive not only because of the similarity of their deaths but because of the importance of the name Lycidas. Lycidas is the young poet-shepherd of Vergil's ninth *Eclogue* who, in an obvious post-war setting, hears the story of old Moeris (*Ecl.* 9.3–4) and who, naively singing, wants to move to the city of Rome. Who is the Lycidas whom Lucan lets die in the waves near Massilia? Is he a poet? Is he a symbol for the tale of woe that must be remembered and honored in the new world, a world that arises from the waves of Massilia, Naulochus, and Actium? Here, Lucan's often intrusive narrator remains silent. He ends the book with a remarkable adversative sentence: "But

Brutus was victorious on water and first conferred on Caesar's warfare glory at sea" (3.761–2). Washed ashore, the truncated bodies of the dead are not distinguishable anymore. The Massilian women do not recognize whom to embrace and to bemoan (3.756–61), but Brutus has got Caesar the honor of his first great success. This success, we might deduce, does not count.

Notes

1. Markus Kersten conceptualized and began to write this article in Vandœuvres. He is most grateful for the hospitality of the Hardt Foundation. Christiane Reitz added some suggestions. All dates refer to the calendar before it was changed by Caesar.

2. The standard commentary is Hunink 1992.

3. For general remarks on structures of epic poetry, see Reitz and Finkmann 2019, esp. the introduction in vol. 1.

4. That Caesar was Pompey's father-in-law is the emblematic reason for the civil war being "worse than civil" (1.1): since it is thus a war between family members.

5. The Massilians claimed indeed to stay "neutral" (cf. Caes. *BCiv.* 1.34–35; Cass. Dio 41.19), which, however, would have been especially useful for Pompey. The absence of the Pompeian general Domitius from Lucan's Massilia enhances the heroism of the Massilians.

6. See Rosner-Siegel 1983; Feeney 1986; Leigh 2010.

7. See Reitz 2017.

8. Cf. Hom. *Il.* 22.300–301; *Od.* 11.488–89: the Homeric characters live in great fear of death.

9. On Pompey's dreams, see Walde 2001, 389–410.

10. On Pompey's imitation of Agamemnon, see Cic. *Att.* 7.1.2; Plut. *Pomp.* 67.5; App. *BCiv.* 2.67; Cass. Dio 42.5.3–5.

11. Metellus pompously but, we may infer, with vain religiosity utters the sentence, "this rank of mine finds gods to avenge its violation" (3.125–26) before shifting to the rather economic argument that Caesar need not plunder the Roman temple since he could conquer foreign cities. See Hunink 1992, on 3.123 for the structure of the speech.

12. "To this extent the love of gold alone knows no fear of sword or death" (*usque adeo solus ferrum mortemque timere / auri nescit amor*), echoing the desperate question of Vergil's Aeneas, "What acts do you not compel the hearts of men to commit, accursed hunger for gold?" ("*quid non mortalia corda cogis, / auri sacra fames?*" *Aen.* 3.56–57).

13. See Cic. *Att.* 7.21.2; Caes. *BCiv.* 1.14.1.

14. Cf. Cic. *De or.* 2.199; Liv. 2.1.8.

15. Cf. Aug. *RGDA* 1.1.

16. See Hunink 1993, on 3.134. It may be instructive to consider whether we should conceive of Lucan's Caesar as somebody who knows that he contradicts the form of conventional epic fashion.

17. "*libertas*" inquit "*populi quem regna coercent / libertate perit.*" The sentence is not easy to understand. The *Commenta Bernensia* offer two explanations: (1) the alleged freedom of the people is destroyed by the freedom of the tyrant (who, like Caesar, takes possession of the treasury), or (2) their freedom is destroyed when somebody (like Metellus) asserts the right of free speech. Although most commentators tend toward (2)—thereby somewhat confusingly inferring that Cotta himself does not make use of free speech when he formulates this disillusioning sentence in public—the ambiguity of Cotta's words cannot be solved.

18. To our mind, it is not necessary to judge Cotta as negatively as Hunink 1992 did.

19. To style Caesar as *dominus* ("master") may be a clarifying reaction to Figulus's prophecy "that peace brings a master" (1.670 *cum domino pax ista uenit*).

20. On this matter, see Reitz 1999.

21. On Lucan's catalogues in general, see Bexley 2014, 3848–49.

22. Cf., e.g., Hes. *frag.* 26.12; Luc. 1.64, 5.73; Stat. *Theb.* 6.355–57.

23. This is further enhanced by the mention of Cirrha. At 1.64 Lucan describes Apollo as "controlling Cirrha's secrets" (*Cirrhaea secreta mouens*) and refuses the god's inspiration for writing the poem. On the implications of this lack of divine authentication for the narrator and the narrative, see Erler 2012.

24. The prophesy of the Delphic oracle at 5.71–236, which is by no means substantial, is perfectly in line with this kind of divine refusal.

25. The narrator, although often interested in rational explanations, expresses a strong feeling for poetic license, cf. his remarks at 9.359–60.

26. Rather, by associating Pompey with the Trojans, the motif of the beheaded Priam / Pompey (*Aen.* 2.558; cf. Lucan 1.685–86) gets reinforced.

27. On catalogues in more general terms, see Reitz, Scheidegger Lämmle, and Wesselmann 2019 and Reitz 2021.

28. On Lucan's "hydrology," see Walde 2007.

29. See the *Adnotationes* on Luc. 3.261; on Nero as a poet and his remaining verses, see Reitz 2006, 23–25.

30. See 1.417–19 and 5.176–89 on the inaccessibility of any "heroic" knowledge about the world.

31. In Libya, he has to share his fame with the Roman Scipio, cf. 4.656–60.

32. One telling exception is his non-Roman cavalry, who are framed as bringing about his defeat at Pharsalus, see 7.506–44.

33. Batinsky 1992; Radicke 2004, 244.

34. Reitz 2013, 233; Batinsky 1992.

35. See Hunink 1992, 141, and see note 5 of this chapter.

36. As the speech of the Massilians makes clear at 3.310–14.

37. On the difficulties of this sentence, see Hunink 1992, *ad loc.*

38. See also 1.30–32, 1.303–5.

39. Cf. Rowland 1969.

40. For an explanation of Caesar's false comparison, see Hunink 1992, *ad loc.*

41. On this as well as on Pers. 1.70, see Fantham 1996, 148.

42. See Phillips 1968; Dyson 1970; Rosner-Siegel 1983, 175–76; Leeman 1985, 203–211; Thomas 1988a; Degl'Innocenti Pierini 1990, 97–100; Ozanam 1990; Hunink 1992, 167–187; Masters 1992, 25–29; Green 1994; Fantham 1996; Santini 1999; Leigh 2010a; Panoussi 2003; Augoustakis 2006; Papaioannou 2012; Day 2013, 136–43; Chaudhuri 2014, 159–65; Pypłacz 2015, 59–109; Tola 2016.

43. The Greek word ὕλη, like the Latin word *silua*, means "wood" as well as "poetic material"; ἐνάργεια means "vividness," which in poetic contexts is achieved by the poet's diligent work.

44. Nevertheless, it is necessary to notice the motifs and conventions that our text shares with the scenery evoked in rituals and sacrifices particularly in Sen. *Thy.* 648–95; *Oed.* 530–58; [Sen.] *Herc. O.* 1618–41; see Garrison 1992, 100–101; Santini 1999, 207–8; Pypłacz 2015, 75–109.

45. On intertextual relations between these both texts and Lucan, see Phillips 1968; Degl'Innocenti Pierini 1990, 97–102; Keith 2011, 125–27.

46. On this example of "metapoetic realism," see Kersten 2018, 71.

47. Cf. Ov. *Met.* 8.877–78 (yet, this version need not be an invention by Ovid). In Callimachus, Erysichthon stays alive as a beggar, but his father wishes that Apollo had struck him (Callim. *Hymn* 6.100–101).

48. The scholia refer to the story of Lycurgus. On the significance of that myth, see Leigh 2010a, 213–15.

49. On this issue, see Thomas 1988a.

50. One reader, closer to Lucan, was Statius. At *Theb.* 6.90–106, the preparations for the funeral of the dead child Opheltes trigger a catalogue of trees. It is the only catalogue in the whole of the *Thebaid* that bears conventional traces and is not convincingly motivated by the plot. The astonishing masses and species of trees in this catalogue point rather, we would suggest, back to Lucan and to Lucan's allusion to Vergil.

51. On the significance of Verg. *G.* 2.513–15 for Lucan's account, see Hunink 1992, *ad loc.*

52. Masters 1992, 27.

53. On this matter, see Kersten 2018, 61–97.

54. Leigh 2010a, 202 and 219–28 on the Augustan transformation of landscapes and its impact on epic ekphrasis.

55. Leigh 2010a, 202.

56. See, e.g., Utard 2016, 189.

57. On this matter, see Hunink 1992 on 3.405; Ambühl 2015, 259–76.

58. Cf. Saylor 2003.

59. On Lucan's relation to epic and historiographic tradition, see Opelt 1957; Rowland 1969; Panoussi 2003; Utard 2016.

60. Caesar's own version of the battle(s) is also very different (cf. Caes. *BCiv.* 1.56–58; 2.1–7).

61. See Hunink 1992, *ad loc.*

62. Cf. Plut. *Ant.* 65.5; Cass. Dio 50.31.

63. See Hunink 1992, *ad loc.*

4

Book 4

The Triumph of Paradox and Exemplarity

Paolo Esposito

Book 4 comprises three large episodes: the Battle of Ilerda (4.1–401), the suicide of Vulteius's men (4.402–581), and the defeat and death of Curio (4.581–824).[1] These three scenes alternate in the outcome of the military operations for the two opposing sides. The second half of the book places more emphasis on setbacks for Caesar's men, while the first shows a decisive victory for the Caesarians; however, this victory comes after a series of ups and downs and only after their opponents seem to be on the verge of ending the war and achieving peace.

Historical Background

The Battle of Ilerda

These, in summary, are the facts.[2] In May 49 B.C.E., Caesar entrusted his military operations at Marseille to Trebonius and Decimus Brutus. He then marched with three legions through the Pyrenees to Spain, where he was reunited with the forces of his lieutenant, C. Fabius, who had already clashed at Ilerda with Pompey and was, at that time, in obvious difficulty. The Pompeians, meanwhile, had divided their forces. L. Afranius, the legate of Nearer Spain, had gathered five of his seven legions south of the River Ebro near the border with Gaul. Three were under his direct command and two were assigned to M. Petreius, legate of Lusitania. The other two legions were under the command of the legate of Further Spain, M. Varro. Afranius and Petreius, instead of exploiting their superior numbers to crush Fabius permanently, had adopted a tactic of wait-ing; their plan was to settle on Ilerda and the nearby hills.

The city of Ilerda was located on a hill looking over the right bank of the River Sicoris, a tributary of the Ebro; it sat opposite the only stone bridge con-necting the two banks. The Pompeians had settled in the city and had placed the supplies in the town and their troops in trenches on a deserted hill facing the town from the south (modern Gardeny). They believed that they were safe there because their elevated position would protect them from any famine. Their oppo-nents, unable to use the stone bridge at Ilerda, would be cut off by the Sicoris on the shore where they were encamped, and in that position they would be sus-ceptible to famine.

Fabius had established the Caesarian camp north of Ilerda and was build-ing two wooden bridges upstream to access the left bank of the river for food supplies, but this action was being hampered by the cavalry of Afranius and Petreius. Between the two sides, therefore, for a few weeks there were only minor skirmishes of this kind. Suddenly, around May 23, the Sicoris flooded and swept away one of the wooden bridges. The troops of Fabius had already crossed it, and now Afranius failed to prevent their return by the other bridge.

Two days after Caesar came to assist Fabius he repaired the damaged bridge and deployed his army near the Pompeian trenches in order to stretch Afra-nius's line. He quickly set up a camp on the slopes of the hill occupied by the Pompeians and simultaneously tried to occupy another hilltop located between the enemy camp and Ilerda, but this attempt was foiled. A second flood brought down the two wooden bridges and flooded the camps and surrounding villages. Caesar seemed to be isolated and contained, but he soon reacted by building a new wooden bridge by which he reopened the connection to Gaul.

Fearing that Caesar would cross the Sicoris, Afranius and Petreius attempted to transfer the fighting south of the Ebro, but Caesar waited until they were in particularly rough terrain to attack them. The exhausted Pom-peians tried to fraternize with opponents, while Afranius ordered the retreat to Ilerda. The two armies camped a short distance from each other, and Caesar began the encirclement of the enemy. The men of Afranius—without energy, wood, fresh water and adequate food supplies—were forced to surrender, the terms of which were negotiated by their commander (through his son): Afra-nius and Petreius had to leave Spain and immediately retire their local Span-ish forces; other troops would be withdrawn at the border between Gaul and Italy. No one would be forced to join the ranks of Caesar nor would they suffer any harm. The Pompeians accepted (July 2, 49). In forty days and with low casu-alties, Caesar had been able to take away from Pompey the only veteran troops still willing to support him and had taken the control of Nearer Spain from the republic.

The Suicide of Vulteius's Men

This event took place on the coast of Illyria, where Caesarian forces under Antonius were under siege by the Pompeians.[3] Three rafts loaded with Caesarians attempted to escape to the neighboring island of Curicta. To prevent their escape the Pompeians had drawn a long line of chains below the surface of the water. The first two rafts evaded the chains, but the third became entangled in them. The occupants of the raft, a cohort of men from Opitergium (modern Oderzo), were thus blocked and surrounded by overwhelming enemy forces as night fell. This pause was exploited by their commander, Vulteius, who convinced his men to commit mass suicide, so as not to give the enemy the glory of their inevitable success and, at the same time, to prove their determination to sacrifice everything for their cause and defend their freedom. The suicide was enacted the following dawn, under the watchful eyes of allies and enemies.

This was not a prominent moment in the war and was inessential to its outcome. For this reason, it was easier for Lucan to expand it and shape it to his own ends compared with more famous characters and events of the war: he seized upon these kinds of minor events to increase the point and drama of his story. The need to respect the essential historical coordinates of the civil war prompted him to give priority to less well-known figures and episodes and to lesser moments and details within episodes of particular relevance to the themes of his epic. In his treatment of these moments he exploits their full potential, freely inventing action, figures, and events that in his poem assume a thematic breadth and significance that a faithful retelling of the historical events could not have conveyed. Lucan himself comments only briefly on this event later in the poem (at 5.38–39 "the enemy lies overwhelmed in Illyrian waves"), but Quintilian (3.8.24, 30) offers good testimony on the potential significance of this episode: he groups it with the mass suicide of the Saguntines, who were besieged by Hannibal in 219 B.C.E., as illustrating an example of how in rhetorical exercises (*suasoriae*) on this topic, the actions of Saguntines and Vulteius's men only ostensibly stem from necessity but in reality are based on expediency. It has been observed that the mass suicide of Vulteius and his men creates in Lucan a miniature vision of the civil war: Lucan transforms the deaths of these men into a symbol of his entire epic; in a sense, they commit all the crimes of war by their action.[4] Vulteius represents a *uirtus* ("courage, bravery") that is perverted: he dedicates his courage wrongfully in the service Caesar.[5]

Lucan distorts the function of the traditional epic *aristeia* as a key moment in which the hero expressed his *uirtus*.[6]

The Defeat and Death of Curio

Gaius Scribonius Curio was one the most controversial and complex figures of the last period of the republic.[7] He had been a follower of the senatorial party but became a staunch supporter of Caesar after his allegiance had been bought with favors and money. Suspicions still lingered that his conversion to Caesar's cause was a ploy since his political maneuvering appeared to some designed to keep him at arm's length from both Caesar and Pompey.[8] Moreover, Curio's conduct during the ill-fated expedition to Africa in which he met his death appears no less controversial in the ancient sources. Some of the decisions taken by Curio in that expedition were certainly reckless and arrogant, but a number of unfortunate circumstances also intervened from the beginning, and these turned out to have greater influence on events than the great disadvantage of Curio's enemy in terms of men and resources.[9] Lucan's version has a unique and valuable place among the ancient sources on Curio's African campaign, since it is the only totally negative view;[10] but scholars have stressed Lucan's excessive concentration and simplification of the historical facts.[11]

Book 4 ends with an invective against Curio that divides into three parts: (1) the role played by Curio in the outbreak of civil war (4.799–809); (2) an apostrophe to Curio (4.809–13); and (3) the invective proper (4.814–24).[12] The tirade ends with a *sententia* in which Curio is contrasted with those who have had mastery over the city of Rome: while his predecessors brought the city to ruin, only Curio was able to sell it—an obvious allusion to the fact that he had been bribed by Julius Caesar:

> ius licet in iugulos nostros sibi fecerit ensis
> Sulla potens Mariusque ferox et Cinna cruentus
> Caesareaeque domus series, cui tanta potestas
> concessa est? emere omnes, hic uendidit urbem.
>
> (4.821–24)

> True, mighty Sulla and fierce Marius and bloody Cinna
> and the chain of Caesar's house created for themselves
> the power of the sword over our throats. But who was ever granted
> such great power as he? They all bought, but he sold Rome.

The placement of Curio's death at the end of book 4 conforms to a practice that was widespread in historiography, in which the death narratives of prominent men occurred at the ends of books.[13] Lucan's account of Curio's death also plays off the conviction of the Stoics that it was only at the moment of a man's death that he could truly reveal his *uirtus*. The story of this character, however—a sort of *alter ego* of Caesar—stands as an example of the corrupting influence of money and luxury: vices that had been described by Lucan as among the causes of the civil war (1.159–60). His death is an atonement and a punishment because he is a true instigator of the war, and it anticipates the fate of Caesar. His blind confidence in Fortune is the cause of his destruction.[14] Lucan himself recalls this story in book 5 when he states, "on Libya's barren fields Curio has fallen—a large part of Caesar's Senate." (5.39–40).

Unity and Coherence

The representation of clashes between highly unequal forces provides an internal coherence to book 4. Another unifying factor is the often-paradoxical performance of gestures and actions inspired by *uirtus*. The book's three episodes illustrate a distortion of Roman values: a common theme in the book is the tragic and paradoxical triumph of a *uirtus* that both leads to voluntary self-destruction and acts as an accomplice to an uncontrollable military *furor* ("madness"). This *uirtus* becomes a negative force that enhances the evil of civil war and acts at the same time as a symbol of the whole work and its theme: the civil war.

In the first half of the book the action begins with the events around Ilerda. The military operations in Spain are further proof of the invincibility of the Caesarians, in spite of their initially unfavorable situation. In the Ilerda episode, despite the obvious strategic and military superiority revealed by Caesar's men, Lucan emphasizes the decisive contribution of fate to their success. Even those moments of apparent setback for the Caesarian party in the next two episodes are presented as infrequent exceptions to an almost unstoppable run of triumphs.

The strictly military section of the narrative is very brief (4.11–47) and consists of the representation of a clash that is primarily a war of position and one characterized by stalling and lack of development owing to the equivalent power of the two armies. Suddenly, the battle narrative is dominated by the capricious mutability of the weather (4.48–49), and there is a long succession of wonders: alternating droughts and torrential rain, burning thirst and excessive consumption of water, destructive fury and the desire for peace and brotherhood (4.48–120). None of these moments lasts, as each is generated by its opposite in an uninterrupted sequence of scenes, but these scenes are unified by Lucan's strong emphasis on the flow of events, as well as by the disproportionate nature of the gestures enacted by both sides. While reason and common sense appear to prevail at times, the leaders' ruthless instincts suddenly re-emerge: instincts that Lucan explicitly denounces as being unjustified.

The flood that strikes Ilerda serves to prefigure, conversely, the torments of thirst that Caesar inflicts upon the Pompeians in order to induce them to surrender (4.292–336). This scene contains a detailed description of the sufferings of the Pompeians, who are first victims of a thirst that destroys them and then cut off by a sudden overabundance of water. Here we can see Lucan's special fondness for analytical and expressionistic descriptions, especially ones that are set in a macabre context or describe paroxysms such as soldiers struggling to the last drop of blood, magical reanimations of corpses, and a wide host of pathological symptoms. Nor could Lucan miss this opportunity for an invective against luxury and everything that falls outside the limits of the most basic natural needs, which he suggests are very small and easy to fulfil (4.373–81).

Lucan's idiosyncratic depiction of battle can also be seen in the clash in which the Caesarians, under the command of Vulteius, are trapped by deception on a raft off the Illyrian coast. At first, they desperately try to resist an enemy whose strength is overwhelming:

> inter tot milia captae
> circumfusa rati et plenam uix inde cohortem
> pugna fuit, non longa quidem; nam condidit umbra
> nox lucem dubiam pacemque habuere tenebrae.
>
> (4.470–73)

> there was a battle between
> the many thousand spread around the captured raft and on board
> hardly a full cohort: not a lengthy battle, it is true, since night hid
> with shadow the faltering light and darkness brought on peace.

After the cessation of fighting overnight and Vulteius's words of incitement, which prove capable of conquering every man's fear, the soldiers, at the rising of the new day, quickly turn their weapons against themselves and commit a dramatic mass suicide (4.539–660).

Similarly unusual is the end of the narrative of Curio's African campaign. As the deception conceived by the Africans becomes apparent, Curio and his men are seized by a paralyzing astonishment, and are unable either to flee or to organize a desperate defense:

> obstipuit dux ipse simul perituraque turba.
> non timidi petiere fugam, non proelia fortes
>
> (4.748–49)

At that moment the leader and doomed host alike were stupefied.
The fearful did not seek escape, the brave did not seek battle

In keeping with this paralysis of the Roman soldiers, Lucan highlights the unusually apathetic and indifferent attitude of their horses, which do not respond to any type of stress (4.750–53). The reason, as pointed out by Lucan's final comment, is that both the horses and riders are not really motivated to go into battle but are almost dragged unwillingly into the assault, thus offering an easy target to their enemies:

> iamque gradum neque uerberibus stimulisque coacti
> nec quamuis crebris iussi calcaribus addunt:
> uulneribus coguntur equi; nec profuit ulli
> cornipedis rupisse moras, neque enim impetus ille
> incursusque fuit: tantum perfertur ad hostis
> et spatium iaculis oblato uulnere donat.

(4.759–64)

And now they quicken their pace, not compelled by whips
and goads or commanded by the spurs however frequent:
the horses are driven on by wounds. And no one gained
by ending his steed's delay, as neither charge nor attack
was possible: he is only carried towards the enemy
and shortens the space for the javelins by presenting a target.

The peculiarity of the scene is formally indicated by a stylistic feature favored by Lucan: an abundance of negated statements that highlight the contrast between the reality of the situation and what one would normally expect.[15] The strangeness of the description is accentuated by the fact that not even the most common and predictable elements (the whips and goads) are present. In view of the work as a whole, this is a decision consistent with the essential outlook of the poem, whose aim is to celebrate an event that is unique in its scope and gravity.

After Curio's infantry suffer the same fate as the cavalry, any remaining doubts about the outcome of the battle begin to wane and death itself prevails (4.769–72). At this point, Lucan employs a favored battle description: a dense concentration of entangled people in confined spaces. Surrounded on each side and forced into a tight space, the victims are submerged under the weight of every kind of weapon, which together form a single mass of iron that falls inexorably over them. In such conditions, it becomes impossible to run or fight hand to hand:

> neque enim licuit procurrere contra
> et miscere manus. sic undique saepta iuuentus

comminus obliquis et rectis eminus hastis
obruitur, non uulneribus nec sanguine solum,
telorum nimbo peritura et pondere ferri.

(4.772–76)

And in fact there was no chance of running to attack
and joining battle. So, totally surrounded, the soldiers
are crushed by spears sent slanting from nearby and straight
from a distance, doomed to die not by wounds
and blood alone but by the rain of weapons and the weight of iron.

The narratives of Vulteius and Curio have two further elements in common: both involve men trapped and surrounded on all sides by the enemy (4.462–64), and the decisive factor for the development of both episodes is the *fraus* ("deception," "stratagem") that dominates the scene and determines the outcome of the events (4.465, 730).

Courage, Love of Death, Madness

In Lucan's Ilerda narrative, military *uirtus* ("courage") and *furor* ("madness") are distorted to such an extent that they merge with each other. Initially *uirtus* is stifled, as the action takes place in confined spaces where maneuvering is impossible, and the equivalence of the opposing forces creates a stalemate. Subsequently, however, it is Caesar who with studied calculation prevents an encounter so as to prevent any opportunity for the Pompeians' fervor (4.271–80). It will ultimately be one of the Pompeian commanders, Petreius, who rekindles the military spirit of his men. He urges them to give up their outrageous peace with the enemy and to resume the assault against their relatives and friends with renewed vigor (4.211–35). In this way, roles and responsibilities are reversed. The Pompeians, the supporters of a just cause, become more contemptible through their cowardice than their opponents, whom they had denounced as bound by oath to heinous crime (4.228–29); by re-igniting hostilities they contribute to the total annihilation of decency (4.251–52). In this role reversal, Caesar, whom Lucan usually depicts as the incarnation of all evil, leaves it to his opponents to take the lead in committing crimes. Petreius's speech has the power to awaken the worst instincts of the Pompeian soldiers; invoked by their oath of loyalty, they furiously attack the relatives whom they had just been embracing moments before:

inter mensasque torosque
quae modo conplexu fouerunt pectora caedunt;

et quamuis primo ferrum strinxere gementes,
ut dextrae iusti gladius dissuasor adhaesit,
dum feriunt, odere suos, animosque labantis
confirmant ictu.

(4.245–50)

Among the tables, among beds
they slay the breasts which they had warmly hugged just now;
and though at first they unsheathed their weapons with a groan,
when the sword, discourager from justice, clings to their hands,
they hate their friends as they strike them and every blow reassures
their faltering spirits.

Lucan emphasizes the savage nature of Pompeians' behavior with a simile that compares them to wild beasts:

sic, ubi desuetae siluis in carcere clauso
mansueuere ferae et uultus posuere minaces
atque hominem didicere pati, si torrida paruos
uenit in ora cruor, redeunt rabiesque furorque
admonitaeque tument gustato sanguine fauces;
feruet et a trepido uix abstinet ira magistro.

(4.237–42)

Just so the wild beasts unlearn the ways of the woods
and grow tame in the locked prison, dropping their threatening looks
and learning to submit to man, but if their parched mouths
find a little gore, their rabid frenzy returns
and their throats swell at the memory of the taste of blood;
their anger seethes, hardly sparing the trembling keeper.

Lucan contrasts Petreius's speech with the speech in which the other Pompeian commander, Afranius, discusses with Caesar the terms of surrender of his men. Here Lucan uses a type scene familiar from earlier in the poem,[16] that of a defeated man who preserves his dignity in the face of the enemy commander. Afranius is depicted as a figure of great nobility since he is able to ensure that his soldiers, although defeated, are not incorporated into Caesar's army, according to a widespread and favored practice of Caesar's propaganda. But here the defeated men, after recognizing the merits of the conqueror, not only refuse to fight under his banner but wish to lay down their weapons and become spectators of the war (4.356–62). Lucan presents the battle in Petreius's camp as being of considerable importance to Caesar, since it prompts a moral re-evaluation of him: compared with the atrocious actions of the Pompeians, who have taken the initiative in massacring their relatives, Caesar represents, at least briefly, the better cause (4.254–59).

Something similar is found in the episode of Vulteius, which should be read in parallel with the *aristeia* of Scaeva (6.118–332).[17] Both situations are characterized by a confrontation between unequal forces and by the manifestation of immoderate *uirtus*. These factors are highlighted by a narrative form, which emphasizes the paradoxical nature of scenes that are almost unbelievable. The term *uirtus* is dominant in both episodes. It introduces the solemn speech of Vulteius when the narrator tells us that, "in this calamity, valour (*uirtus*) did all that valour could" (4.469–70). Within his speech Vulteius states that *uirtus* is likely to be crushed and to vanish in an ordinary battle (4.491), but their raft happens to be well in sight of those ashore and thus ideally placed to display their true worth. During the massacre itself, the value of Caesar's troops lies not so much in being willing and able to die as in their ability to kill their comrades without hesitation (4.556–60). *Virtus* also appears within the closing lines of the episode, when the narrator emphasizes how easy it is to find the courage to escape slavery (4.576–77) and hopes that death itself could be a reward of such courage:

> mors, utinam pauidos uitae subducere nolles,
> sed uirtus te sola daret.
>
> (4.580–81)

Death, I wish that you would not remove the fearful from life
but that you could be bestowed by valour alone!

Virtus is thus a major motif of Vulteius's speech and the mass-suicide of his men. The latter is simultaneously an act of "great valour" (*magna uirtus*, 4.512), but it is "not an arduous act of valour" (*ardua uirtus*, 4.576): its constitutive elements and raison d'être lie in its visibility, its spectacular nature, and above all in the mutual killing of men of the same contingent. An action that is inherently aberrant and monstrous is therefore depicted in a positive light.

In Vulteius's exhortation to his men, two other ideas predominate: *amor mortis* ("love of death")[18] and *furor* ("madness"). The first concept, which runs throughout the poem, has a privileged place in book 4 where its presence is more noticeable and persistent. In the Vulteius episode, the phenomenon is very striking. Death, when procured by the soldiers themselves, is justified and ennobled at an ethical and moral level: Vulteius emphasizes the glory that comes from death, regardless of the length of life that it is interrupting (4.478–80). The enemy, by witnessing the suicide of Vulteius's men, assist them in their gesture: the Pompeians find themselves in the presence of enemies who do not allow themselves to bend and will therefore fear their fury and their readiness to face death to such an extent that the Pompeians will rejoice that so few Caesarians were captured (4.505–7). We find a similar *amor mortis* elsewhere in the poem in the words of Scaeva, declaring to the enemy that his love of death is greater than their attachment to the cause of Pompey and the senate (6.245–46). Similarly, Vulteius describes himself as "wholly driven by the spurs of coming death," a state of mind that he describes as a *furor*: "this is an obsession" (4.516–17). The exaltation of this moment then leads to Vulteius's suggestion that the "blessing" of death is a privilege granted only to those who are close to it; those who have longer to live cannot experience this, for ignorance of it is necessary in order to continue to bear the burden of life (4.517–20). Thus through a series of gradual steps, Vulteius argues for a moral and ethical framework that represent the complete opposite of normality: he champions the ennoblement of defeat, which is celebrated as a victory, and considers death preferable to life.

For Vulteius *amor mortis* and *furor* are inseparable (cf. 4.517–20 and 505–6), but it can be argued that the former is the cause of the latter. Contempt of death and war rage are trademarks of the brave soldier, and it is not strange to find them among Caesar's troops, whose firmness and motivation were proverbial. But in the case of Vulteius's men, we are not in the presence of a normal episode of military virtue; rather we are confronting a very abnormal gesture. The decision to commit suicide engenders a contempt for life, and the determination to hasten the end produces an indifference and insensitivity to the war. Their "confidence of death" (*fiducia mortis,* 4.538) replaces *uirtus* and makes it possible for them to face the initial clash with the enemy at dawn (4.533–38).

There is thus, as it were, a "double fault": on the one hand *furor* is accentuated, which deforms *uirtus* and transforms it into *amor mortis*; on the other, mass suicide is presented as spectacular and exemplary. Just as Scaeva incites his fellow soldiers to anticipate the impact of enemy weapons, to break enemy javelins with the weight of their chests and to blunt swords with their throats (6.160–61), the same notion appears in the suicide of Vulteius's men when breasts are struck against swords and throats press against the thrust of the hand that bears the sword (4.560–62). But for all the similarities between the two episodes, Scaeva sacrifices himself in fighting and dying by enemy hands, Vulteius and his men die by their own hands.

Virtus makes its last appearance in book 4 in Curio's final moments and death, but once again the context and sense are highly unusual. On seeing the massacre of his own soldiers, Curio realizes he is unable to survive the defeat.

Without considering escape he resolves upon death, which he goes to meet, strengthened paradoxically by his desolation and total absence of hope: "[he falls] amid the wreckage of his own men, vigorous for death and brave with necessary valour" (*uirtute coacta*, 4.793–98)

The Gaze

Spectatorship plays a very important role in book 4. The visibility of what is narrated is essential to the logic of the book's narratives, which are all constructed with two separate but converging viewpoints in mind. On one side is the (external) observation of the reader / viewer; on the other is the (internal) gaze of figures within the narrative, who are consistently presented as the spectators of the most decisive moments. Spectacle is such an important factor that the same flow of events varies and takes on a different value according to the way in which it is viewed and assessed by its internal and external audiences.

During the Battle of Ilerda, the theme of visibility is brought to our attention at various times. The proximity of the two camps allows the opposing sides to see each other at 4.169–72; the ability to make out the faces of enemy soldiers and recognize them immediately reveals the wickedness of the civil war (4.192–94). The mass killing set in motion by Petreius is marked as especially serious because it is clearly visible (4.243–45), and after it is over, Lucan says that the Pompeians were pleased to commit their crimes under the eyes of the commanders, because they were afraid that their gesture would lose effectiveness if kept hidden (4.252–53). When the Pompeians obtain permission from Caesar to retire from the war, they are framed as happy because they are now detached spectators of an act of war that no longer involves them (4.400–401).

The suicide of Vulteius's soldiers in particular is conceived as exemplary: its main function is that of a spectacle. Their actions must be seen by the widest audience possible because what they are doing is an extraordinary and paradoxical action.[19] What happens during the carnage suffered by Curio and his men is quite different. When compared with similar examples in the same poem, the difference is the absence of visibility, which makes the African episode exceptional and abnormal. That the battle is occluded by dust and therefore impossible to see is a clear strategy on Lucan's part to withhold notoriety from an enterprise that is doubly shameful because it is located within a larger illicit war and because it results in a victory for foreign forces over whom the Romans have previously triumphed (cf. esp. 4.788–93).

Vergilian Intertexts

Lucan certainly composed book 4 with Vergil in mind (the same could be said of all the books of the *Civil War*).[20] However, the way that Lucan uses Vergil is varied, and the use he makes of his model is not always immediately evident. After the Battle of Ilerda, lines lamenting wartime life (4.382–92) are followed in quick succession by lines praising the life of peace (4.393–401). The Caesarians are to be pitied because, as winners, they are doomed to fight on and keep winning. The Pompeians, on the other hand, in being defeated will benefit from the advantages of peace. In his paradoxical evaluation of the condition of the two opposing sides, we can see the characteristically Lucanian idea that in this civil conflict, the best moral case belongs to the war's losers, not its winners.[21] To describe the condition of bliss enjoyed by the defeated Pompeians, Lucan uses the beginning of a famous passage from the *Georgics*, in which Vergil celebrates the bliss of rural life. One scholar has aptly called it "a beatitude on the man who understands the working of the universe."[22] Lucan begins his praise of the peaceful life thus:

> Felix qui potuit mundi nutante ruina,
> Quo iaceat iam scire loco.
>
> (4.393–94)

> Happy is the man who has already learned the place where he must lie when the world's collapse is tottering.

Compare Vergil:

> Felix qui potuit rerum cognoscere causas,
> Atque metus omnis et inexorabile fatum
> Subiecit pedibus strepitumque Acherontis auari.
>
> (Verg. G. 2.490–92)

> Blessed is he who has succeeded in learning the laws of nature's working, has cast beneath his feet all fear and fate's implacable decree, and the howl of insatiable Death.

Lucan quotes these lines almost verbatim in order to capture the enormous breadth of perspective contained in his Vergilian model. This is typical of the way Lucan avails himself of the conceptual framework of Vergil's poetry. The full weight and complexity of Vergil's lines must be understood in the context of overcoming the horrors and massacres of the civil wars and of striving after the goal of peace—not only as the end of war but as a personal and intimate search for an ultimate truth. However, this is a message that is completely incompatible with Lucan's views, since he considered all hope of a return to a free society after the war as in vain and any future perspective as illusory. He does not want to find deep explanations in philosophy to give specific meaning to human events. In contrast to Vergil, who considers happiness to be the result of a spiritual fulfillment, Lucan merely celebrates modest certainty for soldiers leaving the war that they can end their existence at home, among their loved ones.[23]

At 4.542–44 Vulteius provokes his men by saying he wants to see who among them will be the first to strike their commander:

> primus dux ipse carinae
> Vulteius iugulo poscens iam fata retecto
> "ecquis" ait "iuuenum est cuius sit dextra cruore
> digna meo certaque fide per uulnera nostra
> testetur se uelle mori?"
>
> (4.540–44)

> The vessel's captain,
> Vulteius himself, was first now to demand death with throat laid bare:
> "Is there any of my soldiers," he says "whose hand is worthy
> of my blood, who can prove his wish to die by sure proof
> through my wounds?"

Scholarship has largely missed the clear reference in this passage to Lucan's Vergilian model for Vulteius's opening question:

> "ecquis erit mecum, iuuenes, qui primus in hostem?
> en," ait et iaculum attorquens emittit in auras,
> principium pugnae, et campo sese arduus infert.
>
> (Verg. Aen. 9.51–53)

> "Who's going to join me in being the first at the enemy, soldiers?
> Look!" Then he spins off a well-torqued javelin high towards heaven,
> marking the start of the fight. Then he prances in pride on the meadows.

Turnus's speech in the above passage incites his men to attack, and he immediately casts the first spear of the war against the Trojans in Italy. The usual exhortation of the commander to his troops, which in Vergil leads to action against the enemy, becomes in Lucan's poem a provocation to the soldiers to strike within their own camp, starting with the commander himself.

The mythological excursus treating Hercules and Antaeus at 4.593–660 is without doubt the most studied episode of the fourth book. Two reasons in particular have contributed to its special relevance: (1) it prepares the reader for the clash between Curio and Juba; and (2) it alludes to a very authoritative and famous paradigm, that is, the fight between Hercules and Cacus in Vergil's *Aeneid* (8.190–305).[24] Contrary to what happens in Vergil, where the myth is proposed as realistic and the narrator adheres completely to the story as it is told, in Lucan, the distinction between myth and history is clear, as is the narrator's distance from the mythical tale and its adhesion to historical reality.[25] The allusion is important because it shows once more that Lucan always strives to differentiate himself from his model: note that the entire section that does not concern the duel between the two contenders is omitted.

Conclusion

The fourth book of Lucan ends a section of the poem in which the two opponents, Caesar and Pompey, never meet. It is, in a certain sense, a transition to a subsequent step in which the direct clash will be inevitable. This section of the work contains, clearly and explicitly, all the main features of the *Civil War*. Above all, it carries Lucan's conviction that this is a war against nature for which it is impossible to find any kind of justification. Though the book focuses on minor or marginal episodes of the war between Caesar and Pompey, the disastrous and monstrous nature of the conflict emerges clearly. The events of this book are a prelude to the disaster of Pharsalus: small calamities and abnormal behaviors of the characters anticipate what will happen later in the work, when Pompey's fate will be fulfilled in Thessaly and with it, the fate of Rome.

Notes

1. A detailed, word-for-word analysis of all of book 4 can be found in Esposito 2009; cf. also Radicke 2004; Asso 2010. The English translations of the *Aeneid* are from Ahl 2008; those of the *Georgics* are from Fairclough 2001.

2. Further details at Caes. *BCiv.* 1.62–82; App. *BCiv.* 2.42–43; Cass. Dio 41.20–23; Plut. *Caes.* 36; cf. also outlines at Flor. 2.13.26–28; Suet. *Iul.* 34.2, 75.2; Oros. 6.15.6. Among the best analysis of this episode are Saylor 1982; Masters 1992, 43–90; Leigh 1997, 41–68. Rambaud 1960 compares Lucan's version of events to the historical record.

3. Cf. Livy *Per.* 110.4–5; Suet. *Iul.* 36; App. *BCiv.* 2.47; Flor. 2.13.31–33; Cass. Dio 40.1–2; Oros. 6.15.8–9. Its absence in Caesar may be a result of a lacuna in the manuscript tradition, see Avery 1993. A residual trace may be recognized in a note in the *Commenta Bernensia* on Lucan 4.462.

4. McGuire 1997, 88–89.

5. Martindale 1976, 47.

6. See Gorman 2001; cf. also Saylor 1990; Zlobec 1999; Owen Eldred 2002; Vitelli Casella 2016.

7. Cf. Cic. *Att.* 6.3–4; Vell. 2.48.4; Val. Max. 9.1.6; Plut. *Caes.* 29.3, *Pomp.* 58.1–2, *Ant.* 5.2; Tac. *Ann.* 11.7.2; Suet. *Iul.* 29.1; App. *BCiv.* 2.26; Cass. Dio 40. 60.2–3; Serv. *ad* Verg. *Aen.* 6.621.

8. Cf., e.g., Caes. *BGall.* 8.52.4.

9. See Caes. *BCiv.* 2.37.42; App. *BCiv.* 2.45–46; Cass. Dio 41.42.3–5; Frontin. *Strat.* 2.5.40.

10. Lucan's approach to Curio may be influenced by Livy, whose account is now lost to us. On Curio in Caesar's commentaries, see Carcopino 1968, 440–43; La Penna 2000.

11. Rambaud 1960, 156; Lintott 1971, 491.

12. On the structure, see Morford 1967, 4–5. The apostrophe has been studied by Faber 2005, 338–39. It is very likely that Claudian used this section of Lucan's book 4 in composing the final part of his invective against Rufinus (especially *Rufin.* 2. 498–527).

13. Cf., e.g., the death of Catiline at the end of Sallust's *Conspiracy of Catiline* (60.7).

14. See Marti 1970, 15–16. Lucan's Curio, both in book 4 and book 1 (1.266–91), exerted a clear influence on the negative treatment of Dante's Curio (*Inferno* 28.91–92).

15. For this feature of Lucan's style, see Esposito 2004.

16. Cf. the characterization of Domitius Ahenobarbus at 2.507–25.

17. On which, see esp. Conte 1988; cf. also Marti 1966. For a comparison of the Vulteius and Scaeva episodes, see Ahl 1976, 117–21; Long 2007, 187–88; Hömke 2010; Blaschka 2015.

18. See Rutz 1960.

19. See Leigh 1997, 182–83.

20. Thompson-Bruère 1968, 152. For book 4 and *Aeneid* 4, see Casali 1999; for an overview of Vergil's importance to Lucan, see Cowan (chapter 11) in this volume. Of the three examples that follow in this section, the first and third have been identified and discussed by scholars (see note 23), while the second is new and has largely been ignored in studies on this book of the poem.

21. Cf. 7.706 *uincere peius erat* "it was worse to win" (Lucan's apostrophe to Pompey after the battle of Pharsalus).

22. Thomas 1988b, 2.253.

23. The relationship between these lines of Lucan and the *Georgics* are much more substantial and widespread, see Palla 1983 for an overview. For Vergil's *Georgics* and Lucan more generally, see Paratore 1943; Kersten 2018; for the key allusions in book 4, see Esposito 2009.

24. See Hardie 1993, 66–67. On Curio and Antaeus, see Saylor 1982. On the Hercules and Antaeus episode see, e.g., Grimal 1949; Martindale 1981; Asso 2002; Uhle 2006. In addition to Vergil, the clash between Hercules and Achelous narrated in Ov. *Met.* 9.31–88 can also be considered one of Lucan's models; see Von Albrecht 1970, 294–95. Note also the importance of tragic models for the Vulteius episode—Cadmus, Eteocles, and Polynices—signaled in the simile at 4.549–56; on Lucan's mythological similes, see Esposito 2012b and more generally Aymard 1951; Schindler 2000.

25. In the description of the clash between Hercules and Antaeus, according to Seewald 2008, 264, Lucan also reveals a degree of technical competence in conducting a wrestling match.

5

Book 5

Mortal Authority and Cosmic Order

CHRISTOPHER L. CATERINE

Preliminaries

Lucan uses book 5 to explore two sets of interrelated questions: (1) What is the basis of a leader's power and to whom does he answer? and (2) What is the nature of the relationship between leaders, their supporters, and fate? Repeated invocation of these concerns binds the narrative together and indicates that these issues are central to Lucan's understanding of the civil war's progress in 49–48 B.C.E. For all that these questions produce thematic unity, however, the answers provided to them are consistently ambiguous or contradictory. This fact makes it hard to determine which outlooks abide in the poem's world—a matter complicated by Lucan's use of a "fiery and excited" persona who lacks the omniscience of a traditional epic narrator and is deeply invested in the events he relates (*ardens et concitatus,* Quint. *Inst.* 10.1.90).[1] Consequently, although it is possible to follow the thread of a given answer for a certain length of time, our poet inevitably weaves it into a web whose overall form is chaotic and indistinct. Attempts to find a consistent outlook—to establish the "real Lucan's" views—are necessarily a fool's errand.[2]

This chapter will investigate how the questions posed in book 5 affect the audience's experience of the text and its narrative of civil war. By identifying what Lucan takes for granted, what limits he sets for debate of the above questions, and where crucial tensions lie in the Romans' memory of their past, we can better understand how the maddening, terrifying world of his epic stirs the thoughts and emotions of an audience deeply implicated in its plot.

The book is divided into five tightly knit episodes arranged in interlocking order:

1. Pompey's appointment as head of the senatorial army (5.1–70)
2. Visit of the discontent Appius to the Oracle at Delphi (5.71–236)
3. Mutiny of Caesar's troops returning from Spain (5.237–373)
4. Caesar's crossing to Greece and battle with a storm (5.374–721)
5. Pompey's separation from Cornelia and their farewell (5.722–815)

Scenes 1, 3, and 5 focus on theme (1) What is the basis of a leader's power and to whom does he answer, while scenes 2 and 4 focus on theme (2) What is the nature of the relationship between leaders, their supporters, and fate. There is, in fact, some blending of these concerns within individual episodes, but the outline generally holds. Focusing still on structure, note also that two episodes about Pompey frame three focused on Appius and Caesar. Lucan's narrator will comment on Appius's insignificance, however, and the questions introduced by his scene largely anticipate those raised during the climactic storm. Leaving aside this minor character's intrusion, then, book 5 at its heart explores the leadership style and cosmic significance of Pompey and Caesar.

"Order Your Leader to Be Great"

The book opens in December 49 B.C.E. Lentulus wishes to address the exiled senate one last time as consul and uses the opportunity to recommend entrusting his armies to Pompey.[3] From the start, the narrator identifies this as a moment when the "venerable order [the senate] taught the nations that their faction did not belong to Magnus, but that Magnus was a member of their faction," 5.13–14).[4] These lines clearly echo a passage from earlier in the epic and so may appear to affirm the view espoused on that occasion—that Cato can guarantee Pompey's dedication to the Roman constitution ("Then let him conquer with me as his soldier so he may know he does not conquer for himself," 2.322–23).[5] As the scene develops, however, we must reassess any simplistic connection between these episodes. Lentulus initially claims that his audience is the true Roman senate and that the Roman government resides wherever these men assemble (5.17–30). Yet a few lines later, he admits that Caesar possesses a senate of his own that stands in opposition to their gathering (5.31–40). This reversal undermines his initial claim and draws our attention to the questionable status of this "senatorial" meeting. Indeed, even if most attendees were rightful members of the senate, they had evacuated Italy on Caesar's advance and were meeting—against convention—in a camp instead of a temple (*castra*,

5.12). Lentulus doth protest too much: insisting the exiled senate has a right to act on behalf of the Roman people underscores a problem of legitimacy he could have glossed over. The progression of his speech thus casts the senate's standing into doubt, inviting us to question what constitutes a legal gathering of that body.

Despite this wrinkle, the speech is successful. Pompey's acceptance of the command nevertheless invites us to ask whether our narrator was correct to insist that this event confirmed his loyalty to the senate's cause. The scene's epilogue suggests it has not. Pompey's first action is distributing honors to cities and kings that include Rhodes, Sparta, Athens, and Phocis; Sadala, Cotys, Deiotarus, and Rhascypolis; Libya; and Egypt's Ptolemy XIII (5.47–57). Notably absent are western communities and the Romans at whose head he is supposed to stand. This omission suggests that Pompey sees the war as a conflict between the Greek and Roman worlds and himself as leader of the eastern camp. This dynamic may not refute the narrator's claim at the episode's start, but it does pose a challenge: not only has the legitimacy of the exiled senate been questioned, but Pompey is now shown acting in a manner reminiscent of Hellenistic kings like Alexander, by whose title he is identified throughout the epic (μέγας / *Magnus,* "the Great").[6]

None of these issues mean that Caesar holds a greater claim to legitimacy. Let us jump ahead for a moment to the elections he holds for 48 B.C.E. (5.381– 402). This digression highlights the normal procedures that were *not* followed when Caesar was named consul: officials divide the votes of *absent* people, tribes are drawn from an *empty* urn, augurs *overlook* ill omens (5.392–96, a device called "negative enumeration"). Lest we miss the point, our narrator reminds us that these actions should invalidate the proceedings and insists that this was the first occasion emperors learned to manipulate the rituals that sanctify elected magistrates (5.385–92). If Pompey's right to lead the republican cause is undermined by questions about the legitimacy of the senate in exile and his own behavior, Lucan makes it clear that Caesar has no proper claim to the consulship of 48 B.C.E.

Although we are never given a positive vision of political legitimacy in these scenes, we are primed to consider the issue in certain ways. Notably, it is assumed that leaders should be installed through election by a group authorized to represent the entire *populus* (people). For Pompey that group is the senate, for Caesar the Centuriate Assembly. Narrative suspense does not derive from the outcome of these elections but from the disputed authority of the electing groups. As we have seen, Pompey's status is tainted both by the fact that the senate—if he fights for it at all—may not represent the Roman people and by his own king-like actions. The Centuriate Assembly, meanwhile, is cast as a farce, a once-meaningful body hijacked by men seeking power for themselves. Lucan gives us no basis to determine which of these views has greater claim to truth. Instead, he emphasizes the blurred lines of political legitimacy. It matters little whether Pompey fights for the senate or Caesar's election is valid: Lucan's point is that civil war has undermined Rome's traditional determiners of authority. In such a world, contests for power are necessarily decided by force of arms.

"Which of the Gods Is Lurking Here?"

If readers feel uneasy with Pompey, they soon learn they are not alone. That concern drives Appius Claudius Pulcher (consul in 54 B.C.E., censor in 50 B.C.E.) to Delphi to learn what the future holds for himself and Rome (5.64–70).[7] By way of introducing this scene, Lucan discusses the relationship between Apollo and fate, the physical causes of inspiration, and the value of prophecy to men (5.71–127). As he moves from one topic to the next, however, he creates a jarring contradiction: after relating a story from the *Homeric Hymn to Apollo* to explain Phoebus's power over Delphi (5.71–85), he rhetorically asks what god possesses the site and ponders whether prophecy reveals what is fated or if future events are fixed by the Pythia's speech (5.86–93).[8] This uncertainty is soon reiterated when he presents rival theories on the mechanics of inspiration and expresses faith in its power even though fear of kings condemned the oracle to silence (5.93–120).

This progression is not easily untangled. An opening with clear epic precedent gives way to natural-philosophical questions that undermine the poet's earlier claims by offering competing explanations of how the oracle works. To make matters worse, our narrator says his information is not based on experience because the oracle stopped working before his day—presumably the 60s C.E.[9] This sequence makes mutually exclusive explanations of science and tradition butt heads while our narrator denies having firm knowledge to resolve the tension: the god ruling Delphi may or may not be Apollo; fate may be fixed before the Pythia speaks or after; inspiration may occur when "a majority of *Jupiter's* entirety" (*Iouis*, 5.95; emphasis added) seeps from the earth and overtakes the priestess—or perhaps it does not.

One lifeline in this sea of possibilities is identifying what Lucan takes for granted. He seems certain, for instance, that the oracle works and provides real information to mortals. This point is reiterated later: the Pythia's verses are "fixed and cannot be changed by any mortal" (5.105), and any woman the god overtakes (*deus*, 5.116) is doomed to an early death—empirical proof of Delphi's power (5.116–18). In fact, the oracle's efficacy is not questioned anywhere in the scene, and we eventually learn its ambiguous response was valid, even if Appius misinterpreted its meaning (5.224–36).

Fate is likewise accepted as real within this episode, suggesting that human events in the poem do not proceed by chance. While we may not know who rules the universe, how control is exerted, or when outcomes become unavoidable, the *Civil War* gives no indication—at least here—that a fatalistic view of the world is essentially invalid.[10] Instead, the episode raises questions about the people fate affects. When Appius learns his role in the civil war (he will die in Euboea, 5.224–35), Lucan highlights the insignificance of minor actors in relation to the larger players on whom history itself is said to hinge. Indeed, for all that the Pythia resists Apollo (*Paean*, 5.167; *Phoebe*, 164 and *passim*), when she finally assumes his knowledge she struggles to find Appius's lot among the great fates to which she now has access (5.161–89). We are not told here who these individuals are, but within the *Civil War* men like Pompey and Caesar will readily come to mind.

One final issue is raised amid this prophecy. Apollo allows the Pythia to tell Appius where he will find "rest from civil war" but forces her to suppress details about the war's outcome (5.189–97). This comment prompts the narrator to curse the god, asking whether his silence is due to fear, the unfixed nature of fate at that time, or a desire to see Brutus win fame as a tyrannicide (5.198–208). On the one hand, these questions echo concerns from the scene's opening and give further attention to the operation of fate as it relates to oracles. Seen from this vantage point, we may infer that Pompey's defeat is not yet certain—a situation that invites readers to pinpoint that watershed moment for themselves and thus creates dramatic tension in a narrative whose end is already known. At the same time, the outburst confirms our suspicions about which players are central to Roman history: Pompey and Brutus (and so, implicitly, Caesar) are important enough to warrant fate's intervention.

Yet even this matter is not so tidy. Mention of Brutus opens another can of worms by casting the *telos* (endpoint) of history—and so, perhaps, the poem itself—into doubt. To this point, Lucan's tale of civil war has focused on Pompey and Caesar, and its dark tone has often seemed to lament the collapse of the Roman republic; thus we might expect fate as portrayed in the epic to be directed at the establishment of the kingship so often criticized by our narrator. Instead, the poet raises the possibility that fate is not working toward that end at all but embraces Caesar's victory as a precondition for a second Brutus to attain glory for eliminating a despot. Does this mean we have been shortsighted in thinking the contest is about Caesar and Pompey? Perhaps. But if so, then our narrator—even here—is subject to the same myopia: why stop at

Caesar's assassination when there remains the Second Triumvirate, the Battle of Actium, or the ascension of Nero? Although Lucan does not dwell on the question, suggesting an endpoint we may not have considered forces us to view fate's operation in a new light: its power may be real, but we cannot know how far ahead it really aims.[11]

"Now I Shall Truly Wage War for Myself"

Lucan next turns to Caesar. The general has just defeated Pompeian forces in Spain, but the gods threaten "his fate's advance" with a mutiny of troops sparked by restlessness or lust for power (5.237–44). This crisis is said to be the worst threat Caesar faced, the moment he learned that swords belong to soldiers, not their general (5.244–60). This simple introduction draws our attention to the relationship between a leader and his men, paving the way for a pair of speeches in which two visions of that dynamic can be proposed. Throughout the episode, the troops and Caesar will try in turn to define the role played by the other and to determine once and for all whether leaders in civil war are dominant over the rank and file or become their equals through shared crime (thus the soldiers at 5.289–90).

In assessing this scene, we must differentiate between the speeches and narratorial comments about them. The latter are useful, as often, for directing us to issues the poet seems eager to explore.[12] Given the emphasis Roman education placed on rhetoric, however, we must also consider how arguments within the speeches are constructed and respond to one another.[13] Taking both into account allows us to see with greater clarity how Lucan broadens his discussion of leadership: whereas earlier the issue was an election's validity, here we see how an army's support or acquiescence can help fate elevate a general to terrifying new heights.

We may begin with the orations. The soldiers speak first, insisting they have been faithful subordinates and are innocent of any wrongdoing because they have won no material gain from civil war (5.261–73). Next, they criticize Caesar's limitless desire and opine that their only reward for committing grave crimes on his behalf will be a bloody death away from home (5.273–83). Their complaints thus far draw on common rhetorical tropes but become more interesting in the speech's second half. Here the men argue that (1) crossing the Rubicon erased the status differential between Caesar and themselves, (2) Caesar has been unfair in crediting his victories to *Fortuna* instead of them, and (3) if Caesar allows their anger to fester, they can bring about peace against his wishes (5.284–95).

The first of these arguments is legalistic, holding that Caesar's authority—which derived from the *imperium* he held as proconsular governor—was lost when he touched Italian soil. Although the men do not say so expressly, it is implied that they no longer feel bound by the oath they swore upon enlisting, that they now view Caesar as a private citizen. This suggestion expands the book's earlier discussion of political authority by portraying another way in which a leader's position could be viewed as tainted for having abused a traditional source of legitimacy.

The soldiers' second complaint concerns giving credit where it is due, but its significance is cosmic and builds on themes from the Delphi episode. Caesar has apparently been acting as if he owes his victories to the favor of a supernatural being. His men reject this interpretation of history and insist that their actions are responsible for his success. This claim is tantamount to saying that they possess free will (a view that, taken with their rejection of a deterministic universe, is stereotypically Epicurean) and that their general must take their desires into account if he expects them to support his goals. Their final threat to make peace against his wishes is best understood as an affirmation of this view: claiming that the civil war cannot proceed without an army is tantamount to saying that the destiny Caesar will achieve—to become a name synonymous with absolute power—is really in their hands.[14] This vision of human affairs obviously cannot coexist with the one they attribute to Caesar, and readers may in turn wonder what forces drive this poem's world—which is of course synonymous to our poet with the real world of Roman history. Does fate exist? And if so, was it working on Caesar's side?

Caesar does not balk at this challenge. He paints his troops' complaints as cowardice and bids them go (5.319–24). This gambit is bold, but Caesar is confident his fate will remedy the loss: new soldiers will replace the old, since Fortune wants others to enjoy the benefits of his success (5.325–34). He next mocks the men for thinking they impact history: the human race exists for the benefit of a few, and fate thinks little of casting aside pawns to advance the cause of men like himself (5.335–43). This is a crucial turn, for in it we see that Caesar's men did not misstate their general's position: he really does think they are inconsequential. Next, he takes the accusation a step further by arguing that Labienus—after enjoying successes under Caesar—suffered losses as a Pompeian (5.343–47). This historical *exemplum* gives the claim the ring of truth and invites the reader to think about how Caesar's vision of reality relates to the factual events the poem depicts.

The most immediate point of contact is the previous episode. There, it will be recalled, the Pythia struggled to find Appius's fate amid the lots of greater actors. This difficulty seemed to indicate that certain people in the poem's cosmos were more important than others, and the determination found a degree of support in the truth of the prophecy the Roman received: since the oracle worked, the explanation of the Pythia's delay appears credible. Caesar's views in the mutiny episode align quite closely with those of the Delphic god: both insist fate is unconcerned with minor players, since the real action lies with those whose fortunes shape the lives of all mankind. Without staking a claim on whether this lends credence to the view of human history that Caesar expounds, we can at least say it cements his vision as one outer limit in the debate about the relationship between fate, leaders, and their men.

Caesar's speech soon circles back to his argument that the men should leave the camp if they wish to be private citizens (*Quirites*, 5.358), but he abruptly ends on a different note: the raw recruits should arrest the ringleaders and learn through their punishment how to kill and die (5.359–64). This call to action moves us from direct speech to the moment of resolution: the men were stunned and afraid that their weapons would obey Caesar against their will (5.367–68), and the general also feared the outcome until the troops exceeded his expectations—offering their swords *and throats* (5.364–70). At this point, they strike a revised compact, with the mutiny's ringleaders serving as a sacrifice to establish new terms of service. Caesar's vision has won out, and his troops will not question his authority again.[15]

Before leaving this episode behind, we must consider Lucan's narratorial comments. Here we find a string of contradictions that draw our attention to the nature of the leader rather than the dynamics of leadership. Recall first the "dread" that Caesar felt while awaiting his soldiers' response (*pauet*, 5.369)—an emotion that is plainly consistent with what he experienced when the mutiny broke out (*timuit*, "he feared," 5.241). Despite this, the interlude between the speeches posits a different mental state: "Was there any leader that disturbance could *not* have terrified? Yet Caesar was accustomed to hurl his fate headlong and comes forth rejoicing to test his fortune against the greatest dangers" (5.300–303, emphasis added). As the adversative subsequently makes clear, the narrator's rhetorical question is emphatic: Caesar remains levelheaded in circumstances that would vex any other leader. Indeed, we soon find him welcoming the revolt as a chance to stoke his soldier's greed, to make them *want* to commit offenses on his behalf (5.304–9).

In the span of 130 lines, then, our narrator has told us that Caesar is both afraid and unafraid—a patent contradiction. This change can perhaps be explained if we remember that the episode is focused on how leaders interact with their men. Relationships of that sort depend on *public* appearances and the willingness of subordinates to accept the leader's vision of himself. That Caesar's troops (eventually) do so is made clear by the epilogue. Yet by making it ambiguous whether Caesar feels fear during the mutiny, Lucan highlights the gulf that can exist between public presentation and private experience. While dissimulation of this sort may be a common theme in epic—think of *Aeneid* 1, where Vergil's hero suppresses despair to embolden his men—it enjoys special privilege in the *Civil War* (cf. Italians facing Caesar in book 1; Caesar's election later in book 5; the Egyptian reaction to Caesar in book 10). Lucan's subtle questioning of Caesar's fear in this episode seems to invite us to consider the artifice lurking beneath his self-styled persona and so perhaps to question the cosmic truth of the new communal ideology that underlies his relationship with his troops.

"Keep My Battered Body Amidst the Waves"

After treating Caesar's entry into Italy and election to the consulship (5.374–402, discussed above), Lucan comes to "Caesar and the Storm." This is the book's longest episode, a favorite among scholars, and subject of a stand-alone commentary by Monica Matthews (2008). As Lucan's meditation on the relationship between a leader, the gods, and fate continues, he blows the conceptual limits of the discussion wide open, casting Caesar as a figure with the potential to shape the very forces we expect to shape him.

Before we can have the storm, Caesar must get from Italy to Greece. In recounting this action, Lucan emphasizes Caesar's eagerness to engage with Pompey and his impatience for delay: he is compared to a pregnant tiger as he races through Apulia (5.403–8), mocks his men for refusing to sail during winter (5.409–23), and compels them to proceed even when stranded mid-sea (5.453–60). Throughout these verses we find tacit indications that Caesar seeks a contest with nature itself. Before chastising his men, he claims the sea is open even to those who are unlucky and insists a storm would be a blessing: it would hasten their arrival and prevent Pompey from holding Greece unchallenged (5.411–21). Although the troops—wholly loyal after their abortive mutiny—do heed this call, nature resists: the wind fails when they are halfway across, and the narrator smirks at the paradox of sailors praying for a squall (5.450–53). Eventually, though, the wind returns, and the contingent makes its crossing.

This sequence warrants scrutiny. First, it reveals Lucan's fondness for situations in which characters experience the opposite of what is demanded by a rhetorical trope (*locus communis*). Such inversions are typical of his style, likely reflecting an attempt to innovate within a highly prescriptive literary context.[16] More significantly, the sequence shows the extent to which Caesar's men have internalized their general's point-of-view: for all that their prayers are paradoxical, they accord with the very event Caesar said they should want a few lines earlier. This echo keeps the mutiny scene fresh in our mind and draws our attention to the result of the last conflict in which Caesar's vision of reality had been challenged. Third, the progression suggests that nature—if Caesar is, in fact, pitting himself against her—does not intend to give up without a fight. The wind does eventually carry the men across, but its initial failure creates a delay we know Caesar was keen to avoid (5.409–10). Specific attribution of malice to nature may seem premature in this context but will become more credible as the narrative advances.

Caesar can now turn his attention to Pompey—or so we thought (5.461–75). Lucan only tells us here that half the fleet remained in Italy under Antony's command (5.476–81), leading to a rehearsal of the events and themes just described: Caesar again chafes at delay and again mocks a subordinate for yielding to weather. His speech accordingly grows sharper, and he pressures Antony with assurances that he is holding back the gods and fate; that *Fortuna* wants him to play a decisive role in the war; and that the men will endure shipwreck if it means joining their general (5.482–94). Despite his increased force and repetition (*terque quaterque*, 5.497), this time Caesar fails: Antony remains unmoved (5.497–98).

Caesar now has reason to return to Italy. Fearing further delay, he sneaks from camp at night and, upon reaching the sea, finds the ferryman Amyclas asleep and unconcerned with war (*securus belli*, 5.526). Although Caesar promises him great riches, this poor man insists that sailing is a bad idea: nature gives signs of a coming storm that his little skiff could never survive (5.538–59). There are good reasons to trust him. Amyclas demonstrates knowledge of astronomical, meteorological, and zoological signs; finds confirmation of them in the direction of the wind (5.560–76); and is ultimately proved right when a storm arises that is so massive that it threatens the physical structure of the universe (5.597–653, esp. 615–36). Caesar nevertheless dismisses his concerns, deeming his own person and *fortuna* greater guarantees of safety than experience or scientific knowledge (5.577–93). Like the soldiers in the previous scene, Amyclas promptly obeys, apparently accepting Caesar's worldview as he heaves off amid the rising tempest (5.593–96).

This narrative sequence displays an obsession with *securitas* (a term meaning both "freedom from anxiety" and "safety"). The concept first occurs when we are told poverty guaranteed the helmsman a carefree life: the skiff that forms one of his hut's walls is described as "safe" (*secura*, 5.515), and Amyclas is said to be "unconcerned with war," knowing that his meager possessions are not their object (*securus belli*, 5.526). An apostrophe on rustic life casts this notion in positive terms but turns out to be a setup: Caesar's first words to Amyclas are an order to "expect more than [his] modest prayers" (5.532).[17] This command leads to promises of wealth and enticements for the helmsman to entrust his fate to "the god now eager to fill his home with riches" (5.534–37). The contrast here is plain. Poverty allowed Amyclas to live without a care (*securitas* from *sine cura* "without concern"), but in Caesar's presence he is offered a life of luxury requiring concern for the future: the words *expecta* ("expect," 5.532), *uotis* ("wishes, prayers," 5.532), and *spes* ("hope," 5.533) are all forward-looking concepts that indicate strong commitment to an event turning out a certain way. Compare the situation of Pompeian troops who stop fighting after Caesar defeats them in book 4: they become "free" (*securus*) to enjoy a simple family life because as private citizens they are no longer impacted by a Caesarian or Pompeian victory (4.382–401). The situation for Amyclas is reversed: instead of giving up concern and obtaining *securitas*, he is compelled to accept a wealth that brings with it worry and fear.[18]

Exchanging poverty for riches and calm for anxiety is not all there is to this dynamic. In ordering Amyclas to ignore the signs of the impending storm, Caesar says the helmsman will be safe under his protection (*tutela secure mea*, 5.584). This third occurrence of *securus* adds a layer of complexity. Caesar, it seems, did not just strip Amyclas of the *securitas* poverty had ensured him, but replaced that type of *securitas* with a new one. As far as Caesar is concerned, the helmsman can sail without concern because Caesar's own presence is sufficient to shield him from harm. There is, of course, one crucial problem. Caesar is no longer speaking of how riches resolve the fears of poverty but suggesting that a major storm the helmsman knows is coming cannot actually inflict the damage normally threatened by such tempests. In a rational world, boasts like this would be nonsense. But this is the *Civil War*, and the figure in question is Caesar. Assertions of grandeur are the norm, and our general now appears ready to place himself par with nature.[19]

Fortunately for us, Lucan is heavy handed and often spells out his subtler points. As the storm reaches fever pitch, Caesar deems its threat worthy of his fate (*credit iam digna . . . fatis esse suis*, 5.653–54). Breaking into direct speech, he mocks the gods for struggling to destroy him and declares his willingness to die if they can really do the deed (5.654–59). These lines make it clear that he places himself on the same level as the gods and that he balances his own *fatum* against the world's. Yet the reason for his equanimity is chilling: after listing his deeds in the curt mode of *res gestae* (5.661–64), he boasts that a death at sea will prevent everyone except *Fortuna* from knowing that he dies a private citizen (*priuatus*, 5.665–68).

Although scholars dispute the meaning of this last claim, any consideration of it must start with the questions about the legal status of commanders that

Lucan has raised throughout the book.[20] Seen in this context, there are fewer reasons to get tied in knots: Caesar's words make good sense. The poem meditates compulsively on the nature of power in civil war and particularly on how the conflict's outcome defines reality. For Lucan's protagonists, Pharsalus determines sinner and saint in much the same way that opening the box determines whether Schrödinger's cat is alive or dead. Reality is not established until the crucial moment. Caesar here acknowledges an analogous situation: despite holding the offices of consul and dictator, he is still simultaneously a private citizen until the war is decided. Although such a formulation would be contradictory under normal circumstances, it makes perfect sense in civil war, where words collapse on themselves and paradox reigns supreme.[21]

A similar line of argument helps account for the bit about *Fortuna*. Stating the obvious first, Caesar's death at sea would prevent people from knowing the war was truly over: Lucan's narrative is clear that nobody saw him leave the camp, and without a corpse there can be no proof he is gone. He would seem instead to have disappeared entirely, swept from the earth (like Romulus in Livy 1?) and leaving Pompey the victor *by default*. But to a Roman, wars must be decided by the sword, by a final battle that makes plain which side is better and which side the gods support. The stakes in civil war are doubly high for the reason noted above: without a victor, participants remain simultaneously *ciues* (citizens) and *hostes* (enemies of the state). Caesar's putative death at sea would rob Pompey of the opportunity to end the conflict the Roman way and leave the world to question eternally whether he was a legitimate *dux* (general) all along. *Fortuna*, that embodiment of good luck who always finds a path for Caesar's success, would be the only one to know for sure that his acts were criminal.

The anonymity of this drowning also introduces the speech's final threat, where Caesar mocks the powers that roused the storm: "I have need of no funeral, o gods: keep my wounded body amidst the waves and let my mound and pyre lack *me*—provided I am always feared and awaited by every nation" (5.668–71, emphasis added). We cannot overstate the significance of this boast. Caesar is claiming that ignorance of his death will condemn the world to anxiety in expectation of his return. This realization provides the basis for his confidence and equanimity: he knows his physical destruction will only bolster his reputation's power. If the gods—whoever they are in this chaotic poem—are willing to accept that outcome, Caesar is happy to be stricken down. He dares them to act knowing that the game is already rigged in his favor.

We can never know whether this boasting is idle or an accurate portrayal of the reality the *Civil War* purports to represent. An author like Vergil might have used a "Council of the Gods" to show where Caesar fits in some cosmic plan, but Lucan's abandonment of the divine apparatus denies us certain knowledge of how his universe works. Even so, the narrative's progression suggests that the gods may be listening, that this storm *has* been a conflict between them and Caesar, and that they, like everyone else Caesar confronts, ultimately accept his vision of reality.

As soon as Caesar's speech is over, a miraculous wave drives his disabled ship to shore, bearing it around jagged rocks to deposit it safely on the sand (5.672–76). The crossing may have failed, but Caesar's landing "restored [for him] so many kingdoms, so many cities, and his own good Fortune" (5.676–77). We may well ask whether this turn is just good luck. Although we cannot say for sure, the sequence hints—if only faintly—that the gods have played a role and that Caesar really is the force of history he claims to be. This possibility, at any rate, is soon reiterated: when the army finds Caesar driven ashore, they chastise him for his risk, emphasize his importance to their lives and safety, and beg him to save his luck for battle with Pompey (5.682–99). All the issues raised amid the storm are here mentioned again according to Caesar's vision. And when the ships he needed so badly at last cross to Greece (5.703–21), it is tempting to think he was right all along—that even gods give way to Caesar's onslaught.

"What Power Lawful Love Exerts on Level Heads!"

The final episode of book 5 finds Pompey reluctant to leave his wife Cornelia before the war's decisive battle. The elegiac tone of the speeches they exchange contrasts sharply with Pompey's earlier public persona and Caesar's terrifying ferocity in the previous scene. Although Pompey could risk the fate of Rome and the world on Pharsalus, he could not bear to wager his wife (5.728–31). He consequently passes the hours "indulging in sweet delay (*mora*), drawing out events to come and stealing time from Fate" (5.732–33). Unlike Caesar, whom we saw ready to fight and threatening the gods, Pompey is somber when duty calls. His speech to Cornelia drips with pessimism:[22] he views life as a burden, suggests catastrophic destruction is at hand, and anticipates Caesar's victory by calling Lesbos a happy refuge (5.740–59). Nowhere is there any hint that he expects to win. Instead, he casts defeat as a likely, even welcome, outcome that will reunite him with Cornelia: "the separation from me that you suffer will not be long: calamitous outcomes are coming" (5.745–46).

Cornelia is more duty driven. Although she admits that marriage binds them with a single fate, she says she will commit suicide if Pompey loses and prays that she be the last to learn the war's outcome (5.769–79). She goes on to insist that Pompey must protect himself if he is defeated: since Caesar will seek *him* wherever *she* is, he must not flee to Lesbos (5.782–90). Although Cornelia likewise expects the worst, she at least holds out hope for victory: she anticipates dreading the sight of every ship in her exile—even one bearing good news (5.777–81). Here again *securitas* is a key concern. When Pompey explains why they must part, he says he is ashamed to enjoy carefree sleep (*securos . . . somnos*) in the midst of war (5.749–52), and Cornelia picks up on this term by asking—albeit sarcastically—whether he considers death a carefree lot (*secura . . . sors*). This repetition demands a closer look.

According to Pompey, his love for Cornelia prevents the chaos around him from affecting his psyche: dawn's trumpets may pull him from her embrace (5.751–52), but her presence in bed relieves the day's anxieties. The sentiment is sweet—and problematic. As Pompey admits, enjoying such pleasure in camp is inappropriate. A general is *supposed* to worry about war, which is why it is a trope for leaders to lie awake while soldiers slumber (cf. Cato in book 2: "[Brutus] found the man mulling the people's fate and the city's lot with sleepless care, fearing for all but unconcerned for himself" (*securumque sui*, 2.239–41). This discrepancy between expectation and reality accounts for Pompey's "shame" in his behavior (*pudet*, 5.750).

Yet the *securitas* Pompey claims to enjoy is peculiar and limited: rather than depending on something permanent or internal, it rests on Cornelia's physical presence. Ironically, this external cause of "sweet dreams" invites worries that are dangerous for a man in Pompey's position. They risk tempting him to betray his duty, put his wife at risk, and—to invoke the language of the Delphi episode—privilege the fate of minor players over that of the entire world. Pompey simply is not acting as head of the senate's cause. His attitude in the present scene thus underscores the doubts about him that were raised earlier and forces us to realize that one side of this conflict is unprepared to do what victory requires. Pompey's "lack of concern" is that of a private citizen, not a leader.

Cornelia's response offers a different sentiment. While imagining she will die apart from Pompey, she mocks him for thinking—if only by implication—that death grants freedom from cares (*secura uidetur | sors tibi . . . perisse*, 5.771–72). The reason for her scorn comes in the adversative clause hidden in the ellipsis: "though even now you formulate hopes for the future" (*cum facias etiamnunc uota*, 5.772). Earlier critics have struggled with this phrase,[23] but the point is not hard to unravel in the context of Pompey's speech. Cornelia differentiates between the *securitas* granted by death and the worry suffered by people uttering prayers: if you want events to happen a certain way, you cannot live without anxiety. Pompey is essentially faulted for espousing contradictory views—a shrewd critique of a speech that blends fatalistic acceptance (Caesar has already won) and insistence on meaningful action (Pompey must focus on fighting). As far as Cornelia is concerned, death may well offer "freedom from care," but Pompey cannot enjoy it while still attached to mortal outcomes.

The epilogue focuses on Cornelia's grief, ending with a reminder of the couple's fate: they would indeed be reunited but only after Pharsalus (5.813–15). These lines underscore the book's driving point that Pompey and Caesar are not equally matched. The one is indecisive, committed alternately to the senate and his wife, to life and to death; the other is driven to make men—and perhaps gods—accept his vision of reality (cf. 1.129–57). In a contest for the world's fate, only one of these leaders is up to the task.

Conclusion

Lucan uses book 5 to explore leadership in civil war, reflecting on the nature of power and the relationships between the movers of history, their subordinates, and fate. Unlike other epic poets, however, Lucan gives little indication that an intelligible system governs the cosmos. Although he raises questions and outlines answers, we as readers are ultimately left to decide for ourselves whether events are causally connected or sit together through mere coincidence. The result is a dizzying narrative that makes us more aware of how we *could* understand the civil war but painfully unsure of how we *should*. As book 5 comes to a close, readers may not know whether the fate of the world is fixed, but can be certain that Caesar's victory is now inevitable.

Notes

1. *Contra* D'Alessandro Behr 2007. Perkell (2002) interprets Vergil's contradictions about the Golden Age in a manner similar to my reading of Lucan.

2. See also Caterine 2015; Kimmerle 2015.

3. See Barratt 1979 *ad loc.* for the ancient sources.

4. I have used the Latin text of Shackleton Bailey 2009; translations are my own.

5. On Cato as *exemplum*, see Fantham 1992a, 122–39 on 2.234–325; Seo 2011.

6. On Alexander in Lucan, see esp. Rutz 1970; Maes 2009.

7. Cf. Oros. 6.15.11 (quoted by *Commenta Bernensia* 5.68); Barratt 1979 *ad loc.*

8. This opening is traditional in the hymnic genre, but invoking it *after* telling Delphi's foundation myth breaks the scene's logical flow. It seems doubtful that Lucan is alluding to how Dionysus (Bacchus) held partial control of the oracle, as that god is never mentioned except—perhaps—through the verb *bacchatur* ("run wild," "act like a Bacchante," 5.169).

9. This claim is problematic. Barratt 1979 *ad loc.* follows Duff 1932 *ad* Juv. 6.555–56 in accepting it, but comparison of the sources that Duff cites reveals that their confidence is overstated.

10. Cf. Lucan's frequent description of omens, on which, see Dick 1963, 1965; Morford 1967, 59–74; Korenjak 1996, 15–20. On fate in Lucan, see esp. Dick 1967; Ahl 1976, 293–305.

11. Cf. Vergil's teleological view of history in the *Aeneid* and W. H. Auden's criticism of "history in the future tense" in his poem *Secondary Epic*.

12. *Contra* D'Alessandro Behr 2007.

13. For a full treatment of this scene, see Caterine 2014, 242–60, and 2015, 346–49.

14. See Henderson 1987, an indispensable but challenging piece of scholarship.

15. The historical Caesar would face another mutiny after the narrative of Lucan's epic breaks off. On Lucan's conflation of the two uprisings, see Fantham 1985.

16. On rhetoric in Vergil and Lucan, see Narducci 2010.

17. Cf. Matthews 2008 *ad* 527–31 for the positive aspects of this apostrophe.

18. Cf. the narrator's insistence before Pharsalus that he will make readers experience *spes* ("hope") and *metus* ("fear"), then offer *uota* ("prayers") for a Pompeian victory (7.207–13). This consistency may suggest that Lucan wants his readers to view *securitas* as an ideal philosophical state even as his verse compels us to feel its opposite.

19. Lucan anticipates this move when he has Caesar urge Amyclas to entrust his fate "to the god" that was eager to fill his house with riches (*deo*, 5.536); the identity of that god is never specified, but looking back it is hard not to think that Caesar had himself in mind.

20. See Matthews *ad loc.* for discussion and bibliography. Caesar's troops insist that he was their *dux* ("general") in Gaul but their *socius* ("ally") after crossing the Rubicon (5.289–300); the narrator echoes this language at the end of the episode, observing that the army had been "about to make [Caesar] a private citizen" (5.365–66).

21. See Henderson 1987.

22. Lucan's Pompey is usually a pessimistic and uninspiring speaker; cf. his exchange with Cicero (7.45–123) and speech before Pharsalus (7.337–84). His attempt to rally the battle's survivors is more spirited (8.262–327), but Lentulus rejects his proposed course of action (8.327–455).

23. See Barratt 1979 *ad loc.*

6

Book 6

Thessalian Preludes

Andrew Zissos

Structure and Models

Among the ten extant books of the *Civil War*, the sixth stands out for its complexity, offering a series of episodes that bring to the fore Lucan's subversive approach to generic convention. The book enjoys particular notoriety for featuring two of Lucan's most outrageous figures: the centurion Scaeva and the witch Erictho. It begins with the historical matter of the confrontation between Caesar and Pompey near the coastal city of Dyrrachium (6.1–332), in the rendering of which Lucan engages closely with the corresponding account in the third book of Caesar's *Civil War*. It concludes with an ahistorical flight of fancy, a detailed and grotesque account of necromancy performed by the aforementioned Erictho (6.413–830), in the rendering of which Lucan's "antiphrastic" engagement with Vergil's *Aeneid* operates both structurally and thematically. In between these major episodes, a geographical excursus on Thessaly (6.333–412) helps to set the stage not so much for the immediately following necromancy as for the decisive encounter of the civil war, the Battle of Pharsalus, which will be recounted in book 7. The sixth book, then, comprises three major episodes; it can also be thought of as being divided asymmetrically into two parts, based on its two geographical settings: Epirus (6.1–332) and Thessaly (6.333–830). In combining relatively faithful (as can be surmised from other sources) renderings of historical incidents and outlandish fabrication, the sixth book raises with particular cogency the question of Lucan's commitment to the prevailing norms of historical epic.

An attempt to identify the structural significance of the sixth book neces-sitates speculation on the intended overall form of the incomplete *Civil War*. It is inherently likely that Lucan's epic on the death spasms of the legitimate (as he saw it) Roman political order, like Vergil's on its birth, was to have a clear and unified architecture. For present purposes, it will be assumed, with per-haps the majority of modern scholars, that a twelve-book epic was the author's intention. Within this scheme, the sixth book participates with the seventh in the construction of a poetic center. In narrative terms, these are the decisive books of the poem; in many respects, they need to be read together as forming a crucial thematic unit. As already indicated, a key function of book 6 is to set the stage—to "lay the ground" both topographically and metaphorically—for the disaster of the Battle of Pharsalus in book 7. The two books, then, consti-tute a narrative unit and will be assumed to comprise the intended physical and thematic center of a notional twelve-book epic. This is clearly *not* a Vergil-ian structure, and yet, as will be seen, the Erictho episode constitutes an intri-cate intertextual engagement, both thematically and structurally, with the *Aeneid*.

One unifying feature of the two "central" books is geographical: both lay heavy emphasis on Thessaly as the locus of Roman disaster. Caesar's victory at Pharsalus is for Lucan the central event in Roman history (just as for Vergil it was Octavian's victory at Actium). By an insistent, ubiquitous hyperbole, the collapse of republican Rome resulting from the Battle of Pharsalus is conceived as a global catastrophe—or even, invoking Stoic cosmology, as universal cata-clysm.[1] There is something bizarre about Lucan's insistence on Pharsalus as the decisive and irremediable catastrophe of the civil war—even against the developments of his subsequent narrative and the declarations of his charac-ters. The connection between Thessaly and (Roman) civil war, an established convention in earlier Roman poetry, is so forcefully asserted in the *Civil War* that in later episodes the word *Thessalia* ("Thessaly") frequently serves as a metonymy for the disaster itself. In the sixth book this treatment is initiated by the geographical excursus on Thessaly (6.333–412); book 7 ends with an extended apostrophe to the same region (7.847–72), thereby "rounding out" the textual sequence and bringing it to a close.

Another unifying feature of books 6 and 7 is that these are the only ones in which Caesar and Pompey square off face-to-face, at the head of their respec-tive armies. Such direct military confrontation is something that Caesar has sought from the outset and that Pompey has been shrewdly (given his strategic advantages) avoiding. Book 6 gives us the first major encounter between these two celebrated generals of the late republic (Dyrrachium 6.1–332, in which Pom-pey emerges victorious) and book 7 the second and last (7.123–727, Pharsalus, in which Caesar triumphs). Crucially in Lucan's treatment, the second encounter is inconceivable without the first.

In its linear chronological scheme, with no device to focus the action *in medias res,* Lucan's poem more closely resembles an historical chronicle than a conventional epic. As a history, though, the *Civil War* is selective rather than exhaustive: criteria for inclusion of particular events have to do with broader ideological, thematic, and artistic strategies. So, for example, with respect to the account of military activity in book 6, Lucan has passed over events in theaters of war other than Dyrrachium (cf. Caes. *BCiv.* 3.31–38) in order to keep the focus on the showdown between Caesar and Pompey.

Episodes with a strong historical basis are often intricately engaged with Caesar's *Civil War,* as is the case for the extended account of the conduct of the conflict in the vicinity of Dyrrachium (6.1–332). This episode sometimes makes reference to events and details in so obscure a manner as to virtually compel the reader to seek out the fuller account of the Caesarian commentary.[2] But here as elsewhere, Lucan's intertextual engagement with Caesar operates in a starkly transformative manner. As Gowing observes, Lucan's epic "completely rewrites the history of this war, promoting a very different memory from that transmitted by Caesar himself or by any subsequent historian."[3] This is particularly the case for events at Dyrrachium. The sequence of events starting with Caesar's circumvallation, continuing with Scaeva's *aristeia,* and concluding with Pompey's successful breaching of the siege works, is, as Sklenář well notes, the most "Iliadic" of the entire poem.[4] This effect works on many levels: not just the subject matter but also the style, including many striking similes and elevated epic language, to say nothing of direct Iliadic echoes and overt allusions to Trojan myth (6.48–49). In the immediately following description of Thessaly, Lucan has made heavy use of geographical writers, but he has also drawn on the Homeric catalogue of ships (*Il.* 2.681–759). Part of what is at work here is a self-conscious epicizing of Caesar's matter-of-fact account in the third book of his civil war commentary. In terms of poetic models, though, Vergil's *Aeneid* is generally preeminent, and critics have over the last several decades widely embraced the notion of Lucan's *Civil War* as an "anti-*Aeneid.*"[5] It is arguably the case that book 6 features the most sustained instance of negative modeling of the *Aeneid* (see Thessalian Abomination, below).

Caesarian Megalomania

The *Civil War* is a fervently anti-Caesarian poem: Lucan's epic repeatedly insists not only on Caesar's innate viciousness and immorality but also his megalomania and concomitant tendency to transgress natural limits. And yet Lucan's "ambivalent fascination with Caesar's heroic energy" will be apparent to even a casual reader.[6] Epic is a narration of extraordinary and consequential events; in the *Civil War*, as Martindale observes, "Caesar is, inevitably, the main actor, the creator and controller of the plot, as he overleaps the moral boundaries in the footsteps of Hannibal and Alexander the Great (as developed by the rhetoricians, the type of the tyrant and overreacher)."[7]

The first episode of book 6, the account of the campaigning in the vicinity of Dyrrachium (6.1–332, which, in historical terms, took place between April and July 48 B.C.E.) exhibits the overreaching and transgressive character of Caesar and his adherents with particular clarity. The book opens with the opposing armies setting up their respective camps on neighboring heights near Dyrrachium, an Epirote coastal city of considerable strategic importance. When Caesar undertakes a covert maneuver to capture the city, Pompey counters by occupying the nearby height of Petra, thereby offering an indirect defense (6.11–18). The resulting situation is something of a stalemate, which plays to Pompey's strategic advantages: time is on his side. In these frustrating circumstances, Caesar conceives of a breathtakingly ambitious and counterintuitive strategy: to enclose Pompey's numerically superior forces within a vast siege wall. This impromptu circumvallation shows Caesar's heroic energy at its apex: it registers on a sublime, almost superhuman, scale. In conceiving of and undertaking this monstrous project, Caesar, in Lucan's treatment, demonstrates "impiousness towards nature, a refusal to respect the boundaries or limits in things. . . . The enormous labor, the size and compass of the wall, its hubristic, unnatural character" all attest to Caesar's megalomania, his mad ambition.[8] In order to convey these qualities, Lucan has recourse to both mythical and historical *comparanda*:

> uetus Iliacos attollat fabula muros
> ascribatque deis; fragili circumdata testa
> moenia mirentur . . . Babylonia Parthi.
> en, quantum Tigris, quantum celer ambit Orontes,
> Assyriis quantum populis telluris Eoae
> sufficit in regnum, subitum bellique tumultu
> raptum clausit opus.

> (6.48–54)

> let ancient legend praise the walls of Ilium
> and ascribe them to the gods; let Parthians . . .
> be amazed at the walls of Babylon built of brittle brick.
> Look: as much land as Tigris and swift Orontes encircle,

as much of eastern earth as satisfies Assyrian peoples
for their realm, is enclosed by hasty building-work,
hurried on by the turmoil of war.

Caesar's circumvallation defies conventional military logic, not least because
the Pompeians had the sea to their rear, as well as complete control of the sea-
ways, and so could be resupplied almost at will: whence the paradoxical situation whereby the besieged are better fed than the besiegers (6.114–18). Moreover,
the hemming in of a larger force by a smaller one inevitably involves attendant
perils—and Pompey shrewdly augments those perils by spreading his forces
over a vast area and constructing an inner wall of his own around them, thereby
obliging Caesar to extend the circumvallation well beyond his original intent,
leaving his lines dangerously thin (6.64–79). Yet the circumvallation does exert
a debilitating effect, and at length a plague strikes Pompey's forces (explained
"scientifically" as arising from the interaction between the decaying carcasses
of horses deprived of fodder and stagnant air, 6.88–90).

After suffering this and other hardships, Pompey resolves upon and exe-
cutes a complex breakout, exposing Caesar's thinly drawn forces to grave danger at various points. At one location the massed Pompeian forces are held at
bay by the heroics of a single centurion, Scaeva, whose superhuman feats are
described in a lengthy epic *aristeia* (6.118–262). The Scaeva episode, in fact,
offers Lucan's only fully elaborated instance of the *aristeia*, and it pushes this
type scene to its breaking point. Lucan follows the epic pattern of reporting in
detail a single hero's combats, complete with invocations, apostrophes, lineages
(in this case specifying socioeconomic origins and military rank rather than
genealogy as such), and verbal exchanges between combatants. In terms of epic
antecedents, the Roman poet has drawn, inter alia, on the heroic feats of Ajax
in *Iliad* 12–15. But Lucan undertakes a hyperbolic magnification of the Homeric
model, forsaking any aspiration to realism and offering instead an almost cartoonish treatment of the intrepid centurion single-handedly holding off a whole
army (6.191–92), generating huge piles of Pompeian casualties in the process
(6.180), and sustaining an impossible assortment of wounds: as the *aristeia*
draws to a close, Lucan states that the forest of javelins sticking into Scaeva's
torso was so thick that it served to protect him from, by leaving no place for,
further injury (6.193–94)! This hyperbolic treatment is all the more noteworthy inasmuch as Lucan's poem is an historical rather than mythological epic,
and Scaeva is an historical figure. A veteran of Caesar's Gallic campaigns,
Scaeva had risen through the ranks to the level of centurion. Caesar and other
sources recount a less prodigious and more collaborative feat of bravery at an
earlier stage of the Dyrrachium engagement. Lucan repositions the centurion's

feats to the climactic encounter of the campaign, singles him out, and magnifies his heroics to an impossible degree. The historical Scaeva survived his stalwart exploits and was, along with others at his outpost, handsomely rewarded by Caesar (Caes. *BCiv.* 3.53). Lucan's outlandish account would appear to imply that he died after sustaining an impossible accumulation of wounds (6.265–67). But Scaeva evidently survives in the epic *Civil War* as well, for he reappears at the very end of the narrative as we have it, in the serried ranks facing down Caesar's Egyptian assailants in the royal palace at Alexandria (10.543–46).

In an insightful analysis, Marti has demonstrated that Lucan's *aristeia* is an ingenious reinvention of the story of Scaeva, particularly in its echoes of Homeric and Vergilian epic, its use of epic themes, its rhetorical deployments, and its negative framing of Scaeva's heroism.[9] To put it in Roman terms, an *aristeia* amounts to sustained demonstration of martial *uirtus* and so would normally be a positive and uplifting element of martial epic. But Lucan repeatedly insists on a fundamental problem, of which Scaeva is the poem's most perfect embodiment: in civil war, to demonstrate *uirtus* is to be implicated in a *crimen* (crime) since one's nominally heroic actions are perpetrated not against the enemies of Rome but against fellow citizens (6.257–62). Beyond Caesarian excess, then, Scaeva represents the untethering of martial *uirtus* from patriotism and morality, which is, in Lucan's implicit diagnosis, the essential precondition for the civil wars that brought an end to the Roman republic. Scaeva's *aristeia* is inspired by a perverse sense of *pietas* ("duty, loyalty") that applies to Caesar alone.[10] He constitutes "the most conspicuous, compendious symbol of . . . the civil war mentality of Caesar vis-a-vis that of Pompey."[11]

Pompeian Tragedy

Although the Scaeva episode highlights a kind of jarring extremism that works to Caesar's advantage, it should not be forgotten that its perverse heroics unfold in the broader context of a significant Pompeian victory achieved through Pompey's adept generalship. Beyond that, the importance of the Dyrrachium episode resides in its illustration of Pompey's character. Schröter has identified four key aspects to the figure of Pompey in the *Civil War*, which Lucan blends more or less coherently: he is (1) Caesar's personal rival in a bitter and violent struggle for power; (2) the leader of the republican oligarchy, champion of the senate, and defender of "freedom"; (3) a tragic figure, portrayed with great sympathy in his downfall and death; and (4) a figure associated with mythological epic heroes, notably Aeneas (but also Hector and others).[12] The initial episode of book 6 deals especially with (1) and (3).

At the opening of the *Civil War* Pompey is portrayed as fully Caesar's equal in depravity but, unlike the latter, a weak and ineffectual leader whose best days are behind him (1.89–157). As the narrative advances, however, Lucan increasingly warms to Pompey, who proves, after all, to be a proficient military commander and who, more importantly, undergoes an ethical evolution from unscrupulous *triumuir* in book 1 to republican champion in books 5–7.[13] This transformation has been fully achieved by book 6 and is much in evidence there.[14] If Caesar is a subverter of Roman custom and the destroyer of the senate, Lucan's Pompey gradually emerges as a morally upright supporter of that body. A crucial historical datum is that much of the senate, and certainly its most significant elements, accompanied Pompey on his initial retreat from Italy to Greece. Lucan insists on this exiled group as the only legitimate instantiation of Rome's supreme political body (cf. 5.9–14).[15]

Book 6 also puts on display Pompey's strengths as a military commander. If Caesar's irrepressible activity generally drives Lucan's plot, here the narrative dynamic is less one-sided. As already noted, Caesar's massive circumvallation is ingeniously countered by Pompey's inner defensive wall (6.70–77); Pompey eventually seizes the initiative in breaking out and dealing Caesar a crushing defeat. Though Pompey's initial attempt to break the siege is, as discussed above, repulsed by Scaeva's heroics, a second breakout maneuver at the southern extremity of the circumvallation proves to be more successful. Caesar is (uncharacteristically) slow to react; when he learns of the breach, he hastens to the spot and impulsively attacks a squadron of Pompeians under the command of Torquatus. The latter gathers his men behind a defensive wall, and, when Caesar engages that position, Pompey himself, coming from the outside, pins the Caesarians between his own and Torquatus's forces, thereby catching them in a deadly trap and inflicting heavy losses (6.288–99; cf. 7.315–17). In this advantageous situation, Pompey declines to press home his advantage fully and finish Caesar off, as a more ruthless figure, such as a Sulla, might have done. He thereby misses an opportunity to conclude the civil war and forestall the various republican calamities that will follow (6.299–311). Above all, "Pharsalia could have disappeared from destiny" (6.312–13). In making this assessment, Lucan aligns himself with a widespread tradition that probably goes back to Livy and has its roots in Caesar's own assessment (*BCiv.* 3.70). Appian reports Caesar saying, "Today my opponents would have ended the war, if they had had a commander who knew how to drive home a victory" (2.62). Uniquely among our sources, Lucan attributes this missed opportunity not to an excess of prudence on Pompey's part but to a lingering sense of familial *pietas* toward Caesar (6.299–313). The fact remains, though, that Pompey had inflicted a crushing blow upon his opponent: "though he had not administered the *coup de grace*, his plan appeared to have triumphantly succeeded. Caesar was to all intents and purposes beaten."[16]

In the wake of his shattering defeat at Dyrrachium, Caesar is obliged to abandon the present military theater, relocating to the fateful region of Thessaly (6.314–15). Immediately upon his rival's departure, Pompey summons a war council to consider the appropriate response, at length resolving to follow his opponent eastward rather than return to Italy (6.316–29).[17] This was probably the right strategy: as one modern historian has put it, "Caesar was too dangerous a tiger to be left at large in Greece."[18] Lucan's textual sequence underscores the degree to which the tables have been turned: earlier in the epic it was Pompey who fled Italy in panic with Caesar in pursuit; for the span of time between Dyrrachium and Pharsalus, the hunter has become the hunted. Lucan thus makes the Dyrrachium episode the highwater mark of Pompey's generalship in the poem: his prudence and sound strategy is repeatedly contrasted with Caesar's rashness. He refuses to be drawn into uncertain battle; he foils Caesar's attempt to steal a march and capture Dyrrachium; he countermaneuvers effectively against Caesar's circumvallation; and then, at a well-chosen moment, he initiates a bold and sophisticated breakout maneuver, with a series of well-coordinated attacks from land and sea that break the siege and inflict a significant defeat on his opponent. This Pompey, this inventive strategist and vigorous military leader, seems a far cry from the "shadow of a great name" (1.135) that Lucan introduced in his initial analytic sequence or the flustered republican leader who abandoned Rome in panic on the mere report of Caesar's advance.

The presentation of Pompey as a superior military commander carries over into the opening of book 7, in which he, as Lucan would have it, advocates and initially continues his "Fabian" strategy of avoiding decisive engagements and using his superior resources to wear Caesar down in the confident expectation of an eventual and comparatively bloodless victory.[19] He is at length—and against his better judgment—turned from this strategy by impatient members of his own camp, Cicero chief among them, who insist on a decisive battlefield showdown.[20] These advocates were confident of final victory in the wake of Pompey's resounding success at Dyrrachium, which had indubitably left the enemy forces in a weakened condition.

There is much raw material here for a tragic reading of events. In the estimation of one modern historian, Pompey's *peripeteia* was "more pathetic and more truly tragic" than that suffered subsequently by Caesar on the Ides of March in 44 B.C.E.[21] The pattern of elevation (Dyrrachium) before final catastrophe (Pharsalus) is, of course, very much in the tragic vein. Earlier writers had picked up on this, including Caesar himself, who made Pompey's victory at Dyrrachium the beginning of his demise according to the familiar tragic sequence: initial success—hybris—downfall. If the Pompeians (as opposed to Pompey himself) had not become overconfident and impatient after the victory at Dyrrachium, they would not have compelled their leader to abandon his "Fabian" strategy of avoiding engagement and instead to risk a winner-take-all battlefield showdown at Pharsalus. With respect to the overall trajectory of events, Lucan refines the widespread tragic formulation by implying that had Pompey not undergone a personal evolution, had not become a true adherent of senatorial governance, he would not have yielded, against his own better judgment, to the consensual view of that body. In other words, it is *because* Pompey becomes a genuine republican (and so an oligarch rather than an autocrat) that he suffers final defeat. This tragic failure of (republican) decency constitutes an expression of the cosmic *discors machina* ("discordant mechanism," 1.79–80) on the political level. Disaster at Pharsalus might have been averted had Pompey not felt obliged to defer to Cicero and his senatorial peers. Here as elsewhere, the *Civil War* ingeniously exploits the historical Pompey's strategic and tactical lapses in order to highlight his moral improvement and underscore his newly acquired senatorial *bona fides*.

Lucan's Pompey is presented as a flawed human being who starts out with the same autocratic tendencies as Caesar but gradually undergoes a *political* conversion from wicked triumvir to constitutionalist, defender of the republic and champion of the senatorial oligarchy. This, indeed, is what Lucan forthrightly declares at 5.13–14: Pompey is assimilated into the senatorial party rather than the reverse. The poet should be taken at his word here: Pompey fights under the banner of the republic, having received the authorization of the senate in exile at Epirus (5.45–49). By the time of the decisive Battle of Pharsalus, Pompey has morphed into a champion and defender of the republic, of the senatorial order. To be a true champion of the senate, an individual, no matter how great, must subordinate himself to the oligarchic collective.

Dyrrachium and Pharsalus are, therefore, mutually implicated episodes: in the former Pompey acts according to his own judgment and without oligarchical interference and succeeds; in the latter, he acts under the influence of senatorial pressure and fails. In Lucan's treatment Pompey is the one man who could have saved the Roman political order, but in line with his republican "conversion," he is no longer free from constraint, no longer able to act independently. This amounts to something more than simple tragedy: it is a devastating political diagnosis on Lucan's part. According to this view, ruthless autocrats of Caesar's caliber will tend to succeed precisely because they are not constrained by decency or regard for the views of others. Underwriting Lucan's narrative account, then, is a conceptual fault line between political principle and battlefield efficacy: in late-republican Rome these prove to be ruinously antithetical. If the *Civil War* thematizes the triumph of evil in the universe, incarnated in the figure of Caesar, then a necessary corollary must be that Pompey's progressive moral "improvement" as the narrative advances makes his demise inevitable.

Thessalian Abomination

In the wake of the arrival of the armies of Caesar and Pompey in Thessaly, the narrative is suspended for a geographical excursus that elaborates upon that region and its sinister associations (6.333–412). On one level, this Thessalian excursus constitutes an elaborate "digression" that delays the progress of Lucan's historical narrative at the decisive moment. But there is, of course, more to the passage than that: in conjunction with the subsequent Erictho episode, it sets the scene for the climactic battle of the civil war by providing a sinister and malevolent backdrop for it. The reader is confronted with a veritable topography of abomination: Lucan freights the region with a series of originary negative associations, through allusions to myths of violence and deplorable cultural developments. A noteworthy feature of the Thessalian excursus is that, through the device of "ring composition," it begins and ends with the Gigantomachy. This is a suggestive touch: elsewhere in the poem Lucan repeatedly makes figurative use of conflicts between celestial and chthonic forces to represent the civil war between Pompey and Caesar.[22] And these gigantomachic references are merely the beginning (and end) of Lucan's Thessalian harangue. Thessaly is an ill-fated land that emerged in geological times when a vast inland lake drained through the Vale of Tempe; it would have been better for humankind, the poet bitterly remarks, had it remained forever submerged (6.349–50). Thessaly is the terrestrial homeland of monstrosities such as the hybrid race of centaurs (6.386–87); it is the place where the great hero Hercules died an excruciating death (6.365–66, 391–92); it is the land in which the seeds of human warfare first came into being (6.395). The region is, in Lucan's conception, a perpetual dystopia, a perverse and ill-fated land and, as such, the appropriate setting for a battle that will spell the end of the Roman republic and *libertas* ("freedom"), thereby visiting a culminating catastrophe on the human race.

Following Lucan's lurid description of Thessaly, the narrative briefly resumes on the eve of the Battle of Pharsalus, at which point, the poet declares, "it is clear that the hideous hour of greatest crisis is approaching" (6.415–16). But deferral of this central martial narrative is now prolonged by the notorious Erictho episode, a massive digression that accounts for nearly half of book 6 (6.423–830). The episode begins with an unexpected and ahistorical presence—that of Pompey's younger son Sextus, in his twenties at this time, whom Lucan contrafactually locates with his father at Pharsalus. Though not yet figuring in the unfolding conflict, Sextus is a figure of considerable histori- cal importance: after his father's death, he would lead the resistance to the Caesarians until his own demise in 35 B.C.E.[23] Roman sources are almost uni- formly hostile to Sextus, and Lucan, perhaps somewhat surprisingly, adopts the "official" (which is to say Augustan) line, introducing Sextus as "a son unwor- thy of Pompey the Great" (6.420) and repeatedly laying stress on his corrupt and craven nature. Lucan's Sextus does not follow his father's spiritual and politi- cal evolution: in his initial encounter with Erictho, he characterizes himself as an aspiring "master of the world" (*dominus rerum*, 6.594), thereby excluding himself from genuine adherence to the republican cause.

It is Sextus's trepidation on the eve of Pharsalus and his consequent desire for knowledge of the future that motivates Erictho's necromantic consultation. The account of this ghastly undertaking begins in the foreboding and digres- sive spirit of the Thessalian excursus, with a description of the region's most notorious class of inhabitants, namely, its witches. Their awesome powers are enumerated (6.438–506), including the ability to control nature and to compel the gods above. Lucan prefaces this enumeration with the remark that "their art is the unbelievable" (*quidquid non creditur, ars est*, 6.437), a characteristic instance of literary self-consciousness. The incredible abilities of witches have a rich pedigree in both Greek and Latin poetry, and Lucan certainly engages with this literary tradition.[24] But here, as elsewhere in the episode, it seems clear that "Lucan . . . knew something about magic as it was being practiced, not just from literary models."[25] After the general enumeration, Erictho, a witch even more formidable than her Thessalian peers, is now introduced: her appalling practices and immense powers are catalogued (6.505–68). She is presented as a kind of superwitch, of whom even the gods live in terror.

Following these preliminaries—which, from the perspective of the inter- rupted master narrative amount to digressions within a digression—the action resumes with Sextus seeking out Erictho, addressing her flatteringly, and requesting foreknowledge concerning the outcome of the war (6.569–603). The witch is happy to oblige and indicates that fulsome and accurate prophecy calls for the dark art of necromancy—more specifically, she resolves temporarily to bring back to life the corpse of a recently slain Pompeian soldier and to elicit a mantic utterance from it (6.604–24).[26] Erictho's immense power and her assur- ance of full disclosure inevitably induce high readerly expectations for her vatic project. What follows is arguably the most gruesome passage in Lucan's epic: Erictho selects a corpse suitable to her purpose, a recently slain Pompeian soldier from the dead strewn about on the battlefield—a curiosity inasmuch as no battles have yet been reported in this location,[27] and drags it to a hellish cavern. There, with Sextus looking on apprehensively, she pierces the breast, fills it with noxious poisons, and mutters a terrible incantation (6.625–93). Erictho then utters a "prayer" to the forces of the underworld, requesting their assistance in temporarily returning the spirit of the dead soldier to its body (6.693–718). In evident response, the spirit appears beside the corpse—but hesitates to reincarnate. The witch, outraged by the hesitation, lashes the corpse with a snake and makes a second, more threatening address to the underworld powers (6.719–49). The corpse immediately revives, and Erictho prevails on it to reveal to Sextus what he wishes to know (6.749–76).

The reanimated corpse begins with a general description of the famous Roman dead it saw in the underworld (6.779–99). With unabashed partisanship, Lucan splits these figures along ideological lines:[28] the *optimates* (aristocratic conservatives) are in Elysium, the *populares* (members of the senatorial aristocracy regarded as radicals and revolutionaries) in Tartarus. This clear-cut eschatology has, however, been thrown into turmoil: Tartarean miscreants such as Marius and Catiline have burst their chains and are exultant at Caesar's looming victory; Elysian champions of the republic, such as Camillus and Sulla, are dismayed for the same reason. Of the pious (optimate) Roman shades, Brutus alone evinces a measure of satisfaction, consoled by the fact that his descendant and namesake will lead the successful plot to assassinate Caesar (five years hence, in 44 B.C.E.). In broader terms, the corpse's prophecy here suggests that "all of Rome's history can be read in Pharsalian terms as a battle between *optimates* and *populares*. Pharsalus is thus the culmination of ever-inherent Roman conflict."[29] In conjunction with Caesar's victory and subsequent assassination in Rome, the necromantic prophet foretells the defeat of Pompey and his subsequent death in Egypt. Concerning Sextus's own fate the oracle is somewhat vaguer, instructing him to seek a further prophecy after his father's death (6.811–15). Sextus's reaction to all this is not reported.[30] With the prophecy completed, Erictho returns the dead soldier's spirit to the underworld and accompanies Sextus back to his father's camp.

The triumph of evil in the world, embodied in the figure of Caesar, inevitably problematizes the traditional epic notion of divine providence. This notion is recast in many passages as a malignant force supporting (or at least acquiescing in) the success of wicked humans. But the poem raises other possibilities: that the gods themselves are under constraint or that they are indifferent to human affairs. Such theological vacillation is intrinsic to the *Civil War*, a poem that repeatedly puts on display a profound epistemological uncertainty. Nowhere is this given a more full-throated articulation than in the series of authorial questions on the relationship between divine power and witchcraft at 6.492–99. Such uncertainty renders the poet unable clearly to account for historical and metaphysical causation. And unlike Attic tragedy, in which the power and controlling activity of the Olympian gods is taken for granted but made inscrutable to the audience, Lucan sometimes raises a more radical possibility—that these gods may be subject to malevolent beings vastly more powerful than themselves. This is one of the chief suggestions of the Erictho episode; here more than anywhere else Lucan articulates a vision of the working of a sinister and irrational metaphysics.

For all its breathtaking novelty, the Erictho episode, like many other parts of Lucan's poem, unfolds in part as a process of pattern negation, creating an antithesis of Vergil's epic of Roman glory. The broad parallelism with the *Aeneid* that governs much of the poem is particularly in evidence here. A cursory examination suffices to ascertain that significant inspiration for the elaboration of the Erictho episode is drawn from the Vergilian underworld sequence in *Aeneid* 6—though, as Narducci rightly points, a sense of the grotesque and macabre distinguishes Lucan's treatment from the atmosphere of hallowed mystery in the Vergilian model.[31] The poetic strategy of pattern negation extends to the provision of Vergilian "stand-ins"—figures who unmistakably evoke their Vergilian archetypes but are stripped of every vestige of their Vergilian glory.[32] Although it is generally Pompey who serves as Lucan's antithetical counterpart to Aeneas, in the Erictho episode that role is filled by his son Sextus, who characteristically inverts key aspects of his Vergilian counterpart. If *pietas* is the driving force behind Aeneas's consultation of the dead, Sextus is motivated by fear (6.423) and has recourse to the *nefas* of Thessalian witchcraft rather than licit divinatory practices (6.424–37). While Aeneas gains admission to the underworld through religious ceremonies and signs of divine approbation, Pompey's son gains access to the nether realm by quite the opposite means (6.430–34). By a similar intertextual logic, Lucan's Erictho stands as the perverse intertextual counterpart to Vergil's Sibyl. The witch is referred to as *Thessala uates* ("the seer of Thessaly," 6.652), a clear evocation of Vergil's designation *Amphrysia uates* ("the seer of Amphrysus," *Aen.* 6.398) for the Sibyl. She serves as Sextus's underworld "guide," just as the Sibyl does for Aeneas in book 6 of the *Aeneid*.[33] Sextus even addresses her as if she were, like the Sibyl, a benefactor of humankind (6.589–90). Furthermore, Erictho's speech at 6.605–23, a programmatic explanation of the task at hand, corresponds to the Sibyl's speech to Aeneas at *Aen.* 6.124–55. Rounding out Vergil's necromantic trinity is the dead Pompeian soldier, who stands in for the shade of Anchises, whom Aeneas seeks out in the nether realms in *Aeneid* 6. Perhaps most importantly, the cadaver's catalogue of Roman historical figures at 6.779–99 is clearly based on *Aen.* 6.756–886: the similarities extend to the actual names invoked by the two poets, though the ideological impact is, of course, reversed: instead of the promise of future greatness, Lucan's antiphrastic reworking offers a vision of Rome's irremediable demise.

As Vessey observes, "book 6 [of the *Civil War*] is a counterblast to book 6 of the *Aeneid* in its literary genetics, in its characters, language, atmosphere, and purpose."[34] The careful parallelism extends beyond episodic "mirroring" to include elements of structural mirroring as well: like Vergil, Lucan uses the concluding episode of his sixth book for an encounter with the dead and a foreshadowing of the future.[35] This calls to mind the dyadic structure of the *Aeneid*, composed in twelve books. But this local Vergilian structural parallelism is not part of a more overarching design. Lucan, for example, does not offer a disjunctive medial proem early in book 7; to the contrary, as already observed, he creates a strong poetic center by forging a thematic unit out of books 6 and 7.[36]

If one were to select a single passage to illustrate that Lucan's *Civil War* is something other than versified history, it would surely be the Erictho episode. With this baroque textual sequence, the narrative veers away from the normative content of historical epic and into a realm of grotesque fantasy. The events described are completely ahistorical: the Thessalian witch Erictho is an exuberant product of Lucan's fertile imagination, and Sextus Pompey, though an historical figure, was not in Thessaly at this point to consult her.[37] With respect to both literary models and thematic content, the contrast with the initial narrative of book 6 could hardly be more stark. In stylistic terms, the Erictho episode is clearly important for an anticlassical epic that strives to embody an unrestrained "aesthetic of the gruesome." Like the Scaeva episode before it, it constitutes an "extreme" textual sequence that seems at times to raise the question of dark humor in the *Civil War*.[38]

Erictho is an emblematic figure in Lucan's epic inasmuch as she unabashedly derives pleasure and profit from the carnage and devastation of Roman civil war. For Ahl, the episode of the witch "brings to a final climax Lucan's vignettes of the disintegration of the Roman world." [39] It also forms a bridge between *Civil War* 6 and 7: in the view of Dinter, Erictho "embodies the *nefas* (sacrilege) Lucan does not want to spell out when he describes the battle, at which point he ostentatiously renounces his topic (7.552–54)."[40]

The Thessalian superwitch is arguably Lucan's most remarkable creation, a figure destined to assume a prominent place in the Western literary tradition. Because of her notoriety and renown, it is easy to forget that, like Vergil's Sibyl in *Aeneid* 6, Erictho is a secondary figure in Lucan's epic, confined to a single episode. In this respect, she fits W. R. Johnson's well-calibrated category of "momentary monsters." For one critic, "the figure of Erictho refuses to be exorcised," because of the chasm between her vast powers and her insignificant duties.[41]

Conclusion

Critics have not always been kind to Lucan's sixth book. Writing late in the nineteenth century, Heitland summarily dismisses it as misconceived and extraneous to the overall scheme of the epic: "Half of it is devoted to the affair of the witch, which, though irrelevant, is better than the first half. The book is a poor one, and the least essential of the ten."[42] Other scholars of the era were no less scathing, and this remained the prevailing state of affairs until the late-twentieth century. In line with recent "recuperative" critical trends, this essay has argued that book 6 is integral to Lucan's overall poetic design. It has also stressed the importance of taking books 6 and 7 together, as constituting a poetic center and enacting a tragic sequence at the heart of Lucan's thematic design. With respect to the latter, these books contain the two great military confrontations between Pompey and Caesar, the first at Dyrrachium, the second at Pharsalus. Like other ancient authors, Lucan posits a causal connection between the two battles as forming a tragic arc: in this conception, the disaster at Pharsalus is inconceivable without the Pompeian victory at Dyrrachium.

Notes

1. See Lapidge 1979.
2. Examples of this phenomenon include *letum . . . minantis | . . . ignotis dubias radicibus herbas* ("doubtful herbs which threaten death from unfamiliar roots," 6.112–13), an oblique reference to *chara*, an otherwise unknown local plant with which Caesar's troops sated their hunger (cf. Caes. *BCiv.* 3.48), and *gemini Martis* ("twofold warfare," 6.269), a decidedly oblique way of indicating that Pompey attacked both by land and by sea (cf. Caes. *BCiv.* 3.62).
3. Gowing 2005, 82.
4. Sklenář 2003, 46.
5. Starting with Narducci 1979, who at the same time acknowledges the limits of that useful formulation. For a convenient overview of the matter, see Casali 2011.
6. Paleit 2013, 214.
7. Martindale 1993, 71.
8. Saylor 1978, 247–48.
9. Marti 1966, 246–48.
10. Saylor 1978, 251.
11. Saylor 1978, 244.
12. Schröter 1975.
13. The degree to which Lucan's version of Pompey corresponds to the historical figure is for present purposes beside the point; but it is worth noting that the Roman poet was not inventing "Pompey the republican" out of whole cloth.

14. Cf. Dilke (1972, 66–67): "The change of heart begins to be visible in the second half of book 2. . . . From the beginning of book 3 idealization of Pompey and ranting hatred of Caesar become more prominent. Pompey is frequently called by his *cognomen* "Magnus" ("the Great").

15. See Caterine in this volume.

16. Pocock 1959, 80.

17. Tracy (2014, 26) notes that Lucan's Pompey holds war councils, Caesar does not; the difference speaks to the former's more "senatorial" ethos.

18. Pocock 1959, 80; cf. the assessment of Appian (*BCiv.* 2.65) that returning to Italy "would have been best."

19. Masters (1992, 2) has observed that Lucan's Caesar frequently resembles Hannibal, and is sometimes explicitly likened to him, whereas Pompey, champion of *mora* ("delay"), resembles Hannibal's Roman nemesis Quintus Fabius Maximus, nicknamed *Cunctator* ("the Delayer").

20. A significant departure from the historical record: Cicero was with Pompey at Dyrrachium but not at Pharsalus. In his correspondence, moreover, Cicero criticized Pompey for risking everything in a decisive battlefield showdown (*Fam.* 7.3)—that is, the very decision that Lucan's Cicero advocates.

21. Pocock 1959, 80–81.

22. See Feeney 1991, 297.

23. On the historical Sextus Pompey, see Welch 2012.

24. Fox 2012, *ad loc.*

25. Bremmer 2003, 77.

26. Ogden (2001, xxix) points out that Lucan not only provides antiquity's most elaborate portrayal of necromancy but also makes the single greatest innovation in the literary tradition by having Erictho resort to the technique of reanimation necromancy.

27. O'Higgins (1988, 218–19) argues for a deliberate play with narrative time rather than an oversight on Lucan's part.

28. As Ahl (1976, 136) well puts it, "Heaven and hell are populated along strictly party lines."

29. Dinter 2012, 73.

30. As Dinter (2012, 72) points out, "this signposts that [the prophecy] is not only voiced for him but also for us."

31. Narducci 1979, 56.

32. Ahl 1976, 148.

33. Although Erictho and Sextus do not actually descend to the underworld in the manner of Aeneas, Lucan manages to echo many of the effects from the Vergilian *nekuia*. In particular, the cavern in which the necromancy is performed is said to be physically close to the nether realms and is described in explicitly "Tartarean" and "Stygian" terms (6.646–53).

34. Vessey 1973, 243.

35. Ahl 1976, 147–48.

36. On the medial proem in ancient epic, see Conte 1992.

37. Though the sequence appears to be inspired by an incident that involved Sextus (see Plin. *NH* 7.53) and, as discussed below, unfolds as a process of pattern negation vis-à-vis Vergil's *Aeneid*.

38. Ahl 1976, 148; see also Johnson 1987, 22–23.

39. Ahl 1976, 148.

40. Dinter 2012, 73.

41. Gordon 1987, 231.

42. Heitland 1877, xxxiii.

7

Book 7

Things Fall Apart

Paul Roche

Symmetries, Scale, and Structures

Most individual books of the *Civil War* narrate discrete scenes and are easily divisible into obvious panels of narrative. Book 7 is different in that it concentrates on the events of just one day, August 9, 48 B.C.E. (lines 7.786–872 include the following morning).[1] It moreover stays within the very restricted geographical scope of Thessaly, the region in northern Greece where the Battle of Pharsalus took place. In fact, as we have seen in the previous chapter, the reader's concentration has been focused here since 6.332, when Pompey arrives in pursuit of Caesar. This restricted geography and concentration on just one event sits in contrast to the vast implications of the battle. Its consequences are measured by stretching back in time to Romulus's foundation of the city (7.438–39), and they are felt most keenly in the loss of a political freedom that had existed at Rome since the expulsion of the kings and dawn of the republic, traditionally dated to 509 B.C.E. (7.440–41). The battle's consequences likewise extend forward in time. They continue to be felt even in Lucan's Neronian present (e.g., 7.455–59, 641–66, 695–96) and look even further ahead to the emotional reactions of Lucan's future readers (7.207–13). They also expand outward in geographical space to encompass the whole of the Roman empire (e.g., 7.419–25, 870–72). One of the primary goals of book 7 is to convey properly the true significance and enormity of the losses incurred at this battle. The burden of such a goal is plain from the narrator's summation of the battle at 7.131–33 as "the day . . . which will establish the destiny of human life forever . . . [and] the battle [that] will decide what Rome will be." For this reason, Lucan constantly intervenes as narrator in this book and has persistent recourse to hyperbole and paradox in an attempt either to capture or drive home the full meaning of events, or to engage his reader in the intellectual process of thinking them through. We can see one example of the narrator grappling with the cumulative effects of the defeat when he states:

> maius ab hac acie quam quod sua saecula ferrent
> uulnus habent populi; plus est quam uita salusque
> quod perit: in totum mundi prosternimur aeuum.
> uincitur his gladiis omnis quae seruiet aetas.
>
> (7.638–41)

> From this battle the peoples receive a mightier wound
> than their own time could bear; more was lost than life
> and safety; for all the world's eternity we are prostrated.
> Every age which will suffer slavery is conquered by these swords.

We likewise see him expressing one of the fundamental paradoxes of the poem when he apostrophizes the defeated Pompey, in flight from the catastrophe:

> quidquid in ignotis solus regionibus exul,
> quidquid sub Phario positus patiere tyranno,
> crede deis, longo fatorum crede fauori,
> uincere peius erat.
>
> (7.703–6)

> Whatever you suffer in unknown lands, an exile alone,
> whatever you suffer subject to the Pharian tyrant,
> trust the gods, trust the Fate's long-lasting favor:
> to win was worse.

Such interventions are typical of the poem as a whole and are especially concentrated in book 7 as Lucan constructs and confronts the meaning of Caesar's decisive moment of victory at Pharsalus.

The prospect of narrating a summative encounter between an epic's main protagonists makes *Iliad* 22 and *Aeneid* 12 major points of comparison. However, if the reader comes to book 7 with these epic models or Caesar's own prose account of Pharsalus (*BCiv.* 3.82–99) in mind, one surprise must surely be how little space is actually devoted to narrating the climactic battle. This occurs at 7.460–646 and appears to grind to a halt altogether at lines 7.545–56 when Lucan says he will remain silent about what happened at the center of the battle where Caesar's forces came into direct contact with Pompey's (the battle narrative continues by turning to Caesar's frenzy, Brutus, and Domitius). This intervention, extraordinary for an epic narrator, comes as the most extreme moment in a series of delaying tactics that have deferred his retelling of the battle since the poem's beginning and has intensified in book 7 as the crucial moment draws closer. In this respect, Lucan's narrator is not unlike the rising sun at lines 7.1–6 that strenuously resists illuminating Thessaly on the fateful day but is compelled to against its will by "the eternal law" governing the universe. Such delaying tactics are common to epic narration but take on an explicitly ideological dimension in Lucan and come to a head in book 7 because the poem's narrator is openly opposed to Caesar's victory: he resists narrating it—even though it is the subject matter of his poem and his own claim to fame as poet—and seeks to retard Caesar's progress because it means the permanent loss of liberty.[2]

Readers should also be struck by a number of conspicuous deviations from even basic patterns that recur in epic narratives of war. There is, for example, no arming scene, such as we see repeatedly in the *Iliad* and at *Aeneid* 12.81–111, where Turnus and Aeneas are each described donning their armor prior to their final confrontation.[3] In Lucan's account of Pharsalus, there is no narrative of an individual warrior's *aristeia*, his glorious moment of supremacy in battle; there is not even room for something akin to Scaeva's frenzy in book 6. In the *Iliad*, the *aristeia* has been aptly called "the main compositional unit of battle narrative," and each of the major warriors in the *Aeneid* receive one.[4] There is, in fact, no narration of *any* individual battle between warriors. The narrator goes out of his way to pass over such a narrative at 7.617–31 ("When the world is dying, I feel shame to spend my tears on the innumerable deaths and to follow individual destinies"). The questions that the narrator says he will *not* ask at 7.619–30 ("whose guts did the fatal sword pass through? Who trampled on his vitals spilling on the ground?") are a travesty of the kinds of inquiries made by epic narrators at the beginning of such *aristeia* narratives: compare, for example, *Iliad* 5.703–4 "Who then was the first to be slain and who last by Hector, Priam's son, and brazen Ares?" or *Aeneid* 11.664–65 (the narrator to Camilla) "Fierce maiden, whom first, whom last do you strike down with your weapon? How many bodies do you lay low on the earth?" It is against the backdrop of such relatively standard inquiries that we should set the two most extreme of Lucan's questions:

> quis pectora fratris
> caedat et, ut notum possit spoliare cadauer,
> abscisum longe mittat caput, ora parentis
> quis laceret nimiaque probet spectantibus ira
> quem iugulat non esse patrem.

(7.626–30)

who strikes his brother's
breast, cuts off the head and throws it far away
so he can plunder the familiar corpse? Who mangles
his father's face and proves to those who watch by his excessive wrath
that the man he slaughters is not his father?

These speak to a concentrated thematic insistence in book 7 upon kin killing, the fundamental *nefas* ("evil") of civil war foreshadowed in the epic's proem (1.4 "[we sing] of kin facing kin"). Perhaps most radically, there is no confrontation between Pompey and Caesar, which is in many respects the most basic component to be expected in a book of epic holding out *Iliad* 22 and *Aeneid* 12 as its models. The closest we will get to a confrontation between them will be deferred until the end of book 9 (9.1010–1108), when Caesar "confronts" Pompey's decapitated head in the harbor of Alexandria.

Taken as a unit, book 7 may be considered as dividing (in a slightly lopsided fashion) into a long section that builds to and repeatedly delays this battle narrative (7.1–459), the brief battle narrative itself (7.460–646), and a shorter section treating the immediate consequences of Caesar's victory and Pompey's flight (7.647–872).[5] Several motifs and themes that emerge before and are reprised after this battle narrative help structure the book and shape the reader's response to it. Thus, Pompey's pre-battle dream of the Roman plebs fervently applauding him in his own theatre at 7.9–12 is balanced by the dream of the Caesarians who are terrified by apparitions of murdered citizens, brothers, and fathers from the battle, all of whom haunt Caesar (7.760–86). Rome's loss of Pompey's burial at 7.36 (to become a major theme in book 8) is recalled in Caesar's denial of burial to the Pompeian forces at 7.797–99. The lightning, fireballs, and meteors falling on the Pompeian army as it approaches Thessaly (7.151–60) are mirrored by the gore, flesh, and human limbs dropped by carrion birds on the Caesarian army as it marches away from the plains of Pharsalus at 7.838–40. Finally, the ghosts of kinsmen who afflict the Pompeians before battle (7.179–80) are balanced by the murdered kinsmen who haunt the Caesarians during the night following the battle (7.773–76).

Also threading through the book and offering an additional structural principle are four major interventions by its narrator. It is characteristic of Lucan's impassioned narrator frequently to intrude on and comment upon his own narrative, but the restricted focus of book 7 means, uniquely in the poem, that he returns in four extended passages to draw the reader's attention to different aspects of the same pivotal event. At 7.201–13 he declares that when the events of the poem are read by future generations they will evoke hope and fear and elicit prayers, and that to their audience they will seem like events that are yet to come and not yet past—a detail indicative of Lucan's commitment in book 7 to vivid narration, called "enargeia" by ancient rhetoricians—and that this future audience will side with Pompey. At 7.387–459 the narrator reflects on the permanent consequences of the battle: its devastating impact on future Roman generations, the desolation of Italy, the end of Roman imperialism, and the loss of Roman liberty. He states that if Jupiter will watch Pharsalus without stopping it, Rome has the means of her revenge upon the pantheon of gods by making her own divinities out of deified emperors. At 7.617–46 he states that he won't recount individual deaths, decries the battle for bringing permanent slavery to Rome, and laments that subsequent generations were given no opportunity to fight against the tyranny into which they were born. The book ends at 7.847–72 with a bitter apostrophe to Thessaly: it ought to have been abandoned for all time had subsequent civil war battles not spread throughout the world and made even her guilt relative.

The Gods

Lucan's poem is obsessed with religion and the gods.[6] One of the masterstrokes that gives the poem its distinctive energy—and makes it possible in the form it takes—was Lucan's decision to withhold from the reader's view any scene of the gods in speech or action. This position of basic ignorance regarding the gods extends to the poem's narrator. He has a vantage point in history from which he knows what happened: that is to say (as he puts it at 1.128) that "the conquering cause pleased the gods but the conquered pleased Cato." But he does not know why this was the case, why the gods allowed Caesar's victory to come to pass. Since he has foregone the divine assistance of Apollo, Dionysus, and the Muses—the daughters of Zeus and Mnemosyne, memory personified (cf. 1.63–66)—he is unable properly to account for the causes of events. We can see one effect of this in book 7 in the multiple inconclusive attempts offered to explain phenomena such as Pompey's dream (7.19–24 "perhaps . . . perhaps . . . perhaps . . .") or the augury of the unnamed Cornelius (7.197–200 "perhaps . . . perhaps . . . perhaps . . .");[7] elsewhere he is constrained to questions regarding divine motivation (e.g., 7.58–59, "Does it give you pleasure, O gods above, when universal ruin is your plan, to add this guilt [i.e., the demand for the battle] to our mistakes?"). One might consider as a point of contrast the divine framework of earlier epic. To give just two examples, at *Aeneid* 1.297–304, Jupiter's sending of Mercury to Libya accounts for why Dido does not withhold hospitality from the Trojans, and at *Aeneid* 12.791–841, the discussion between Jupiter and Juno offers a framework for understanding why Juno drops her enmity against the Trojans and desists from further preventing their establishment in Latium.[8]

No such frame of reference exists in the *Civil War*. The divine machinery that brings about Caesar's victory in the poem remains inscrutable to the reader, the characters, and the narrator, all of whom must rely on evidence and outcomes to deduce divine support or hostility. We can see this limited human viewpoint, as well as the pathos and various types of irony that they generate, at many points in book 7. Cicero cannot conceive that the gods do not support the republican cause at 7.76–77. Pompey senses that the gods have turned against him from the evidence of his mutinous camp at 7.85–86 and realizes that Caesar's prayers must have had more efficacy than his own by his soldiers' wish to fight at Pharsalus at 7.113–14. The Pompeian forces advancing to the plain at 7.151–84 do not register the significance of the inauspicious supernatural signs that accost them, and these are attributed variously to Fortune and the gods; the narrator is not even sure if they are divinely sent or a psychological result of excessive fear (7.172–73). Caesar "has never seen the gods so near" when he realizes the battle is imminent (7.297–98, cf. 301–2), and it is the sight of the Caesarians marching onto the plain at 7.337–38 that makes Pompey realize that battle on this day was approved of the gods. At 7.349–50 Pompey tells his army that the "better cause" bids them to hope for favoring gods, that the gods will guide republican weapons into Caesar's body, that they will wish to "sanction Roman laws" in his blood, and that if they had wanted Caesar to rule they could have hurried Pompey's old age to an end: "to preserve Pompey as leader is not the act of gods angered with the people and with Rome" (7.354–55). This is either empty rhetoric or a delusion into which Pompey has relapsed after his earlier realization that they have turned against him. The irony of Pompey's statement is multiplied by its evocation of 1.128 (Lucan's gods are not interested in the "better cause," only the "conquering cause"), by its contradiction of earlier statements in the poem that the gods are angered (1.617, 2.1), and by Pompey's inadvertent allusion to a tradition that grew after his defeat and death, that it would have been better if he had in fact died before Pharsalus, when he was gravely ill in the summer of 50 B.C.E. (cf. Cic. *Tusc.* 1.86, Juv. 10.283–84).[9]

The climax of these "human responses" to evidence of divine support for Caesar's victory in book 7 comes from the narrator. As the two sides charge at each other he unleashes an embittered tirade in which he states that if there is no intervention from the gods to stop the battle (lightning, darkening of the day), then the notion that Jupiter rules in heaven is a lie: that there are no gods for the Romans, that blind chance sweeps along human affairs, and that human affairs are of no concern to the gods (7.445–55). He follows with one of the

poem's most brilliant and sardonic paradoxes, a demolition of state religion during the principate: humanity will have her revenge upon the gods for their
indifference at Pharsalus by creating second-rate divinities out of the deified
emperors who will rule as a result of Caesar's victory. As Lucan puts it, "in the
temples of the gods Rome will swear by ghosts" (7.455–59).

This theme diminishes in frequency once the battle is joined. At 7.647 it
is the evidence of the turning battle as observed by Pompey that makes him
realize that the gods had transferred their allegiance from him. At 7.725 the
sight of Pompey in defeat elicits tearful recriminations against the gods from
the townspeople of Larisa. A final instance of this theme occurs on the morning after battle when Caesar "sees his fortune and his gods" in the blood covering the plain at 7.796.

Pompey and Caesar

In contrast to the success he had enjoyed in book 6, the Pompey we meet in
book 7 ominously reverts to the characteristics described in his first introduction in the poem and his comparison to an aging oak tree at 1.129–43. He identifies as and refers to himself as an old man (cf. 1.129–30): at 7.14 he dreams of
being a young man, while at 7.352–53 and 382 he calls attention to his own
senescence.[10] He is backward looking (cf. 1.134–35 "he relied chiefly on his former fortune"), as can been seen, for example, in his dream of long-past success described at 7.7–27 (not invented by Lucan but chiming brilliantly with
the themes of his poem) and in the narrator's inference that "perhaps at the
end of success his mind, distressed by troubles, fled back to happy times" (7.19–
20). Further contributing to this impression is the narrator's comment that after
his defeat Pompey now has leisure to look back on happier times (7.686–88).
Pompey is concerned about his reputation with others (cf. 1.131–32 "seeking
fame, . . . generous to the crowd, wholly driven by popular winds, rejoicing in
applause"), as can be seen, for example, in the concern that his name will be
either hated or pitied by the people at 7.120–1 (cf. also line 112). After his defeat,
Lucan notes that "much endures of [his] mighty name" (an example of Lucan's
relentless punning on Pompey's "name," *Magnus*) and that Pompey has now
become inferior only to himself, that is, his previous reputation (7.717–19): a
foreshadowing of a theme to be developed in book 8, that in defeat Pompey's
worldwide fame has now become a burden to him.

The introductory description of Pompey as one who had "unlearnt the general's part" (1.131) is also highly relevant in book 7. It is tragically ironic that at
the beginning of our book Pompey's strategy is working well and promises

success. He points this out to his own troops at 7.92–101, and it is confirmed
by the detail that Caesar is about to move his troops to plunder crops when he
first appears in the book at 7.235–36.[11] The crucial shortcoming of Pompey in
the arena of generalship is the tenuous authority he exercises over his soldiers.
We see this most clearly in his first speech at 7.85–127, in which he yields
immediately to his camp's demand for war even though he can see that this is
madness and likely to bring about his and their defeat.

Pompey's capitulation to his army's wish, a crucial moment in the book,
should be compared with a number of other speeches, all of which redound to
his discredit or confirm his shortcomings. He evokes Vergil's ineffectual Latinus, who at *Aeneid* 7.594–600 yields to an angry crowd of Latins clamoring
around his palace and calling for a war against Aeneas, which they are destined to lose. In Vergil's words, Latinus thereby "lets go the reins of affairs"
(*Aen.* 7.600). Lucan echoes this phrase—Pompey "lets go their reins as they rage
with anger" (7.124–25)—before developing the image of his forfeited authority
in a crushing simile comparing Pompey to a sailor caught in a violent sea
storm who concedes control to the winds and "is swept along, a useless cargo
on his ship" (7.125–27). His speech should also be compared with Caesar's
version of the same speech (*BCiv.* 3.86.2–5). While Caesar's Pompey may be
wildly overconfident, he is at least an agent in events rather than Lucan's passive respondent, and he makes known a strategy for the battle (encircling Caesar), on which topic Lucan's Pompey is silent. His failure to withstand the will
of his rank and file should be read against Pompey's first speech to his troops
in *Civil War* (2.526–609), in which he utterly fails to rouse them to action (cf.
esp. its impact at 2.596–600); it should likewise be compared with the speeches
made by Caesar and Cato when their own troops revolt against their authority
(5.319–64 [Caesar]; 9.217–93 [Cato]): both men immediately cow their armies
back into submission.

Caesar, too, adheres closely to the characteristics that dominate his introduction in the poem. The relentless, unstoppable, and destructive energy established and compared to a lightning bolt at 1.143–57 sets the tone for the Caesar
we see in book 7, who makes his first appearance in the book as one who has
prayed for a summative battle a thousand times and "is sick of delay and blazing with desire for power" (7.238–40). The momentary lapse of energy when
his frenzy diminishes and his mind is "stopped in doubt" at 7.247 is one of
only two times he pauses of his own volition in the poem (the other is on the
banks of the Rubicon before the image of *Patria* [1.194]: one of a number of links
between the first and seventh books).[12] Much more typical is Caesar's insistence
upon the ability of victory to legitimate the part played by himself and his
army in the civil war (as at 7.261–63, echoing the proem's promise to sing of

"legality conferred on crime," 1.2) and his order to "rule, and let me take the blame" (7.269): a position that contrasts well with Pompey's handwringing about his reputation (7.120–21).

While Pompey has only limited authority over his army, Caesar rejoices that Fortune has entrusted him to his men, celebrates his close familiarity with the rank and file—whose javelins he will recognize as they fly through the air, and reads their menacing faces as a sure sign of victory (7.285–89). It is no accident that in this rhetoric he sounds like Livy's Hannibal: compare the Carthaginian's speech to his own soldiers before he inflicts defeat upon the Romans at Ticinus in 218 B.C.E. (Livy 21.43.17). Caesar himself had drawn the comparison between his own invasion of Italy and Hannibal's at 1.303–5, and Caesar will surpass his model in implacable anger and inhumanity at 7.799–803 by denying burial to the dead at Pharsalus in contrast to Hannibal's burial of Aemilius Paullus at Cannae. The mutual identification of Caesar with his soldiers (in his words they are "the essence of my fortune," 7.250) reaches the level of complete assimilation in the narrator's (slightly hallucinatory) comments upon the Caesarian army marching into battle: "if in the deadly warfare you had placed so many fathers-in-law of Magnus [i.e., if every soldier had been Julius Caesar] . . . they would not be rushing into battle with such headlong speed" (7.334–36).

Another telling point of contrast between the two heroes is Pompey's essentially human position compared with the inhuman extremity occupied by Caesar. At 7.369–76 Pompey asks his troops to imagine that they fight under the imploring gaze of their mothers hanging from city walls, aged senators begging them in supplication, Rome herself running to them in fear, and present and future peoples bringing them their prayers. These conjured objects of filial devotion and responsibility sit in contrast to the "visions" Caesar encourages in his own troops: at 7.292–94 he tells them that he "seems to see" rivers of blood, kings trampled underfoot along with the senate, and "nations swimming in an endless slaughter." At 7.304–6 he asks his soldiers to picture the crosses and chains awaiting them, his own decapitated head nailed on the rostra, his limbs scattered, and the mass executions that Rome witnessed when Sulla came to power. Pompey is connected to family in book 7, as elsewhere in the poem,[13] and he assumes that the same is true for his soldiers, whom he orders to win back with the sword "land and house-gods dear, children, marriage chamber, the ties . . . left behind" (7.346–48). Pompey needs and feels love, a theme that will take on great significance in book 8:[14] Cornelia is one reason he flees from the battle (7.675–77), and the narrator consoles him with the knowledge that he is genuinely loved by the people of Larisa because they support him after his defeat.[15]

Caesar, in contrast, forbids his soldiers from allowing any image of *pietas* (here, the "duty" owed by children to their parents) to prevent them from killing family members if they encounter them in the battle (7.320–25). He personally goads his troops on to madness and criminality in the center of the battle like the war goddess Bellona or Mars himself (7.557–85); and on the following morning, he enjoys a macabre breakfast amid the piled corpses of his countrymen in a place "from where he can discern the faces and the features of the dead" (7.789–94). Caesar's order to his army to destroy their own camp before going into battle (7.326–28)—although it is historically accurate and not unparalleled as a means of motivating troops to fight courageously (by removing any possibility of retreat)—accords perfectly with the suicidal imagery that accretes around Caesar in the poem and acts as a dominant metaphor for the civil war he initiates.[16]

One aspect of Pompey's humanity that book 7 sets in sharp relief is a tendency to plead excuses or cite conditions preventing him from extreme action ("if" seems to be his special conjunction). This can be observed in his carefully qualified desire that the first spear cast in the battle might kill him (emphasis added):

> "prima uelim caput hoc funesti lancea belli,
> si sine momento rerum partisque ruina
> casurum est, feriat"

> (7.117–19)

> "I wish that the first lance of deadly war may strike
> this head, *if* it can fall without influence upon events
> or the ruin of our party"

Pompey is convinced that his army fights out of personal loyalty to him and that if he should fall in battle his entire army would die with him.[17] This very conditional death wish contrasts with similar unqualified statements from the poem's other heroes. Compare how Cato wishes to devote his life:

> "o utinam caelique deis Erebique liceret
> hoc caput in cunctas damnatum exponere poenas!
> deuotum hostiles Decium pressere cateruae:
> me geminae figant acies, me barbara telis
> Rheni turba petat, cunctis ego peruius hastis
> excipiam medius totius uulnera belli.
> hic redimat sanguis populos, hac caede luatur
> quidquid Romani meruerunt pendere mores."

> (2.306–13)

"O if only this head, condemned by heaven's gods
and Erebus,' could be exposed to every punishment!
When Decius offered his life, enemy squadrons overwhelmed him:
let me be pierced by twin battle-lines, let Rhine's barbarous
horde aim its weapons at me, let me, exposed to all the spears,
standing in the midst, receive the wounds of all the war.
Let this my blood preserve the people, let this my death
atone for all the penalties deserved by Roman morals."

Cato's commitment to self-sacrifice may be underwritten by the reader's knowledge of the historical Cato's suicide at Thapsus in April 46 and by his unyielding characterization by Lucan in books 2 and 9. Also contrasting with Pompey's conditional death wish is Caesar's flat avowal that he will commit suicide if any of his troops should so much as look back before total victory is achieved (7.308–10): the words in which Caesar makes this prediction, "he will see me stabbing my own guts" (*fodientem uiscera cernet | me mea*), echo the opening of the poem and its promise to tell of "a mighty people attacking its own guts with victorious sword-hand" (*populumque potentem | in sua uictrici conuersum uiscera dextra*).[18] When Pompey makes such grand gestures in the poem they are undermined by his flight from the summative encounter, his often mistaken sense of self, and a tendency to excuse himself from extreme action. Thus, in the second speech to his troops (7.337–84) he states that he would grovel before the feet of his troops *if only* he could do so "with the dignity of his high office intact" (7.376–79). Cut from similar cloth is the remarkable conclusion to Pompey's exhortation, in which he states that unless his side prevails he will be an exile, a laughing stock (i.e., to Caesar), and a disgrace (i.e., to his troops) and, shockingly, that he hopes not to learn how to be a slave in his old age: that is, to live under Caesar' autocracy (7.379–82). His prayer before fleeing the battle is similarly disappointing:

"parcite," ait "superi, cunctas prosternere gentes.
stante potest mundo Romaque superstite Magnus
esse miser."

(7.659–61)

"Refrain, gods," he says, "from overthrowing all the peoples.
With the world still standing and Rome surviving, Magnus can
be ruined."

The conditions of "the world still standing" and "Rome surviving" lead the reader to expect that Pompey's antithesis will be "Magnus can die" (*potest . . . Magnus | mori*) or similar: Pompey's compromise position of living on as a wretch rather than dying in battle is sharpened by the crucial phrase *esse miser* being delayed in enjambment.[19] Finally, compare the narrator's comment as Pompey leaves the battlefield that he did not lack courage to face the enemy and receive his death blow, *but* he thought that *if* he were to die, "the whole world would crash down on its leader," *or else* he wanted to remove his death from Caesar's gaze (7.669–74).

Philip Hardie has observed that when Pompey looks out over the military disaster unfolding on the plains—"so many weapons aimed at his own death, so many bodies laid low and himself dying in so much blood" (7.652–53)—and decides to flee battle, his survival constitutes an inversion of the "one for the many" pattern by which the kind of self-sacrifice he invokes at 7.117–19 is supposed to take the place of mass casualties.[20] At Pharsalus, to Pompey's eye, the many are dying for the sake of the one: the precise concern complicating his death wish at 7.117–19. An alternative interpretation is offered by the poem's narrator, that Pompey is deluded in this belief. The narrator assures us that after Pompey left the battle, the most important part of it remained: the battle between freedom and Caesar, the same gladiatorial pair, he notes, that have been a match ever since (7.689–96).

Pompey's flight from battle and the senate's decision to remain is a key moment in Lucan's presentation of this theme, but we should not take the narrator's interpretation at 7.689–97 as the last word on the matter. The question of the motivation of Pompey's forces—whether personal or ideological—and the related issue of the nature of Pompey's own motivation—whether he fights for himself or for the senate—resist easy resolution. Throughout books 1 to 9 of the poem a number of speeches and scenes offer information regarding the motivation of either Pompey or his troops. The issue is first raised at 2.322–23 when Cato enters the war so that, in his own words, Pompey will not think he is conquering for himself. Later, the Pompeian general Afranius explains to Caesar at 4.348–50 that his forces and he are not driven by party zeal and that they did not go to war to oppose Caesar's plans. At 5.13–14 the narrator tells us that the senate proves to the world by assembling in Epirus that it is not Pompey's party but that Pompey is in their party. In book 7, Pompey's camp complain that he is dragging the war out because he is addicted to world rule (7.52–55), and Cicero tells Pompey that if he is the senate's leader and war is being waged for them (i.e., and not for Pompey's own benefit), then the men should fight on whichever field they wish (7.79–80). Immediately prior to his flight, Pompey goes around to troops who are rushing to their deaths and denies that he is worth so great a price (7.666–69). Any sense that the matter is finally resolved by the narrator's intervention at 7.689–97—as it appears to be—is

undermined in book 9 when one of Cato's soldiers explains to him that they
fought only out of personal loyalty:

> "nos, Cato, da ueniam, Pompei duxit in arma,
> non belli ciuilis amor, partesque fauore
> fecimus."
>
> (9.227–29)

> "We—give pardon, Cato—were led to fight by love
> of Pompey, not of civil war; we turned partisan
> out of goodwill."

In making a theme of this issue, Lucan does more than draw a contrast between
the steadfast personal devotion of Caesar's troops, the immovable ideological
position held by Cato and the less clear-cut position occupied by Pompey. He
reflects an historical ambiguity found in a variety of contemporary sources. In
September 46, in a speech before Caesar, Cicero carefully parsed his own motivation for entering the war:

> Hominem sum secutus priuato officio, non publico, tantumque
> apud me grati animi fidelis memoria ualuit ut nulla non modo
> cupiditate sed ne spe quidem prudens et sciens tamquam ad
> interitum ruerem uoluntarium.
>
> (Cic. Marcell. 14)

> I followed a man [i.e., Pompey] because of personal rather than
> public duty; and so much force did the loyal memory of a grateful
> heart have with me that—without any greed and even without
> hope—deliberately and knowingly I rushed as if to a voluntary death

Two Caesarian Travesties: Crastinus and Domitius

Lucan was not only polemically opposed to Caesar's progress in his own poem
but often to the pro-Caesarian version of events as portrayed in Caesar's *Commentaries*.[21] Book 7 offers us two moments of pointed contrast with Caesar's
narrative in Lucan's treatment of the Caesarian Crastinus (7.470–75) and the
Pompeian Domitius (7.599–616). Crastinus, a re-enlisted veteran, is twice given
individual attention in Caesar's account. At *Bellum Civile* 3.91, he is described
as a man of singular courage (*singulari uirtute*) and given two short, direct
speeches. In the first he affirms Caesar's pretext for beginning the war: "This

one battle remains; when it is over, he will regain his position (*dignitas*) and we our freedom (*libertas*)" (3.91.2). Here Crastinus echoes Caesar's rationale for war at *Bellum Civile* 1.7.8 and 1.22.5: defense of his *dignitas* and restoration of his *libertas* and that of the Roman people. In the second speech Crastinus pledges to fight in such a way as to earn Caesar's gratitude whether he survives the battle or dies in it (3.91.3). Caesar notes that he then led the charge into battle from the right wing. At the end of Caesar's battle narrative, attention returns to Crastinus, who is found among the dead and showing heroic wounds. Caesar reminds the reader of his earlier speech, confirms his veteran's outstanding courage in battle, and acknowledges his debt to Crastinus (3.99.2–3). Livy (*frag.* 42) appears to have been the first to record the variation (or additional detail) that it was Crastinus who cast the first spear in the battle. Caesar's mention of Domitius Ahenobarbus's part in the battle comes at the very end of his account of Pharsalus and can be quoted in full: "Lucius Domitius fled from the camp to the hills, but when he succumbed to exhaustion he was killed by the cavalry" (3.99.5).

Lucan's account of these same men seems deliberately to respond to Caesar's. Where Caesar accords praise, Lucan is searing in his indictment. Where Caesar notes a cowardly escape ending in an ignoble death, Lucan presents the ostensible glory of a steadfast republican, heroic in death, confronting Caesar with his dying breath. Lucan reinterprets both men through the prism of epic poetry and its paradigms to radically different effect. Crastinus is presented in the tradition of epic heroes who cast the first spear in battle: Vergil's Turnus (*Aen.* 9.51–53) or more appositely, the Homeric truce-breaker Pandarus (Hom. *Il.* 4.104–40) and his Vergilian version Tolumnius (*Aen.* 12.258–68). By evoking these models Lucan is able to cast Crastinus in an utterly negative light. Where Caesar celebrates Crastinus as a man of extraordinary courage, Lucan presents a rash lunatic ("O impetuous frenzy! When Caesar wielded weapons was there found a hand to act before his?" 7.474–75), whose cast breaks the momentary hold of *pietas* over the armies when the combatants see fathers and brothers in the opposite lines (7.466–69). In the poem it is not unusual for Caesar's soldiers to have a moment's hesitation prior to committing an act of *nefas* ("unspeakable crime"). They pause, for example at 1.353–56, struck by *pietas* and their ancestral gods at the beginning of their invasion of Italy. They also hesitate at 3.429–31, stunned by the majesty of a sacred grove Caesar has ordered them to fell. In both cases it is Caesar who overwhelms such hesitation: love of the sword and fear of Caesar at 1.356; fear of Caesar's anger at 3.439, which is more formidable to his soldiers than the wrath of the gods. These moments contextualize the crime of Crastinus in Lucan's eyes, since his cast breaks the spell of *pietas* and nudges the two armies over the brink into actual fighting. Where Caesar names and thereby immortalizes Crastinus in his narrative, Lucan damns him with an altogether different kind of immortality: "May the gods give to you, Crastinus, not death—a penalty awaiting everyone— but feeling in your corpse after death: your hand hurled the lance which started the fighting and was the first to stain Thessaly with Roman blood!" (7.470–73).

Just as Lucan removes any glory from Caesar's Crastinus, he utterly transforms the inglorious death of Domitius Ahenobarbus. His death scene conforms to a pattern whereby a dying hero is taunted by his opponent and responds by predicting the imminent death of his assailant at the hands of a more powerful warrior. Thus Patroclus promises Hector that he will die by the hand of Achilles (Hom. *Il.*16.818–61), Hector promises Achilles that he too will die at the hands of Paris and Apollo (Hom. *Il.* 22.326–66), and in Vergil's version of the scene the dying Orodes promises Mezentius that the same fate (death in battle) "watches over" him as well (*Aen.* 10.739–46). We should pause before interpreting Lucan's epic transformation as glorifying Domitius. When read against these models, Domitius's hope that Caesar "will be subdued in savage war and pay a heavy penalty to Pompey and to me" (7.614–15) appears as utterly deluded. His misreading of the situation is especially egregious in light of the description of Caesar raging like Bellona and Mars in the center of battle (7.557–85) and the fact that Domitius lies amid an enormous heap of patrician corpses (7.597–98). Domitius's hope strongly foreshadows that Pompey will not confront Caesar at Pharsalus at all: the philosophical composure with which he dies (7.612–13) is completely unfounded. As problematic as it is, however, Domitius's death in battle offers the reader an explicit model of behavior—fighting to the death in defiance of Caesar—that his general Pompey fails to follow.

The deaths of Patroclus, Hector, and Orodes foreshadow the deaths of their assailants in the *Iliad* and the *Aeneid*, but the death of Domitius seems only to foreshadow the demise of his own general Pompey in the following book, since Domitius acts as an inferior substitute for his general in the kind of confrontation with Caesar that book 7 promises but Pompey flees battle to avoid. The ironies of the scene are sharpened by Lucan's Caesar appearing to "know" the version of events in which Domitius dies as a deserter (note Caesar's jibe "*iam Magni deseris arma*," "now you abandon Pompey's army," 7.606); by the grandiose epic formula describing his moment of death, "life left him and thick darkness closed his eyes" (7.616)—sitting at odds with his minimal presence in the battle;[22] and by our knowledge that Domitius was the great-great-grandfather of the emperor Nero and thus dies in the attempt to prevent Caesar's establishment of his own descendant's power.

Notes

1. Roche 2019, 1–28 provides a more detailed overview of the book.

2. For a classic exposition on this aspect of the poem, see Masters 1992.

3. There may be very compressed and oblique glimpses at this conventional scene at lines 7.139–43 (Pompeians) and 7.330 (Caesarians).

4. Quote from Schein 1984, 80.

5. There are a number of possible schemes for the structure of the book. Another option is to count the battle as beginning at 7.214 with the descent of Pompey's troops to the plain (as do, e.g., Radicke 2004, 374, and Lanzarone 2016, 1–4) or at 7.385 with the commencement of the initial charge. In favor of a briefer "battle narrative," from 7.460–646, are the pre-battle exhortations of both Pompey and Caesar at 7.250–329 and 342–82 and that Crastinus's casting of the first javelin in the battle does not occur until 7.470.

6. It may surprise the reader that the gods are referred to more frequently in the *Civil War* than they are in Vergil's *Aeneid*. For Lucan and religion, see Feeney 1991, 250–301; Arampapaslis and Augoustakis in this volume.

7. One effect of these multiple explanations is to bring Lucan closer in rhetoric to didactic poetry or history.

8. Both moments discussed by Feeney 1991, 141, 147–51.

9. Leigh 1997, 118–25.

10. Note that historically Pompey and Caesar were only six years apart in age. His old age in Lucan casts him in the mold of older epic warriors who often fall to the insurmountable energy of younger opponents.

11. Lucan has simplified Caesar's motivation compared with the account found in Caesar's own version at *BCiv.* 3.85.2: there he does strike camp to find provisions more easily but also on the chance that there would be an opportunity of battle from the Pompeians while he was en route and because he thought it would exhaust Pompey's army, which in Caesar's opinion was unused to hard work.

12. Cf. Caesar's mention of the Rubicon at 7.254–55.

13. Cf. esp. book 5 and 8.

14. Cf., e.g., his final words in the poem, 8.635 *gnatus coniunxque . . . amant* ("my son and wife . . . love me").

15. Cf. the emphasis upon family and love in book 8.

16. Cf., e.g., the lightning that strikes its own quarter of the sky at 1.151–57 or the lion that goads itself to anger and leaps onto hunting spears, driving them deeper into its chest at 1.205–12: both similes for Caesar.

17. Pompey gives voice to a similar belief at 7.659–66 as he justifies his imminent decision to flee the battle: here if he remains at the battle his army will perish to a man.

18. Hardie 1993, 55.

19. That is, being delayed until it is the first word or phrase of a new line: a technique for adding emphasis in Latin poetry.

20. Hardie 1993, 54–55.

21. For the issue of Lucan's reception of Caesar's writings, see Ginsberg in this volume.

22. It is based upon the death formulas of the major Vergilian characters Camilla (Verg. *Aen.* 11.831) and Turnus (Verg. *Aen.* 12.952).

8

Book 8

The Remains of the Day

MARTIN T. DINTER

Defined in terms of poetic structure, the eighth book of Lucan's *Civil War* is its *volta* ("turning point").[1] The seven preceding books narrate a struggle between two factions, the Pompeians and the Caesarians. By the start of book 8 the former have clearly been defeated by the latter, and by the end of book 8, Pompey himself will have been removed from the equation. Hence, insofar as a war entails conflict between two opposing parties, the "war" element of the *Civil War* indeed ends in book 8.[2] Although we cannot know for sure how Lucan would have finished his epic, the final two books as they now stand do not admit of any possibility that the Pompeians—now led by Cato—will turn things around. What remains of that party after Pharsalia is further decimated by a harsh desert march and poisonous snakes (9.218–949), and while Caesar finds himself in mortal danger (10.332–546), he has undoubtedly come out ahead relative to his opponents.

As the leitmotif *plus quam* ("more than," 1.1) indicates, however, the *Civil War* strives to exceed expectations from the very beginning.[3] Accordingly, Lucan does not bind his work with traditional constraints such as length and genre but instead distinguishes it by introducing a wealth of characters and perspectives.[4] The multiplicity of the *Civil War* is so pronounced that scholars have been hard-pressed to identify a single hero: Caesar, Pompey, and to a lesser extent Cato are all viable candidates for that position.[5] In addition, even within single books Lucan eschews fixed focalization, preferring to communicate his story through a wide variety of viewpoints.[6] Book 8 is one of the more "settled" books in this respect, for the majority of the narrative is anchored to Pompey's gaze, but it also contains a major shift in perspective: the council scene in the Egyptian court is told from Ptolemy's point of view (8.472–560).[7]

Lucan's penchant for diversity also manifests in his wide variety of narrative techniques, themes, and motifs, four of which predominate in book 8. Fame shadows Pompey throughout his final days, manifesting both overtly in mentions of *Fama* and subtly within epitaphic gestures. The Egyptians' act of treason moreover provides opportunities for ethical discourse, which Lucan seizes by peppering the evildoer Pothinus's speech with moralizing *sententiae*. In addition, Lucan employs repetition in innovative ways: the repeated adjective *incertus* ("not fixed, not decided, not certain") marks "points of divergence" where Pompey could have escaped death, while the recurring leitmotifs of "death in small boats" and suicide foreshadow that event. The body imagery running through Lucan's epic moreover comes to a "head" in this book, where Pompey's decapitation leaves the Roman state body leaderless and enables Lucan to reflect on the hazards of misrepresentation.[8] These aspects of Lucan's epic technique feed into the suspense of book 8, which builds from its very first lines toward an undesirable and yet inexorable conclusion.

Fama

The opening verses of book 8 describe Pompey's escape from the battlefield. The images of past renown that had dominated his pre-battle dreams—applause, triumph, and a seat in the senate (7.9–19)—have been snatched away by the outcome of the Battle of Pharsalus. Indeed, Pompey has "fallen from his lofty eminence" (*summo de culmine lapsus*, 8.8), and in this reduced state *Fama*-as-rumor presents itself as an enemy rather than a friend.[9] Lucan highlights this reversal by attaching *Fama* to the participle *prodente*, which carries a double meaning: fame is not only in the course of "revealing" Pompey's defeat but also midway through "betraying" it (8.15).[10] The qualification that *Fama* has "not yet" finished this task (*nondum*, 8.15) on the one hand attests to the speed of his flight and to the breakdown of relations between Pompey and Rumor on the other. He is forced to perform duties that conventionally fall under *Fama's* remit, such as "reporting his own defeat" (8.16–17).[11]

This reading gains credence from Lucan's wider use of *prodere* ("betray") and its cognate noun, *proditio*, to denote "treason." During the siege of Ilerda, the Pompeian generals Petreius and Afranius refuse to consider "unspeakable betrayal" until they run out of water supplies (*nefandae / proditionis*, 4.220–21). The verb again appears in Lucan's epitaph for the perfidious Curio, at whose hands "laws of the senate were betrayed" (*prodita iura senatus*, 4.820). Hence,

the presence of *prodere* in the opening verses of book 8 does not merely emphasize the newfound hostility between *Fama* and Pompey but also foreshadows
his betrayal by the Egyptians. What is more, *Fama* has a history of causing harm
to Pompey by intimidating his soldiers. To name but one example, in book 2
Caesar weaponizes rumor so successfully that the Pompeians withdraw from
battle (emphasis added by author to the Latin and translation throughout):

> sensit et ipse metum Magnus, placuitque referri
> signa nec in tantae discrimina mittere pugnae
> iam uictum <u>fama</u> non uisi Caesaris agmen.
>
> (2.598–600)

> Even Magnus sensed their fear himself, and decided to recall the
>   standards
> rather than to send into the crisis of a battle so immense
> a force already overcome by <u>rumour</u> about Caesar as yet unseen.

Pompey's problematic relationship with *Fama* instills him with a logical desire to
avoid it: "[he] would choose to pass safely through the cities with a name unknown
to fame." (8.20–21).[12] However, while he had previously been able to do so—in
book 2, he had escaped Caesar's rumored forces by fleeing from Brundisium to
Epirus—after Pharsalia he can no longer run from his own infamy. As a result,
he now finds *Fama* onerous, an impression that Lucan conveys to the reader by
emphasizing the "weight of renown" (*pondere famae*, 8.21–23). Pompey's wish to
cast off this burden highlights his utter military and ideological defeat:

> It is as if Pompey, as the defeated representative of a legitimate
> Roman tradition, were trying to shake off the burden of fame and
> destiny that Aeneas, Atlas-like, takes up at the end of *Aeneid* 8, in the
> shape of the shield of Roman history, 731 *attollens umero famamque et*
> *fata nepotum* ["lifting onto his shoulder the renown and destiny of
> his descendants"].[13]

To paint Pompey as a "shirker" of his own renown is nevertheless simplistic.
Even though *Fama* has turned against him, he does not cease to value it. His
adherence to this concept is perceptible from his reaction to the "excessive sorrows" of his wife Cornelia, who faints as she watches him disembark onto Lesbos (8.71). Noting that she cannot hope to achieve glory either as a statesman
or a general, he argues that his defeat provides her with the "avenue to fame
that will endure for centuries" (8.72–74).[14]

His focus on the legacy that a wife can gain from her husband's sufferings
is reminiscent of the speech made by Marcia in book 2. There, she convinces

Cato to remarry her even though the civil war will doom their union, stating that she wants only to be known as "Marcia, wife of Cato" (2.343–44).[15] She does not choose this epitaph out of mere sentiment but rather out of concern for posterity: "Let not the question be disputed in future eras . . ." (2.344).[16] Pompey's use of this trope to reassure his wife therefore attests to the rapport between them: he understands her desire for glory and chooses language that has proved effective in consoling similarly minded women.[17]

When read alongside his own desire to remain hidden, Pompey's advice to Cornelia initially appears hypocritical. A closer reading, however, reveals how seeming inconsistencies add to Pompey's characterization as a tragic and heroic figure. His reference to *Fama* is in itself a sign that he has not yet been destroyed by defeat; at heart, he remains the "seeker of fame" that he was at the beginning of the epic (*famae . . . petitor*, 1.131).[18] Moreover, the contrast between Pompey's private despair and his composure before Cornelia attests to his Stoic mind-set: he does not allow his emotions to overtake his strong facade.[19] Since Pompey is still in command of himself, his epic career is not yet over; in his own words, "Magnus lives on after the battle; only his fortune has died" (*uiuit post proelia Magnus / sed fortuna perit*, 8.84–85).

Pompey's death of course comes as no surprise, for it is preceded by numerous epitaphic gestures. Foremost among these is his use of the *cognomen* (honorary epithet) Magnus ("the Great") to refer to himself in the third person. He thus encourages Cornelia to "be the sole follower of Magnus" (*incipe Magnum / sola sequi*, 8.80–81) and, we have seen, describes his own legacy as the continued survival of "Magnus."[20] Having been invested with the role of Pompey's *Fama*, Cornelia contributes to his self-monumentalizing efforts by using the appellation "Magnus" twice in just five lines:

> "mallem felicibus armis
> dependisse caput: nunc clades denique lustra,
> Magne, tuas. ubicumque iaces civilibus armis
> nostros ulta toros, ades huc atque exige poenas,
> Iulia crudelis, placataque paelice caesa
> Magno parce tuo."
>
> (8.100–105)

> "I had rather
> paid for successful warfare with my life: now at least you can expiate
> your disaster, Magnus. Cruel Julia, you have avenged
> our marriage-bed with civil war; now, wherever you lie, come here,
> exact the penalty and, placated by your rival's death,
> spare your very own Magnus."

As this passage highlights, both instances of "Magnus" in its various inflections occur as the first word in a verse; Cornelia's use of the epithet thus forms a mirror image of Pompey's own use of that term, which he instead positions as the last word in a line (cf. 8.80 and 84 above).[21] The role that Cornelia envisions for herself is nevertheless more passive than the active deeds typically associated with *Fama*. Lucan contrasts Julia's agency against Cornelia's passivity by making the former the subject of imperative verb forms such as *exige* ("exact [the penalty]") and *parce* ("spare [Magnus]"); by contrast, the latter speaks in hypotheticals, as encapsulated in her use of the counterfactual imperfect subjunctive *mallem* ("I would rather have").[22] In eschewing an active role, Cornelia again echoes her husband's thoughts: he had assigned to her a type of renown stemming from innate characteristics, such as her "noble race" (8.72) and her tie to himself (8.78), as opposed to that derived from memorable deeds.[23]

The *cognomen* "Magnus" and Cornelia's transformation into a passive variant of *Fama* are not the only epitaphic precursors to death. Epitaphs commonly include three elements: the deceased's name, place of death, and brief biography.[24] All of these feature in book 8: Pompey describes his name as "one which the world loves" (8.276), raises that possibility that he will "fall at the end of the earth" (8.314–15), and "reviews the whole story of [his] life" (8.316–17). Even while alive, therefore, he has begun to "draft" the renown attached to his posthumous reputation. It therefore comes as no surprise that Pompey's final monologue, spoken in silence to himself, hinges upon the word *fama*:

> "saecula Romanos numquam tacitura labores
> attendunt, aeuumque sequens speculatur ab omni
> orbe ratem Phariamque fidem: nunc consule famae."
>
> (8.622–24)

> "Future ages, which never will be silent about the toils of Rome
> are watching now, and time to come observes from all the world
> the boat and loyalty of Pharos: think now of your fame."

Although Lucan's stated intention is to exalt Pompey's "mastery of mind while dying" (8.636), commentators generally read these last words as a lesser version of the "Stoic good death."[25] As Hardie observes, a true Stoic would not be concerned about worldly *Fama* but only about virtue; hence for him "the motto would better have been *consule uirtuti* ["this of virtue"], not *consule famae* ["think of your fame"]."[26] Similarly, Sklenář acknowledges that all Pompey achieves is a "Stoic posture": his "outward demonstration of Stoic *ataraxia* [equanimity] . . . does not alone constitute the *uirtus* ["virtue"] of wisdom."[27] Within this framework, Pompey's very last lines come across almost as a vain attempt at garnering adoration:

> "tanto patientius, oro,
> clude, dolor, gemitus; natus coniunxque peremptum,
> si mirantur, amant."
>
> (8.633–35)

> "with all the more endurance, pain of mine,
> I beg, suppress your groans; my son and wife, if they admire
> me in death, love me."

Nevertheless, to criticize Pompey for failing to achieve the rank of Stoic sage seems at odds with his characterization throughout the epic. Lucan's characters are defined by their imperfections: Caesar is vigorous but tyrannous and Pompey is principled but insecure.[28] Hence, just because Pompey falls short of perfect virtue does not mean that his death is devoid of value. On the contrary, he stages his death as a Stoic spectacle, demonstrating supreme self-control by refusing to cry out in pain.[29] Read in this context, his mention of his wife and son is not an overture of vanity but rather an invitation for them to witness— and therefore memorialize—his courage.[30] Cornelia-as-*Fama* gladly takes this cue by launching into a spoken epitaph. In her last words to Pompey she includes all three of the epitaphic elements that he had established for himself. She situates his death between Lesbos and Egypt (8.640–41), refers to him as "Magnus" (8.645), and summarizes the key events of his later life by mentioning "the war" and "defeat" (8.648 and 650). Most importantly, she confers upon him— even as he is about to die—the coveted title of eternal life: "You still live, my husband" (*uiuis adhuc, coniunx,* 8.659).[31] By "collapsing" into a deathlike faint, moreover, she attests to the magnitude of his death, which does not only subsume him but also those around him (8.661).

As poet, Lucan also grants Pompey the fame that he desires. Pompey's hasty cremation and insignificant burial marker are viewed as meaningless; since his immortal presence stretches as far as "the Roman name and all the Roman empire" (8.798–99), "that grave will never mar his fame" (*nil ista nocebunt | famae busta tuae,* 8.858–59). Their shabbiness, so Lucan implies, should even be construed positively, for they enable the evidence of Pompey's death to be erased more quickly from memory:[32]

> proderit hoc olim, quod non mansura futuris
> ardua marmoreo surrexit pondere moles.
> pulueris exigui sparget non longa uetustas

congeriem, bustumque cadet, mortisque peribunt
argumenta tuae.

(8.865–69)

One day this will be to your advantage, that no lofty pile
with marble mass arose, to last into the future.
No lengthy time will scatter the heap of tiny
dust, the tomb will fall, and of your death
the evidence will vanish.

This exaltation is heightened when compared with Pompey's dejected state at
the beginning of book 8; there, he had been abandoned by fame and fortune,
but in death he has superseded both these phenomena. During the course of a
single book, therefore, his *fama* has grown from nothingness into something
so great that it no longer requires traditional avenues of commemoration:
Magnus survives even without monuments.

Sententiousness

In addition to the theme of *Fama*, ethical discourse also dominates book 8 in
the form of *sententiae*, defined as pointed formulations often also containing
moral messages.[33] The Egyptian courtier Pothinus makes particularly heavy use
of these sayings to support his ethically corrupt but rhetorically effective case
for Pompey's assassination. This speech supports the impression that book 8
is the single most significant book in the *Civil War*: it constitutes the culmination of sententiousness in Lucan just as Pompey's death constitutes the climax
of *Fama*-related imagery within the epic. Up until this point, Lucan has been
judicious in doling out *sententiae*, reserving them for particularly significant
moments. Accordingly, Pompey's defeat is commemorated by just two *sententiae*, joined together in a single quatrain:

sic longius aeuum
destruit ingentis animos et uita superstes
imperio. (1) | nisi summa dies cum fine bonorum
adfuit et celeri praeuertit tristia leto,
dedecori est fortuna prior. (2)

(8.27–31, divisions added)

So age too long
and life surviving after power destroy heroic

spirits. (1) | Unless the final day coincides with the end
of blessings, by speedy death forestalling sorrows,
former fortune brings disgrace. (2)

Although Pothinus is a relatively minor character, his oration displays no such
economy. In the first ten lines of his speech alone he employs eleven *sententiae*
(8.484–95). This abundant cluster feeds into Lucan's description of Egypt as a
decadent location marked by "excess."[34] Moreover, since *sententiae* usually have
a moralizing function, their misappropriation by Pothinus to advocate for the
morally unacceptable act of killing a guest highlights the intrinsic corruption
of the Egyptian court.[35] The reader cannot help but contrast its degeneration to
the virtuous republic, not only as embodied by Pompey within the epic but also
as encapsulated in the wider rhetorical tradition. In Seneca the Elder's *Suasoriae* ("*Deliberative Speeches*"), republican declaimers similarly make use of *sententiae* to drive home their points, but their arguments are always morally
"correct": out of the thirteen orators quoted in *Suasoria 6*, only one—Varius
Geminus—goes against Roman notions of honor and argues that Cicero should
have begged Antony's pardon (Sen. *Suas.* 6.12).[36]

   We should of course not expect Pothinus's *sententiae* to reflect republican
values. However, they also do not adhere to any recognizable ethical system in
antiquity and are most accurately characterized as "utilitarian." While we cannot identify a single hero for the *Civil War*, Pothinus is most certainly its villain. The principles to which he clings—selective kindness, moral relativism,
and strategic cruelty—are all antithetical to Stoic thought. In the following two
sententiae, for example, he advises Ptolemy to abandon Pompey so as to save
himself from being dragged down with the "losing side:"

> "dat poenas laudata fides, cum sustinet," inquit
> "quos fortuna premit. (1) | fatis accede deisque,
> et cole felices, miseros fuge." (2)
>   (8.485–87, divisions added)

> "loyalty, though praised, pays the penalty when it supports
> the people Fortune crushes (1) | Side with the Fates and gods,
> and court the fortunate; avoid the failures." (2)

The first *sententia* places immense value on Fortune, and the second mandates
that kindness should be doled out on a discriminatory basis: favors should be
granted only to those who are "prosperous." Both of these maxims are antithetical to Senecan morality.[37] Seneca holds that "Fortune" is not a boon but rather
a bane: "While all excesses are hurtful, the most dangerous is unlimited good

fortune" (Sen. *Prov.* 10). Moreover, Seneca encourages his readers to enrich others rather than those who are already rich: "we must add every possible kindness [to munificence]" (*deinde adicienda omnis humanitas, Ben.* 2.11.4).

Another key tenet of Stoicism is moral absolutism: the world is split into "right" actions (*recta*) and "wrong" ones (*praua, Tranq.* 9.4).[38] These opposites should in no case be conflated; Seneca sees crime as the direct result of "men rising up to level the barriers between right and wrong" (*Ira* 2.9). Furthermore, he admits no possibility of living a good life without the "right" mind-set. Even the prosperous, so he implies, would find their possessions unfulfilling without it, whereas a humble man with a correct sense of judgment has no need for material gain:

> beatus ergo est iudicii <u>rectus</u>; beatus est praesentibus, qualiacumque sunt, contentus amicusque rebus suis; beatus est is, cui omnem habitum rerum suarum ratio commendat.
>
> (Sen. *Vit. Beat.* 6.2)

> The happy man, therefore, is one who has <u>right</u> judgement; the happy man is content with his present lot, no matter what it is, and is reconciled to his circumstances; the happy man is he who allows reason to fix the value of every condition of existence.

Pothinus's *sententiae*, however, instead showcase the contrasting principle of moral relativism. He portrays guilt as a social construct contingent upon arbitrary rules rather than an objective standard of "wrongdoing:" "Ptolemy, the laws of god and man make many guilty" (8.484). In addition, he states that tangible rewards are wholly distinct from what is morally "right": "as stars are different from earth and flame from sea, so profit is from right" (8.487–88). Modern readers may nevertheless find themselves somewhat puzzled as to the problem with these *sententiae*, for they accord with contemporary ethical theories. In very broad terms, twentieth-century ethics can be summarized as a celebration of the individual and his or her subjective experience.[39] Existentialism holds that philosophical thinking—including moral judgment—should derive from an individual's internal matrix of meaning; outside "truths" such as Seneca's "right" and "wrong," do not enter into the equation.[40] Similarly, nihilism represents an alternative to both moral absolutism and relativism: nothing can be described as either "right" or "wrong," for these categories simply do not exist.[41]

These modern conceptions must be put aside if we are to understand book 8 in relation to its original context. In Lucan's world, there were such things

as "right" and "wrong," and the communal institutions of ancient Rome—
beginning with the *res publica* ("republic" or "state," but literally "common
thing")—did not encourage individual interpretations of morality.[42] Within this
framework, Pothinus's *sententiae* cannot be interpreted as anything other than
morally "wrong." Moreover, Pothinus advocates for an approach that is unpalatable even to most modern philosophers: strategic cruelty. In another cluster
of five *sententiae*, he argues that Ptolemy should behave cruelly toward Pompey, both to maintain his own sovereign power and to reserve for himself the
right to commit cruel deeds in future (divisions added):

> "sceptrorum uis tota perit, si pendere iusta
> incipit, (1) | euertitque arces respectus honesti. (2) |
> libertas scelerum est, quae regna inuisa tuetur,
> sublatusque modus gladiis. (3) | facere omnia saeue
> non inpune licet, nisi cum facis. (4) | Exeat aula,
> qui uult esse pius. (5) | uirtus et summa potestas
> non coeunt."

> (8.489–95)

> "All the might of sceptres disappears if it begins to weigh
> justice; (1) | regard for what is honourable overthrows citadels. (2) |
> Unrestricted wickedness is the defence of hated tyrannies
> and limit removed from swords. (3) | You cannot act brutally
> without penalty unless you always do. (4) | Let him who wishes
> to be good leave the court. (5) | Virtue and the highest power
> are not compatible."

This *sententiae*-packed passage makes for a climactic end to Pothinus's excursus, which he immediately follows with a specific plan to kill Pompey (8.496–
535). The immorality of Pothinus's speech is therefore structured as a crescendo:
he begins with maxims that are only mildly unsavory—help the prosperous and
not the poor—but, within the space of ten lines, has arrived at outright exhortations to "slaughter." This rapid escalation feeds into the *topos* of excessiveness
that Lucan applies to the Egyptians; as their representative, Pothinus is immoderate in both thought and speech.[43] Moreover, the provocative language with
which Pothinus transitions into the persuasive section of his speech highlights
his rhetorical shrewdness: by regurgitating *sententiae* thick and fast he endows
himself with irrefutable authority, and the unforgiving pace of his moral maxims encourages the listener to look past their dubious content and simply go
along with his plan.[44] As befits Lucan's "rhetorical epic," this strategy proves
effective: the Egyptians set a trap for Pompey.[45]

Repetition

The four appearances of the adjective *incertus* ("uncertain") within book 8, however, imply that there is possibility yet of an uptick—albeit temporary—in Pompey's fortunes. For this term appears exclusively at junctures where Pompey's fate *could have been* changed. Its first instance is located at the very beginning of book 8; during his escape, Pompey "confuses the <u>uncertain</u> traces of his flight" (*incerta fugae uestigia turbat*). Read at face value, *incerta* suggests his mental and geographical disorientation: by this point in the epic, Pompey is truly "lost" for he has lost sight of his route to both military victory and personal safety. More subtly, Pompey's trajectory serves as a metatextual stand-in for the course of Lucan's narrative; therefore, its uncertainty raises the possibility that both Pompey and the story might err from their path.

Lucan does not negate this hypothetical straight away but directs attention toward another viable point of deviation in Pompey's final journey. While sailing from Thessaly, Pompey finds himself hassled by "wavering doubts" (*incerti pectoris aestus*, 8.166); in particular, he has not yet decided where his destination will be. He rids himself his doubts by conversing with the steersman about navigation, asking how one might travel to Syria and Libya by following the stars (8.169–70). These provinces naturally appear as alternatives to Egypt, since they both are unoccupied by Caesar's forces. By mentioning them, therefore, Lucan imbues the passage with dramatic irony: the reader knows that Pompey can save himself by sailing to either of these destinations but cannot advise him on that choice. The steersman spells out this possibility by asking, "But whither do you bid me shape our course, and with which sheet shall the canvas be stretched?" (8.185–86).

Here as elsewhere, Pompey's downfall stems from his most prominent characteristic: inertia.[46] Instead of making an informed choice, he merely tells the steersman to "leave the West behind . . . all else trust to the winds" (8.187–90). Pompey's indecisiveness limits his options; upon hearing these instructions, the steersman directs the ship to sail south, that is, toward Libya and Egypt but—at least temporarily—eliminating Syria as a possibility (8.195–96). Lucan's comment that "the ship's course was altered" (8.198) thus lends itself to a metatextual reading: through inaction Pompey has not only changed the "course" of his life but also that of the epic narrative.

Indeed, Lucan adds one more teaser that Pompey will change course during a protracted deliberation scene (8.202–471). Initially, Pompey appears to be on the right track. He offers three destinations to the senate but immediately eliminates the first two—Egypt and Libya—so as to advocate for Parthia alone (8.276–89).[47] Pompey suggests that Parthian mercenaries can help to retake

Rome, for their archers are so skilled that "from no arrow is death <u>uncertain</u>" (*a nulla mors est <u>incerta</u> sagitta*, 9.297).

Pompey's faction-member Lentulus nevertheless argues against Parthia by playing upon fears of Eastern decadence, a commonplace in Roman republican rhetoric.[48] He also integrates *incertus* into a phrase about archery, thus creating a linguistic parallel: the typical Parthian bowman, so Lentulus claims, is "crippled by his unreliable bow" (*<u>incerto</u> debilis arcu*). These contradictory statements seem to reflect doubts over the reliability of the Parthians as allies and simultaneously mirror the uncertain direction of the narrative. However, Pompey's staunch adherence to republican values does not allow him to overrule the communal vote (9.455); interfering in the "democratic" process would be tantamount to Caesarian tyranny.[49] This line of thinking is not without irony. For as Lucan demonstrates in the remainder of his epic, the misguided vote is the very deathblow which robs the Pompeians of their leader and therefore allows Caesar to subjugate Rome fully.

The four instances of *incertus* in book 8 are therefore unitive in function; they signpost key verses in which the narrative could have changed course and impose an overall theme—that of "uncertainty"—upon its verses. This leitmotif is necessary, for book 8 might otherwise come across as "scattered"; since the plot tracks Pompey as he swivels from plan to plan and sails from port to port, the reader is at times "not certain" of where Lucan will focus next. However, Lucan also anchors the book within the wider narrative by repeating motifs found in other sections of the *Civil War*. Foremost among these is the idea of suicide. While his death is orchestrated by the Egyptian court, Pompey is not killed by an Egyptian assassin but rather by a former Roman soldier:[50]

> Septimius, qui, pro superum pudor, arma satelles
> regia gestabat posito deformia pilo,
> inmanis, uiolentus, atrox nullaque ferarum
> mitior in caedes. quis non, Fortuna, putasset
> parcere te populis, quod bello haec <u>dextra</u> uacaret,
> Thessaliaque procul tam noxia tela fugasses?
>
> (8.597–602)

Septimius, who—shame on the gods!—had put aside the javelin
and was bearing the degrading weapons of the king, as his minion,
brutal, savage, cruel and no less fierce for bloodshed
than any wild beast. Who would not have thought that you took pity
on the peoples, Fortune, since this <u>sword-hand</u> had no part in war
and you had banished far from Thessaly his weapons so guilty?

By equating Septimius to his "right hand" (*dextra*) in a *pars pro toto* ("part for whole") description, Lucan emphasizes that he is but one limb of the Roman military corps. As Pompey constitutes the "head" of that particular body, his death comes across as "self-inflicted": the renegade "hand" stabs at its own "head."[51] This image does not only intensify the treason underlying Pompey's death and therefore evoke pathos in the reader but also helps situating that event to the wider narrative. The most immediate "intratext" is Cornelia's own suicidal language, which does not only feature in her invocation of Julia (8.100–105, as discussed above) but also in her reaction to Pompey's betrayal:

> aut mihi praecipitem, nautae, permittite saltum,
> aut laqueum collo tortosque aptare rudentes,
> aut aliquis Magno dignus comes exigat ensem.
>
> (8.654–56)

> Allow me, sailors, to make a headlong leap or fit
> the noose and twisted ropes round my neck, or let some comrade,
> truly worthy of Magnus, drive the sword right through.

Despite Cornelia's anguish, Lucan does not engineer her demise either at this pivotal moment or in an act of self-immolation upon Pompey's funeral pyre, a possibility that the Pompeian loyalist Cordus vocalizes while burying his master (8.739–42). Cornelia *cannot* die, for her mission is incomplete: as we have seen, she had been charged by Pompey to propagate his renown by serving as *Fama*.[52] In the process, she is deprived of her own opportunity to win fame by loyally following her husband in death.

Repeated mentions of various forms of self-destruction are not limited to book 8. In the proem, Lucan describes the civil war in terms of a collective suicide: "I tell how an imperial people turned their victorious right hands against their own vitals" (1.3).[53] The civil war is dotted with episodes of heroic quasi-suicidal self-sacrifice: the Massilians fight bravely despite being outmaneuvered by Caesar's navy, and each of their ships is ultimately "defeated by its own blow" (*ictu uicta suo*, 3.564). Suicide-related metaphors also recur throughout the epic, most notably during the Caesarian mutiny in book 5. Almost abandoned by his men, Caesar is described as a "torso maimed by the loss of so many hands" (*tot raptis truncus manibus*, 5.252–53). Lucan explains the rebellion by castigating Caesar's fondness for "the wars now rejected by [his] 'hands'" (*iam manibus damnata tuis*, 5.310–11); in accordance with the conventions of Roman military vocabulary, the noun *manus* (literally "hand") serves as a synecdoche for "armed troop."[54]

The idea of suicide is not, however, the only repeated motif linking Pompey's death to other books of the *Civil War*. That he perishes on a small boat harks back to Vulteius's band of Caesarians, who—crowded onto a raft and surrounded on all sides—slay each other to avoid capture (4.402–581). Caesar himself survives a near-death experience while sailing through a storm (5.476–721) but survives because of his personal invincibility.[55] As the defeat at Pharsalus in book 7 indicates, however, Pompey is no match for Caesar and so cannot be expected to survive the same tribulations that he can. Hence, by describing the assassins' arrival in a "little two-oared boat" (*non longa . . . biremi*, 8.562), Lucan "foreshadows" Pompey's murder one last time, just moments before the act takes place, and highlights the reversal of fortune that this event entails: while in book 4 Caesar's troops had killed themselves to escape Pompey's men, just four books later Pompey himself dies at the "hand" of an ex-subordinate.

Body Imagery

Repeated instances of *incertus*, the motif of suicide, and the *topos* of "death in small boats" thus relate the events of book 8 to other parts of the *Civil War*. The strongest current of imagery that runs through Lucan's epic is nevertheless that of body imagery. The ubiquity of this theme is best illustrated by the numerous appearances of the noun *caput* ("head"), which does not only take center stage in verses about Pompey's death but also binds together the *Civil War* as one of its master tropes.

Fittingly, the first instance of *caput* in the epic foreshadows the dismemberment of the Roman state body. In a portent of war, lightning strikes the geographical "head of Latium" (*Latiare caput*, 1.535), which most scholars take to mean the Alban Mount.[56] The identification of that mountain as a "head" owes itself to two factors. On the one hand, owing to its altitude the summit projects itself over the earth, thus mirroring the superior position of the human head relative to the body. On the other, the location is invested with sacral significance; there Rome's consuls celebrated the *feriae Latinae* ("Latin festivals") each spring, symbolically renewing the pact of the Latin League, a Roman-led confederation originally formed against the Etruscans.[57] That lightning, which typically occurs in epic as a result of Jupiter's displeasure, should strike the location of these unifying rituals therefore foretells Rome's impending division.[58]

Terrified by such omens, the Romans decide to sacrifice a bull to Jupiter; however, as the animal's liver contains two *capita* ("lobes," but literally "heads"), it signals further division rather than divine propitiation (1.627–28). Lucan explicitly frames this instance of body imagery as a metaphor for Caesar and

Pompey: each lobe displays the personal attributes of its associated leader. The "Caesarian" lobe thus "throbs fast and drives the veins with rapid beat," whereas its Pompeian counterpart "droops sickly and flabby" (1.629–30). This metaphor extends itself throughout the epic, for both Caesar and Pompey are perceived by their followers as *caput orbis* ("the head of the world," 5.686 and 9.123–24 respectively). Similarly, before the Battle of Pharsalus Caesar is shown "choosing the gamble of fate bound to plunge one head or the other in ruin" (6.8).

This crescendo of bodily imagery culminates in Pompey's decapitation, an event that can be interpreted as both a resolution and a destruction. On the one hand, the coexistence of two heads is abnormal and has resulted in the equally unnatural state of civil war. Hence, by removing both Pompey's physical "head" and his political role as "head" of the senatorial faction, Lucan returns Rome to a state of normalcy. The "sickly lobe" from Arruns's bull has been excised in favor of the more viable one, and Caesar has scored a decisive victory in his "gamble." On the other hand, for a staunch republican, Caesar is no "head" at all but a mere usurper. From this viewpoint, Rome has only one *caput*— Pompey—whose death therefore dethrones the city from its long-held position as "head of the world" (2.136; 9.123–25).[59] As a close reading of the decapitation scene indicates, however, these opposing readings constitute but two out of many layers of meaning in Lucan's epic:

> impius ut Magnum nosset puer, illa uerenda
> regibus hirta coma et generosa fronte decora
> Caesaries comprensa manu est, Pharioque ueruto,
> dum uiuunt uultus atque os in murmura pulsant
> singultus animae, dum lumina nuda rigescunt,
> suffixum caput est, quo numquam bella iubente
> pax fuit; hoc leges Campumque et rostra mouebat,
> hac facie, Fortuna, tibi, Romana, placebas.
> nec satis infando fuit hoc uidisse tyranno:
> uult sceleris superesse fidem. tunc arte nefanda
> summota est capiti tabes, raptoque cerebro
> assiccata cutis, putrisque effluxit ab alto
> umor, et infuso facies solidata ueneno est.

(8.679–91)

> So that the ungrateful boy can recognize Magnus, that shaggy
> hair by kings revered and locks which graced his noble
> brow were grasped and on a Pharian spear—
> while features are alive and sobs of breath impel
> the mouth to murmur, while unclosed eyes are stiffening—

the head is fixed: when it commanded war, never
was there peace; it swayed the laws, the Campus, and the Rostra;
with this face you stood proud, Roman Fortune.
And the sight of it was not enough for the monstrous tyrant:
he wants proof of his wickedness to survive. Then by their hideous art
the fluid is taken from the head, the brain removed
and skin dried out, and rotten moisture flowed away from deep
within, and the features were solidified by drugs instilled.

In these verses, Lucan describes the metamorphosis of Pompey's head from a living appendage into a lifeless object. This process is tied to the motif of *Fama*, for its constituent actions combine into a grisly form of memorialization. That Pompey's facial features can be so easily "recognized" attests to his renown. Ptolemy's motivation in preserving the head—namely to ensure that it shall "remain" (*superesse*) for future watchers—similarly reveals a desire to "make a monument" out of Pompey. However, this attempt is ultimately unsuccessful, not only because of the inherent irony that arises from trying to immortalize a dead man but also because the embalmment process cannot truly capture the living Pompey: his "sobbing breath" and "stark eyes" are converted into a semi-artificial husk that has been dried in parts and injected with "drugs" in others. The Egyptians' failure to monumentalize Pompey can be read as a meditation on the impossibility of encapsulating dynamic *Fama* within static objects: as we have seen, Pompey's grave is likewise unable to contain his renown.[60]

Imperfect representation brings negative consequences; in this case, the painstakingly preserved skull fails to bring about its desired reaction. The Egyptians believe that their gift will garner praise and gratitude, going as far as to remind Caesar of his great debt to them while presenting him with the head (9.1031). By that time, however, the mummy has deteriorated even further from its appearance in life: "the features, relaxed by death, had changed the aspect of that familiar face" (9.1033–34). As a result, Caesar does not immediately recognize his son-in-law but inspects the head "until he can be sure" (9.1036). Even then, he fails to heap his hosts with the rewards they desire, opting instead to shed crocodile tears (9.1038–39). Far from fulfilling its intended purpose, moreover, the head backfires by generating hostility between Caesar and Ptolemy:

> fortasse tyranni
> tangeris inuidia, captique in uiscera Magni
> hoc alii licuisse doles, quererisque perisse
> uindictam belli raptumque e iure superbi
> uictoris generum.
>
> (9.1051–55)

> You are touched perhaps
> By envy of the tyrant, and feel pain that another had such power
> over captive Magnus' guts, and you complain that warfare's
> revenge has vanished and your son-in-law has been taken
> from the power of his proud conqueror.

At its most basic level, the failure of the Egyptians' ploy can be read as a cautionary fable. Lucan demonstrates from the very first lines that he is not averse to moral commentary; he applies a value judgment upon the entire civil war by terming it a "shared crime" (*commune nefas*, 1.6), and as we have seen, the Pothinus episode serves as a commentary on the insidiousness of Eastern "morality."[61] His intentions nevertheless extend beyond providing a lesson about the "wages of sin." By detailing the preservation of Pompey's head in gruesome detail, Lucan evokes disgust in the reader, who expects that Caesar will react similarly when presented with the actual artifact. Notably, Caesar fails to demonstrate any of the "correct" emotional responses: instead of being nauseated, he is first joyful and then jealous.[62] Lucan thus distances Caesar from the reader and emphasizes the former's inhumanity, a trait associated with the stereotypical Eastern tyrant into whom he is transforming, as his dalliance with an Eastern queen further indicates (i.e., Cleopatra, 10.53–106). Within our metapoetic reading of the embalmment process, moreover, the head's poor reception microcosmically reproduces the tension between artistic purpose and execution. The intention of the artist | assassin is not always successfully conveyed through the artwork | head to the consumer | Caesar.

As these myriad interpretations highlight, body imagery in the *Civil War* comes to a "head" during and after Pompey's death. Nevertheless, these actions are not the only manifestations of *caput* imagery in books 8 and 9. En route from Tripolis to Leptis Magna, Cato and his fellow Pompeian survivors wander into an area of the desert filled with poisonous snakes.[63] Lucan cites Medusa's blood—emanating from her dripping head—as the reason for their venom:

> illa tamen sterilis tellus fecundaque nulli
> arua bono uirus stillantis tabe Medusae
> concipiunt dirosque fero de sanguine rores,
> quos calor adiuuit putrique incoxit harenae.
>
> (9.696–99)

> Yet that barren land and fields productive of no good
> catch the venom from the gore of dripping
> Medusa, a hideous dew from wild blood
> which heat promotes and boils in the crumbling sand.

The Medusa head shares several similarities with that of Pompey. Both heads influence the manner in which their owners are killed: Perseus must behead Medusa so as to neutralize her lethal gaze (9.680), and Pompey's head is extracted from his corpse as evidence of his death. Furthermore, both heads are related to the cosmic body: the former shapes it through its petrifying gaze and also its snake-breeding blood, while, as we have seen, the latter signifies the restoration of universal order, for Pompey's decapitation means that the world is no longer being torn apart by two competing "heads." In addition, both heads affect the Roman state body: the former diminishes it by generating deadly serpents that fell members of Cato's troop, and the latter creates a power vacuum at its summit that Caesar aims to fill.[64] Given these manifold properties, it is only natural that Caesar should seek out another "head" in book 10 as part of his imperial quest: the "hidden source" of the Nile (*arcanum . . . caput*, 10.295).

Conclusion

In this reading of book 8, I have highlighted four of its key themes. After regaining the confidence lost at Pharsalus, Pompey chases *Fama* in his final days, seeming unaware that he can receive it only in death. Meanwhile in Egypt, the courtier Pothinus invests his treasonous plan with authority by subverting the typical uses of moral *sententiae*. Lucan does not treat Pompey's death as a settled matter; the repeated adjective *incertus* marks "points of divergence" where the course of history could have been changed. However, he does signpost that event throughout the *Civil War* by employing the leitmotifs of "death in small boats" and suicide. The most significant motif is nevertheless that of body imagery, which comes to a "head" in this book with the removal, preservation, and presentation of Pompey's physical head. This complex web of intertextual and intratextual allusion showcases the complexity of the *Civil War* and of book 8 in particular, which is not only the *volta* of the whole epic but also its thematic, linguistic, and narrative climax.

Notes

1. Here, I draw from the vocabulary of the sonnet. Not unlike book 8, the *volta* is traditionally present in the latter half of its poem (either at line 9 or 13 out of 14 total) and changes the direction and tone of the narrative (Middlebrook 2009, 33–34).

2. For this conceptualization of war, see Cornwell 2017, 48.

3. Henderson (1987, 135) details the relationship between the comparative *plus quam* and Lucan's "excesses" in subject and language.

4. Roche 2009, 287.

5. Gorman 2001 outlines arguments both in favor and against these three candidates.

6. Roller 1996, 335–36: "The character or group in question focalises the narrator's description of its actions. One such passage is the narrative of Scaeva's deeds (6.165–227); here the narrator regularly refers to Scaeva's Pompeian foes as *hostes* ["enemies"] (171, 173, 185, 206) just as Scaeva does (156)."

7. For further observations on the gaze and focalization in Lucan, see Lovatt 2013 and Esposito in this volume.

8. See Dinter (2012, 9–49) on body imagery in Lucan, especially p. 20 (Pompey's decapitation).

9. On the variants of *Fama* (i.e., as rumor and as renown), see Hardie 2012.

10. Owing to these connotations, Tracy (2014, 135) characterizes *prodere* as a word "fraught with menace."

11. As Guastella (2017, 102) observes, transmitting news is *the* defining property of rumor.

12. Fratantuono (2012, 312) identifies Pompey's avoidant tendency as his fatal flaw: "Lucan made clear . . . that Pompey could have continued the struggle; he had willingly surrendered that chance, just as he had given up his opportunity to crush Caesar before *Pharsalia*."

13. Hardie 2012, 184, emphasis mine and Latin translated.

14. Roman women almost exclusively gain fame through actions that relate to men. Lucretia is lauded for preserving her bodily purity from a man (Sextus Tarquinius), Cornelia Africana is famed for giving birth to great men (the Gracchi), and Cornelia here derives fame from remaining loyal to a defeated man (Pompey).

15. Sannicandro (2007, 83) characterizes Marcia as "the incarnation of the most noble virtue of Roman femininity." This reputation stems in part from her preoccupation with *Fama*, which typically concerns male heroes; by concerning herself with it, therefore, Marcia transcends the limitations of her sex.

16. Iterations of this *topos* recur throughout classical literature. Hector reminds Andromache that she will be remembered as his wife by devising an epitaphic "tagline" for her: "This is the wife of Hector" (Hom. *Il.* 6.459–61). Likewise, the exiled Ovid comforts his wife by drawing her attention to the poetic renown of Homer's Penelope and promising her that she will similarly live on through his works (Ov. *Tr.* 1.6.21–22, 35–36).

17. The intimacy between Pompey and Cornelia leads McCune (2013–2014) to cast them as an "elegiac couple." Pompey indeed corresponds to the trope of the returning lover and Cornelia to the abandoned girl; she had been wandering the shore of Lesbos in a manner resembling Ariadne (cf. 8.45–9 with Ov. *Met.* 3.489–75; Catull. 64.130–35; Prop. 1.3.1–2).

18. The epithet *famae petitor* can be read both positively and negatively. Sklenář 2003, 103: "Pompey is a politician of the worst sort, made complacent by previous success and so enamored of the public's favor that he will do anything to retain it. That pandering, however, is introduced by *famae petitor*; to the extent that *fama* is also *kleos*, *petitio famae* is an accurate description of the epic hero's *uirtus*."

19. Sen. *Const.* 17.1 demonstrates the value that the Stoics placed on an "unruffled countenance" (*frontis . . . firmitas*).

20. Referring to oneself in the third person is common in military historiography, both as a literary convention and as a self-aggrandizing strategy; on which, see Batstone and Damon 2006, 144–5. See also Feeney 1986 on Lucan's recurrent play on *Magnus*.

21. See Dinter 2012, 59.

22. Cf. Mayer (1979, 348) on the force of the potential vs. contrary-to-fact subjunctive in Lucan. Mulhern 2017 outlines the complex relationship between Julia and Cornelia.

23. On the contrast between Pompey's activity and Cornelia's passivity, see Hutchinson 2018, 234.

24. For these elements, see Dinter 2019.

25. Seo (2011, 216) thus considers Pompey to be a mere *proficiens* ("apprentice") in Stoicism at the time of his death: "There is little evidence of latent Stoic qualities, aspirations, or even awareness in Pompey's characterisation until the defeat at Pharsalus."

26. Hardie 2012, 185–86, Latin translated.

27. Sklenář 2003, 126.

28. Pandey 2014, 114: "The civil war itself [entails] a forced choice between two flawed leaders." On the specific character traits of Pompey and Caesar, see respectively Ahl 1993 and Helzle 2008.

29. Braund 2002, 102: "The self-control that Lucan's Pompey shows as he dies . . . represents an important point of intersection between Roman mentality and Stoic philosophy."

30. Bexley 2010, 147: "The dying Pompey perceives himself as both subject and object."

31. On Cornelia's speech, see Tasler 1972, 202–9.

32. Fratantuono 2012, 342; cf. also Rimell (2015, 243), who sees Pompey's grave as an example of *multum in paruo* ("much in little").

33. On sententiousness in Roman literature see, e.g., Dinter 2016.

34. Cf. the feast scene at 10.174–75.

35. Egypt's inherent immorality proves overwhelming even for Caesar, who is consistently depicted as less scrupulous than Pompey. As Tracy (2014, 238) remarks, "Caesar [in book 9] has come to a land that is already infested with the Caesarian type."

36. As Lobur (2008, 144) points out, however, Varius is heavily penalized by Seneca for simply daring to suggest that Cicero beg pardon: "The remarks he makes . . . are dismissed as 'buffoonery' (*scurrilia*), typical from this declaimer."

37. For a summary of Seneca's philosophy, see Mannering 2013, 188–203. Linking a poet's personal life to his work is always problematic, but in this case—as Seneca was a well-known philosopher and tutor to the young Nero—we can safely assume that Lucan, not unlike most Roman intellectuals of his day, was closely acquainted with his uncle's writings.

38. Sellars 2014, 47: "The Stoics follow Socrates in holding a unified, monistic conception of the soul and an intellectualist account of the relationship between knowledge and action."

39. For this approach to ethics see, e.g., Waddington 1960.

40. As Montgomery (2004, 296), observes, in the existentialist writer Camus's works "experience is individual and personal."

41. Harman 1977, 11: "Nihilism is the doctrine that there are no moral facts, no moral truths, and no moral knowledge."

42. As Langlands (2018, 117) suggests, individualism can hardly be identified as a societal phenomenon in ancient Rome prior to the principate.

43. See note 35 in this chapter.

44. Dinter 2012, 111.

45. On the *Civil War* as a "rhetorical epic" see, e.g., Morford 1967.

46. Rosner-Siegel 2010, 192: "The images of Caesar as a fiery striking force and Pompey as inert and stationary run through the entire epic."

47. The seriousness with which he clings to the Parthian option is moreover evident from his decision, before the meeting, to send Deiotarus as legate to Parthia (8.211–38); on the "despotic implications" of that command, see Tracy 2014, 27–29.

48. See, e.g., Cic. *Mur.* 20: "That Asia of yours, so crammed with wealth and luxury."

49. Leigh (1997, 151) observes on Pompey's previous address (2.531–95): "Pompey gives great emphasis to the authority conferred by the Senate and by Rome." This statement pertains to the epic in its entirety.

50. Fucecchi 2010, 238n6: "Septimius was a tribune of the Roman army and fought with Pompey against the pirates before becoming a servant of Ptolemy. His portrayal perfectly suits the Caesarians."

51. Consider also Seo 2011, 216: "By transforming Pompey's death into a Catonian *mors uoluntaria* ('suicide'), Lucan enables Pompey's death to be seen as a *deuotio* ('sacrifice') that 'restores' the Republic, albeit temporarily."

52. See above section on *Fama*.

53. Cf. the similar sentiments expressed at Verg. *Aen.* 5.670–72 and Hor. *Epod.* 7.9–10.

54. *OLD manus* 1 and 22.

55. For a detailed reading of this episode, see Matthews 2008.

56. For this interpretation, see Nix 2008, 289; Dinter 2012, 19; Ambühl 2015, 82. A minority read *Latiare caput* as the "ancient capital city of Latium," that is, the settlement of Alba Longa (e.g., Spentzou 2018, 261). Nevertheless, in practical terms these locations are almost the same: Alba Longa was built at the foot of the Alban Mount (Liv. 1.3.3–4).

57. Dinter 2005, 302. On the *feriae Latinae* more generally, see Warren 1970, 50–52.

58. On the oft-discussed connection between lightning and divine disapproval, see, e.g., Currie 2006, 362.

59. Hardie 1993, 7: "It is the individual Pompey who is decapitated, but this is equated with the loss of Rome herself as 'head of the world' (*caput mundi*)."

60. See 8.858–59, as discussed above.

61. See above section on *sententiae*.

62. As Bartsch (1997, 98) suggests, Caesar's inappropriate response toward Pompey's head—which shocks even the immoral Egyptians—reinforces his negative characterization: "Demonic Caesar cackles over the carnage on the battlefield and has the sickening temerity to weep over his enemy's head."

63. On the significance of the Medusa passage in creating a new myth of "Stoic heroism," see Fantham 1992b.

64. Malamud (2003, 38) likewise interprets Pompey's head as a vector of authority: "As Caesar takes possession of the Gorgonic head of Pompey, he reveals the control over speech and gesture that gives him his terrifying power."

9

Book 9

Author and Authority, Caesar and Liberty

Michael Dewar

If Lucan had decided to finish his grim account of the civil war with the death of Pompey near the end of book 8, he would not have been departing significantly from the conventions of epic poetry. His poem would in fact have reached its conclusion and its climax much as Vergil's *Aeneid* did, with the brutal elimination of the predestined loser. Or he could have ended it just a little later and, as it were, buried the republic along with Pompey's ashes on Cordus's makeshift fire. That would even have given a bitter, and hence a satisfyingly Lucanian, twist to the way in which Homer ends the *Iliad*, not at the moment when Hector is slain in battle but as the Trojans gather in grief around his pyre. History, though, is often less tidy than poetry, and even if it was at Pharsalus that the constitutionalists suffered their true deathblow, resistance to Caesar, for a time, continued. Another army remained in the field, in northern Africa, commanded by Cato the Younger. In this poem with too many heroes, or too few, a new hero, or would-be hero, accordingly demands our attention.

Indeed, it almost seems—over six thousand lines from the beginning—as if Lucan is only now really getting going. Pompey's vacillations disappeared when he saw that death at the hands of a rogue Roman assassin was about to follow defeat at the hands of his own father-in-law, and Lucan gives him a stirring interior monologue in which he exhorts himself to earn eternal fame by meeting it with courage:

> "spargant lacerentque licebit,
> sum tamen, o superi, felix, nullique potestas

hoc auferre deo. mutantur prospera uita,
non fit morte miser."
(8.629–32)

"Though they tear and mangle me,
still fortunate am I, O gods above, and no deity has the power
to deprive me of this. In life prosperity is changed;
death does not make men unhappy."

When we move on to book 9, we find that this elevation of Pompey continues
in a dramatic and unexpected manner, as his soul bursts from his body and
soars aloft to join the stars:[1]

prosiluit busto semustaque membra relinquens
degeneremque rogum sequitur convexa Tonantis.
(9.3–4)

it leapt up from the tomb and, leaving half-burnt limbs
and the ignoble pyre, it heads for the Thunderer's dome.

We thought he was dead, but he turns out to be immortal. We also thought he
was done with earthly cares, but no sooner does he reach those stars than he
descends again, to inspire Brutus and Cato to avenge him:

hinc super Emathiae campos et signa cruenti
Caesaris ac sparsas uolitauit in aequore classes,
et scelerum uindex in sancto pectore Bruti
sedit et inuicti posuit se mente Catonis.
(9.15–18)

From here it flitted above the fields of Emathia, the standards
of blood-stained Caesar and the fleets dispersed upon the sea
and, avenging wickedness, it settled in the sacred breast
of Brutus and stationed itself in the mind of invincible Cato.

It is a brilliant stroke, prolonging the narrative but also filling it with new vigor.
The poem that could have ended continues, and this book will, in fact by over
two hundred lines, prove to be the longest yet. A more traditional epic poet
might have appealed for fresh inspiration to the Muses,[2] but Lucan has as little
time for the Muses as for any of the other gods of traditional epic poetry. He is
his own inspiration, and his is therefore the only authority we have for Pompey's having rediscovered his courage as death came for him, let alone for
Pompey's apotheosis. There is much more to this than a desire to surprise.
Lucan's authoritative rhetoric seeks to redefine Pompey for us, to banish the

weak man who had rested on his laurels and could not resist the demonic power of Caesar's energy and to replace him with a demi-god who can inspire the fight against Caesar even from beyond his humiliating grave on Egypt's lonely shore. This startling assertiveness at such a critical point in the narrative helps prepare us, not only for the continuing struggle but for a book that lays out with similar boldness the poet's claims to authority, to autonomy, and to his right to tell a well-known tale as his genius compels him.

True, book 9 is in some ways like those that have preceded it. Pharsalus, the poet told us, did not so much end civil war as transform it into an eternal gladiatorial contest between competing ideologies:[3]

> par quod semper habemus,
> libertas et Caesar, erit.
>
> (7.695–96)
>
> that pair of rivals always with us—
> Liberty and Caesar.

In particular, just as in earlier books we saw how not only the whole of Italy but also Gaul, Spain, and Thessaly were affected by this war between two factions of the governing classes of the imperial capital, so in this one we see how the war spreads yet further, to the Aegean, to Asia Minor, and, above all, to Africa. It also takes us back to Egypt, where book 8 had ended and book 10 will begin. Now, however, resistance to Caesar will take a philosophical form, that of the resistance of the spirit, and, with Pompey eliminated, the hoary old question of who is the poem's hero is also given a new twist.[4] And yet, though civil war continues, it is also kept in a kind of suspense for over a thousand lines, since, although we are given brief accounts of how Cato's troops crush the opposition offered them by the city of Phycus (9.39–41) and later occupy Cyrene (9.297–99),[5] we are in effect spared the sight of Roman fighting Roman. Instead, even though we are introduced to yet another new corner of the Roman world, and indeed pass beyond the empire's frontiers into the sun-blasted African desert, this time the landscape itself becomes the enemy, not only an active participant but the deadliest combatant of them all.

That hostile geography will serve as the true testing ground for our new protagonist, but first Lucan establishes Cato's moral superiority and his right to lead on the human plane. Pompey's widow Cornelia, fleeing by ship, reveals to his son Sextus, and so to us, the sacred command (*mandata*, 9.98) that he had given her to pass on:

> "uni parere decebit,
> si faciet partes pro libertate, Catoni."
>
> (9.96–97)

"One man alone will it be right
to obey, if he takes the side of freedom—Cato."

Cato: A New Hero

When they reach his army in Libya, Cato is not slow to take up the challenge to lead. He first pronounces an obituary that celebrates Pompey's unwillingness to embrace the kind of open tyranny that Caesar so ardently longs for:

"nil belli iure poposcit,
quaeque dari uoluit uoluit sibi posse negari."
(9.195–96)

"He demanded nothing by right of war
and what he wanted to be given, he wanted to be able to be denied him."

The obituary does not, however, take the form of undiluted encomium. Indeed, it begins by cutting Pompey brutally down to size:

"ciuis obit" inquit "multum maioribus inpar
nosse modum iuris, sed in hoc tamen utilis aeuo,
cui non ulla fuit iusti reuerentia . . ."
(9.190–92)

"A citizen has died," he says, "far inferior to our ancestors
in knowledge of the limit of power, but valuable in this age yet
which has no respect for justice . . ."

Cato feels entitled to pronounce judgement along with his praise, and such praise as he gives is bestowed with a lofty consciousness of his own moral superiority:

"scire mori sors prima uiris, set proxima cogi.
et mihi, si fatis aliena in iura uenimus,
fac talem, Fortuna, Iubam; non deprecor hosti
seruari, dum me seruet ceruice recisa."
(9.211–14)

"To know how to die is the warrior's best lot, the next to be compelled
    to die.
And if by fate I fall into another's power, make Juba,
Fortune, behave like this to me; I do not decline to be kept
for the enemy, provided that he keeps me with my head cut off."

Pompey, that is, was forced unwillingly to his death by one treacherous African king, Ptolemy of Egypt, but Cato is entirely prepared to embrace his death of his own free will if King Juba of Numidia should prove similarly ready to betray old loyalties in favor of the rising Caesar. There is great self-conviction here, and self-conviction is a useful quality in a general. We readers, however, may feel that the sharp distinction Cato draws between the two men does not do justice to the Pompey whom we have witnessed—as Cato himself has not—stifling his groans and meeting his death with an admirably Stoic fortitude of his own (8.632–36). Moreover, although it will not be narrated within Lucan's poem as it has come down to us, Cato's self-immolation at Utica was undoubtedly the most famous part of his tragedy, and here we have that celebrated Cato, already obsessively imagining his death and rehearsing for it. Self-conviction and the desire for glorious self-destruction combine in our new hero's character in a manner that, to many readers, disturbingly suggests a megalomania that is a match for Caesar's.[6] Lucan is perhaps warning us not to be too quick to take another egoist at his own evaluation of himself.

If so, however, he immediately shows us how that same self-conviction can inspire others to loyalty and virtue. Tarcondimotus, yet another Roman client-king, this time of Cilicia, leads part of the Roman forces to mutiny, but a comprehensive tongue-lashing from Cato shames them into loyalty and at the same time establishes firmly that Cato is in command (*erupere ducis sacro de pectore uoces*, "from the leader's sacred breast the words burst out," 9.255). His authority thus asserted, he first leads them to subdue Cyrene and then decides to march them across the desert to King Juba's realm. What follows is a stunning sequence of descriptions of the ravages inflicted upon the Roman army by the raw power of nature at her most unrestrained. The appalling heat stifles them, and the absence of natural barriers allows the winds to rage across the desert wastes with perfect freedom. The wind, indeed, seems to attack the Romans with the conscious malice of a living creature, ripping the very ground from under them:

> tum quoque Romanum solito uiolentior agmen
> adgreditur, nullisque potest consistere miles
> instabilis, raptis etiam quas calcat, harenis.
>
> (9.463–65)

> Then too, more violently than usual, the wind attacks
> the Roman army and the tottering soldiers cannot stand firm
> on sands which even as they tread on them are torn away.

Above all, thirst torments them, sending the sweat streaming over their limbs and scorching their throats (9.498–500). To make time for so much hyperbolical action, Lucan takes a difficult journey that Plutarch tells us lasted a week (*Cat. Min.* 56.4) and turns it into a series of labors of two months' duration (*bis positis Phoebe flammis, bis luce recepta,* "twice had Phoebe lost her flames, twice regained her light," 9.940). What sustains them through it all is the heroic example set by their general, which reaches its apogee when, on the discovery of a small stream, a soldier brings him some water in his upturned helmet. Cato upbraids the loyal legionary, treating an act of dutiful respect as tantamount to an accusation of selfish cowardice:

> "mene" inquit "degener unum
> miles in hac turba uacuum uirtute putasti?"
>
> (9.505–6)

> He said: "Degenerate soldier, did you consider
> me the only one in this multitude devoid of heroism?"

Filled with righteous anger, Cato empties the helmet in an arresting gesture of extreme self-denial and solidarity that restores his men's powers of endurance: the water drains into the sand, but, paradoxically, *suffecit . . . omnibus unda* ("there was water enough for all," 9.510).

Snakes: A New Enemy

The greatest challenge, however, is still ahead, and it comes in the form of the most memorable grotesqueries that the poem has to offer apart, perhaps, from the infamous Thessalian witch Erictho, whom we met in book 6. The sands of Libya are free of Caesar's men, but they teem with venomous snakes whose powers to inflict appalling and degrading deaths are as varied as they are horrendous. Cato's men are contending against a new kind of army, and so Lucan honors the serpents with a short but highly stylized catalogue of the kind that Homer created for the Greeks in the second book of the *Iliad* and Vergil for the Italians in the seventh book of the *Aeneid*. He gives us their exotic names and some details of their appearance as if they were human warriors, and in place of the weapons that indicate different ethnic origins in Vergil's catalogue,[7] he documents for us the deadly effects of their various kinds of venom and poisonous exhalations:

> iaculique uolucres,
> et contentus iter cauda sulcare parias,
> oraque distendens auidus spumantia prester,
> ossaque dissoluens cum corpore tabificus seps;
> sibilaque effundens cunctas terrentia pestes,

ante uenena nocens, late sibi summouet omne
uulgus et in uacua regnat basiliscus harena.

(9.720–26)

and flying Jaculus;

and Parias, content to cut a path with its tail;
greedy Prester stretching wide its foaming mouth;
the putrefying Seps, dissolving bones along with body;
the Basilisk which pours forth hisses terrifying all
the beasts, which harms before its poison and orders the entire crowd
far out of its way and on the empty sand is king.

We thought that it was terrible enough to witness the sight of Romans slaughtering Romans on the field of Pharsalus, but here, in this accursed landscape and far from home,[8] young Italians die excruciating deaths that surpass even that horror. Here is poor Nasidius, from the Marsian country a little to the east of Rome,[9] bitten by a prester, whose venom induces terrifying, inexorable swelling:

illi rubor igneus ora

succendit, tenditque cutem pereunte figura
miscens cuncta tumor . . .

. . . .

ipse latet penitus congesto corpore mersus,
nec lorica tenet distenti pectoris auctum.

. . . .

tumidos iam non capit artus

informis globus et confuso pondere truncus.
intactum uolucrum rostris epulasque daturum
haud inpune feris non ausi tradere busto
nondum stante modo crescens fugere cadauer.

(9.791–93, 796–97, 800–804)

A fiery redness set alight his face,

and swelling strains the skin, confounding all his features,
their shape destroyed . . .

. . . .

The man himself is out of sight, buried deep in bloated body,
and his breast-plate cannot hold the swelling of his bursting chest.

. . . .

No longer can the shapeless mass

and torso with its jumbled bulk contain the swollen limbs.

Untouched by beaks of birds and destined to provide for wild beasts
a banquet not without danger, they did not dare consign the body
to the tomb but ran away as it still grew, its limit not yet fixed.

Lucan tells us that at least Nasidius is spared the terrible fate, of being eaten by
wild beasts and birds, that Homer, at the beginning of the *Iliad*, warned us was
awaiting the Greek and Trojan dead.[10] That is, of course, no real consolation for
the new abomination that he thrusts upon us, and we are left wondering when,
and with what gory results, Nasidius, now nothing more than some kind of vast
blood blister, will burst apart.

Here we come up against the core issue with Lucan's aesthetic. Some love
it and some hate it, but few are likely to find themselves capable of remaining
indifferent to it. Lucan, admittedly, is not the only wayward genius in the classical Latin canon whose self-indulgence can, and even in his own day did, leave
some readers recoiling in distaste. Seneca the Elder (*Controuersiae* 2.2.12) tells
the story of how Ovid was asked by some friends to erase three of his lines that
they found crashingly bad. Ovid agreed, so long as they would allow him to
specify three that would be exempt from possible erasure. When they exchanged
notebooks, it was found that Ovid and the friends had listed the very same three
lines. Seneca explains that Ovid was not unaware of the excesses of his poetry
and that the problem was that he simply loved those same excesses. We might
also appeal to the change in the public's taste in different periods to explain
what it is that makes the snake vignettes so divisive. It is, no doubt, all too easy
to aim for impressiveness in style and diction and yet, while achieving it for a
readership or audience one understands, nonetheless lay one oneself open to
the charge of being ridiculous in an age that is less comfortable with that level
of grandeur. Perhaps the most human thing about Lucan's "monsters" is the
very way in which, like all of us, they can slip from the magnificent to the ludicrous depending on the perspective of the audience. As with grandeur, so also
with horror or with pathos: if we laugh at Cato's—that is, Lucan's—ostentation,
maybe it is just that we are not attuned to that kind of pomposity and that our
aesthetic dislike for it interferes with our ability to understand and admire its
cleverness. Parallels from literary cultures closer in time and outlook to ourselves than the Rome of the first century, and changes in those cultures, are
easy to find. Dickens made the Victorians weep, but "[o]ne must have a heart
of stone," Oscar Wilde supposedly said only a few decades after Dickens's death,
"to read the death of Little Nell without laughing."[11]

What we are dealing with, however, is emphatically not *merely* a matter of
taste, whether Lucan's own immaturity or the Neronian age's supposed weak-
ness for ghoulish pleasures. W. R. Johnson identifies the crucial question to

ask: "Why is Lucan enjoying himself here?"[12] The glee and loving craftsmanship with which the snakes are described are palpable. Johnson's own reply to that question still has force: "For me, the snake vignettes are among the poem's glories. Like Erictho, like Cato himself, they possess an uncanny, wonderful verve. Engaging what is more fertile in Lucan's imagination, his wit and his sense of the grotesque, they issue from his imagination as unique poetic creations."[13] For Johnson, Cato and the snakes deserve each other and belong in the same poem because Cato himself is a monster too, a monster of Stoic virtue taken to dangerous but also ludicrous excess: "Cato's virtue is, as Lucan imagines it here, as implausible and fantastic as the snakes that destroy his soldiers. Like his adversary, Caesar, Cato is an expressionist caricature."[14]

Johnson's reading of Cato and the snakes derives much of its cogency from its insistence that Lucan's politics are inseparable from his aesthetics. One passage in book 9 where we can perhaps test for ourselves the power of this argument is the account of how the Roman army, afflicted with thirst, comes across what should be a welcome sight, an isolated spring of freshwater in the desert. At first, however, the legionaries do not dare to drink because the spring is infested with poisonous snakes, cousins of the grotesque creatures whom we will soon see inflicting those terrible deaths on some of their comrades. They were quite prepared to die on the discovery of this life-preserving water, says Lucan, relishing the paradox, had Cato not calmly reassured them, first, with a rational, scientific account of how snake venom is dangerous only when transmitted by a bite directly into the bloodstream and not when ingested with drinking water and then, second, by himself setting the example and drinking:

> dixit, dubiumque uenenum
> hausit; et in tota Libyae fons unus harena
> ille fuit de quo primus sibi posceret undam.
> (9.616–18)

> He spoke and drained the questionable
> poison; and in all the Libyan sand, that was the only spring
> from which he for himself demanded water first.

There is, of course, a pointed contrast between his not drinking the water offered him in the helmet a hundred or so lines earlier and his being the first to drink now, but at the same time the two passages tell us the same thing: Cato puts his men before himself and sets them an example. And yet some readers may also feel that Cato is someone whose self-confidence and belief in his moral and intellectual superiority combine in such a way that he can be relied upon to do the precise opposite of what, in any stressful situation, other men would naturally do—that Cato is, in fact, an unnatural creature himself. Moreover, Cato's own speeches and the poet's editorializing observations draw attention to the singular unexpectedness of Cato's not drinking when others long to and of his drinking when others dread to. The very power of the poet's verbal triumphs can seem to hammer it all home: monstrous setting, monstrous enemies, monstrous hero.

Hero or Fanatic?

There are other elements in Lucan's portrayal of "Cato in the wilderness" that may also cause unease, even in readers who are generally willing to accepts Lucan's aesthetics of hyperbole. For a start, there is the unsettling intratextual resonance between Cato and his nominal antithesis Caesar. Cato possesses *uirtus*, manly courage and virtue, in abundance, and now, in this benighted age, Brutus sees in him Virtue's "sole support" (2.243). We may not feel entirely easy in our mind, however, when Lucan tells us that this "daring valor hopes" that it can overcome the shifting sandbanks of the Syrtes (9.302). Is hope truly enough? This audacious virtue is also *impatiens . . . haerere*, "lacking in the patience to stand still" (9.371). Cato is positively eager to get going and to stride out into the desert, leading his men with him into the most appalling dangers. That should worry us because it reminds us of Caesar and his *nescia uirtus | stare loco*, "never-resting virtue" (1.144–45). Caesar's restless courage starts the war, and Cato's restless courage starts the desert march. Both will get a lot of men killed. Even a critic like Hardie, who is generally sympathetic to Lucan's portrayal of Cato as the poem's hero and scapegoat,[15] acknowledges that "there is something megalomaniac in Cato's altruism."[16] Nor is Caesar the only world conqueror of whom Cato reminds us. The story of the general who nobly refuses water brought to him in an upturned helmet is also told by Arrian of Alexander the Great, on the occasion of his heroic, yet all but disastrous, march through the Gedrosian desert (*Anab.* 6. 26). Arrian thought it an uplifting example both of Alexander's self-control and of his skill in handling his men, and, long before Arrian, much the same story, with evident approval and admiration, had already been told in the Hebrew scriptures of King David when he was caught between Philistine armies stationed in the valley of Rephaim and in the town of Bethlehem (2 Samuel 23:13–17). Perhaps, then, the most natural thing to do when we first read Lucan's account is to give Cato the same kind of credit. And yet Alexander generally gets a bad press in Latin literature, and we may in any case be forced to reconsider the positive image of both Alexander in Arrian and Cato here in book 9 when, in the next book, Lucan brings Caesar to view the embalmed body of his predecessor and role model in world domination, denouncing him as *Pellaei proles uaesana Philippi,* | *felix praedo* ("the crazy off-spring of Pellaean Philip, | the lucky bandit," 10.20–21).[17]

Even if we decline to associate Lucan's Cato with Alexander or Caesar, it can still be hard to avoid the impression that he is self-consciously theatrical. It is almost as if Cato is playing the role of "the great Cato," condemned by the literary tradition about the historical Cato to audition before every audience, inside the poem and outside it, for the part that literature has assigned him. Johnson again puts the issue before us squarely: "To be sure, in Stoic thought the theater was a favorite metaphor both for life and for the struggle to live life virtuously; but for Cato, the metaphor has become all but a reality, fiction has replaced life. For him, what happens in history is merely the fiction from which virtue victoriously emerges; for him, the single reality is his own virtue. In short, virtue becomes solipsistic delusion."[18] Johnson is far from being alone in finding Lucan's Cato an unsatisfactory standard-bearer for the cause of liberty, but there have also been numerous scholars and critics who have felt no such qualm or for whom, though in some measure flawed, Cato remains essentially heroic and admirable.[19] Caterine has even ingeniously argued that we can move "past the interpretive divide"[20] and should accept that Lucan's portrayal of Cato is so thoroughly ambiguous and inconsistent that any attempt to argue definitively for a positive or a negative view of him is doomed to be defeated by the very text it tries to make serve its argument, with the result that the poem "does not recommend any specific interpretation but rather leads its audience into a state of agnosticism."[21] All that, as Caterine goes on to suggest, is in tune with the culture of rhetoric that shaped the writers of Lucan's day and that permeates the whole of his work, a culture and practice of rhetoric that admired ostentation but also encouraged versatility and flexibility in both the speaker and the audience, the writer and the reader. That view can even be justified by reference to the biographical tradition concerning Lucan, since the list of his works given at the end of the *Vita Lucani*, attributed to Vacca, includes a pair of speeches in prose, one against Octavius Sagitta and another, on the contrary, defending him. Those speeches will have dealt with the particularly lurid affair of adultery, disappointed love, and *crime passionel* narrated by Tacitus at *Annales* 13.44. Tacitus dates the trial and conviction of Sagitta to 58 C.E., when Lucan was not yet out of his teens, and even if we could still just about imagine him taking part in a trial at that age,[22] he could hardly have spoken both for the prosecution and the defense. It therefore looks as if these speeches were performance pieces intended to demonstrate their author's command of the rules of rhetoric and his ability to argue either side of a case with dazzling skill. The audience or readers of those speeches in all likelihood overlapped with the readers of *Civil War* and can be presumed to have had similar tastes and expectations. They may have been less troubled than modern readers of Lucan by any inconsistency or may even have relished rather than deplored a Cato who is admirable at one moment and repellent at the next.

This is an attractive line of reasoning and one sensitive to Roman cultural practice. It cannot be accused of naivety, the charge sometimes leveled at those who insist that Cato is a hero, and to many it will seem better grounded in Roman realities than Johnson's appealing but subjective talk of "the bitter levity that can set a cartoon Cato in a desert of cartoon snakes."[23] It is, on the other hand, worth reminding ourselves that this inclusive approach to the literary criticism of Lucan is particularly congenial to the intellectual culture of our own times and fits in well with the taste of the contemporary humanist academy for complexity. It can also be said that some passages in Lucan seem to carry a particular force, with the result that they create a lasting and dominating impression in some readers that overrides any lingering doubts. One such passage is the account of Cato's arrival at the celebrated oracle of Jupiter Ammon (9.511–86). Alexander the Great was known to have consulted the same oracle during his conquest of Egypt and on that occasion had been told by the god that he was Jupiter's own son. Cato is encouraged by Labienus to consult the oracle in his turn. To whom, Labienus asks, would the god more readily reveal his will for the outcome of the war than to "holy Cato" (9.554–55)? Cato, however, refuses point-blank to seek the god's revelation. He already knows all he needs to know in order to be a good man, a good soldier, and a good Roman:

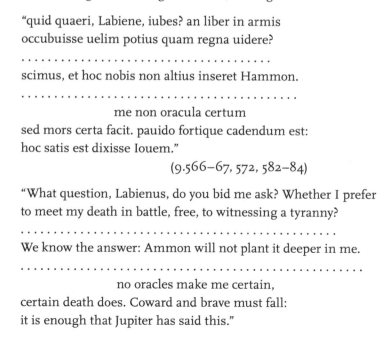

"quid quaeri, Labiene, iubes? an liber in armis
occubuisse uelim potius quam regna uidere?
. . . .
scimus, et hoc nobis non altius inseret Hammon.
. . . .
　　　　　　　me non oracula certum
sed mors certa facit. pauido fortique cadendum est:
hoc satis est dixisse Iouem."
　　　　　(9.566–67, 572, 582–84)

"What question, Labienus, do you bid me ask? Whether I prefer
to meet my death in battle, free, to witnessing a tyranny?
. . . .
We know the answer: Ammon will not plant it deeper in me.
. . . .
　　　　　　　no oracles make me certain,
certain death does. Coward and brave must fall:
it is enough that Jupiter has said this."

If Lucan himself was ever on the fence at all, he now appears to stand firmly on two feet and to be on Cato's side as he cries out:

> ecce parens uerus patriae, dignissimus aris,
> Roma, tuis, per quem numquam iurare pudebit
> et quem, si steteris umquam ceruice soluta,
> nunc, olim, factura deum es.
>
> (9.601–4)

> Look—it is the real father of his country, who most deserves
> your altars, Rome: you will never be ashamed to swear by him
> and you will make a god of him, now, one day,
> if you ever stand with neck unfettered.

There seems little to find ridiculous in Cato's noble declaration of the self-sufficiency of his sincere rational commitment to Stoic principles, and Lucan himself here sounds as if he is speaking with the authority that is traditionally possessed by the epic poet when he intervenes directly in his narrative by openly declaring what he knows or believes. All this also has the ring of conviction because it is so much in Lucan's manner, and so consistent with the avowed anti-Caesarian temper of the bulk of the poem, that he should seize the opportunity to point out that the Romans of his own time are deifying the wrong men.[24] Lucan then moves directly from that open praise to the scene we examined above, of Cato encouraging his men to drink from the serpent-infested pool. Should we really find him ridiculous or cartoonish so very soon after Lucan has personally vouched for his godlike rationality?[25]

The Poet: Playing with Styles

However we choose to interpret the snakes or Cato, we should note that it is precisely in the context of this network of hyperbolic representation that Lucan makes his most explicit claims to poetic independence and authority. Even before we get to the snakes, in fact, we can occasionally sense that Lucan is drawing our attention to what other kinds of a poet he could have chosen to be, had he not decided to be the author of the shocking and gruesome poem he has given us. For example, we may think of Vergil as being peerless among the Roman poets, whether in his *Georgics* or his *Aeneid*, and tell ourselves that his melodious descriptions of the Italian countryside, often suffused with melancholy, are beyond compare, but when Lucan has narrated how Pompey's widow and sons burn, in the absence of his body, his clothes, his weapons, and other

personal effects, he offers us a remarkably lovely imitation of the Vergilian manner and ethos. He compares the scene, quite unexpectedly, to the rustic practice of burning stubble in the fields to help the grass grow back:

> sic, ubi depastis summittere gramina campis
> et renouare parans hibernas Apulus herbas
> igne fouet terras, simul et Garganus et arua
> Volturis et calidi lucent buceta Matini.
>
> (9.182–85)

> So when the Apulian prepares to make the grass grow high
> on plains grazed bare and to renew the winter's fodder
> and warms the land with fire, then together Garganus
> and Voltur's fields and warm Matinus pastures glow with light.

Vergil had, in fact, devoted several lines of his first *Georgic* to the usefulness of
this agricultural process and had provided his readers with a short but learned
disquisition on the possible scientific reasons for its efficacy in renewing the
soil's potency (*G.* 1.84–93). It is Lucan, however, who takes this material and
uses it to enrich epic poetry with a "Vergilian" description that blends the love
of the Italian countryside with a sense of loss, for these are the very lands that
Pompey passed through as he fled before Caesar on his way to Brundisium in
book 2 (*profugus . . . per Apula rura*, "fleeing through Apulia's lands," 2.608),
and these are the lands, Lucan is subtly reminding us, that Pompey will never
see again. He even enriches his Vergilian subject matter further with a rare
word, *buceta*, "cattle pastures," of the kind we might have expected Vergil to
use, though in fact he never does.[26] It seems Lucan may be telling us that he
could produce epic poetry that matched Vergil's achievement if that was what
he wanted to do, if he were not writing the poem he is writing now. Elsewhere,
in the description of the terrors of the Libyan desert that alienates so many readers with its outrageous hyperbole, Lucan may also be reminding us that he
could have chosen to write like Ovid in the *Fasti*, giving learned explanations
for Roman customs and religious beliefs. The African winds, we learn, are so
strong that they rip the very armor and weapons from the legionaries' bodies
and carry them off to distant regions whose inhabitants, when they fall back to
land again, think them dropped there by the gods (9.471–77). That, he goes on
to declare, was "surely" (*profecto*, 9.477) what lay behind the *ancilia*, the sacred
shields carried by the priestly fraternity of the Salii, one of which was believed
to have fallen from heaven in the reign of King Numa.[27] Even the snakes have
their literary antecedents, as perhaps did the learnedly didactic style in which
Lucan describes their horrors. At any rate, the Berne scholiast on line 9.701 tells

us plainly that one of Lucan's possible sources for the names of his serpents was the *Theriaca*, a didactic poem by Vergil's rather older contemporary, Aemilius Macer;[28] though that poem now survives in the form of only a few fragments, Courtney argues, for example, that the smoky trails left by the *chelydri* at 9.711 were inspired by one of Macer's surviving descriptions.[29] Whatever the details of Lucan's debt to Macer in particular may have been, his scholarly descriptions of the snakes are both a contribution to the learned tradition of scientific poetry and a reminder, again, that, had he wanted to do so, Lucan could have written a quite different sort of hexameter poetry.

The greatest tour de force, however, of this kind of literary impersonation in book 9 is Lucan's account of the genesis of the snakes. They were, as he narrates, created by the blood that dripped from the severed head of Medusa as Perseus, flying backward to avoid the terrible gaze of the dead Gorgon, traversed Africa at Minerva's bidding (9.619–99). The whole extended passage can be read as an exercise in the style of Ovid's *Metamorphoses*, a mix of fantasy and horror, of mythological learning and whimsical literalness, as in this account of Medusa's petrification of the local wildlife and human inhabitants:

> e caelo uolucres subito cum pondere lapsae,
> in scopulis haesere ferae, uicina colentes
> Aethiopum totae riguerunt marmore gentes.
>
> (9.649–51)

> From heaven birds fell down with sudden weight,
> the beasts were fastened to their rocks, entire tribes
> of Ethiopians, living near, grew stiff in marble.

The passage can even be read as a virtuoso attempt to fill in a gap in Ovid's text, for Ovid himself, drawing on Apollonius of Rhodes (4.1513–17), gives the same etiological explanation for the serpents of Africa but tells us it in just four more or less business-like lines:[30]

> cumque super Libycas uictor penderet harenas,
> Gorgonei capitis guttae cecidere cruentae,
> quas humus exceptas uarios animauit in angues;
> unde frequens illa est infestaque terra colubris.
>
> (Ov. *Met.* 4.617–20)

> And while he hung victorious over the Libyan sands
> drops of blood from the Gorgon's head fell down
> and the ground received them and breathed life into them as snakes
>   of various kinds.
> And so it is that that land is densely snake infested.

To put that slightly differently, Lucan may be striving to surpass Ovid at his own game by combining the manner of Ovidian epic with pseudo-realistic didactic in the style of Macer, though we shall never know just how many of the details of the serpent description had no direct model in Macer's lost poem and should be understood as Lucan's own gleeful additions.

The Poet: The Truth and Authority

What is clear, however, is that Lucan wants us to read his engagement with the tradition communicated to him by Ovid in such a way that we cannot easily escape the question of poetic truth and authority. Long before he ever introduced us to the snakes, Lucan had reminded us that the African landscape into which Cato was about to lead us had plenty of literary precedent and also reminded us that we should be indulgent to that tradition and to anyone seeking to draw upon it. His readers will have known since they were children that the far west of Africa was where Hercules was sent by Eurystheus to steal, as one of his celebrated twelve labors, the golden apples that grew in the sacred grove of the Hesperides, guarded by a mighty serpent. "There was once a golden wood" (9.360), the poet says, settling in to tell us that familiar story in brief outline as part of his description of the geography of Africa—but not before he first implicitly acknowledges that the story is, in point of fact, plainly incredible even as he insists on the duty of the well-intentioned reader to play along with the poet and not to be so begrudging as to expect a bard to tell the truth:[31]

> inuidus, annoso qui famam derogat aeuo,
> qui uates ad uera uocat.
>
> (9.359–60)

> Spiteful is anyone who takes away from aged time its glory,
> who summons poets to the truth.

If that sounds like a plea for respect and indulgence for the entire guild of poets, it must be admitted that Lucan is ready to break ranks when it suits him. The snakes, he assures us, would have been inexplicable had not earlier poets preserved the etiological account of Perseus's flight that he himself is about to tell at his leisure (emphasis added):

> non cura laborque
> noster scire ualet, nisi quod uulgata per orbem
> fabula *pro uera* decepit saecula *causa*.
>
> (9.621–23)

> no care or toil of ours
> can know; except that a legend, spread throughout the world,
> has deceived the centuries in *place of the real reason*.

The etiological account is, then, the only one he can give us, but this *aetion*, this *causa*, is, he admits, a mere *fabula*, a fiction that has displaced the true explanation. The two passages, taken together, serve as a paradoxical reminder both of the poem's status as fiction and of the part that readers, aware all the time that they are reading fiction, must nonetheless play in sustaining the literary pretense.

All that prepares us for the moment when Lucan brings us to the very fountainhead of all ancient epic poetry, the city of Troy. When he has deposited Cato and what remains of his army, safe at last, in the kingdom of Juba, Lucan suddenly whirls us back across to the opposite side of the Mediterranean and shows us Caesar stopping off at Troy to visit the place where, chronologically, the *Aeneid* began to view the ruins of the city whose sack we already know so well from Vergil's book 2. What Caesar sees on his tour is nothing more than a jumble of broken stones scattered across a hilltop amidst the trees and bracken, so utterly destroyed that it barely even qualifies as ruins—*etiam periere ruinae* ("even the ruins suffered oblivion," 9.969). As he makes his way through the tall grass, a local rebukes him for thoughtlessly treading on the grave of Hector (9.975–77), and his guide then expresses surprise when he seems about to pass nonchalantly by the rubble that is all that remains of the altar of Jupiter Herceus where, in Vergil's poem, we saw Pyrrhus brutally slaughter King Priam.[32] Lucan does not need to name his great Greek and Latin predecessors, for their works were the bedrock of his readers' education. In showing us what is left of the city whose last days Homer and Vergil had chronicled, he seizes the opportunity to make two claims, one traditional and one, though rooted in tradition, also daringly radical. The first claim is that poetry, along with the fame it confers, outlives the monuments. There are only shattered stones here now, but *nullum est sine nomine saxum* ("no stone is without a story," 9.973) and the ghosts of this place "owe much to the bards" (9.963). Lucan probably expects us to see here an allusion to Horace's bold claim for the power of poets to preserve the past and the memory of human deeds down the long centuries:[33]

> uixere fortes ante Agamemnona
> multi; sed omnes illacrimabiles
>   urgentur ignotique longa
>   nocte, carent quia uate sacro.
>   (Hor. *Carm.* 4.9.25–28)

Many a brave man lived before Agamemnon, but all lie buried unwept and unknown in the long night, because they lack a sacred bard.

Agamemnon, the Greek king who overturned the very stones that Caesar is now inspecting and who hurled "the topless towers" to the ground, would now be utterly forgotten and nameless had not Homer sung of the Trojan War. The second claim follows on immediately after Lucan has shown us Caesar obliviously strolling past the altar of Jupiter Herceus, the setting for one of the most moving scenes in the poem that Vergil wrote to preserve the memory of his ancestor Aeneas:

> o sacer et magnus uatum labor! omnia fato
> eripis et populis donas mortalibus aeuum.
> inuidia sacrae, Caesar, ne tangere famae;
> nam, siquid Latiis fas est promittere Musis,
> quantum Zmyrnaei durabunt uatis honores,
> uenturi me teque legent; Pharsalia nostra
> uiuet, et a nullo tenebris damnabimur aeuo.
>
> (9.980–86)

O how sacred and immense the task of bards! You snatch everything
from death and to mortals you give immortality.
Caesar, do not be touched by envy of their sacred fame;
since, if for Latian Muses it is right to promise anything,
as long as honours of the Smyrnaean bard endure,
the future ages will read me and you; our Pharsalia
shall live and we shall be condemned to darkness by no era.

Bards confer immortality on their subjects, as convention has it, and so it follows that if Lucan's poem will be immortal, then Caesar's immortality is also assured. The generations to come will read *"me teque"* ("me and you"), Lucan declares, and the Caesar who will live forever in the imagination and memory will be, not the Caesar of the monuments and the historians, but the Caesar that Lucan chooses to show us. Whatever Lucan's vices may be, false modesty is not one of them.

Caesar: Truth and Mendacity

The Caesar promised immortality in this poem is, then, also the Caesar who ends this book by taking us back to where we began it. On his own arrival on the shores of Egypt, Caesar delivers a third judgement on Pompey, to stand

beside Lucan's own and Cato's from the opening pages of this book. The syco-
phantic courtiers of the young King Ptolemy present Caesar with his defeated
enemy's head, and Caesar, in a masterful performance of a grief he does not
feel, laments aloud that it is no longer possible for him to do as he now claims
he had hoped, to spare Pompey and thereby win Rome's forgiveness for victory
in civil war:

> "tunc pace fideli
> fecissem ut uictus posses ignoscere diuis,
> fecisses ut Roma mihi."
>
> (9.1102–4)
>
> "Then in lasting peace
> I could have helped you in defeat forgive the gods;
> you could have helped Rome forgive me."

It is a rousing, accomplished speech. Lucan, however, assures us that none in
all that crowd believed him (9.1104–6), and so the book ends with Caesar fixed
in our memories as a hypocrite and a poseur. And yet, if the authoritative poet
appears momentarily to cut the ground from under his own character's feet,
he also immediately shows us that Caesar's loss of control is transient, limited,
in effect a mere illusion. While Caesar feigns sorrow and conceals his delight
in his rival's elimination, those whom Caesar's victory enslaves do not follow
his example but instead seek his favor by concealing their own true sorrow and
feigning delight:

> abscondunt gemitus et pectora laeta
> fronte tegunt, hilaresque nefas spectare cruentum,
> o bona libertas, cum Caesar lugeat, audent.
>
> (9.1106–8)
>
> they hide their groans and veil their hearts
> with happy brow, and cheerfully—O happy liberty!—they dare
> to gaze upon the bloody crime though Caesar grieves.

They "dare," says Lucan ironically, to defy Caesar, but their defiance goes no
further than appearing to celebrate the completeness of his victory. If the battle
now truly is between Caesar and Liberty, then Caesar, at least outside the
serpent-infested wastelands, has the upper hand, and the only form that Liberty can take is that of abject servility.[34]

Notes

1. The stirring "apotheosis" of Pompey left such a strong impression on the late-antique Christian poet Prudentius that he refashioned it to describe the ascent to heaven of St. Agnes of Rome on the completion of her martyrdom: cf. in particular lines 9.11–14 with *Peristephanon* 14.89–96.

2. See, e.g., Verg. *Aen.* 7.37–45, Valerius Flaccus 6.33–41, and Stat. *Theb.* 8.373–74.

3. Liberty and Caesar are dramatically opposed as if they are a pair (*par*) of gladiators in the amphitheater, see Leigh 1997, 235.

4. That Cato's devotion to philosophy will not prevent him from taking an active part in civil war when the time comes was made clear to us in his speech to Brutus at 2.286–323.

5. Lucan appears to have simplified and thereby mispresented the situation, as Plutarch (*Cat. Min.* 56.2) tells us that Cyrene had closed its gates against Labienus but welcomed Cato.

6. See Tac. *Dial.* 2 for a perfectly literal tragedy on the subject, the lost *Cato* of Curiatius Maternus. In this book, Cato's readiness for self-immolation aligns him with the deranged Cornelia, who, while the others on board pray for delivery from a storm, prays for their ship to sink (9.113–16).

7. See, e.g., Verg. *Aen.* 7.664–65, 730–32.

8. For the pathos attached to this idea in epic from Homer on, see Griffin 1980, 106–12.

9. The pathos is enhanced if we remember the Marsians in Vergil's Italian catalogue, above all Umbro, the snake charmer who could not save himself in battle but who, we now may reflect, was at least fated to die in Italy and by human hands (*Aen.* 7.750–760).

10. See Griffin 1980, 19–21, 115–18.

11. The attribution to Wilde appears to be apocryphal, but it catches his style and expresses much the same difference in taste and outlook between the Victorians and their twentieth-century successors that infuses, for example, Lytton Strachey's *Eminent Victorians*.

12. Johnson 1987, 52.

13. Johnson 1987, 52.

14. Johnson 1987, 55.

15. Hardie 1993, 30–32.

16. Hardie 1993, 11.

17. For the hostile portrayal in Seneca and Lucan of Alexander as a dangerous megalomaniacal tyrant, see Tracy 2014, 120–21, 253, 255, 278. See also Zwierlein 2010, esp. 416–21, for an analysis of the visit made by Caesar to the ruins of Troy at the end of book 9 that builds on the "recognition that Lucan has fashioned his Caesar as a mirror image of Alexander" (419).

18. Johnson 1987, 63.

19. Caterine (2015, 339–40) with notes 2 and 3 opens with a quick taxonomy ranging the "optimists," those who, generally speaking, see Cato as a true Stoic, a true republican, and a true hero, against the "pessimists," those for whom he serves to make the point that, in Lucan's "dysfunctional world," heroism is no longer possible.

20. Caterine 2015, 340.

21. Caterine 2015, 358.

22. L. Sempronius Atratinus was only seventeen when he took part in the prosecution of Marcus Caelius Rufus and found himself opposite Cicero. See Dyck 2013, 6, 61.

23. Johnson 1987, 57.

24. Contrast the triumphant but acerbic tone of Lucan's assertion at 7.455–59 that the Romans of his day take vengeance for the gods' decision to grant Caesar victory at Pharsalus by raising up mortal men to be their equals and by swearing oaths by mere ghosts. The cult of the deified Caesars provides the material for a bitter epigram, but the cult of the deified Cato, if ever it became reality, would be the ultimate proof of liberty restored.

25. Statius seems to have derived a predominantly positive impression of Cato's role in *Civil War*, whose subject matter, as he summarizes it, includes *libertate grauem pia Catonem* ("Cato stern with a patriot's love of liberty," *Silv.* 2.7.68). If we subscribe to this view of Cato, however, then our radical poet with a fondness for provocation turns out to be largely in line with the standard view taken by the Roman literary tradition. Note, e.g., Hor. *Carm.* 2.1.21–24 *audire magnos iam uideor duces | non indecoro puluere sordidos | et cuncta terrarum subacta | praeter atrocem animum Catonis* ("Already do I seem to hear of mighty leaders, begrimed with a dust

that cannot disgrace them, and of all the world subdued, save Cato's unrelenting soul"). It seems likely that it was Asinius Pollio's account that set the tone for this tradition, see Harrison 2017, 51–54.

26. The word *buceta* seems not have been used by any other extant Latin poet and may have been generally thought too prosaic for verse. Varro uses it at *Ling.* 5.164 and Gellius at 11.1.1. For another simile that may remind us of Vergil, this time with the bees we know so well from *Georgic* 4, see 9.284–93.

27. See, e.g., Fordyce 1977, 275 on Verg. *Aen.* 8.663–66.

28. For Macer, see Courtney 1993, 292–99, and Hollis 2007, 93–117. Ovid, when still very young, attended Macer's recitations of his *Ornithogonia* and *Theriaca*, as he tells us at *Tr.* 4.10.43–44.

29. Courtney 1993, 296, on frag. 8. See also Hollis 2007, 107–9.

30. Translation from Hill 1985. The point being made here is limited to the matter of style(s), but see Fantham 1992b for a sustained analysis of Lucan's engagement with Ovid and his other predecessors in the literary tradition. Fantham argues that the contest between Medusa and Perseus "has allegorical resonances far beyond the context of the ninth book" (96–97) and that, in his exploration of the questions of ethics and heroism, "Lucan has exploited to the full the role of Medusa as symbol of human overreach" (110). In her response to Fantham, Malamud 2003 goes considerably further, seeing Medusa's head as "an emblem not just of civil war, but of Lucan's own artistic production, *Civil War*" (32).

31. Lucan here may remind us of Ovid's similar insistence on the freedom of poets from the respect for fact that binds the historians: *exit in immensum fecunda licentia uatum | obligat historica nec sua uerba fide* ("out in boundless flood goes the fruitful licence of the poets, and does not bind their words with loyalty to history," *Am.* 3.12.41–42). As a satirist calling a spade a spade, on the other hand, Juvenal feels free to heap contempt on both *quidquid Graecia mendax | audet in historia* ("whatever lying Greece dares to tell as history," 10.174–75) and the fictions of the epicists (4.34–36).

32. See Verg. *Aen.* 2.506–58.

33. Translation by Rudd 2004. We also recall Horace's boast that his own poetry will outlast the pyramids of Egypt: *Carm.* 3.30.1–5.

34. And yet, despite Lucan's insistence that the final word in defining Caesar and the world's view of him is his, we can, if we choose, refuse to accept Lucan's Caesar, not least because we can still read Caesar with authors other than Lucan. Agamemnon has left us no personal memoirs of his campaigns, but Caesar has, and it is striking that he merely records that "at Alexandria he learned of Pompey's death" (*BCiv.* 3.106) before passing quickly on to an account of the military situation as he found it in the Egyptian capital. Plutarch tells us rather more, noting that Caesar recoiled from the head in horror and shed tears (*Caes.* 48.2, *Pomp.* 80.5). He gives no hint at all of insincerity, however, and thereby ends his account of the life of Pompey with an implicit endorsement of the stature of the vanquished general and also of the truthfulness of the tribute paid to it by the historical Caesar.

10

Book 10

The Living End

PAUL ROCHE

Lucan's Caesar slackens in intensity after his victory at Pharsalus. This impression may in part be an effect of Lucan's narrative attention to Pompey in book 8 and to Cato in book 9, but there are clear signs of new, nonmilitary interests and broader horizons for Caesar in the closing two books of the epic. The center of the battle line at Pharsalus had shown Caesar at the extremity of his characterization as an overreacher: an elemental force embodying the frenzy and madness of civil war (cf. esp. 7.557–85). When we first encounter him after his breakfast amid the carnage at Pharsalus and his march away from the killing fields amid a rain of human gore and rotting body parts (7.786–846), he is described as "satiated with the slaughter of Emathia" (9.950), a line that answers to 7.802 "with his anger not yet glutted by the slaughter." Although we are told that he is intent upon his son-in-law (9.952), we are almost immediately shown a more discursive pursuit. Caesar quickly diverts to the site of Troy. Here, accompanied by a local guide, he wanders amid the ruined topography of Iliadic myth (9.959–99). In undertaking this detour, Caesar is walking in the footsteps of Alexander the Great, who in 334 B.C.E. had toured this site at the outset of his eastern campaigns. He, too, had viewed the sights of the city accompanied by a local guide, and he had offered sacrifice at the Altar of Zeus Herkeios, the remains of which Caesar inadvertently disrespects at 9.977–79.[1]

For all its relevance to the foundation myth of Rome and its importance to Lucan's place in the epic tradition going back to Homer—for all its symmetry with Lucan's narrative of destruction and his thematic attention to the life cycles of cities and states—Caesar's interest in the site is unrelated to his ambitions in the poem. We are told that he filled his sight with "revered antiquity" (9.987);

his prayer at 9.990–99, while self-glorifying and asserting a personal claim on the state-gods of Rome, has been read as reflecting a newfound understanding of a sight he had previously ill comprehended.[2] The whole episode is inessential to his drive toward sole power and is motivated rather by curiosity: he goes to Troy as a *mirator famae* (9.961 "an admirer of renown") and leaves the site concerned to make up for the diversion (9.1002 *auidus . . . | Iliacas pensare moras*, "keen to compensate for his delays at Troy"). This less severe, more indulgent version of Caesar—accommodating his intellectual pursuits and showcasing encounters with models from revered antiquity—will find more detailed and explicit exposition in book 10.

When he first arrives in Alexandria, Caesar is fearful of the barely muted hostility of the Alexandrian people (10.11–15), and this highly unstable political situation is reiterated when we are told that the wrath of the people is allayed by Ptolemy, whom Caesar keeps "as . . . [a] hostage in the Pellaean court" (10.54–56) in order to be safe. Caesar's atypically fearful response is ironically misdirected: the real source of danger to him in book 10 will be not the populace at Alexandria but the influence of the enervating eastern court upon his martial disposition. Caesar's prowess declines to its nadir at the royal court of Alexandria in the corrupting presence of Cleopatra. After these new aspects of Caesar's characterization have been explored, book 10 will plot a (not uncomplicated) movement back toward the essentialized "epic" Caesar familiar to readers from the poem's earlier books, before the narrative, and Lucan's epic, are cut off at line 546.

Alexander

At 10.14–19 Caesar briefly "tours" Alexandria in a manner recalling his earlier tour of the site of Troy: "he visits the gods' abodes and temples of ancient deity which declare the Macedonian's might of old" (10.15–17). These are the temples in which the Ptolemaic kings, the successors to Alexander the Great, had received cult after their death. In contrast to Caesar's raising of an altar and his elaborate prayer at Troy, in Alexandria we are told that he is unimpressed until he "eagerly descends" to the tomb of Alexander the Great.[3] Caesar's two tours and their framing of a relationship between himself and Alexander dovetail around Alexander having visited Achilles's grave in Troy.[4] Caesar—Lucan's version of triumphing Iliadic wrath in the mode of Achilles—makes no such visit to Achilles's grave but does visit the tomb of Alexander in our book. A direct line of emulation is thus established in the sequence Achilles ~ Alexander ~ Caesar. This sequence is moreover extended another step by the reader's recollection that Caesar's visit has its historical model in Octavian, who had viewed and honored the body of Alexander in 30 B.C.E.[5] There is a thematic link between

Caesar's disinterest in the deified successors of Alexander and the narrator's promise at Pharsalus in book 7 that Rome will have its vengeance upon the gods for allowing Caesar's victory by creating second-rate divinities out of dead emperors (7.458–59). Note that when Octavian had viewed the body of Alexander and a tour of the tombs of the Ptolemies was suggested, he spurned the offer by stating that he wished to see a king, not corpses (Suet. *Aug.* 18.1).

We are meant to see Alexander as Caesar's model because he offers a blueprint for an individual's totalizing drive to world domination. His centrifugal rush outward from Macedon amid human devastation (10.28–31) recalls Caesar's destructive round of the Mediterranean through similar carnage in books 3–7. Alexander is also linked to Caesar as the cause of both an autocratic world empire and as the founder of a line of divine rulers in the Ptolemies and Roman emperors respectively. The connection is unmissable when Alexander is compared to a bolt of lightning that strikes the nations equally (10.34–36), just as Caesar had been programmatically described as a lightning bolt that terrifies the panicked nations (1.151–57). But Alexander's phenomenal military success and personal hegemony offers an enticing model to more of Lucan's heroes than just Caesar. In a poem that examines the destructive power of "rivalry in excellence" (*aemula uirtus*, 1.120), we are meant to conceptualize Alexander as the unattainable benchmark to which all combatants of the poem aspire. In his introduction at 10.21 as "a lucky bandit" (*felix praedo*), Alexander is further described as monopolizing *felicitas* (a personal "good fortune" that brings about victory and success), a quality to which so many of the protagonists in this and previous Roman civil wars have aspired: Marius (2.74), Sulla (2.221–22), Pompey (e.g., 2.582, 9.80), and Caesar (e.g., 3.296, 7.702).[6] Alexander "the Great" is moreover the original archetype of the "great name" that Pompey inherited and to which he can no longer measure up (cf. 1.135).[7] Not all of Lucan's heroes straightforwardly aspire to be the new Alexander. Cato makes no claim upon *felicitas* in the poem, and he swerves away from Alexander's precedent when he flatly refuses to consult the Oracle of Zeus Ammon at Siwah (9.544–86): it was here that Alexander was addressed as the son of the god in 331 B.C.E.[8] But not even Cato is totally immune from his example. The mutiny of his war-weary soldiers in Libya (9.217–93) replays the mutiny of Alexander's demoralized army at the Hyphasis River in India in 326 B.C.E.[9] Cato's angry response to a soldier who offers him water in the desert at 9.498–510 is an unpalatable adaptation of an anecdote illustrating Alexander' generosity, greatness of spirit, and self-control (Curt. 7.5.9–12, Arr. *Anab.* 6.26.1–3, Plut. *Alex.* 42.5–10).[10] And Cato's march west from Cyrene to Leptis en route to Utica at 9.218–949 may recall for the reader that at the time of his death Alexander was planning an expedition from east to west across North Africa to Spain and had determined to build a road through Libya for this purpose (Diod. 18.4.4).

While Alexander is a model for the would-be autocrat, he is at the same time "a useless example for the world" (*non utile mundo | exemplum*, 10.26–27). By casting him in these terms, Lucan invokes a concept familiar from Roman education and ethical thinking. An *exemplum* was a figure, case, pattern, or model showing behavior to be imitated or vices to be avoided.[11] Alexander as *exemplum* holds no profit for the world because the world—we, Lucan's readers—did not apply the lesson of being subject to his autocracy. Alexander's case was so extreme that it should have taught the world ever after to cast off and guard against tyranny. This is why the narrator says that Alexander's body should have been dismembered and his limbs scattered over the world instead of being interred in a sacred shrine (10.22–23).[12] Lucan's point—and his withering observation that Alexander's body was preserved to be an object of mockery if ever Liberty and the world should be reunited (10.25–26)—would have had particular poignancy for his Roman readers, who could contemplate these words while gazing upon the Temple of the Deified Julius Caesar in the Roman Forum or the Mausoleum of Augustus in the Campus Martius.

Lucan's invective against Alexander at 10.20–52, which casts his personal ascendency and legacy as both unending and antithetical to world liberty, should remind us of his impassioned interjections at Pharsalus: because of that day Liberty went into permanent, self-imposed exile from Rome (7.432–36); because of that battle Rome was reduced to a condition of never-ending slavery (7.638–41); after that battle the eternal gladiatorial pairing will be liberty and Caesar (7.695–96). On the other hand, for all its destructive potential, there is another side to the *exemplum* of Alexander. When Lucan ends his invective by noting that the sarissa, the characteristic weapon of the Macedonian army, is more feared by the people of the east than the Roman javelin, the *pilum* (10.47–48), he laments a lost positive model of imperial expansion into foreign territory as opposed to internecine conflict. This is a dichotomy that Lucan had established very early in the poem at 1.9–12. The point is driven home at 10.51–52 by reference to the failed Parthian expedition of Crassus, who offers an early positive model of Roman expansion and whose expedition is presented as the unfinished business that should have taken precedent over internal conflicts at 1.10–12.

Cleopatra

Cleopatra presents one of the most formidable threats to Caesar's power in Lucan's poem.[13] She is marked as significant to the *Civil War*'s concerns from her first appearance, when she is described as conveying herself "into the

Emathian halls" (10.58), a phrase that recalls the poem's central subject matter, "wars across Emathian plains" (1.1), by alluding to the "Emathian," that is Macedonian, origin of the Ptolemies. The adjective is significant because it is Lucan's only use of *Emathius* to mean "Macedonian" in the poem: elsewhere he uses terms such as *Pellaeus*, *Lagus*, or *Macetae* to convey "Macedonian." Her description as a "deadly Erinys" at 10.59 further evokes the huge Erinys (a fury) hovering over the city of Rome at the outbreak of the war at 1.572 and which at 4.187–88 has become a metaphor for the civil war itself. Cleopatra's sudden appearance to Caesar at court is moreover a neat inversion of Aeneas's sudden appearance to Dido amid her own courtiers at Vergil, *Aeneid* 1.586–95. This is an early marker of Cleopatra's primary epic model (soon to be developed), and it cues the reader to the possibility that Caesar will be delayed and diverted from his imperial mission in Africa, as had Vergil's Aeneas. It is also the first indication of Cleopatra's dangerous and deceptive agency (cf. 10.57 "with the guard bribed"), qualities that sit in contrast to Caesar's passivity in her presence; note that as she enters the court, his ignorance of her arrival is explicitly drawn to our attention (10.55, 58). Her comparison to Helen of Troy (10.60–62) is certainly cast in terms that convey a national threat: the narrator immediately develops an anachronistic description of Cleopatra in the full horror of her danger to the Roman state at the Battle of Actium in 31 B.C.E., such as we find her in Augustan poetry (10.63–67; cf. Hor. *Carm.* 1.37 and Verg. *Aen.* 8.685–713). But, as Helen, Cleopatra is also connected specifically to Caesar's most recent concerns: she is like "the Spartan women [who] . . . knocked down Argos and the homes of Ilium" (10.60–61), while Caesar has just arrived to Alexandria from viewing the ruins of "Assaracus' houses" during his "delays at Ilium" (9.967, 1002).

The encounter between Cleopatra and Caesar is framed from the outset as amplifying her power and diminishing his. We are told that the spirit that will drive Cleopatra's ambitions for world domination at Actium was acquired by her on her first night in bed with him at 10.68–69. On the other hand, for Caesar the affair is both enervating and strategically disadvantageous. The narrator observes that "the fire [of love] devoured Caesar's stubborn heart" (*durum . . . Caesaris hauserit ignes pectus*, 10.71–72). This marks a dangerous weakening of Caesar's normative "hard," "stubborn," or "pitiless" (*durus*) masculinity: compare, for example, the Massilians who try in vain to deflect Caesar's "unbridled fury and pitiless mind" (*duramque . . . mentem*, 3.304) or his own men who address him as "pitiless Caesar" (*dure . . . Caesar*, 5.682). Lucan also tells us that Caesar "let the routed party gather strength (*coalescere*) in Libya's furthest realms, while he spends time disgustingly on love beside the Nile" (10.79–80). Caesar's military strength has been thematized throughout the poem as "concentrated," "coalescing," or "coming together" in contrast to the "dissipating" or "scattered" strength of his opponents: compare how Caesar concentrates "scattered cohorts" (1.394–95) into "gathered might" (1.466) to attack Rome; or how the republicans had scattered from Rome before his invasion (1.490–510); or how in Greece, Pompey had seen "the supreme crisis of pitiless war as Caesar's troops combine from everywhere into full strength" (5.722–23). Note finally that the affair with Cleopatra also has the effect of putting a break upon his relentlessly solipsistic drive to power: he now prefers to make a gift to Pharos (i.e., Egypt) and "not to conquer for himself" (10.81).

The luxurious feast that Cleopatra gives for Caesar at 10.106–71 provides a vivid and extensive illustration of her corrupting influence over him, and her own "dangerous beauty" is set and described in the very center of the scene at 10.137–43. The same scene marks the nadir of Caesar's martial bellicosity, and yet it is also in this scene that we see the first embers of his renewed intensity begin to glow. A number of models and influences help us to read this passage. A banquet scene was a set piece of ancient epic: the earliest archetype is Homer's description of the reception of Odysseus at the palace of Alcinous (*Od.* 7.80–333), but a more direct epic model for Lucan is Vergil's description of the banquet given by Dido for Aeneas (*Aen.* 1.637–42, 697–756). These scenes and their emphasis upon the refinements of his host's palace are focalized through the astonished gaze of the weary hero, whose point of view is sharpened by his arriving at a low point in his fortunes and resources; both Odysseus and Aeneas, for example, arrive to their hosts after a devastating storm at sea. Lucan's Caesar swerves from this tradition by arriving after a summative victory and at the head of an army, but the awed wonder of his models remain, and we witness his reaction to expensive servants (10.129–31), citrus tables set on ivory legs (10.144–45), and the exotic fair served to the guests (10.169–70). Cleopatra's luxurious entertainment of Caesar was not an invention of Lucan (Plut. *Caes.* 49.4, Suet. *Iul.* 52.1), and it seems to have been the subject of criticism in antiquity (Frontin. *Strat.* 1.1.5). Lucan's readers must also have thought of the scandalous luxury of the entertainments of Marc Antony and Cleopatra (cf. Plut. *Ant.* 26.4–28.7), and the extravagances of contemporary Rome are also made a point of comparison when the narrator states that "the place itself was equal to a temple which an age more corrupt would hardly build" (10.111–12).

The imagery and components of luxurious banquets are commonly presented in negative terms in Roman literature and thought in a number of contexts. In the philosophical tradition golden statues and halls bedecked with silver and gold could be presented as superfluous to the needs of the body or as corrupting to the soul (Lucr. 2.24–28, Sen. *Ben.* 7.9); to Roman historiographers luxurious banqueting was a powerful index of decadence and moral decline

(cf. Livy 39.6.7–9, Sall. *Cat.* 13.3, Sall. *Iug.* 85.39–41);[14] Roman satire and declamation had adopted the same basic stance.[15] There is a certain paradox that this
conspicuous luxury, normatively enervating, reanimates Caesar's martial
appetites and desire for war. We see this reawakening develop through Caesar's
focalized reactions to the display, as he comments on the blonde hair of Cleopatra's servants (10.129–30), as we are told he had never seen such ivory and citrus wood tables (10.144–46), as the narrator interjects to decry the potential
danger of setting such rewards before Caesar (10.146–49), and as ultimately it
is plainly stated:

> discit opes Caesar spoliati perdere mundi
> et gessisse pudet genero cum paupere bellum
> et causas Martis Phariis cum gentibus optat.
>
> (10.169–71)

> Caesar learns to squander the riches of a plundered world;
> it shames him to have waged a war against his impoverished son-in-law
> and he prays for pretexts to fight the Pharian peoples.

In this motivation for war, Caesar mirrors on a personal level the "public seeds
of war" (*publica belli semina*) cited by the narrator as the first of his original
causes of the outbreak of civil war at Rome (1.160–67).

Acoreus

Caesar's inquiry of Acoreus at 10.172–92 may be taken as the extremity of his
intellectual interests in the *Civil War* and as the poem's most sustained inquiry
into natural phenomena, a topic of concern threading through the epic.[16] Caesar's question and the reply it receives should be compared with the previous
scenes in epic that they evoke: the song of Demodocus in Homer's *Odyssey*
(8.487–520) and the song of Iopas in Vergil's *Aeneid* (1.740–46), both sung at
banquets before the hero as guest in a sumptuous foreign court. The latter
model is especially important, since it continues the framing of Cleopatra and
her feast as a version of Dido's entertainment of Aeneas. In the *Odyssey*, the
hero self-interestedly asks the court bard to recount a version of the Trojan horse
story starring himself (as he says at 8.494–95), while in the *Aeneid*, Iopas per-
forms unasked and offers a didactic song about the origins of humans and animals and astronomical and meteorological phenomena. Although Acoreus's
discourse is not explicitly presented as a song, Lucan's scene resonates in various ways with these predecessors. We can see a version of Odysseus's desire to

be glorified by Demodocus's song in Caesar's self-aggrandizing comparison with Plato and Eudoxus: "If your ancestors taught their mysteries to Cecropian Plato, what visitor ever more deserved to listen or could better comprehend the universe? . . . nor will my year be worsted by Eudoxus's calendar" (10.181–83, 187). Caesar's intellectual curiosity is here shown to be possessed of the same competitive drive and uncompromising ambition as are his military and political ambitions, and he even links the term *uirtus*, usually describing martial courage, to his "love of the truth" and desire for knowledge (10.188–91).

Although scholars have differed on the precise significance and meaning of Iopas's song, it is clear that Vergil's bard offers a scientific explanation of the world in a poem that shows the power of divine causation and fate; he has thus been read as illustrating the limitations of human knowledge.[17] Whereas Iopas is atypical of the framework of the epic in which he appears, Acoreus's professed ignorance of the origin of the Nile moves closely in step with the narrator of the *Civil War*, for whom the true causes of events are also beyond certitude.[18] Moreover, his disproportionate, digressive, and inconclusive response, which detains Caesar for 138 lines only to withhold from him the object of his desire, has much in common with the narrator's strategy of obsessively delaying Caesar's march to victory.[19] It is difficult to escape the feeling that Acoreus is cannier than his disavowal of knowledge and the rambling structure of his answer may suggest when he lectures Caesar on the tyrants of history—Alexander, Sesostris, and Cambyses (10.268–85)—who have come in search of the same answer and have gone away frustrated in the attempt. As partisan readers of Lucan's poem we may especially sympathize with Acoreus's decision to detain and divert rather than simply admit he doesn't know, since Caesar has put so high a price on the issue of knowing the source of the Nile: he even claims that he will abandon the civil war if he attains knowledge of it (10.192). It may be significant in this context that at Apollonius Rhodius *Argonautica* 1.492–515, Orpheus had sung a spellbinding didactic song to avert internecine conflict from erupting on the *Argo*.

(Just Like) Starting Over: Alexandrian Revisions

When war erupts in Egypt, Lucan offers us the first battle narrative since Pharsalus.[20] For readers there is a strong sense of déjà vu. Set pieces and echoes from earlier in the poem are reprised and feed into the poem's sense of unending cycles of internecine conflict. Lucan takes great pains to stress that this is another chapter in the same civil war:

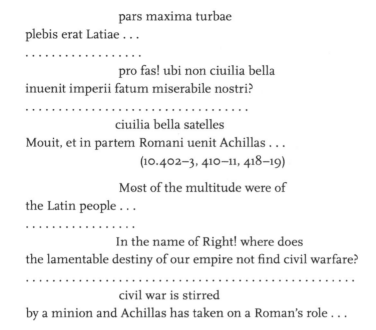

> pars maxima turbae
> plebis erat Latiae . . .
>
> . . . .
>
> pro fas! ubi non ciuilia bella
> inuenit imperii fatum miserabile nostri?
>
> . . . .
>
> ciuilia bella satelles
> Mouit, et in partem Romani uenit Achillas . . .
>
> (10.402–3, 410–11, 418–19)
>
> Most of the multitude were of
> the Latin people . . .
>
> . . . .
>
> In the name of Right! where does
> the lamentable destiny of our empire not find civil warfare?
>
> . . . .
>
> civil war is stirred
> by a minion and Achillas has taken on a Roman's role . . .

At its outset the battle contains the most emasculated image of Caesar in the poem: hiding in the palace, a mix of anger and fear, "like an unwarlike boy or a woman in a captured city" (10.439–59).[21] And yet in these same lines a more threatening and elemental incarnation of Caesar is described and holds out the prospect of his destructive eruption. He is like a caged animal: a recollection of his comparison to the self-destructive force of a wounded lion in book 1 (10.445–46; cf. 1.205–12) and perhaps also of Alexander, who is described at the beginning of book 10 as breaking loose from his lair to enslave the world (cf. *latebras* "hiding places" at 10.441; cf. 10.28–29). Caesar is also compared to trapped fire raging in Mount Etna—"no differently would your flame rage in the caves of Sicily if Etna's summit, Mulciber, were blocked" (*nec secus in Siculis fureret tua flamma cauernis, | obstrueret summam siquis tibi, Mulciber, Aetnam,* 10.447–48)—a reminder of the omens at the start of the war, when "fierce Mulciber unclosed Sicilian Etna's mouths" (*ora ferox Siculae laxauit Mulciber Aetnae,* 1.545), and a return to the chthonic energy that has been used throughout the poem to describe the war and Caesar in terms evoking a gigantomachic assault on cosmic stability.[22]

At several points in the battle, scenes from earlier books are evoked to suggest Caesar or his fortune "improving" upon earlier models. When Achillas's troops decide not to attack Caesar in the palace during the feast and therefore let slip the opportunity of victory over him (10.425–30), they are reprising

Pompey's failure to press his advantage at Dyrrachium (6.290–313).[23] When Caesar is besieged in the palace, the scene reprises elements from Caesar's own siege of Pompey at Dyrrachium (6.29–137). Achillas's men have no battering ram and no machines of war (10.480–81), whereas Caesar as besieger had earlier built a wall that no battering ram or any machine of war could overthrow (6.36–37). Moreover, in the siege itself, Caesar reprises the restless, all-consuming energy we have last seen in the center of the battlefield at Pharsalus: "Here Caesar, maddening the people and goading them to frenzy, goes ranging around the troops, adding fires to spirits already blazing" (7.557–58). Compare his actions at Alexandria where his is energy is so great that he paradoxically assumes the aggressor's role:

> sed adest defensor ubique
> Caesar et hos aditus gladiis, hos ignibus arcet,
> obsessusque gerit, tanta est constantia mentis,
> expugnantis opus.
>
> (10.488–91)
>
> Everywhere is Caesar present
> In defence: he repulses these attacks with sword and these with fire,
> and while blockaded—so great is his firmness of mind—he performs
> the work of a besieger.

Finally, when Caesar breaks out and takes the island of Pharos, he returns to characteristic form: he is "successful always in his use of headlong speed and warfare" (10.507–8), recalling the headlong speed of the Caesarians we have seen at Brundisium, Massilia, and Pharsalus (2.706, 3.391, 7.336, 7.496). He moreover "improves" upon his earlier failure to contain Pompey at Brundisium: then to prevent the republicans from escaping Italy he had blockaded the port, but despite his best efforts Pompey had escaped to the open sea (2.660–736); now without complication "he deprived the enemy of a passage out, and the outlet to the deep" (10.513).

An especially ironic pointer to Caesar's inevitable victory comes in the final thirteen lines of the poem, when it is claimed that "Caesar then was on the point of defeat, but without bloodshed" (*uincendus tum Caesar erat sed sanguine nullo*, 10.541). As readers we know to put little stock in such claims because the last time this was said of Caesar was on the eve of his summative victory over the republicans at Pharsalus: this formula reprises a theme from Pompey's speech to his camp:

> "potuit tibi uulnere nullo
> stare labor belli; potui sine caede subactum
> captiuumque ducem uiolatae tradere paci."

$$(7.92–94)$$

> "The toil of war could have cost
> you no wound; I could have handed over to the peace which he defiled
> their leader, a prisoner, tamed without slaughter."

Lucan's Pompey was here recasting his own overconfident boast in Caesar's account: "We will . . . finish the war with no danger to the legions and practically without a wound" ("*sine periculo legionum et paene sine uulnere bellum conficiemus*," 3.86.4).

The End

As the battle narrative develops a number of counterfactuals, uncertainties, and paths not taken are flagged for the reader. These are not merely a reflection of Lucan grappling with the expression of material that is *nefas* (literally "unspeakable," i.e., "evil")[24] but have the cumulative effect of investing the fixed trajectory of the historical and narrative past with a sense of live contingency. This effort to reopen the closed past and momentarily sideshadow alternate realities should be seen as one aspect of the narrator's multidimensional strategy of resisting the narrative he is telling.[25] We have seen versions of this, for example, in the narrator's incessant obstruction of his own narrative by interjections, apostrophes, and digressions;[26] we have seen it in his praying for alternate outcomes to the events he narrates (4.110–20); and we have seen it in his dictating to his audience how they will react to the poem's events (7.210–14). An interest in alternate outcomes had been foreshadowed for the reader at the outset of book 10:

> pugnauit fortuna ducis fatumque nocentis
> Aegypti, regnum Lagi Romana sub arma
> iret, an eriperet mundo Memphiticus ensis
> uictoris uictique caput.

$$(10.3–6)$$

> the general's fortune and the destiny of guilty Egypt
> fought would Lagus's kingdom be subdued by Roman
> force or would the sword of Memphis remove the head
> of conqueror and conquered from the world?

The question is implicitly answered when the siege of the palace in which Caesar hides ultimately fails: "The fates say no and fortune maintains the function of a wall" (10.485). Lucan more typically keeps this question open throughout the siege and battle narrative: note the narrator's comments "if fate does not ward off their hands from Caesar's blood, their side will win" (10.420–21) and "Caesar's blood might have been shed among the royal cups and his head might have settled on the table" (10.423–24). Caesar seems to symbolize a narrative with an interest in straying from destiny when "with uncertain path he roams and wanders through the halls" (10.460).[27] Caesar's own plans encompass the possibility of his defeat: he keeps Ptolemy nearby "to exact retribution and welcome atonement *should he die*" (10.462), and Ganymede's momentary successes against Caesar are cast as coming close to changing the course of history: "that single day could have passed into glory and the centuries because of Caesar's utmost danger" (10.532–33).

These uncertainties reach their culmination in the final thirteen lines of the poem as it survives (10.534–46), lines that also constitute one extremity of the narrator's opposition to Caesar.[28] All bodes ill for Caesar. He is close packed and surrounded by enemies on all sides in a poem that thematizes death in densely packed crowds: we have seen it in Pompey's forces at Pharsalus (7.492–95), in Curio's forces in Africa (4.777–83), and in Sulla's victims (2.203–4). Caesar's emotions are brought before the reader; hope typically describes his state of mind throughout the poem,[29] but here we see dread (10.536), confusion (10.542), and doubt wavering between fear and the wish to die (10.542–43). We are flatly told there is no escape: "no path of safety is there, no flight, no heroism; hardly can he even hope for honorable death" (10.538–39). Caesar's final act in the poem is an enigma. He "looks back" in desperation to Scaeva in the closely packed ranks (10.543–46). Had Scaeva not died in book 6 (cf. 6.250–62)? Does Caesar literally look back (*OLD respicio* 1a), and must we make one final revision of an event that seemed closed so far back in the poem? Or is the verb used figuratively (*OLD* 3a "to look round for someone one needs," *OLD* 5 "to look back on past events")? Is Caesar looking for a soldier or looking for inspiration on how to fight his way out of a desperate situation? In the poem's final lines, Scaeva is described as blockading Magnus by himself, returning us to the poem's supreme illustration of the power of "the one" versus "the many" in a context where the many have the upper hand.[30] At line 10.546 the poem breaks off, literally giving Pompey the last word (*Magnum*). A civil war had carried off its author,[31] but Lucan has already told us that "the frenzy did not disappear once the author of the madness was removed" (10.529–30). The poem may stop, but the war rages on.

Notes

1. Plut. *Alex.* 15.4–5, Arr. *Anab.* 1.11.7–8; see Bosworth 1988, 38–39. On Lucan's scene see, e.g., Tesoriero 2005; Zwierlein 2010, 418–19.

2. Tesoriero 2005, 212. On the prayer see, e.g., Feeney 1991, 294; Zwierlein 2010, 423–30.

3. On Alexander in Lucan, see Celotto 2018 with refs at 325n2; especially influential are Morford 1967, 13–19; Ahl 1976, 222–30.

4. Plut. *Alex.* 15.4–5; cf. Cic. *Arch.* 24: the story was very well-known and lies behind Lucan's apostrophe to Caesar at 9.980–86.

5. Suet. *Aug.* 18.1, Cass. Dio 51.16.5.

6. Cf. Henderson 1987, 129.

7. It is in contrast to Pompey that Caesar is formally introduced to the reader as having "not *only* a general's name and reputation" (1.143–44).

8. On Alexander's consultation of the same oracle, see Curt. 4.7.22–28, Plut. *Alex.* 27.3–6, Diod. Sic. 17.51.1–4, Arr. *Anab.* 3.3; see Bosworth 1988, 71–74.

9. Curt. 9.2.10–3.19, Arr. *Anab.* 5.25–28; see Bosworth 1988, 132–33.

10. See Leigh 2000, 100; cf. Maes 2009.

11. On this concept, see Roller 2018; Langlands 2018.

12. A notion that resonates with the fate of Caesar's opponent Pompey, whose dismembered remains are buried on the shore of Alexandria; the narrator wishes he personally could return them to Rome for veneration at 8.842–50.

13. On Lucan's Cleopatra, see Zwierlein 1974; Turner 2010; Tracy 2014, 53–56, 123–26.

14. On the banquet as a subject for moralizing, see Edwards 1993, 186–88, 199–204. For moralizing historiography and the outbreak of the civil war, see Roche 2009, 38–39.

15. See Bonner 1966, 271–22; Coffey 1996, 89–92.

16. On Acoreus, see D'Alessandro Behr 2007; Walde 2007; Barrenechea 2010; Tracy 2014: 144–224.

17. Perkell 1999.

18. On Acoreus and Lucan's narrator, see Tracy 2011: 35–38. On Acoreus in Lucan more generally, see Day 2013, 162–64.

19. See Masters 1992, esp. 1–10.

20. On the siege of the palace and the eruption of battle at Alexandria, see Day 2013, 159–64; Tracy 2014, 227–37.

21. See Cowan (chapter 15) in this volume.

22. Cf., e.g., 7.144–50. On Etna as an assault on cosmic order, see Hardie 1986, esp. 263–67; Williams 2017, 33–44. On Lucan, Caesar, and gigantomachy, see Feeney 1991, 296–97; Roche 2019, 104–5.

23. See Zissos in this volume.

24. Cf. Allendorf 2013 on the poetics of uncertainty, disorientation, and obfuscation in Seneca's tragedies.

25. On sideshadowing, see Bernstein 1994; for its use in Latin poetry, see Pagan 2002, 54–57; Cowan 2010, 2018.

26. See, e.g., Masters 1992, 5–6, 87–90; D'Alessandro Behr 2007, 1–15.

27. See Dinter in this volume on narrative open-endedness thematized by the adjective *incertus* ("uncertain").

28. On the poem's final lines, see Day 2013, 159–60.

29. Roche 2019, 20.

30. Hardie 1993, 3–10.

31. Cf. Henderson 1987, 122.

11

Charging the Canon

Lucan and Vergil

Robert Cowan

Epic poetry is obsessed with its own tradition and especially with its great predecessors in that tradition. Homer's *Iliad* and *Odyssey* loom large over the whole of Greek and Latin epic, not least over Vergil's *Aeneid*, which constituted an ambitious attempt to combine and surpass those Greek classic poems so as to create a Roman epic that would have the same cultural and political centrality. Vergil succeeded. Even before its publication after Vergil's death in 17 B.C.E., the elegist Propertius wrote that "something greater than the *Iliad* is being born" (Prop. 2.34.66). His contemporaries and successors immediately and unceasingly imitated, alluded to, parodied, and in every imaginable way reacted to what was now the canonical Roman epic, and even the canonical Roman poem.[1] Its centrality in Roman culture (including the Roman system of education) meant that any allusion to any part of it would be recognized and interpreted by the educated readers of later poems. As such, it stands as a relatively "safe" text on which to build intertextual interpretations, since the inevitable question "but would a reader recognize that as an allusion?" can be confidently answered "yes, because every educated Roman knew the *Aeneid* virtually by heart." However, as well as a central cultural artifact, it was also an intensely political poem, inextricably bound up with the question of what it was to be Roman, and especially with the answers to that question offered by the pre-eminence of the emperor Augustus. Engagements with the *Aeneid* thus tend to be themselves political, whether they endorse or challenge its triumphalist message or even propose through imitation that the *Aeneid* is itself subversive. No intertextual engagement with the *Aeneid* was more overtly political than Lucan's.[2]

Intertextuality and allusion are among the most important tools for the interpretation of classical texts.[3] The slightly smug, elitist practice of including obscure allusions to earlier poetry in one's own poetry so that discerning readers could spot them is undeniably part of the game being played in a literary culture in which both poets and readers were expected to be "learned" (*doctus*). However, it is the way in which intertextuality generates meaning that is its most interesting and most important function. Inevitably, meaning is generated at the point of reception, and the potential for different readers to respond differently to different texts increases exponentially when they are responding to two or more texts and deciding whether the relationship between them is comparative, contrastive, or something more complex still. Nevertheless, without appealing to the old-fashioned notion of authorial intention, it is still possible to observe strategies in the text that guide the reader in a particular interpretive direction, even if she retains the option of going her own way.

Allusions affect the reader's interpretation of the text that is alluding (the "target text"), and we read Lucan's Pompey differently because we make associations with Vergil's Aeneas. They can also change the reader's response to the text being alluded to (the "source text"), with the target text acting as a sort of creative commentary, so that we read Aeneas differently because of his similarities to Pompey. Allusions can draw parallels or contrasts and can challenge the reader to assess which relationship is more appropriate in a particular case. It can pervert, debase, and even parody, as Lucan often does to Vergil, but this raises the further question as to whether he is constructing an unimpeachably noble *Aeneid* to which the *Civil War* stands in grotesque contrast or whether he is subverting and undermining the *Aeneid* itself. This chapter will try to indicate some of the different ways in which a number of Lucan's allusions to the *Aeneid* can be interpreted. However, it by no means exhausts the possible interpretations and neither does it rule out the possibility that more than one can, however inconsistently, be in play at once. Finally, intertextuality can operate on various levels of magnitude, from a tiny two-word phrase, through larger episodes, through the on-going depiction of individual characters, to the relationship between two epics taken as a whole. This chapter will start at the smallest level and pan out, offering examples of different types of allusion that will enable readers to approach others throughout the poem.

The Devil in the Detail: Small-Scale Allusions

Some allusions seem, on the surface at least, to set up a relatively simple relationship between the "source text" and the "target text." The situation and its implications are similar in both texts, and the allusion serves to consolidate that sense of similarity, possibly adding by association some details that are explicit in the source text but not in the target text. This is not to say that such allusions have to be read this simply, and there is always the potential for the reader to complicate their implications, perhaps emphasizing some details rather than others or interpreting the relationship as contrastive rather than parallel. In book 5, Caesar is rushing (as always) from putting down his troops' mutiny at Placentia in northern Italy to the port of Brundisium in the south, from where he can sail to Epirus in pursuit of Pompey. However, he is disappointed when he arrives:

> curuique tenens Minoia tecta
> Brundisii clausas uentis brumalibus undas
> inuenit et pauidas hiberno sidere classes.
> turpe duci uisum rapiendi tempora belli
> in segnes exisse moras, portuque teneri
> dum pateat tutum uel non felicibus aequor.
>
> (5.406–11)

> Reaching the Minoan homes of curving
> Brundisium, he finds the waves hemmed in by winter winds
> and his fleets afraid of wintry constellation.
> To the leader it seemed disgraceful that the moment for hastening war
> had extended into slow delays, disgraceful to be kept in harbour
> while the sea is safely open to others, even the unlucky.

The whole passage is utterly characteristic of Lucan's depiction of Caesar, with his insistence on rapid and constant movement, his impatience of any delay, his perverted idea of what constitutes disgrace, and his arrogant confidence in his superiority even to the forces of nature.[4] This picture is further reinforced by an allusion to book 4 of the *Aeneid*. When the narrator, focalizing through Caesar so that the reader sees and interprets the situation through the character's eyes, describes the "fleets afraid of wintry constellation" (*pauidas hiberno sidere classes*, 5.408), there is a strong verbal echo of Dido's words to Aeneas when she discovers that he is abandoning her and sailing away from Carthage: "What? Are you hurrying to build a fleet even under a wintry constellation (*hiberno moliri sidere classem*) and to go through the deep in the midst of the North Winds, cruel man?" (*Aen.* 4.309–11).

On one level, the situations are rather different: a distraught woman desperate to understand why her lover is abandoning her even when the conditions for departure are unfavorable and a group of experienced sailors justifiably trepidatious about embarking outside the sailing season. Nevertheless, both are fundamentally about attempts to restrain an epic hero from continuing what he considers his fated mission, regardless of the human or natural obstacles in his way. Dido and the ships' captains are mere mortals, swayed by the everyday considerations of rough seas and destructive storms and standing in the way of Aeneas and Caesar, who are above such things. On this level, the parallel is clear, but the relationship between Aeneas and Caesar remains negotiable. Pious Aeneas leaves Carthage to fulfill his manifest destiny, a mission assigned by Jupiter and Fate and communicated by ghosts, oracles, dreams, prophecies, and even the direct epiphany of the gods. Caesar's mission is an impious one of unspeakable crime and transgression, to achieve tyranny by means of civil war. The allusion could be taken as contrastive, a grim parody, even suggesting that Caesar himself is under the delusion of being another Aeneas, though he is in many ways his opposite. Alternatively, the parallel between the two characters could be all too close. The allusion may suggest an altogether darker reading of the *Aeneid*, where the will to power that leads Aeneas to destroy so many lives to establish the Roman people is indistinguishable from Caesar's drive to establish the principate. Even the smallest and apparently simplest of allusions can have wide-reaching implications for how we read both poems and the relationship between them.

Allusions to Vergil can also be ironic, almost suggesting that characters have either misread or failed to listen to the warnings of the earlier text. After his flight from the defeat at Pharsalus, Pompey holds a council of senators at Syhedra in Cilicia to discuss what to do next (8.202–455).[5] Pompey himself proposes that they go to Parthia because he has faith in neither the Numidian king, Juba, nor the Egyptian king, Ptolemy XIII, saying of the latter, "I do not trust the youth of the tyrant of the Nile, because loyalty in adversity requires mature years" (8.281–82). He is opposed at considerable length by Lentulus, who attacks his suggestion of an alliance with the Parthians and insists on the wisdom of going instead to Egypt:

> "sceptra puer Ptolemaeus habet tibi debita, Magne,
> tutelae commissa tuae. quis nominis umbram
> horreat? innocua est aetas. ne iura fidemque
> respectumque deum ueteri speraueris aula;
> nil pudet assuetos sceptris: mitissima sors est
> regnorum sub rege nouo."
>
> (8.448–53)

"The sceptre which boy Ptolemy holds he owes to you;
it was entrusted to your guardianship. Who would shudder at

the shadow of a name? His age is innocent. Justice, loyalty,
regard for the gods—do not look for these in an aged court;
nothing shames men grown accustomed to the sceptre: mildest is the lot
of realms beneath a new king."

Lentulus's argument wins the day and Pompey sails to Egypt, where the agents
of the young Ptolemy treacherously murder and decapitate him. Every reader
of the speech would have known the disastrous consequences of its acceptance
and appreciated numerous ironies throughout.

Among these is Lentulus's insistence that, contrary to Pompey's assertion
that only the mature display "loyalty in adversity" (*aduersa . . . fides*), in fact, it
is the young who are more likely to be trustworthy and that the old do not show
"justice [and] loyalty" (*iura fidemque*).[6] Although these two concepts might seem
to go naturally together, the phrase itself is found only once before in Latin, in
the same metrical position, and in a highly significant context. During Aeneas's
narration of the sack of Troy in *Aeneid* 2, the elderly Trojan king Priam rebukes
the young Greek warrior Pyrrhus for his impious behavior, contrasting the
respectful treatment that Pyrrhus's father, Achilles, had offered him when he
was ransoming his son Hector's body: "he showed blushing respect for the
rights and trust (*iura fidemque*) due to a suppliant" (2.541–42). Pyrrhus mocks
Priam's invocation of Achilles and ruthlessly kills the old man at the altar of
Jupiter.

Even read solely on their own terms, the Vergilian passage reveals the weak-
ness of Lentulus's argument, as *iura fidesque* are shown to be the preserve of
the elderly and mature, like Priam and Achilles, not the young, like Pyrrhus.
However, the allusion takes on much greater resonance because Vergil's depiction of the death of Priam itself alluded to the historical death of Pompey.[7] Lucan
creatively indicates that he recognized this allusion by in turn alluding to Priam
in *his* depiction of Pompey, most strikingly when the possessed *matrona*
cries "him I recognize, lying on the river sands, an unsightly headless corpse"
(1.685–86).[8] Lentulus is assigning justice and loyalty not only to the wrong age
group but more specifically to the wrong person, since Ptolemy is both the historical inspiration and the Lucanian imitation of Vergil's Pyrrhus. Even Vergil's use of Pyrrhus's alternative name, Neoptolemus, signals his status as "the
new Ptolemy" (Greek *neos Ptolemaios*).[9] By referring to the Egyptian king as
"the boy Ptolemy" (*puer Ptolemaeus*)[10] and the "new king" (*rege nouo*), Lucan—
through the mouth of the unwitting Lentulus—signals his status as the new
Neoptolemus.

Sometimes Lucan alludes to two or more passages of Vergil simultaneously,
a technique called "combinatorial allusion."[11] By doing this, Lucan enriches the

implications of the scene he is narrating by evoking its parallels with multiple Vergilian scenes, complicating the "target text" through its relationship with different parts of the "source text." At the same time, the act of creative imitation serves as a commentary on the "source text," suggesting a connection between the two, seemingly disparate passages alluded to. Among the portents and prodigies that attend the beginning of the civil war, signaling divine displeasure and a general disturbance in the force, is the appearance of an Erinys, or Fury:

> ingens urbem cingebat Erinys
> excutiens pronam flagranti uertice pinum
> stridentisque comas, Thebanam qualis Agauen
> impulit aut saeui contorsit tela Lycurgi
> Eumenis, aut qualem iussu Iunonis iniquae
> horruit Alcides uiso iam Dite Megaeran.
>
> (1.572–77)
>
> a huge Erinys was circling Rome,
> shaking hissing locks and a pine-tree with its blazing
> top turned downwards—like the Eumenis who drove
> Agave of Thebes and hurled the weapons
> of fierce Lycurgus; like Megaera, who on resentful Juno's order
> caused Alcides to shudder, though he already had seen Dis.

The choice of mythological figures in the simile is not arbitrary. Agave, Lycurgus, and Hercules all killed members of their family while driven mad by divine influence.[12] Kin killing is a key metaphor, in Lucan and elsewhere, for the killing of brother-citizens in civil war, and the narrator frequently describes the impulse to civil war as madness.[13] The Erinys here doubles as an external force driving Rome to fratricidal frenzy and as a metaphorical personification of that frenzy.

However, the detail that Megaera, the Fury driving Hercules, is acting on the commands "of resentful Juno" (*Iunonis iniquae*) forges a connection with two passages of the *Aeneid* where that same phrase is used in the same metrical position at the end of the line.[14] In the first, Venus reminds Cupid what Aeneas has suffered "because of the hatred of resentful Juno" (*odiis Iunonis iniquae*, Aen. 1.668).[15] In the second, a hymn to Hercules performed by Evander's Arcadians at the future site of Rome refers to the labors he had to complete "because of the fate imposed by resentful Juno" (*fatis Iunonis iniquae*, Aen. 8.292). The *Aeneid*'s internal verbal echo reinforces the connection between Aeneas and Hercules as persecuted but resilient heroes.[16] Lucan's combinatorial allusion, positioned within a simile about Hercules whose tenor is about Rome, signals that he too has recognized Vergil's association of the founder of the Roman people and the Greek hero. However, with a characteristically dark twist, he perverts the Vergilian parallel he has just identified. In Lucan, divine hostility does not lead to the Stoic endurance of *pius Aeneas* and of the laboring Hercules but to the frenzied kin killing of 49 B.C.E. Romans and of *Hercules furens*.

A similar technique is employed when Lucan alludes to a passage of Vergil alongside one or more passages from other poets. Sometimes the Vergilian passage is itself alluding to the earlier passage, a so-called window allusion, and thus Lucan is not only alluding to the two passages but also to the very act of allusion.[17] Sometimes the "source texts" have a more equal status, being treated as independent passages to each of which Lucan alludes without regard to any relationship between them. The distinction between these categories, as ever with intertextuality, is both blurred and subject to individual readers' generation of meaning at the point of reception.

In book 10, Lucan alludes to a marked phrase that occurs in Lucretius, Vergil, and Ovid. Whether he is alluding to each of these independently, or to Ovid's allusion to Vergil and Vergil's to Lucretius, is a matter for the reader to decide. The description of Cleopatra's banqueting hall, itself strongly alluding to that of Vergil's Dido, concludes with the eunuchs in attendance:[18]

> nec non infelix ferro mollita iuuentus
> atque execta uirum: stat contra fortior aetas
> uix ulla fuscante tamen lanugine malas.
>
> (10.133–35)

and there were boys unfortunate, enfeebled by the sword, castrated of their manhood: opposite there stands a stronger age-group, yet with hardly any down darkening their cheeks.

The phrase referring to the down on their cheeks (*lanugine malas*), placed emphatically at the end not only of the line, but of the whole verse paragraph, also occurs in three earlier texts, all by poets to whom Lucan regularly alludes.

In *Aeneid* 10, Vergil describes the narrow escape from Aeneas of a Latin warrior, Cydon, who is in love with the beautiful youth, Clytius, "his cheeks growing blonde with their first down" (*flauentem prima lanugine malas*, 10.324).[19] The status of the Egyptian eunuchs as passive objects of homoerotic desire and indeed penetration, always implicit when beautiful, ephebic cup-bearers are mentioned, is emphatically signaled by the connection with the *eromenos* Clytius. Yet where Vergil's beautiful youths, such as Euryalus, Lausus, and even

Turnus, often combine sexual desirability (considered effeminate) with military valor (unambiguously masculine), Lucan's youths have had their manhood (literally "man," *uirum*) excised, their encounter with the sword was enfeebling castration rather than empowering warfare, and even the ostensibly "stronger" (*fortior*) age group lack the physical markers of that strength.

If the allusion to Vergil emphasizes the erotic associations of the eunuchs, those to Ovid and Lucretius focus on their unnatural and monstrous quality, a central motif in Lucan's depiction of Cleopatra's court. Ovid uses the phrase when describing the miraculous rejuvenation of Iolaus, Hercules's elderly squire, who was "virtually a boy and shades his cheeks with doubtful down" (*paene puer dubiaque tegens lanugine malas*, Ov. *Met.* 9.398). Lucan's eunuchs are a grotesque parody of the rejuvenated Iolaus. The act of rejuvenation is already controversial in the *Metamorphoses*, and Ovid stages a divine squabble about which favorites should be allowed a second youth (*Met.* 9.400–441). Yet it still constitutes a positive marvel, as Iolaus, at Fate's command (*Met.* 9.430–31), truly regains his youth and, though Ovid does not mention this detail, traditionally did so in order to fight in defense of Hercules's children against Eurystheus. Lucan's eunuchs, in contrast, are disfigured not by Fate but by cruel slave owners, destined not for war but for sexual exploitation, not truly rejuvenated but reduced to a paradoxical situation in which their youthful faces belie their ageing bodies.

This paradox is further emphasized by the allusion to Lucretius. Lucretius's use of the phrase is part of his logical proof that centaurs could not possibly exist because the horse part would be declining into old age just when, for the human part, "youth is dressing its cheeks in soft down" (*molli uestit lanugine malas*, DRN 5.889). Lucan's evocation of Lucretius's centaur, an impossible hybrid, adds to his depiction of the eunuchs as monstrous and unnatural beings. More specifically, their unnaturalness is manifested by their embodying the very paradox that Lucretius used to disprove centaurs' existence, the combination of adolescent downy cheeks with a mature body.[20] Thus, Lucan's seemingly throw-away reference to downy cheeks uses Vergil, Ovid, and Lucretius to suggest sexual exploitation and monstrosity, evoking the contexts of the multiple source texts but also parodying and perverting them, pointing to the grim contrasts as much as the parallels.

Scene Before: Allusive Episodes

Panning out from Lucan's micro-allusions to individual Vergilian phrases, the reader can also see whole scenes and episodes that echo scenes and episodes from the *Aeneid*. This repetition and remodeling of earlier scenes is very much a characteristic feature of epic's obsession with its own tradition. Many scenes in the *Aeneid* itself—shipwreck on a seductress' shore, funeral games, a descent to the underworld, pursuit of and duel with an antagonist—are clearly designed to recall and surpass scenes in Homer's *Iliad* and *Odyssey*. Vergil's aggressive emulation of Homer runs parallel with Aeneas's emulation of Achilles and Odysseus and with his transformation from a Trojan victim to a proto-Roman victor, inflicting the defeats he and his people had suffered in the *Iliad*. Lucan's reworking of Vergilian scenes—some of them already reworkings of Homer— also combines poetics and politics. Lucan takes on Rome's national epic but also perverts, debases, and even parodies its political meaning.

Although a number of scenes in the *Civil War* can be seen as more distant imitations of those in the *Aeneid*—such as the centurion Scaeva's single-handed battle as a sort of epic *aristeia*—Lucan generally avoids jarringly anachronistic episodes. Vergil's Aeneas inhabited the same mythological universe as Homer's Achilles and Odysseus, so there is no awkwardness in having him receive a divinely crafted shield or encounter a cyclops. Fantastical scenes are not unthinkable in historical epic, and a generation later, Silius Italicus's *Punica*, set in the third century B.C.E., would depict Scipio fighting a river like Achilles (Sil. 4.570–703). By contrast, Lucan limits his closest imitations of Vergilian scenes to those away from the battlefield and especially those politically charged episodes that connect the poem's action to the past and the future. The prophecy of Vergil's Sibyl at the start of *Aeneid* 6 is imitated three times in three contrasting ways.[21] The possessed *matrona* who closes *Civil War* 1 has a vision of bloody war very similar to the Sibyl's. But where the latter urges perseverance ("don't give in to misfortunes," *Aen.* 6.95) and offers hope of a road to salvation (6.96), the *matrona*'s vision is of an unending, repetitive cycle of civil war ("The factions rise again, again I travel through all the world. Let me gaze on different sea-shores, different land: already have I seen Philippi," 1.692–94). Phemonoe, priestess of Apollo at Delphi, is a more obvious equivalent of his priestess at Cumae, but her first prophecy to Appius is a sham and then, when the god genuinely and brutally possesses her, he also prevents her from giving more than the most truncated form of the truth. The narrator, rather than the prophetess, predicts the death of Pompey and Brutus's assassination of Caesar. The third version of the Sibyl is the most grotesque parody of all, the Thessalian witch Erictho, whose combination of power and evil makes her very much at home in the world of the *Civil War*. However, Erictho does not prophesy anything herself but rather resuscitates the corpse of a soldier to perform a necromancy. This scene is a bitter response to the parade of heroes that Vergil's Aeneas witnesses in the underworld, with a running commentary by his dead father, Anchises. The civil war between Pompey and Caesar is mentioned in Vergil's parade, but the overwhelming emphasis is on the greatness of Rome's future (from Aeneas's perspective), climaxing in the world empire of Augustus. Lucan's corpse tells of civil war among the Roman dead and the rejoicing of the populist villains from Rome's history. Both the message and the medium are grim perversions of Vergil's parade of heroes.

Book 8 of the *Aeneid* is central to the poem's vision of Rome, stretching back into the even earlier mythical past and forward to the Augustan present. Even before the more explicit depictions of Aeneas's future and Vergil's past on the shield made by Vulcan (itself a retooling of the Homeric shield of Achilles), Aeneas's visit to Pallanteum, the kingdom of Evander, includes two episodes heavy with political significance: his tour of the future site of Rome and Evander's narration of the myth of Hercules and Cacus. The *Civil War* includes imitations of both these episodes and, as might be expected, they are debased and distorted imitations. Aeneas's tour of the landscape that will eventually become Rome is full of none-too-subtle foreshadowings, as each part of the undeveloped countryside can easily be recognized (by the Augustan reader) as the site of a major landmark in the contemporary city: the hill that will be the Capitoline is bristling with thickets (*dumeta*) and the future Forum is a paddock grazed by cattle. These adumbrations of the eternal city resonate with the *Aeneid*'s themes of Rome's predestined, teleological rise from the humblest origins to its current status as the most powerful city in the world.

In *Civil War* 9, Caesar visits not the site of the future Rome but that of the past Troy:[22]

> iam siluae steriles et putres robore trunci
> Assaraci pressere domos et templa deorum
> iam lassa radice tenent, ac tota teguntur
> Pergama dumetis: etiam periere ruinae.
> (9.966–69)

> Now barren woods and trunks with rotting timber
> have submerged Assaracus's houses and, with roots now weary,
> occupy the temples of the gods, and all of Pergamum
> is veiled by thickets: even the ruins have perished.[23]

Here is the same wild landscape occupying the same space as a civilized cityscape, but the temporal trajectory is reversed. Instead of the promise of future greatness, there is the result of decline and decay, the descent from Troy in its pomp to the ruins of ruins. The mighty river Xanthus is reduced to a trickle in the dust, Hector's tomb lies concealed in long grass, and the altar where Priam died is only scattered rocks (9.974–79). The sightseeing of *Aeneid* 8 is shifted from the site of Rome to *Aeneid* 2's landscape of Trojan destruction, in keeping with the *Civil War*'s reversal of Vergil's teleology, heading toward dissolution rather than foundation. Yet alongside this serious, if bleak, message there is a mocking sense that Caesar's sightseeing does not have the almost numinous significance of Aeneas's but is rather an empty, meaningless act of tourism. He is shown round not by an important figure of Rome's prehistory like Evander but by a professional tour guide (*monstrator*, 9.979). His failure to notice the Xanthus or Hector's tomb is a sign not only of how far they have fallen but of how little they mean to Caesar. Once again, the form of the Vergilian scene as well as its content is perverted and debased.

The other episode in *Aeneid* 8 that links mythical past, narrative present, and Augustan future is the story of Hercules and Cacus. Evander offers an etiology or origin story for a festival of Hercules, narrating how the hero, returning from Spain with the cattle of Geryon, killed the fire-breathing monster Cacus, who had stolen two of the cattle and incidentally terrorized the local countryside. Although the episode has prompted conflicting interpretations emphasizing the brutality and self-interest of Hercules, and his disturbing similarity to Cacus, the surface meaning of the story is an almost allegorical triumph of hero over monster, civilization over barbarism, and order over chaos, as well as a model of the colonizer mastering hostile territory.[24] As such it offers an exemplary model for Aeneas to emulate in his conflict with Turnus and the other "native" Italians. However, because it stands as an exemplary mythical narrative within the larger exemplary mythical narrative that is the *Aeneid* itself, it also dramatizes the way in which such narratives can be read. The reader is invited to interpret Aeneas in the same (or a different) way as Aeneas interprets Hercules, as a positive (or negative) model for Augustus.

Lucan's imitation of this myth narrates how Hercules defeated the giant Antaeus in a wrestling match by denying him the strength that he derived from contact with his mother, the Earth.[25] Just as with the tour of Pallanteum, the myth is narrated not by a figure as significant as Evander but by a nameless, uneducated local (*rudis incola*, 4.592). The audience is no Aeneas, and not even a Caesar, but the corrupt and inept Caesarian tribune, Curio, in Libya to fight the Pompeian forces there. However, unlike Caesar's tour of Troy, the myth itself is not an obvious or overt debasement of Hercules and Cacus but can be read relatively "straight" as a similar victory of order over chaos, with the colonizing element even more prominent because of Antaeus's closer association with the very land of Libya. In fact, it could be argued that it is the very "straightness" of the myth that emphasizes how poorly such myths fit into the world of the *Civil War*. Curio, as an internal audience, reads the victory of Hercules and of subsequent "heroes" like Scipio as signs that he, too, will conquer the land of Libya and its inhabitants, but this is a misreading:

> Curio laetatus, tamquam fortuna locorum
> bella gerat seruetque ducum sibi fata priorum,
> felici non fausta loco tentoria ponens
> inclusit castris et collibus abstulit omen
> sollicitatque feros non aequis uiribus hostis.
>
> (4.661–65)

> Curio was delighted, as if the fortune of the place would wage
> his wars and maintain for him the destiny of former leaders,
> and pitching his unlucky tents on lucky ground
> he spread wide his camp and robbed the hills of their good omen
> and with unequal strength provokes a fierce enemy.

Curio's army is destroyed by the forces of King Juba, and he himself is killed. However, it is not simply that there is a mismatch between the hero's victory in the glorious myth and the contemporary hero's defeat in the inglorious narrative. Curio is the object of an extended obituary that extols his glorious potential but condemns his corruption as the man who "sold Rome" (4.799–824, quoting the book's final words). He is no Hercules or Aeneas or Augustus, or if he is, then the reader must reassess her valuation of those figures. More complicatedly still, the forces of Juba are those of Pompey and the senate so that the better side (from the narrator's partisan perspective) is aligned with Antaeus and with the ghosts of Rome's archetypal enemy, Hannibal and the Carthaginians (4.788–93). In the world of civil war and of the *Civil War*, where all relationships and distinctions are confused and confounded, Lucan challenges not just the interpretation of inset myths and framing narratives but the very ability of such myths and narratives to offer any meaning at all.

Playing Aeneas: Intertextual Characters

Various characters in the *Civil War* echo characters—or certain facets of characters—in the *Aeneid*. Sometimes a Lucanian figure is a complex and jarring combination of more than one Vergilian antecedent. As Pompey is sailing away from Italy for what proves to be the last time, he sees the ghost of his dead wife Julia in a dream (3.8–35).[26] The visitation by a dead wife as the hero is leaving his homeland inevitably recalls Aeneas's first wife, Creusa. Lost in the flight from Troy, she appears to him as a ghost to offer comfort, a prophecy of his future prosperity, and instructions to move on from her and remarry in Italy (Verg. *Aen.* 2.771–94, esp. 783–84: "There you will gain success, a kingdom, and a royal bride; drive away your tears for your darling Creusa"). Julia's message to Pompey is the precise opposite, reproaching him for his unfaithfulness, condemning his remarriage to Cornelia, predicting his defeat and death, and staking her exclusive and eternal claim to him: "Never, Magnus, by the ghosts and by my shade, will you stop being [Caesar's] son-in-law; in vain you sever with the sword your pledges: civil war will make you mine" (3.31–34). Her speech not only serves as an inversion of Creusa's but also aligns her with another woman Aeneas left behind, the bitter and vengeful Dido ("Go, pursue Italy with the winds, seek your kingdom across the waves. As for me, I hope, if dutiful gods have any power, you will drink down your punishment on the rocks and often call on Dido by name," *Aen.* 4.381–83). As ever, the connection between the two texts affects how the reader responds to each of them. The depiction of Pompey as a failed or inverted Aeneas is compounded by the way his supportive Creusa morphs into an implacable Dido. But Lucan also invites us to read *Aeneid* 2 and 4 in a different light, forging connections between the two very different women Aeneas leaves behind to pursue his Italian destiny and his Italian bride, perhaps making us wonder whether Creusa's farewell, for which we only have Aeneas's own testimony, was really as affirmatory as he claimed.[27]

Sometimes different facets of a single Vergilian figure are distributed among a number of Lucan's characters. We have seen how the abandoned Dido's bitterness is manifested in Julia's ghost. Yet in Cornelia, Pompey's current wife, Lucan evokes the passionate, clinging Dido who begs Aeneas not to leave but whose love has not yet turned to hatred. This very different Dido lies behind the scene where Pompey sends Cornelia to Lesbos for her own safety (5.722–815) and especially her last plea to accompany him to the Egyptian shore: "Where are you going without me, cruel man? Am I deserted a second time, kept away from Thessaly's disaster?" (8.584–85). Yet another Dido is embodied in the *femme fatale* Cleopatra of book 10, whose luxurious banquet for Caesar offers a subtle commentary on Dido's for Aeneas in *Aeneid* 1. As when Lucan's Pompey recalls Vergil's Priam recalling the historical Pompey, so his Cleopatra evokes the Cleopatra—if not the historical one, at least that of Augustan propaganda—behind Vergil's Dido. The multifaceted complexity of Dido is revealed by Lucan's distributed allusion, but in turn his own female characters gain depth and nuance from their relationship with the infinite variety of Vergil's Carthaginian queen.[28]

Unsurprisingly, it is Aeneas who is embodied most often and with the greatest complexity in multiple Lucanian avatars. Some of these are relatively minor characters who appear center stage only once, such as Appius at Delphi,

Curio in Libya, or Sextus Pompeius consulting the witch Erictho. It is arguably more helpful to approach these through the lens of each episode's intertextual relationship to a Vergilian episode featuring Aeneas rather than
focusing on them as allusions to the character of Aeneas himself, but the connection between Aeneas and his momentary avatar always remains relevant.
However, it is the different ways in which the *Civil War*'s three main protagonists, Pompey, Cato, and Caesar, echo and contrast with Aeneas that are most
significant.

Cato embodies the *pietas* of Aeneas, his devotion to his duty to the gods
and his country and willingness to endure immense suffering and labors to
serve them. Aeneas subordinates his nostalgia for Troy, his love for Dido, and
feelings of despair and exhaustion all to the will of Fate, most poignantly when
he tells the uncomprehending Dido "against my will, I follow Italy" (*Italiam non
sponte sequor, Aen.* 4.361). When he is mentally devastated by the Trojan women's
burning of the ships, the old Trojan Nautes comforts him with the injunction
"let us follow where the Fates lead and lead us back again" (*quo fata trahunt retra-
huntque sequamur, Aen.* 5.709). Similarly, the more explicitly Stoic Cato, equally
unable to grasp the large plan of providence, tells Brutus that "where the Fates
lead, confident will Virtue follow" (*quo fata trahunt uirtus secura sequetur,* 2.287).
Yet where Aeneas was faced with the agonizing but comprehensible conflict
between personal emotion (love or despair) and public duty, Cato's unflinch-
ingly virtuous following of Fate paradoxically risks tainting him with the guilt
of civil war. As he says in the same speech to Brutus, "civil warfare is the greatest crime" (2.286) and "to make guilty even me will be the gods' reproach"
(2.288). In the perverted universe of the *Civil War*, Fate is either a fiction mask-
ing anarchic randomness or, as a sort of Stoic nightmare, a malign, nonprovi-
dential Destiny driving Rome through the horror of civil war to the even worse
horror of tyranny. Can values such as *uirtus* and *pietas* operate in such a meaningless or malignant universe, and what can a good man do? Cato's predica-
ment shows how hard it is to be Aeneas when you are not in the *Aeneid*, but it
may also raise questions about whether Vergil's hero, his destiny, and his devotion to duty—a devotion that killed Dido, Turnus, and many others—are themselves untainted. Likewise when Cato leads his men on their march across the
Libyan desert—"hard is the path" (*durum iter,* 9.385) just like that which *pietas*
overcame bringing Aeneas to his father in the underworld (*Aen.* 6.688)—his
austere endurance and the terrible encounters with thirst and snakes can be
read as translating Aeneas's enduring labors across the Mediterranean into an
alien world or as bitterly parodying them, or even as diminishing the grandeur
of the Vergilian original. The effect of intertextuality on the reader can be
guided, but it can never be controlled.

Pompey is a failed or even anti-Aeneas, one who never moves on from the despair and aimlessness shown by Vergil's hero at the sack of Troy and whose physical and political journey is an inversion of Aeneas,' moving further and further away from the city of Rome and from the power it symbolizes.[29] As Pompey sails out of the port of Brundisium, leaving Italy for the last time, the narrator apostrophizes him: "You go, driven out with wife and sons and taking all your household-gods to war, accompanied by nations, an exile but still great" (2.728–30). The reader inevitably recalls Aeneas sailing away from the ashes of Troy, "carried onto the deep as an exile, with comrades, son, household-gods and great gods" (*Aen.* 3.11–12). The similarities and the differences are equally significant. Pompey is in a very similar situation to Aeneas, leaving his ruined homeland as an exile. However, the departure from Troy is the start of Aeneas's journey westward toward the destined goal, the *telos*, of Italy and the future glory that will be Rome. Pompey is sailing away from Italy, from Rome, and from glory, toward the east, toward defeat, failure, and death. Likewise, at the start of the next book, Pompey is the only one looking back toward Italy, significantly called *terra Hesperia*, the mysterious "land of the West" often used in Vergilian prophecies and other references to Italy.[30] In this he is just like Aeneas at the start of *Aeneid* 5, except that Aeneas is looking back at Carthage, the land he loved but knew he had to abandon to pursue his destiny in Italy. For Pompey, Italy is the land he loves *and* the land of destiny, but it is *his* destiny to abandon both. Throughout the remainder of his appearances in the poem, he continues his role as an anti-Aeneas, inverting or falling short of his Vergilian predecessor, moving back toward the east, until he ends up in his version of the sack of Troy, a headless corpse like Vergil's Priam.

If Cato is *pius Aeneas* and Pompey a failed Aeneas, then Caesar is the impious, all-too-successful dark avatar of Vergil's epic hero. With characteristic self-confidence, he lays personal claim to his Julian ancestor, "my Aeneas" (9.991), the poem's only explicit name check of the latter. Like "his Aeneas," Caesar is a man of destiny, but while destiny in the *Aeneid*, at least on a surface reading, is a providential drive toward the victory of order over chaos and the establishment of peace and "empire without limits," the destiny that drives Caesar and that he himself seems sometimes to control is aimed toward crime, civil war, and tyranny. Caesar is Aeneas without the weaknesses that, despite his detractors, make Vergil's hero human. The prospect of dying in a storm at sea plunges Aeneas into despair (*Aen.* 1.92–101), but Caesar embraces the notion, seeing it as a measure of his equality with the gods and a means of inspiring even greater fear after his death (5.654–71). Aeneas's genuine love for Dido almost derails his divine mission (*Aen.* 4), but Caesar's lustful, politically opportunistic liaison with Cleopatra aligns perfectly with his single-minded ambition (10.53–171).

Even the controversial ending of the *Aeneid*, when a frenzied Aeneas kills the suppliant Turnus to avenge his friend Pallas, whatever else it does, shows the all-too-human emotion that lies beneath his devotion to duty (*Aen.* 12.930–52). Caesar, in contrast, does show mercy, his vaunted virtue of *clementia*, but only as a cynical political tactic to demotivate and humiliate his enemies (2.508–25). Yet once again, the reader has a choice. Caesar can be read as a dark perversion of Aeneas, as what the man of destiny looks like in a world of civil war. Alternatively, he can be read as a close parallel to a man who followed his destiny, through a proto-civil war, to establish (eventually) the Julio-Claudian principate. Perhaps Lucan's Caesar is simply Vergil's Aeneas with the true nature of his mission laid bare.

Lucan versus Vergil

Panning out one last time, the entire *Civil War* can be taken as an extended and sustained allusion to the *Aeneid*. This global intertextuality is built up by the smaller allusions, episodes, and characters we have already examined, and, in turn, the overall relationship between the poems informs how the reader interprets each smaller allusion. Broadly speaking, the poem's overall intertextual relationship can be taken in three different ways. There is considerable overlap between each of them, and there is no sense that the reader needs to choose one to the exclusion of the others. Whether the *Civil War* truly has a fractured voice or not, it certainly dramatizes its own inconsistency of tone and attitude, in keeping with the unstable world of civil war.[31]

The most common interpretation of the *Civil War* is as an "anti-*Aeneid*," taking the message and medium of Vergil's epic, then inverting, perverting, and even parodying it. Vergil's poem is a foundation story, relating and dramatizing in a teleological narrative the fated rise of the Roman people from the disaster of Troy's sack to the Golden Age of Augustus and empire without limits. Lucan's teleological path, though no less linear and inevitable, is one of decline, the loss of empire through self-destructive civil war, leading eventually to the dissolution of a Stoic cataclysm but without that philosophy's expectation of cyclical regeneration. We have seen this model underlying many of Lucan's allusions to the *Aeneid*, including Pompey's journey away from Rome and Caesar's visit to the ruins of Troy. Such a reading involves an impossibly simplistic and monolithic interpretation of the *Aeneid* as a triumphant manifesto of Augustan imperialism. We need not assume—though we can never know—that the historical Lucan read the *Aeneid* in this way, ignoring Dido, Marcellus, Creusa, and the *lacrimae rerum* ("tears shed over things," *Aen.* 1.462).

However, it is a common technique for a "target text" to construct an oversimplified (especially an over simplistically optimistic or triumphalist) interpretation of a "source text," so that it can more fully subvert and debase that interpretation. Lucan could well have been a "Harvard-school," pessimistic reader of the *Aeneid*, but that would not necessarily have prevented his constructing a phantom Augustan *Aeneid* against which to react.[32]

The second broad approach is to take Lucan the Harvard-school reader of the *Aeneid* more seriously and see his pessimistic allusions to Vergil as highlighting the pessimism that he detected as already there in the earlier poem. Many modern—not to mention ancient, mediaeval, and early modern—readers have recognized that the *Aeneid* is a poem about civil war, fought between the Trojans and Latins who are both proto-Romans. Many, too, have detected greater or lesser degrees of discomfort, anxiety, grief, and even condemnation for the actions of Aeneas, and of the gods and mortals on his side. When Lucan exposes the moral chaos of civil war and expresses pity and rage at the defeat of freedom, it may be that he is not contrasting his vision with that of an Augustan Vergil but rather encouraging his readers to interpret the *Aeneid* as expressing the same worldview, albeit less overtly and explicitly than in the creative commentary that is the *Civil War*.

Finally, instead of a sharp contrast between the poems, or a close alignment of them in subject matter and worldview, it is possible to see the *Aeneid* and the *Civil War* as telling the same basic story but having diametrically opposed attitudes to it. Although one strand of Lucan's pessimism imagines an endless cycle of civil war and another a linear precipitation toward cosmic dissolution, a third, perhaps the dominant one, sees his epic and the historical process it embodies as moving ineluctably along the teleological path toward tyranny. The notion is most startlingly and paradoxically expressed by the astrologer Nigidius Figulus, who ends his prediction of the future:

> "cum domino pax ista uenit. duc, Roma, malorum
> continuam seriem clademque in tempora multa
> extrahe ciuili tantum iam libera bello."
>
> (1.670–72)

> "The peace we long for brings a master. Rome, prolong your chain
> of disaster without a break and protract calamity
> for lengthy ages: only now in civil war are you free."

The *Aeneid* is about the long, linear journey through time and space to the establishment of the Augustan (and hence Julio-Claudian) principate. The *Civil War* is about exactly the same journey. With whatever layers of irony we read them, Lucan's invocation of Nero makes exactly this point: "But if the Fates could find no other way for Nero's coming, . . . then we have no complaint, O gods; for this reward we accept even these crimes and guilt" (1.33–38). Both poems depict Rome's journey through civil war to the establishment of tyranny. Caesar is not a dark Aeneas but Aeneas is as dark as Caesar. Pompey *is* a failed Aeneas but only because his political aspiration to be a tyrant is indivisible from his intertextual aspiration to be Aeneas. The plots of the *Aeneid* and the *Civil War* are not so very different. It is just that Lucan hates them both.

Notes

1. On the *Aeneid*'s early reception, see esp. Thomas 2001.

2. Space forbids discussion of Lucan's engagement with Vergil's earlier poem, the *Georgics*, though this is of great significance. Vergil's depiction of the recent civil wars and Caesar's assassination at the end of *Georgics* 1 is of particular importance in the omens of book 1 and the curse of Thessaly at the end of book 7. On Lucan and the *Georgics*, see Paratore 1943; Kersten 2018; Esposito in this volume.

3. See esp. Fowler 1997; Hinds 1998; Edmunds 2001.

4. On the storm episode, Matthews 2008; Pitcher 2008; Day 2013, 143–56; and Caterine in this volume.

5. On the debate, see Pogorzelski 2011, 159–64; Tracy 2014, 17–49.

6. Tracy 2014, 77–78 notes how the following episode at Ptolemy's court also refutes Lentulus's claim, since it is the elderly Acoreus who is the champion of *fides*.

7. Moles 1983; Bowie 1990; Morgan 2000.

8. Narducci 1973; Hinds 1998, 8–10.

9. Bowie 1990, 478.

10. The Greek adjective νέος (*neos*) means "young" as well as "of recent date" and in the plural can simply mean "boys."

11. Hardie 1989.

12. In Euripides's *Herakles*, it is the personification of madness, Lyssa, who makes the hero kill his family, though still on Hera's orders. The Fury Megaera is responsible in the *Hercules Furens* of Lucan's uncle, Seneca. Most versions have Agave and Lycurgus maddened directly by the god Dionysus. Lucan's use of Furies fits with the "hellish energy" that drives much post-Vergilian epic, as well as the second half of the *Aeneid* itself, instigated by the Fury Allecto. On hellish energy: Hardie 1993, 57–87.

13. For example, "kin facing kin," 1.4; "Rome's first walls were drenched with a brother's blood," 1.95; "What madness was this, O citizens?" 1.8.

14. Ovid's two uses of the phrase, the only others before Lucan, are also significant. His Deianira, Hercules's second wife, also applies it to Hercules's labors (*Her.* 9.45), with particular emphasis on the very Vergilian motif of Juno's enduring anger (*ira . . . longa deae*, 9.46; cf. *saeuae memorem Iunonis ob iram*, *Aen.* 1.4). In the *Metamorphoses*, Aeacus describes the plague that wiped out the people of Aegina as caused by Juno's resentment of a land named after her husband, Jupiter's, lover (*dira lues ira populis Iunonis iniquae / incidit exosae dictas a paelice terras*, *Met.* 7.523–24).

15. Most editors of Vergil print the variant reading *Iunonis acerbae*, with little or no explanation, but *iniquae* has equally good manuscript authority (including a fifth-century papyrus) and is the version read by ancient commentators such as Servius and Donatus.

16. Miller 2014, 442; Fratantuono-Smith 2018, 401; O'Hara 2018, 57.

17. On window allusions in general (sometimes called double allusions or window references), see Thomas 1986, 188–89; McKeown 1987, 37–45; Cowan 2014.

18. On the banquet, see Tucker 1975; Coffey 1996, 86–92; Tracy 2014, esp. 123–34; and Roche (chapter 10) in this volume.

19. For a further complex allusion, with wordplay, to Vergil's own phrase *lanugine mala* ("apple with down") at *Eclogue* 2.51, see Boyd 1983.

20. Lucan's "mature age-group" (*fortior aetas*) may also echo Lucretius's reference to how the horse part's "strong powers fails in old age" (*ualidae uires aetate senecta | . . . deficiunt, DRN* 5.886–87).

21. On all three characters: O'Higgins 1988; Day 2013, 93–105; *matrona:* Roche 2009, *ad loc.*; Phemonoe: Masters 1992, 91–159; Erictho: Masters 1992, 180–96; Pillinger 2012, 63–73.

22. On Caesar at Troy, see Rossi 2001; Spencer 2005; Tesoriero 2005.

23. Braund's translation "the ruins have suffered oblivion" certainly conveys one implication of *etiam periere ruinae* but misses the full (very Lucanian) hyperbolic paradox that even the ruins, the result of buildings perishing, have themselves perished.

24. A representative subversive reading is Lyne 1987, 27–35; a more complex interpretation is Morgan 1998.

25. On Hercules, Antaeus, and Curio, see Ahl 1972; Martindale 1981; Saylor 1982; Asso 2002.

26. On Julia, see Batinski 1993; Chiu 2010; Mulhern 2017; and the articles in the next footnote.

27. The combinatorial allusion is further complicated by Julia's strong resemblance to the ghost of Cynthia, the beloved of the elegiac love-poet Propertius (Prop. 4.7), whose assertion of an eternal claim on the poet ("Let others possess you now; soon I alone shall hold you: you will be with me and I shall mix and grind my bones on yours," Prop. 4.7.93–94) adds an element absent from the depiction of Creusa, who lets Aeneas go, and Dido, whose love turns to hate and who is reunited in the underworld with her first husband, Sychaeus (*Aen.* 6.471–76). On Lucan and elegy, including Julia and Prop. 4.7, see Caston 2011; McCune 2013–2014; Littlewood 2016.

28. On Lucan's reception of Dido, see Thompson-Bruère 1968; Kubiak 1990,

29. Rossi 2000.

30. 3.4–7. Hesperia in the *Aeneid*: 1.530, 569; 2.781; 3.163, 185–86; 503; 4.355; 7.4, 44; etc.

31. On the fractured voice, see esp. Masters 1992.

32. "Harvard-school" is a shorthand widely used to refer to scholars who interpret the *Aeneid* as critical, subversive, pessimistic, or at least ambivalent toward the Augustan regime. Examples include Putnam, Thomas, and Lyne. "Augustan" or "optimistic" readers see it as relatively straightforwardly glorifying Augustus and the values he promoted. They include Galinsky, Cairns, and many German scholars.

12

Religion and Ritual in Lucan

KONSTANTINOS ARAMPAPASLIS AND ANTONY AUGOUSTAKIS

> A religion is a unified system of beliefs and practices relative to
> sacred things, that is to say, things set apart and forbidden—beliefs
> and practices which unite into one single moral community called a
> Church, all those who adhere to them.
>
> —Durkheim 1995, 44

Any attempt to come up with a single definition of religion that would apply
universally to cultures past and future seems futile. In the epigraph above,
Durkheim accounts for religious change and diversity diachronically. From
the deification of natural elements and polytheism to the establishment of
monotheism with a precisely defined dogma and standardized rituals, religion has gone through many stages and transformations as it adapts to specific cultural environs. It should not strike us as odd, therefore, that Roman
religion was distinct from those systems prior to its formulation or from its
modern counterparts.

By contrast to the adherents of modern western religions, the Romans
focused strictly on what scholars call *orthopraxis*, that is, the correct and precise performance of established rituals.[1] Their religious behavior was not regulated by any set of principles or orthodoxy. The immediate result of the lack
of a dogma was that Roman religion was open to alternate exegesis and speculation about the nature of the world and gods, as long as the individual fulfilled
the obligation of attending or practicing rituals. Any religious prohibitions or
duties were imposed on the people solely based on their social status. In other
words, religion was closely linked to the position somebody occupied within

the community and not to their spiritual decision (e.g., baptism or conversion). This strong social aspect of Roman religion justifies the absence of an ethical code governing religious relations. Religious relations were regulated by the same rules as other social relations.[2] Such differences with modern religions justify why a discussion on Roman religion should entail two aspects to be complete: the nature and role of the gods and the practice of rituals.

Depictions of gods in action and descriptions of rituals are important components of epic composition in general. Evidently, gods are a literary device serving specific purposes in the narrative, and as such they should be considered highly refined poetic creations. But in their essence, they are still modeled upon (and modified from) contemporary concepts of the divine.[3] As modern readers we should always keep in mind that poets tend to incorporate religious materials in their works based on popular beliefs and experiences. That said, when interpreting the divine machinery and rituals in the epics, one should take into account the impact of the author's social and ideological milieu on his work.[4] Lucan is no exception as his use of religious elements is in harmony with the topic of civil war and the turbulent years of the reign of Nero, both of which had contributed to the decline of the *mos maiorum* ("ancestral customs") according to the authors of the period.[5] Certain excerpts also reveal a Stoic influence on the poem's theology, which can be attributed to Lucan's philosophical education.[6]

This chapter offers an introduction to the topic of religion and ritual in Lucan's *Civil War*.[7] The first part of this essay engages with passages relevant to the gods' absence from the narrative and with Lucan's attempt to substitute the conventional deities with the figures of Nero and Pompey after they have undergone their apotheosis as well as with the deified forms of *Fata* ("fate") and *Fortuna* ("fortune," "chance"). The second part details several passages of divine consultation, such as the episodes involving Arruns, Appius, and Ericho. Finally, we argue that the failure of these rituals is absolutely justified in conjunction with the absence of the epic's divine machinery. Lucan deviates from the norms of epic poetry by depicting his gods as passive in an effort to criticize traditional Roman religion and, especially, the changes that were brought by the establishment of the principate.

Lucan's Ragnarok

The abandonment of divine machinery is a distinctive feature of the *Civil War*, while at the same time references to the gods abound. The divine figures are mentioned both collectively and individually with their names or characteristic epithets by the narrator and the protagonists.[8] Less frequent, but still notable in number, are the references to divine plans and deeds. However, the reader does not see the gods performing any action toward the plot's conclusion:[9] long gone are their traditional, epic appearances in front of mortals to warn them of an unforeseen development or advise them on the proper course of action; divine councils and arguments between gods are totally absent as well as their engagement in battles and conflicts, as last seen in the Latin tradition, for instance, in Ovid's *Metamorphoses*.

This realization might come as a surprise to modern readers since the supernatural element fits prominently in the first book.[10] When Caesar is about to cross the Rubicon, a vision of the fatherland (*Patria*) appears before him, addressing the general. The use of vocabulary suitable for a deity appearing in a dream (*ingens uisa duci patriae trepidantis imago*, "the general saw the mighty vision of his fatherland in fear," 1.186) argues for the deification of *Patria* but also sketches the apparition as an omen, the first of a series of omens with which book 1 reaches its climax (1.522–83).[11] At the beginning of the catalogue of prodigies in book 1, Lucan makes clear that the divine machinery is still functioning in the background of the narrative by revealing their origin: *superique minaces | prodigiis terras inplerunt, aethera, pontum* ("and the menacing gods fill the earth, the sky, and the sea with prodigies," 1.524–25). These omens, however, constitute the only instance of the gods' active interference with mortal affairs before and during the war. More specifically, when Lucan enumerates the causes of the civil war at 1.67–182, he excludes divine agency, thus deviating from the tradition established by his predecessors and adopted by contemporary poets: for Homer, the cause of the Trojan war was divine (Zeus's will, *Il.* 1.5), just as the adventures and wars in the *Aeneid* were all instigated by Juno's wrath (*Aen.* 1.4). Her hatred for Rome is also instrumental to the commencement of the war in Silius (1.38). The lack of divine causation and the catalogue of the signs in book 1 as the only divinely ordained event in the narrative boldly underline the reversal of natural order and the transgression of epic conventions. The reason is that, in the narrator's view, the abomination of the civil war (brother pitched against brother, son against father, and so on) cannot be the result of divine machinery, and this is further affirmed by the gods' displeasure at Caesar's marching to Rome despite the monstrous signs.[12]

Divine wrath climaxes early in the *Civil War*, at the beginning of book 2, and eventually leads the gods to abstain from the war altogether:[13]

Iamque irae patuere deum manifestaque belli
signa dedit mundus legesque et foedera rerum

praescia monstrifero uertit natura tumultu
indixitque nefas.

(2.1–4)

The gods' wrath was already evident, and the world gave clear signs of
war; foreknowing nature overturned her laws and pacts with monster-
bearing turbulence, and declared the wicked deed.

Even though divine anger in Lucan does not actively contribute to the plot as
does Juno's wrath in the *Aeneid*, it still leads to the commencement and conclusion of the civil war and, consequently, the poem's narrative. In Vergil, the
goddess's hatred for the *gens Troiana* ("Trojan race") is the primary, active force
that sends Aeneas to his wanderings on land and sea; conversely, anger in the
Civil War is revealed and immediately leads the gods to disengage themselves
from mortal affairs and withdraw from the narrative, thus rendering them
passive observers whose presence, nevertheless, looms in the background.

The narrator has successfully figured out the origin and meaning of the
omens, namely divine displeasure at the reversal of natural order. But this is as
far as he can get, and subsequent lines suggest that he has absolute ignorance
of the situation in the divine realm.[14] In the reader's mind, the conditional conjunctions (*siue . . . siue* "whether . . . or," "perhaps . . . perhaps") introduce two
contrary and mutually exclusive hypotheses, creating a form of disjunction with
the *manifesta signa* ("clear signs"):[15]

siue parens rerum, cum primum informia regna
materiamque rudem flamma cedente recepit,
fixit in aeternum causas, qua cuncta coercet
se quoque lege tenens, et saecula iussa ferentem
fatorum inmoto diuisit limite mundum,
siue nihil positum est, sed fors incerta uagatur
fertque refertque uices et habet mortalia casus

(2.7–13)

Perhaps the creator, as soon as he took up the shapeless realm of pure
matter after the conflagration had stopped, established the eternal causes,
binding himself as well by universal laws, and with the immovable
boundary of destiny arranged the world to endure the prescribed ages; or
perhaps nothing is preordained, but chance randomly wanders, bringing
change over again, and rules on mortal affairs

As Shadi Bartsch observes, the narrator "obsessively addresses the question of
what the gods' status might be;"[16] but all the questions do not lead to any

successful answers necessarily, and such "Unsicherheit" ("uncertainty") characterizes the poem in general.[17] The narrator is equally puzzled as one of his characters, Nigidius Figulus, at 1.639–69. Both, in their effort to understand who runs the affairs of the universe, express the same alternative views on the nature of fate.[18] The narrator argues that everything happens as a result of predetermined causation set by Jupiter within the boundaries of fate (*fatorum immoto limite*), which also binds the father of gods (*se quoque lege tenens*), or that the universe is regulated by a nonteleological randomness (*fors incerta*). These lines verbally echo Nigidius Figulus's interpretation, who claims that either fate is a preordained force (*si fata mouent*, 1.644) or pure chance (*nulla cum lege | incerto . . . motu*, 1.642–43) rules the universe.[19] These ideas correspond to the doctrines of the two major philosophical schools during Lucan's time. The belief of a deterministic world derives probably from the poet's Stoic upbringing while that of the randomness of events can be attributed to the Epicurean tradition.[20]

Whether *fortuna* and *fata* control whatever happens in the world, and more specifically in the human realm, is of great value for the denouement of the narrative. Lucan's intention is to raise a more important point about the poem's universe, and that is divine indifference, which allows evil to accomplish itself unopposed. Although confusion about the situation in the world of the gods persists for the largest part of the *Civil War*, the narrator comes to a ground-shaking realization in book 7:[21]

> sunt nobis nulla profecto
> numina: cum caeco rapiantur saecula casu,
> mentimur regnare Iouem. spectabit ab alto
> aethere Thessalicas, teneat cum fulmina, caedes?
> . . . mortalia nulli
> sunt curata deo.
>
> (7.445–48, 454–55)

No deities aid us, we lie when we say Jove reigns, since it is blind chance that drives the world along. Would a Jupiter grasping the lightning bolt gaze idly from high heaven at Pharsalia's slaughter? . . . Mortal affairs are the concern of no god.

It is by no coincidence that *fortuna* is used in book 7 by the narrator sixteen times, more than any other book.[22] Upon a first reading, the ideas expressed in this passage might seem identical with those of Nigidius Figulus and the narrator, in books 1 and 2 respectively. But such a statement seems cursory and is not entirely accurate, since this excerpt argues that either luck regulates everything, and thus the gods are powerless or nonexistent, or even worse, they exist, but they do not care about human affairs, in accordance with Epicurean tenets.[23] The realization that the gods have forsaken the Roman people is used as a springboard that serves to externalize the narrator's massive tantrum against the chief Roman god and protector of Rome, Jupiter Optimus Maximus.[24] For Lucan it is inconceivable that the greatness of Rome, which was the longtime result of divine providence and plan in Vergil's *Aeneid*, is now led to destruction by the same forces.[25]

One might be led to assume that the judgment in book 7 represents Lucan's last words on the issue.[26] This conclusion, however, could only be supported by the absence of references to the gods in subsequent passages—and this is not the case—thus the statement holds no truth whatsoever. A few lines later, at 7.690, the narrator addresses Pompey, urging him to summon the gods as witnesses (*ac testare deos*); at 7.705 he asks the general to trust both the gods and fate (*crede deis, longo fatorum crede fauori*). The discrepancy illustrates the "fractured voice" of the narrator who is constantly at odds with himself throughout the poem.[27] The deficiency in certitude about his own narrative is justified because Lucan has broken the first significant rule of the genre set by Homer and Hesiod: instead of the Muses, he invokes the deified Nero for inspiration. This modification severely impacts his task since the function of the Muses is to help the poet remember the events and their order in the plot.[28] Without their presence, Lucan's thoughts are diffused, and his narrator is not omniscient: he lacks the knowledge of a traditional, Vergilian narrator.[29]

So far, we have discussed the passages indicating that the gods are absent from the narrative of the *Civil War*; let us now move to those which suggest possible substitutes for the divine machinery. We will examine the deified figures of Nero and Pompey as well as *Fata* and *Fortuna* as possible replacements of divine machinery. Since the last two are used with various meanings in different contexts, we will narrow the discussion only to some excerpts that refer to the deified forms of these abstracts.

A New Holy Trinity: Nero, Fortuna and Fata

Nero is addressed in the beginning of book 1 (1.33–66): after a short prelude that rationalizes the civil war as the means of his ascension to power (1.33–45), Lucan continues with the emperor's apotheosis (1.45–59). As part of the tradition established by the Augustan poets, namely Ovid, Horace, and Vergil, this apotheosis follows the conventions of panegyrics to Roman emperors:[30]

> te, cum statione peracta
> astra petes serus, praelati regia caeli
> excipiet gaudente polo: seu sceptra tenere

seu te flammigeros Phoebi conscendere currus
telluremque nihil mutato sole timentem
igne uago lustrare iuuet, tibi numine ab omni
cedetur, iurisque tui natura relinquet
quis deus esse uelis, ubi regnum ponere mundi.

(1.45–52)

When you complete your duty and seek the stars at a later point, you will
be received by your chosen court of heaven with everyone up there
rejoicing. Whether it pleases you to hold the scepter or to climb the
fire-bearing chariot of Phoebus and with moving fire to wander around
the earth (as it fears not the changes of the sun), every god will yield to
you, and nature will leave it up to you to decide which god you would like
to be, where to place your kingdom of the world.

The passage starts with the apotheosis or catasterism (*astra petes*): a standard
process that will elevate Nero to divine status. The phrase *sceptra tenere* ("to hold
the scepter") implies his assimilation with Jupiter since the *sceptrum* was the
sign of regal power;[31] the emperor is also identified with the sun god while
mounting his chariot (*flamigeros Phoebi conscendere currus*, "to climb the fire-
bearing chariot"). The choice of the specific deities is not accidental, and it is
related to either contemporary public imagery of Nero or the tradition of Augustan panegyrics.[32] Lucan goes even further by explicitly ranking the deified
Nero even above Jupiter and by having all the gods yield to his power. Such
changes to divine hierarchy shock the realm of the gods with unforeseeable
results.[33] This passage also marks a breaking from the oldest and most significant rule of epic poetry, namely the invocation for divine inspiration. Lucan pro-
claims Nero a deity before his death and invokes him as a substitute for the
traditional Muse or Bacchus:[34]

sed mihi iam numen; nec, si te pectore uates
accipio, Cirrhaea uelim secreta mouentem
sollicitare deum Bacchumque auertere Nysa:
tu satis ad uires Romana in carmina dandas.

(1.63–66)

And for you are already a god. Nor, if I receive you in my heart as a poet/
prophet, would I want to bother the god who controls Cirrha or to take
away Bacchus from Nysa: you alone are enough to give me power to
compose Roman songs.

The main reason for invoking the emperor instead of a conventional deity is
probably the topic of the poem. The civil wars in the second half of the first

century B.C.E. gradually led to the establishment of the imperial regime. The only divine or godlike figure who cannot feel disgust at the events of the civil war is a successor of Caesar, precisely because the civil wars created the principate.[35] If the invocation is ironic, and Lucan criticizes contemporary religious life, then this passage could be construed as an indirect critique of imperial cult and the excessive worship of mortal figures.[36]

Such an idea is further supported in book 7:[37]

> cladis tamen huius habemus
> uindictam, quantam terris dare numina fas est:
> bella pares superis facient ciuilia diuos,
> fulminibus manes radiisque ornabit et astris
> inque deum templis iurabit Roma per umbras.
>
>   (7.455–59)

And yet we have a revenge for this slaughter, such as the gods are allowed to give to mortals: the civil wars will create gods equal to the Olympians, Rome will decorate the dead with thunderbolts and rays and stars, and she will swear by ghosts in the temples of the gods.

The deification of mortals in Rome was an old practice, and the people had some sense of the divine in man as we can infer from the custom of worshiping the spirit of the dead in private cults.[38] However, the worship of a deceased individual became part of the official state religion by Octavian as the first action of the Second Triumvirate (January 42 B.C.E.), which ultimately led to the creation of the imperial cult.[39] Beginning with Augustus, the emperors were deified upon their death pending senatorial approval, even though certain divine honors could be conferred upon them while still alive.[40] The passage alludes to the designation *diuus* ("divine"), while the ornaments mentioned, namely the thunderbolts, rays, and stars, are drawn from the representations of Augustus and Claudius in contemporary art.[41] Lucan's strong feelings against this practice are also evident in 6.809, where the corpse reanimated by Erictho ridicules the idea that the emperors can become gods upon their death and, functioning as the poet's mouthpiece, urges readers to condemn their worship.[42]

Pompey's apotheosis (9.1–18) is not surprising since it concludes a set of passages from book 8 that discuss the possibilities of the general's religious exaltation (cf. 8.793–805, 835–50, 856–64, 871–72). Some scholars regard these lines as the poet's call for cult worship, but given Lucan's critique of the practice of deification in general, and his contempt of the imperial cult in particular, such a supposition seems unlikely.[43] Upon his death, Pompey's soul detaches from the body (*at non in Pharia manes iacuere fauilla | nec cinis exiguus tantam compescuit umbram*, "but his soul did not stay in the Pharian ashes, nor could a small piles of ashes contain such a mighty shade," 9.1–2). It travels to the sublunary region between the earth and the ether that is the space reserved for the virtuous and innocent:

> qua niger astriferis conectitur axibus aer
> quodque patet terras inter lunaeque meatus,
> semidei manes habitant, quos ignea uirtus
> innocuos uita patientes aetheris imi
> fecit et aeternos animam collegit in orbes.
> non illuc auro positi nec ture sepulti
> perueniunt.
>
> (9.5–11)

Where the dark air is connected to the star-bearing heavens, the space which lies open between the earth and the paths of the moon; there shades half-divine live, whom fiery virtue made to endure the lower ether, since they were blameless while alive, and gathered their soul into the endless spheres. Those laid in gold or buried with incense do not reach this place.

From there Pompey's soul contemplates the vanity of human affairs, and it is consoled by the harmony of the cosmos, for the violent treatment of his body:

> illic postquam se lumine uero
> impleuit, stellasque uagas miratus et astra
> fixa polis, uidit quanta sub nocte iaceret
> nostra dies risitque sui ludibria trunci.
>
> (9.11–14)

There after it filled itself with real light and marveled at the wandering planets and the stars fixed in the poles, it saw in what darkness our day lies and laughed at the mockery of the truncated body.

This account differs from Nero's apotheosis 1.43–59, most importantly because it takes place within the narrative, not in the foreseeable future.[44] Contrary to the emperor's ascension, which will allow him to assume divine status and dwell in the celestial palace (the Milky Way), Pompey's soul reaches only the air, which, in the context of Stoic cosmology, belongs to the mortal sphere, whereas the ether constitutes the sphere of the immortal.[45] But instead of residing in this part of the sky designated for the heroes (*semidei manes*, literally "shades half-divine"), eventually it transmigrates in Cato and Brutus (9.15–18). The discrepancy with Nero's apotheosis is justified since the two narratives are based on different premises. More specifically, the apotheosis in 1.43–59 adheres to the propaganda of the imperial regime while Pompey's catasterism is in accordance with the Stoic doctrine, modified to agree with Lucan's personal views and to fit the general lack of divine forces in the poem.[46] The image of the soul leaving the fields of the blessed to sink into Brutus's and Cato's breast is in no way equivalent to the process of metempsychosis, which presupposes a real rebirth. Lucan's imagery then adopts a rather traditional folk belief than philosophical doctrine.[47] He portrays the transfer of the commanding power to Cato by means of a remarkable image, and by naming Brutus, he alludes to Caesar's future murder and the revenge of Pompey's death. After the general's death and ascension to the regions of the stars, the survivors, who until then have acted only on orders, must be authorized to act independently in the future. This unexpected deviation from the orthodox Stoic tenet also cancels the general's apotheosis and renders him useless as a divine character in the narrative.[48]

Fortuna[49] and *fata* are constantly employed in the narrative with various meanings, and Lucanian scholarship from the end of the nineteenth century onward has focused on the problem of their function in the poem.[50] Although in 2.7–15 and 7.445–55, *fortuna* and *fata* are described as mutually exclusive, subsequent passages suggest that Lucan uses them interchangeably.[51] Elsewhere, especially when related to Caesar, the words seem identical (1.227, 262–65, 393–94).[52] Together, as an inseparable entity, they have assumed control of the divine realm, and since they seem to overlap (5.500–502), it does not really make a difference whether Lucan uses the binaries *di* / *superi* ("gods") or *fortuna* / *fata*.[53] The assimilation between *fata* and *fortuna* also occurs, though rarely, in the *Aeneid*.[54] The essential difference, however, is that Lucan renders these same powers that function in harmony with the gods and their decisions in Vergil as the only active supernatural forces in his poem. For Lucan, *Fortuna* is the sole divine agent responsible for the orchestration of the civil wars, both between Marius and Sulla and Caesar and Pompey (2.230, 3.96–97). Conventional deities have withdrawn from the narrative, powerless to resist her capricious choices (3.448–49, 5.1).[55] Powers that were reserved for the gods have now been transferred to *Fortuna*: in 1.524–25 it is the gods who sent the omens to warn the Romans for the upcoming destruction, but in 7.151–52, Lucan reveals *Fortuna* as the harbinger of negative signs before the Battle of Pharsalus. Such statements function cumulatively, and they serve the poet's main goal, that is, to throw anathema on Caesar's luck, which led to his victory and eventually the creation of the principate. At the same time, certain passages (most notably in 5.581–93) illustrate Lucan's intention to criticize Roman religion and the changes brought by Caesar's victory.

In 5.581–93, Lucan narrates one of the most successful stories of Caesarian propaganda:[56]

uectorem non nosse tuum, quem numina numquam
destituunt, de quo male tunc Fortuna meretur
cum post uota uenit . . .

. . . .
                    quaerit pelagi caelique tumultu
quod praestet Fortuna mihi.

(5.581–83, 592–93)

to not know who your passenger is, whom the gods never abandon, who is ill-treated by Fortune then when she comes after his prayers . . . by the turmoil of sea and sky, Fortune seeks to favor me.

The initial purpose of the story was probably to create an image of Caesar as the protégé of the goddess. This idea is further supported by the representation of *Fortuna* with a rudder on the coins of Sepullius Macer, issued while the dictator was alive. Furthermore, it serves as an etiological myth pertaining to the new cult of *Fortuna Caesaris* ("the Fortune of Caesar").[57] Even after the dictator's assassination, the exploitation of *Fortuna* for personal benefit continued by his successors: for instance, after his victory at Actium, Augustus introduced the *Fortuna* of Antium as a protectress of seafarers, a function that originally belonged to the traditional gods.[58] With this development, the power to stop the winds, which later became a common claim for emperors such as Augustus and Nero, is transferred to *Fortuna*.[59] Although we do not possess much evidence for her significance in the Neronian period, Tacitus attests that Nero had ordered golden statues of *Fortuna* to be placed on the throne of Jupiter on the Capitolium in 62 c.e. at the event of his daughter's birth, an action illustrating the important position of *Fortuna* in imperial Roman religion.[60]

Ritual Anomalies

Since traditional deities are absent from the narrative, one end of the reciprocity that regulates human–divine relationships—a reciprocity distilled in the phrase *do ut des* (lit. "I give so that you may give")—is de facto missing from the *Civil War*. Therefore, all religious rites addressed to the gods are destined to be ineffective at best. The rituals detailed in the narrative are mostly connected with popular religion and superstition, and their failure reveals Lucan's strong criticism for such practices. Here we discuss the *lustratio* and the interpretation of the omens in book 1 by Arruns and Nigidius Figulus, the prophecy to Appius in book 5, and the scene of necromancy in book 6.

After Italy is filled with prodigies of civil war (1.522–83), the Etruscan prophet Arruns comes in procession to the city and attempts the ritual of *lustratio*, a purificatory rite to appease the gods and cleanse the city from miasma (1.584–638). And yet Arruns utterly fails:[61] the bull led to sacrifice keeps resisting, and when immolated, the entrails, the heart, and the liver betray unwavering signs of disaster to follow. In the finale of his speech, Arruns underscores the inevitability of the upcoming *nefas* ("evil") and appeals to the gods, who, however, have had no role in the narrative at all:

> "non fanda timemus,
> sed uenient maiora metu. di uisa secundent,
> et fibris sit nulla fides, sed conditor artis
> finxerit ista Tages." flexa sic omina Tuscus
> inuoluens multaque tegens ambage canebat.
> (1.634–38)

> "We fear things which ought not be said, but disasters greater than fear shall come. May the gods turn these signs into a better outcome, and may there not be any trust in the entrails. Perhaps the inventor of this skill, Tages, has made things up." Thus the Etruscan was prophesying convoluting the winding omens and covering them up by much ambiguity.

As has been observed, Arruns ends on a pathetic note.[62] The direct attack against the credibility of his own *disciplina* ("learning") sounds hollow. Especially so since Nigidius Figulus immediately afterward confirms that "imminent destruction is at hand" (*paratur | . . . matura lues*, 1.644–45). The astrologer then goes on to raise more questions than answers (1.645–49).[63]

Mantic instability and unreliability are, however, raised by the narrator in the episode of Appius Claudius's consultation of Phemonoe, the Pythian prophetess in Delphi in book 5 (5.64–236).[64] The ritual is unusually upset, as the priest "forces" the priestess to utter a prophecy (*corripuit cogitque*, 5.127). Such effort results first in Phemonoe's tricky speech (5.130–40), which is then followed by a real prophecy only under force (5.146): in utmost fear (*pauens*, 5.146), Phemonoe reveals that a grim future awaits Appius on the Euboean shore (5.194–96). This unexpected ritual violence forced upon Phemonoe by a fellow priest is symptomatic of the fragmented religious world of the poem: it is not just that "knowledge of the future is bound to be fragmented," but that "once put to the test it is inadequate."[65]

Likewise Sextus Pompeius's visit to the Thessalian witch Erictho in search of knowledge about the outcome of upcoming events offers another glimpse into the upset world of ritual and religion in the poem.[66] One of the most striking passages in the necromancy in terms of an outlook toward the divine comes at the end, when the resurrected soldier announces the end of the house of Pompey and the future deaths of both father and son:

> properate mori, magnoque superbi
> quamuis e paruis animo descendite bustis
> et Romanorum manes calcate deorum.
>
> (6.807–9)

Hasten to die, and proud of your great spirit go down to the underworld, albeit from your small tombs, and trample the shades of the Roman gods.

Is Lucan reflecting on imperial apotheosis and all the *principes* to become *Romani dei* one day after death?[67] Once again the narrator, this time through a corpse, exults in the elimination of the divine from the world and the triumph of *nefas* ("evil"). As we have seen in this selective analysis of passages related to religion and ritual in the *Civil War*, Lucan's universe is governed by forces outside the purview of the traditional, epic divine machinery, where random chance rather than a well-established divine "Weltplan," a plan for the world,[68] get to decide which party will win this unwinnable civil war.

Notes

1. Scheid 2003, 18; Rüpke 2007, 86.

2. Scheid 2003, 5–40, discusses these concepts and the problems of methodology in studying Roman religion. Our discussion on the differences between Roman and modern religions is heavily indebted to Scheid's analysis on pp.18–21. See Rives 2007, 13–53; Ando 2008, 13; Scheid 2016, *passim* on the nature of rituals.

3. For the function of divine machinery in epic generally, see Feeney 1991; Louden 2005 can be read as a brief introduction on the topic, but he also includes a discussion on a non-Greco-Roman epic, *Gilgamesh*; for the role of gods in Vergil, see Woodworth 1930; Hardie 1986; Harrison 1970.

4. Feeney 1991, 4.

5. Tac. *Ann.* 14.20.10–24 is indicative of the moral degeneration during the Neronian Age; on moral values in the *Civil War*, see Hardie 2013, 229–31. On religion in the Neronian Age, see Erker 2013, esp. 126–29 on the literary representations.

6. Lucan is said to have studied under the prominent Stoic philosopher Cornutus, who was also the teacher of Persius (*Vita Persi* lines 21–22). For Cornutus's influence on the *Civil War*, see Most 1989, 2053–56.

7. All translations are our own.

8. For example, Bacchus occurs six times, Bromius two; Ceres is found seven times, and Bellona two. As Tucker 1983 observed, the god whose name or characteristic epithets occur more frequently than any other deity is Apollo.

9. Feeney 1991, 270; for the absence of the divine agent from Lucan's narrative, see Feeney 1991, 250–301; Roche 2019, 5–7.

10. Feeney 1991, 270–72.

11. Roche 2009, 206–7, citing primarily Verg. *Aen.* 2.772–74 as a parallel, notes that *uisa* is commonly used in the introductory formula for dreams and apparitions, paired with the word *imago* (Ov. *Fast.* 2.503). The use of *ingens* as an adjective modifying *imago* is frequent in the context of dreams where gods and the dead appear to mortals; see also, for example, the use of *uasta effigie* for the ghost of Phrixus appearing in Aeetes's dream in V. Fl. 5.231–45.

12. Le Bonniec 1970, 174–78, argues that for Lucan, Caesar's victory was not compatible with the belief in divine providence; Jal 1962, 170, underlines the contradiction between the disapproval of the gods' passive role and the critique of the civil war as irreligious in Lucan.

13. Fantham 1992a, 77–79, notes that the opening lines of book 2 can be linked to the proem of the entire epic (1.1–32) through several verbal echoes. Perhaps these verses also function as a second, appropriate *prooemium* to the *Civil War* since the theme of divine anger is so prominent, just like in the *Odyssey* and the *Aeneid*.

14. Feeney 1991, 278.

15. For an analysis of the passage, see Fantham 1992a, 80–81.

16. Bartsch 2012, 87; cf. also 97: "a figure both confused and compromised by the paradoxes of his project."

17. Erler 2012 discusses extensively the narrator's "Unsicherheit" ("uncertainty").

18. Feeney 1991, 279.

19. On the connections between Nigidius Figulus's views and the Epicurean and Stoic traditions, see Roche 2009, 365–66; cf. Casali 2011, 92–95, on Nigidius Figulus on the antipodes of Vergilian Jove.

20. Feeney 1991, 280; for Lucan's Stoicism in general, see Due 1962, 1970; Wanke 1964, 163–66; Schotes 1969; Lapidge 1989; George 1992; Sklenář 2003; D'Alessandro Behr 2007.

21. On the passage, see Lanzarone 2016, 366–71; Roche 2019, 172–73.

22. See the statistics by Walde 2012, 74.

23. Feeney 1991, 282; Chaudhuri 2014, 173–75, "a powerful battery of attacks on traditional epic theology, as if the narrator at last offers an explanation for the strange character of the poem thus far."

24. Feeney 1991, 281n136.

25. Hardie 2013, 227; The idea of Lucan's poem as anti-*Aeneid* is noted in Hardie 1986, 381; Henderson 1987, 142–43.

26. For example, Due 1962, 101–2; Ahl 1976, 280–81.

27. Feeney 1991, 282–83. An earlier generation of scholars had assumed that the narrator's confusion is the result of Lucan's youthfulness and poetic immaturity (see, e.g., Dilke 1960, 40–41, and Le Bonniec 1970, 178). For an opposite view, suggesting that this confusion is an important element of Lucan's narrative technique, see Syndikus 1958.

28. The function of the Muses and the aspects of their invocation have been extensively discussed in many studies. On the issues of knowledge, memory, poetic craft, and performance, see, e.g., Murray 1981 and Finkelberg 1990.

29. Feeney 1991, 278.

30. To Roche's 2009, 129–30, bibliography, add Casali 2011, 89–92; Kessler 2011; Nelis 2011; Galli Milić 2016. On Nero and political attitudes in the poem, see Kimmerle 2015.

31. Roche 2009, 138–39; for the implications of Nero's assimilation with Jupiter, see Feeney 1991, 299.

32. Roche 2009, 139–40. Beginning with the first century c.e., Roman emperors were associated with Jupiter, especially in the context of the imperial cult. Nero was also the first one to issue coins with him holding the aegis of Jupiter (*BMC* 1.122–25, 127–29, 131–34). His assimilation with Apollo as the protector of arts is attested through Nero's alleged singing talent and as the sun god through his participation in chariot races. On different types of the emperor's portraiture, see Bergmann 2013.

33. Granting divine status to living emperors was more frequent in literature than real life: Feeney 1998, 108–14.

34. For a discussion on Nero's invocation, and Lucan's breaking from the epic tradition, see Feeney 1991, 275–76, with annotated bibliography. Johnson 1987, 118, 121–23, raises some very important points about Nero's function as Lucan's Muse.

35. Feeney 1991, 300–301.

36. Extensive bibliography on Lucan's invocation to Nero can be found in Roche 2009, 129–30.

37. Feeney 1991, 298; on the passage, see Lanzarone 2016, 372–74; Roche 2019, 174–75.

38. Ross Taylor 1931, 35–57.

39. For the events before Caesar's deification, and the implications of this process for Octavian as his heir as well as Marc Antony's objections, see Ross Taylor 1931, 78–99; for the date of the official deification, and the procedure followed by the senate, see Weinstock 1971, 386–98.

40. For the worship of emperors while still alive, see Clauss 1999, 503–19.

41. For the links between these lines and the representations of Augustus and Claudius, see Haskins 1887, 250; Dilke 1960, 131.

42. Ahl 1976, 146. For the meaning of *calcite manes*, see *TLL* iii.137.35. Seewald 2008, 40, comments on Lucan's criticism of the deification of the emperors and the long tradition of Cynic-Stoic and Epicurean philosophy, which emphasized the insignificance of funeral rites.

43. Seewald 2008, 33; Le Bonniec 1970, 163, based on 9.1–18 and 8.841–50, assumes that Lucan wanted to elevate Pompey to the rank of a protector of Rome, according to the Greek tradition. In the absence of clear statements, this idea must remain speculative.

44. For a brief discussion of these lines, and the philosophical influence on the content, see Wick 2004, 2.7–8; on the lack of conclusion with the death and apotheosis of Pompey, see Chaudhuri 2014, 188–89.

45. Wick 2004, 2.11; the aerial as the place of residence for semidivine, semihuman spirits also regularly appears in the philosophical-theological context.

46. Grimal 1960, 66n25; Seewald 2008, 8.

47. Wick 2004, 2.16.

48. Seewald 2008, 42. Cf. Sklenář's 2003, 126–27, discussion of Pompey as an unfit character to be catasterized.

49. Weinstock 1971, 112–27. An ancient and popular goddess with her cult in Rome, Fortuna was not purely assimilated to the Greek *Tyche*, since she always favored the brave; the individual whom she assisted was called *felix* (e.g., Sulla). Pompey and Caesar also stressed the role of luck in their military operations: in Cic. *De imp. Cn. Pomp.* 47, Cicero attributed Pompey's earlier success to fortune, and the republican general established himself in 55 B.C.E. a new cult of *Felicitas* that was considered the personification of enduring good luck. In 49 B.C.E., Q. Sicinius issued a coin depicting *Fortuna* on the obverse with the characteristic symbols of *Felicitas* on the reverse. By claiming the favor of *Fortuna*, Caesar gained greater reputation and more supporters, especially those who were less determined but still ready to take the probable winner's side.

50. The word *fatum* occurs 254 times, while *fortuna* 144, but they are not always used as replacements of the divine agent. See Friedrich 1938; Dick 1967; Long 2007; Eigler 2012, 50–2; Walde 2012; as well as the brief discussion by Barratt 1979, 95–6, and Dinter 2012 132.

51. Liebeschuetz 1979, 142–43, 148; Pratt 1983, 51; Feeney 1991, 280. Cf. Sen. *Ben.* 4.8.3: *sic nunc naturam uoca, fatum, fortunam: omnia eiusdem dei nomina sunt uarie utentis sua potestate* ("So now call these *nature, fate, luck*: they are all the names of the same god who is using his power in various manifestations"; emphasis added).

52. Getty 1940, 58 and 80; Friedrich 1938, 407n3: in Manilius's *Astronomica* 4.14–21, *fata* is represented as having the same power as *fortuna*. Thus, they do not seem to be two clearly distinctive forces but rather a multivalent one. On Caesar and *fortuna*, see Walde 2012, 68–69.

53. For an elaborate explanation of this idea, see Friedrich 1938, 405–6. Quite attractive is Pichon's 1912, 175, conclusion that the words fate, fortune, and gods are just different names for the unalterable destiny; see also Friedrich 1938, 408–9.

54. For the assimilation of *fortuna* and *fata* in the *Aeneid*, see Bailey 1935, 235–37.

55. Friedrich 1938, 407n1: the gods are still there, however, because in epic poetry an artistic requirement did not allow heaven to be completely unpopulated.

56. Plut. *Caes.* 38.5; Cass. Dio 41.46.3; App. *BCiv.* 2.57.236. On the role of *fortuna* in book 5, cf. Matthews 2008, 81–82.

57. Weinstock 1971, 127; for a detailed discussion on her cult, see Champeaux 1988, 267–91.

58. Weinstock 1971, 125–26. Cf. Hor. *Carm.* 1.35.

59. Calp. *Ecl.* 4.100.

60. Tac. *Ann.* 15.23.1.

61. Santangelo 2015, 178–79.

62. Roche 2009, 359. On prophecy in the poem, see the relevant commentary in Roche 2009 as well as Masters 1992, 118–215.

63. Dinter 2012, 79; on Nigidius Figulus cf. Casali 2011, 92–95, and Santangelo 2015, 179–80.

64. On the episode, see most recently the extensive analysis by Casamento 2012 with further bibliography, as well as Casali 2011, 101–4, and Santangelo 2015, 180–81.

65. Santangelo 2015, 181.

66. This is an episode widely discussed in Lucanian criticism; see most recently Reif 2016, 415–78, as well as Gowing 2002; Ogden 2002; Tesoriero 2002; Bernstein 2011, 263–65; Casali 2011, 104–9; Dinter 2012, 62–75; Pillinger 2012; Santangelo 2015, 182–85.

67. Korenjak 1996, 232. Is Lucan playing off against Nero's interest in necromancy? See Ogden 2002, 256–57.

68. For an example of this, see Jupiter's speech at Verg. *Aen.* 1.257–96.

13

Philosophy and the Aesthetics of Apostrophe in Lucan

FRANCESCA D'ALESSANDRO BEHR

Stoicism in the *Bellum Civile* and Lucan's Style

From its origins, Latin literature was imbued with philosophy. Not only was poetry an established medium of philosophical exposition and propagation, but philosophy also offered to writers a variety of themes and material that we find in practically all Latin genres.[1] In her seminal study about Latin literature and Stoicism, Marcia Colish affirms that "if any Latin poet can lay claim to the reputation of uniting Stoicism with epic genre, that poet is Lucan."[2] The importance of Stoicism for Lucan's poem is rather evident since the *Civil War* gathers more Stoic material than any other Latin epic written before it. Moreover, "his characterization of Cato of Utica is the most detailed and circumstantial portrait of the Stoic sage to be found in Latin literature,"[3] although Lucan is not particularly interested in maintaining philosophical coherence or adherence to all tenets of Stoicism.

While the presence of a Stoic matrix in Lucan's poem has never been doubted, what has been debated in the last century is how we should interpret it. It is possible to organize the approaches to the theme by dividing commentators in two major groups. The first includes those who believe the poem is oriented toward orthodox Stoic premises and is basically optimistic. In this approach Cato is the poem's Stoic hero.[4] This trend has proved long lasting, and although currently Lucan's alleged orthodoxy has been challenged on account of the many "competing voices" present in the poem, what persists is the idea of his serious engagement with Stoicism and, as a corollary, his commitment to politics. For these commentators, Lucan's multiple deviations from Stoic orthodoxy (above all the dissolution of theodicy, the celebration of the self-sufficiency of the Sage, the lack of acceptance of Fate, and the rejection of Stoic *apatheia*) are not identified with the poet's disillusionment with Stoic philosophy.[5] If a Stoic crisis is discernible it does not prove Lucan's rejection of the creed.

A second group of scholars highlights Lucan's detachment from Stoic faith and argues that he distances himself from it. The realization of "unorthodox" Stoic tendencies in the poem is at the core of this interpretation, which views Lucan's baroque, idiosyncratic, spectacular representation of civil war as the mirror of a chaotic, irrational, markedly non-Stoic universe in which cosmic order and commitment are impossible because all is governed by Chance. On these premises, in a world without rules, whoever behaves according to principles cannot be taken seriously: the Stoic saint must be ridiculed and at times be considered dangerous; indifference and nihilism are the only tenable positions.[6]

In this chapter, it is Lucan's style, and above all his use of apostrophe, that will be interpreted as intrinsically Stoic. With the help of Aristotle, Longinus, and Ankersmit's notion of the sublime, Stoic poetics, and contemporary rhetorical theory on the meaning of the second person in narrative, I shall assess Lucan's apostrophe as a rhetorical tactic drawing attention to the ineluctable role of the readers. His style is influenced by Seneca's dramatic style and a desire to empower the reader against Caesarism: it is as a conscious poetic reaction to the Neronian literary and political environment. Lucan forges a "morality of resistance"[7] visible above all in his apostrophes, which makes possible an activist reading of the poem.

Aristotle and *Mimesis*

Let us start with Aristotle's discussion about the didactic function of tragedy. For Aristotle, tragedy is characteristically the *mimēsis* of events that should not happen, actions that should be avoided at all costs. Tragedy focuses on acts of violence between "close friends or relatives" (*philoi, Poet.* 1453b19–23), actions that compound the repulsion of death and physical suffering with the violation of ties that should supposedly be secured and respected for their sanctity and basis in nature.[8] Violence between *philoi* is clearly the theme of Lucan's *Civil War*; he selects a topic unusual for epic but quite typical for tragedy.[9]

Apart from the subject, Lucan's allegiance to Aristotle is evident in the way he describes the interaction between poetry and audience. According to the narrator, the depiction of the war in his poem will produce hope and fear in the readers:[10]

Cum bella *legentur,*
spesque metusque simul perituraque uota mouebunt,
attonitique omnes ueluti uenientia fata,
non transmissa, *legent,* et adhuc *tibi, Magne, fauebunt.*

(7.210–13)

Whenever accounts of these wars *are read,*
they will stir *hope and fear* alike, and useless prayers;
all will be astonished *as they read* the fates as yet to unfold,
not as [already] happened, and oh *Magnus,* men *will* again *side* with you!

For Aristotle the readers' emotional reaction (i.e., pity and fear, *Poet.* 1449b25–29) produced by *mimēsis* is essential because it reveals a great deal about the readers' moral character. They should feel pity only for good characters, undeserving of their losses; at the same time, the spectators' fear reveals that they, too, are vulnerable to the kind of misfortune suffered by the protagonist.[11] Emotional participation is what Lucan is soliciting as he addresses Pompey, who is implicitly qualified as the decent (if imperfect) protagonist.[12] In the quoted passage, there is a third element that can be connected with Aristotle's poetics. As the narrator invokes Pompey, he reminds us that this is a *mimēsis.* The verb *lego* ("I read") repeated twice highlights the readers' act as such and indirectly Aristotle's distinction between objects and their representation:

> There are things that we see in their actual state with distress, yet we
> take pleasure in viewing the most accurate representation of them [. . .].
> The reason for this is that learning is not only the greatest pleasure for
> philosophers but equally for others [. . .]. They take pleasure in seeing
> representations because *it happens that as they view them they learn and
> draw conclusions* about each thing. . . . (*Poet.* 1448b11–17)[13]

The philosopher endorses realistic fictions for their didactic function. Apart from *catharsis* through which the viewer of a tragedy may experience a change of his emotional and intellectual disposition for the better, the *anagnōrisis* that characterizes the best plot involves a "recognition," a revelation, a moment of insight that might ideally prevent the violent action from happening. Even if the dreadful action is not averted, the central and violent heart of the tragedy "becomes an experience of cognition rather than a transgressive act."[14] In this way Aristotle defends the experience of the theatre as desirable, pleasurable, and useful. Lucan selects the topic of civil war in this perspective and in apostrophe wishes to trigger an *anagnōrisis,* a moment of insight for his readers, a revelation that will not prevent the catastrophic ending but will affect their cognition, minimize the results of the catastrophe, and engender hope for the future. Not accidentally, the passage cited above (7.210–13) invites readers to hope and fear, forgetting that the narrated events have an already established outcome.[15]

Longinus and the Sublime

Intense participation is secured through vivid representation, as had been examined by the ancient critic Longinus, probably a contemporary of Seneca and author of *On the Sublime*, whose beliefs seem to be at work in Lucan's epic.[16] According to Longinus, the employment of *phantasia* ("mental picturing") and *enargeia* ("vividness") (*Subl.* 15.2) brings shock (*ekplêxis*) and rapture. Both qualities allow the reader to be imaginatively present at the event represented in the text while, at the same time, eliciting his emotions.[17] In other words, through *enargeia* the sublime experience is enacted so that "we attain a state of aesthetic dispossession in which we forget who is who, the writer or the reader. By losing the safety of our critical distance, we feel what the poem feels, we despair about what the poem despairs about."[18] That is why poetry is dangerous but also powerful. As Plato suggested, "part of the 'yielding' or 'surrender' contained in the experience . . . is precisely . . . to take on the underlying attitudes and values of the figures with and for whom one feels."[19] Lucan is quite aware of these risks, but like Longinus, he fosters a sublimity that employs emotional heightening without compromising the relevance of the truth and benefitting those exposed to it. Stephen Halliwell qualifies Longinus's sublime as "a process which involves not so much a loss of self as a realization or fulfillment of the soul's inner potential," a movement that is "activated by the words of another" and "brings about a dynamic . . . transformation of the hearer's state of mind . . . and *a surplus of meaning* which provides material for permanently renewed contemplation."[20] In the Longinian sublime, not only are the infinite capabilities of the mind revealed but in it thought and emotion cohabitate and collaborate. This juxtaposition, as we will see, squares well with Seneca's philosophical style and with Lucan's sublime apostrophes, which envision poetic elevation, but also methods that favor enhanced cognition and empowerment of the reader within a specific Stoic matrix.

Stoic Rhetoric and Apostrophe

At a doctrinal level, the Stoics do not elaborate on rhetoric, which along with dialectic (argumentative reasoning) they consider a part of logic. Stoic philosophers recommend that the orator should speak like a philosopher: that is, he should employ clear arguments based on syllogism and aimed at rational persuasion. In the abstract they exclude rhetorical figures. However, when we consider books written for the general public by authors like Seneca, Epictetus, or Marcus Aurelius, who profess themselves supporters of the Stoics, they do not follow these prescriptions but adopt a recognizable style that includes rhetorical strategies and counts on them for persuasive effect. The language of these authors is characterized by abundant rhetorical questions, the employment of irony, continuous commentary on the action, and frequent and sustained apostrophes. Their style hinges on a model of psychological persuasion developed by the Stoics. According to it, emotions produced in response to a work of art are evaluative judgments taking place in a unicameral soul. Poetry is able to educate the audience by shaping or changing these judgments.[21] Poetry can be dangerous because unreflective readers or listeners might be taken in by ambiguously presented ethical dilemmas. Yet in this approach to poetry, poetic images are offered as objects of assent to the scrutiny of the mind for acceptance or rejection.[22] Lucan's apostrophes seem his most important tool for engendering the mental process to help readers to see things as they are, training them "in the formation of the correct propositional content about impressions both epistemologically and ethically."[23]

There are at least 197 instances of apostrophe in the *Civil War*. Through them, Lucan comments on the unfolding actions highlighting good as well as bad behavior. The already mentioned Longinus emphasizes the importance of concealing figures of speech (*Subl.* 17.2), and Aristotle praises the covertness of the Homeric narrator, who, apart from the proem and Muse-invocations, remains invisible as a person in the narration (*Poet.*1460a5–11). While preferring the hidden narrator, Aristotle also theorizes one who at times steps forward in the epic as a person and comments in first-person utterances and interventions. We can credit Aristotle with the anticipation of the modern narratological distinction between a "telling" narrator (who is visible and sums up or interprets what is happening) and a "showing" narrator (who hides so that the story seems to tell itself and the reader by himself must draw conclusions).[24] If Homer and Vergil *show*, Lucan *tells* and does not conceal his presence. His intrusions are an intentional tactic, a programmatic and deliberate attempt to disentangle the reader from the spells of *mimēsis* and to orient him toward the desired evaluation of the represented object.

The issue of helping the reader to assess representation appears even more urgent to the author considering the sociopolitical environment in which he writes and the historical moment captured in his poem. When the reality being described is one in which words and ideas have been manipulated by politicians and have lost their communicative efficacy, readers need intrusive narrators.[25] In his retelling of the war, Lucan reproduces in writing its perversion(s) and

Caesar's exploitation of Roman ethical vocabulary. Yet, within his own ambiguous narrative, the Neronian author tries to recover control through exegesis. If the significance of the narrated events cannot spontaneously emerge from the text, open comments, accusations, and pointed apostrophes are used to highlight problems. Therefore, apostrophic outbursts are used in the poem for two different and opposite purposes: they seek to emotionally engage the audience, creating a surplus of ecstasy and identification, but also to direct reader response. Ismene Lada has underlined the novelty of this approach in which the Stoics effectively developed a form of "reader response theory" that charged the hearer with some responsibility with respect to the fiction.[26] In order to establish how the reader is brought inside the fictional space and what his presence entails, we must consider some apostrophes more closely.

Apostrophe under the Microscope

The inclusion of the reader into the poem occurs, above all, through apostrophe, a rhetorical mechanism that envisions an intruding speaker and an internal addressee. Paolo Asso points out that "for the intrusion to be noted, a third person is necessary"; this third entity is the audience that assents to the demands of the trope and agrees to accept the narrative intrusion.[27] The second-person address encourages the external reader to identify with the apostrophized object. This process can be observed at 1.84–95:

> Tu causa malorum
> facta tribus dominis communis, *Roma*, nec umquam
> in turbam missi feralia foedera regni.
> O *male concordes* nimiaque cupidine caeci!
> Quid miscere iuuat uires orbemque tenere
> in medio? . . .
> . . . .
> nulla fides regni sociis, omnisque potestas
> inpatiens consortis erit. Nec gentibus ullis
> *credite*, nec longe fatorum exempla petantur:
> fraterno primi maduerunt sanguine muri.
>
> (1.84–89, 92–95)

> You caused these evils, *Rome*,
> when you became the property of three masters, never
> the sepulchral pact of a tyranny was shared among so many.

O men in evil accord, blind with excessive avarice!
Why does it please you to join forces and hold the globe
in common? . . .

. . . .

No trust can be found among allies in tyranny, power
tolerates no partner. *Look to no* foreign nations,
examples of this fatal law need not be sought far away:
our newly erected walls were wet with fraternal blood.

The narrator first addresses *Roma* (1.85) and then the *male concordes* triumvirs (1.87), summoned also through the imperative *credite* (1.94). The imperative can also be taken as encompassing Rome and its citizens, those present during the events narrated or reading about them. Essentially the apostrophe bears two "addresses." Explicitly, the narrator sends a message to the narratee, the named character(s);[28] covertly, the message is meant to provoke a response through its reception in a second(ary) communicative circuit, received by the readers of the poem.[29] This "inclusiveness" is an important peculiarity of Lucan's technique, here employed to suggest that all the citizens of Rome are in part responsible for their enslavement, for a guilty behavior that appeared right at the beginning of their history.

We notice the merging between narratee and audience again in book 4 when the narrator apostrophizes the Caesarian Curio:

quid nunc rostra *tibi* prosunt turbata forumque,
        quid prodita iura senatus
et gener atque socer bello concurrere iussi? . . .
has urbi miserae uestro de sanguine *poenas*
ferre *datis, luitis iugulo* sic arma, *potentes.*
felix *Roma quidem ciuisque* habitura *beatos,*
si libertatis superis tam cura placeret,
quam uindicta placet! Libycas en, *nobile corpus,*
pascit aues, nullo contectus Curio busto.
At *tibi nos,* . . .
digna damus, *iuuenis,* meritae preconia uitae.

. . . .

ius licet in *iugulos nostros* sibi fecerit ensis
Sulla potens Mariusque ferox et Cinna cruentus
Caesareaeque domus series, cui tanta potestas
concessa est? Emere omnes, hic uendidit urbem.
          (4.799–824, selected lines)

What does it profit *you* now to have rocked the Rostra and Forum
        what from Senate's right betrayed
from son- and father-in-law commanded to clash in battle? . . .
Such, *men of power*, are the penalties *you pay* to your wretched City—
your life's blood, *your jugulars* given in exchange for war!
O happy *Rome*, mistress of *a long line of prosperous
citizens*, were gods above as pleased to preserve her freedom
as they are to avenge it! But see! *Noble carrion*,
Curio feasts Libya's birds, sheltered by no tomb.
Yet *we to you* . . .
give the praise you deserve, *young man*, for the good you did.
. . . .
Powerful Sulla, ferocious Marius, bloodstained Cinna,
and the chain of Caesar's house may have forged for themselves the right
to hold their swords *at our throats*;
But who among these wielded
power like this? They all bought Rome, Curio sold it.

Generally speaking, the passage is characterized by sublimity and indignation. In it, a vocabulary normally attributed to positive characters describes a depraved man. Curio's death reminds us of Regulus's during the first Punic war.[30] Like a hero he dies bravely (4.798). By employing traditional vocabulary to describe a negative character, Lucan exposes the fragility of a language that employs identical words to portray the demise of worthy heroes as well as that of an unscrupulous schemer like Curio, ready to sell himself to Caesar.[31] Confusion is also triggered by the multiplicity and blurring of the apostrophized characters—*tibi* ("you"), *potentes* ("men of power"), *Roma* ("Rome"), and so on— who are all implicated in the misbehavior. For the apostrophe does not remain still, it gradually expands to include everybody, from Curio, to the *potentes* (4.806), to the citizens of Rome (*Roma*)—those present during the civil war but also Lucan's contemporaries. The content underlines generalization, illustrating the ever-present corruption of the age (*ambitus*, 4.817) and "the fearsome power of wealth" (*opum metuenda facultas*, 4.817) that dragged "weak souls in a torrent of perversity" (*transuerso mentem dubiam torrente tulerunt*, 4.818). At line 4.821 the presence of the adjective "our" (*in iugulos nostros*) contains the throats of Lucan's contemporaries and that of the narrator himself: the idea is that all were guilty and all are paying for their partnership with Caesar and the likes.[32] Like at 7.210–13 (quoted above), the apostrophic movement also involves modern readers, who are called to identify with protagonists and powerfully evoked events and, at the same time, to judge them since what emerges through apostrophe is not forgiveness or acceptance but the narrator's "profound disparagement" of Curio so that while the narrator becomes the singer of Curio's deeds, he also distances himself from Curio's terrible choices.[33]

What has been written about Platonic dialogues and philosophical activities requiring an audience can apply to this apostrophe, "in the theater of presence, watching turns into participating...a watcher 'merges his fantasy with the action he is watching in such a way that he—the watcher—is playing the primary role' (177)."[34] In this scenario, "'you do not care about the hero as much as you care about this new merged entity—yourself in the hero's role' (181). In practice, the philosophical scrutiny and indictment of someone else can feel like a self-indictment."[35] So the reader is the protagonist of the apostrophe and will "exit" the apostrophe in a different state of mind because, as Ann Carson explains,

> A poem, when it works, is an action of the mind captured on a page,
> and the reader, when he engages it, has to enter into that action. And
> so his mind repeats that action and travels again through the action,
> but it is a movement of yourself through a thought, through an
> activity of thinking, so by the time you get to the end you're different
> than you were at the beginning and you feel that difference.[36]

The apostrophe helps this process, which is also consistent with what, according to Paul Roche, is Lucan's goal of making his readers enticed by the heroic behavior and rhetoric of characters like Curio or Caesar only to be told by the narrator that they are not heroic at all.[37] Like protagonists of a tragedy, readers must experience and then realize their *hamartia* ("failure") and the reasons for their fall. They are at first implicated, but by the end of the apostrophic sequence they can pull themselves free because a narrator concerned with what they think and how they feel guides them, acts as their advisor.

The importance of the reader is again manifested in the narrator's apostrophe to the labor of poets in book 9:

> o sacer et magnus uatum labor, omnia fato
> *eripis* et populis donas mortalibus aeuum.
> inuidia sacrae, *Caesar, ne tangere* famae;
> nam, si quid Latiis fas est promittere Musis,
> quantum Zmyrnaei durabunt uatis honores,
> *uenturi me teque* legent; *Pharsalia nostra*
> uiuet, et a nullo tenebris *damnabimur* aeuo.
>   (9.980–86)

> O sacred and immense labor of bards, you snatch everything
> from fate and grant to mortals immortality.

> *Caesar,* do not be touched by envy of sacred fame;
> since, if it is right for Latin Muses to promise anything,
> as long as the honors of Homer (the bard from Smyrna) shall last,
> *future ages* will read *me* and *you; our Pharsalia*
> will live and *we will be condemned* to darkness by no era.

This famous address comes at the end of Caesar's visit to Troy after the general has given his own myopic description of the past "appropriate[ing] the history of Troy as the history of the Julian *gens*."[38] As a reaction to what he has heard from Caesar, in the passage the narrator steps out to warn the reader, revealing that against Caesar's manipulated recollection, he must write his own tale that is the poem we read. So the narrator is responding to Caesar and at the same time thinking about that "third," most essential entity who is part of the dialogue, "those who will come" (*uenturi,* 9.985). The narrator, in this fiction, is a character who "rectifies" wrong readings of the past for future readers.[39] "Our Pharsalia" is a project in which the triad, narrator, internal addressee, and external readers, are all significantly clustered together in the Latin with "readers" coming first (*uenturi me teque,* "those who will come . . . me and you," 9.985), all present and essential.[40] Future audiences can make Pharsalus their own by keeping it alive through the memory they choose to impose on it. Pharsalus stretches its tentacles toward them, the traumatic past reaches into their future, but they can interpret it as they wish and cease to become its victims.[41]

Second-Person Narratives to Implicate the Readers

Recently, several scholars have reflected about second-person narratives and their power to involve the readers. For instance, for Adriana Cavarero the second person acknowledges "the ontological status that binds the reality of the self to the . . . material presence of some*one* other."[42] For Brian McHale "the second person is *par excellence* the sign of relation. Even more strongly than the first person, it announces the presence of a communicative circuit linking addressor and addressee"; through apostrophe the text invites us as readers to place ourselves in the position of protagonist, "to project ourselves into the gap opened in the discourse by the presence of you."[43] Similarly Uri Margolin stresses that the reader is "not just an observer, but the main agent of these events."[44] Lucan's voice, as he addresses his characters and comments on their behavior, draws attention to himself but also to the ineluctable role of readers. In Lucan's hands, the narrative "you" produces effects unobtainable by other persons. The examples above confirm its explicitly transactive nature, its acknowledgement of and reliance on external readers.[45] In apostrophe "the convergence of text and reader brings the literary work into existence";[46] the poem exists for and is realized by its readers who will have to decide on its meaning, following or rejecting the narrator's elucidations.

The role of the reader in the *Civil War* is clearly perceived by Christopher Caterine, who notices that when Lucan's narrator is talking about the geography of Libya, he addresses the reader through a "you" and offers antagonistic theories about that land without choosing a preferred explanation but leaving the decision completely up to him.[47] In this way, Caterine affirms, the poem "places much emphasis on its reader's creation of meaning within the text" but downplays the role of the narrator as a guide.[48] Certainly historically and geographically speaking there is a lot the narrator does not know and cannot understand, but when behavior is being evaluated, neutrality and agnosticism do not seem ever his attitude. On the contrary, Lucan's apostrophes appear as privileged sites for "ethical judgment."[49]

Second-Person Narrative in Seneca and the Control of the Self

The slippery "you" noticed above and the importance of the readers seem inspired by Seneca's way of interacting with his addressee. Not only are Seneca's letters controlled by the implied reader, and apostrophe is a dominant trope of his tragedies, even in his so-called dialogues Seneca "addresses the named addressee . . . in a lively, engaging 'I–you' style, employing frequent rhetorical questions and exclamations. He advocates a particular (generally Stoic) view on the topic of the dialogue and therefore cajoles, exhorts, and chides the addressee and other possible interlocutors, including the reader, to embrace this view."[50] We are tempted to identify Seneca's interlocutor with the dialogue's named addressee—especially when his rejoinders are introduced with the second-person singular form *inquis* ("you say")—but the universal nature of the problems explored in the exchanges encourages us to maintain a more general view of the interlocutor's identity. Seneca's slippery rhetoric of address united with the universality of the situations discussed is meant to involve all readers. Lucan adopts a similar use of the "you" in his apostrophe.[51] Let us elaborate about the ethical implications of apostrophe, what it reveals about the narrator when he talks to his readers, and why this narrator figures so prominently in Lucan's context.

In his book *The Empire of the Self,* Christopher Star describes the role of *imperium* in Senecan philosophy. He notices that Seneca in his work "subordinates the traditional ideal of military and political power over others to the power of commanding the self (*sibi imperare*). When the rule over one's soul is the greatest victory a man can aspire to, tools to obtain this mastery are not of minor importance."[52] Therefore apostrophe and the imperative mood, originally appreciated in the courtroom, become essential psychological instruments in the theatre of the mind. In his letters, when Seneca addresses Lucilius and helps him to re-evaluate facts and ideas, the point is the reshaping of one's soul (*se fingere*, Ep. 18.2; *animos transfigurari*, Ep. 94.48).[53] In his *Civil War*, Lucan addresses his characters, his readers, and himself for the same goal. The apostrophe, especially as it is read by a silent reader or by the author, can be heard as a call to self-reflection, as an invitation or command to believe something and behave consequently. Seneca's letters mimic a conversation in which the speaker wanting to provoke a reaction uses an indulgent or harsh tone. Although he represents himself for his reader as a moral guide and a doctor of sorts, he is quite aware that he is not essentially different from his addressee. For instance, letter 27.1 opens with Seneca's acknowledgement that he is addressing himself as much as his correspondent:

> "Why are you giving me advice" you will ask "perhaps you have already given it to yourself, you have corrected yourself and now you have time for the correction of others (*aliorum emendationi*)?" I am not so dishonest to pretend to heal others while I myself am sick. Instead as if we were in the same hospital, I talk to you about a common disease and I share the medicines (*de communi tecum malo conloquar et remedia communico*). Therefore listen to me as if I talked to myself (*sic itaque me audi tamquam mecum loquar*).[54]

The advice is for the reader but also for he who writes. The address becomes a self-address, and the therapy becomes peer counseling. The identification with the addressee in this case promotes a tolerant tone. Instead, in letter 99 the tone is harsh. Quite aggressively, Seneca addresses Marullus, who is still grieving for his son. He begins, "Are you looking for consolation? Take some abuse instead" (*solacia expectas? conuicia accipe*, Ep. 99.1). The point is to shake the addressee—Marullus, the reader, himself—to make each person see that grief is an error. Seneca's style implicates his readers "as active players in the therapeutic drama, as if licensed and encouraged to rise to the Senecan provocation."[55] We realize throughout Seneca's corpus the Stoic idea of learning as increasing vigilance and wakefulness, in which "the mind learns to repossess its own experiences from the fog of habit, convention, and forgetfulness."[56]

Similar concerns are at work in Lucan's poem. Through apostrophe he talks to his readers; sometimes with biting sarcasm he conveys the folly of Caesar or his supporters, other times in sympathetic, rather consolatory tones, for instance as he encourages Caesar's victims. The cognitive content of the trope enables the readers' reconceptualization and control of the matter in question. A good illustration of the link between control of the self and apostrophe can be found at 7.677–97. Here, the long apostrophic movement through which the narrator accompanies Pompey while the general abandons Pharsalus illustrates the mechanism. Witness to Pompey's defeat, the narrator bids him to read it as a sign of divine favor and reminds him that it is the best option from an ethical point of view:

> quidquid in ignotis solus regionibus exul,
> quidquid sub Phario positus patiere tyranno,
> *crede* deis, longo fatorum credi fauori:
> *uincere peius erat.* prohibe lamenta sonare,
> flere *ueta populos,* lacrimas luctusque *remitte.*
> tam mala Pompei quam prospera mundus adoret.
>
> (7.703–8)

> Whatever you suffer in lands unknown, a lonely exile,
> whatever trials at hands of the Pharian tyrant,
> *trust* the gods, trust the long-lasting favor of Fate:
> *to win was worse!* Allow no sound of lamentation,
> *forbid* the people to weep, *forgo* tears and grief!
> Let the world hail Pompey's woes as they hailed his prosperity!

Lucan commands Magnus not to be sad for a withdrawal that proves his own ethical superiority. No tears should be shed because Pompey's rectitude has not been compromised. The imperatives summon the general but also the reader to favor an ethical choice that privileges what is right over what seems convenient. Already Seneca had observed that in civil war "the better man may win, but the winner is bound to be the worse" (*potest melior uincere, non potest non peius esse, qui uicerit. Ep.* 14.13); Lucan voices Seneca's opinion in a Senecan style. Against Caesar who tries to convince his man that defeat will make them guilty (7.259–60), the narrator endorses an opposite point of view. Just as in Plato's *Republic* Socrates challenged Thrasymachus's doctrine according to which "might is right," Lucan's narrator challenges that view and becomes the supporter of a philosophically charged ethical stance that does not depend on practical success.[57] Philosophical discourse becomes a filter through which the epic world is often explored and Roman *uirtus* requalified. With the help of philosophy, Lucan "deconstructs the binary opposites 'winner' and 'loser,'" on which epic is built.[58] A Stoic approach to defeat is communicated in a Stoic fashion. Lucan's narrator cares about his reader and as a kind of consoler steers him to evaluate defeat in the right light. As Seneca suggested to Polybius, the role of *consolator* ("consoler") can be thrust upon somebody whose own wounds are not healed yet. Polybius can be an *exemplum* for his relatives even if he is still troubled by the death of his brother (Sen. *Pol.* 5.4–5).[59] Lucan's narrator, sounding like a philosopher, can address Pompey even if he is far from the *tranquillitas* ("calmness") of the sage and greatly troubled by the defeat of the republic.[60] As he confesses in book 6, Caesar's victory over an enemy committed to piety is cause for never-ending pain ("it hurts and it always hurt that you fought against a pious son-in-law," *dolet heu semper dolebit . . . cum genero pugnasse pio,* 6.303–5). The sorrow stems from a tragic awareness that morality in the civil war does not accomplish anything.[61] If the ruthless Sulla had fought Pharsalus, final defeat could have been avoided (6.302–3); instead a general rightly preoccupied to preserve as many Roman lives as possible triggers the demise of the republic. Dilemma chokes Lucan's characters and turns the epic into a tragedy. However, the narrator regains a degree of control in this apostrophe when he celebrates defeat and consoles Pompey in the name of ethical decency. He presents arguments that readers can use to reassess events and to regain control over themselves. Moral judgment is not customarily provided in epic apostrophe, but Lucan transforms the trope and makes it a privileged site for didactic evaluation.

Hope and Lucan's "Sublime" Apostrophes

There is one more factor relevant about Lucan's apostrophes to Pompey and their function. Henry Day has argued that we can find two kinds of sublime in the *Civil War*, the "Caesarian" and the "Pompeian" sublime. The first is based upon the sublime experience of nature that, like the encounter with Caesar, overcomes and enslaves; the second, the Pompeian sublime, is linked to traumatic history as described by Frank Ankersmit.[62] Day frames the fall of Pompey and of the republic as the traumatic experience that generates in the viewer a sense of estrangement and loss.[63] Yet, according to Day, there is an essential difference between the sublime and the traumatic: "where the reorientation of identity imposed by trauma is fundamentally negative, characterized by pain and grief, that produced by the sublime, though also spurred by loss, additionally promotes a movement of subjective restitution."[64] The Pompeian sublime "carries with it an implicitly positive charge."[65]

The potentials of the Pompeian sublime can be grasped better in close reading of the text, for example, at 1.135–43 when the reader contemplates Pompey's decrepitude embodied in the metaphor of the tottering yet sublime oak tree (*sublimis quercus*, 1.135) and is invited to "see a previous state in a later one."[66] What is missing and the viewer is asked to re-create with the help of the narrator enlarges the object and makes it alive again.[67] Even more clearly, in book 8 when the narrator apostrophizes Pompey and stares at his tomb, he wants the reader to visualize the general's resurrection:

> Magne, petet, quem non tumuli uenerabile saxum
> et cinis in summis forsan turbatus harenis
> auertet manesque tuos placare iubebit
> et Casio praeferre Ioui? nil ista nocebunt
> famae busta tuae . . .
>
> . . . .
>
> proderit hoc olim, quod non mansura futuris
> ardua marmoreo surrexit pondere moles.
> pulueris exigui sparget non longa uetustas
> congeriem, bustumque cadet, mortisque peribunt
> argumenta tuae. Veniet felicior aetas,
> qua si nulla fides saxum monstrantibus illud,
> atque erit Aegyptus populis fortasse nepotum
> tam mendax Magni tumolo, quam Creta Tonantis.
>
> $$(8.855-59, 865-72)$$

> Which man, Magnus, the venerable stone of your tomb
> and the ashes perhaps dispersed on the surface
> will not draw aside and urge to appease your spirit
> preferred over Casian Jove? This pyre
> will not mar your fame . . .
>
> . . . .
>
> One day, it will be a boon that no high monument of massive marble
> has risen up to remain for posterity.
> A short amount of time will disperse the small pile of dust,
> the grave will fall and will perish
> all proofs of your death. A happier age will come,
> when none will believe those who point out that stone
> and, perhaps, to the generation of our descendants, the tomb of Magnus
> in Egypt will sound like a lie similar to the tomb of Jove in Crete.

The narrator envisions Pompey's fall and rise, so to speak, in the unremarkable tomb that at first marks his collapse and in times to come points to a different fate and triumph. We see here the mesmerizing effect of an address that derives power and presence from absence and ruin. Pompey's makeshift tomb becomes the conduit for his greatness, indeed for his elevation to divine status. Earlier in the text (8.849–50), the narrator imagined the creation of a newly established Pompeian cult "contrasting with the form of deification associated with, and following on from, Caesar."[68] In lines 8.861–62, Pompey's almost invisible grave is qualified as "more venerable than the altars of the winner" (*augustius aris uictoris*) and the myth of Pompey's burial compared to Jove's. The absence of a tomb guarantees Pompey's fame and makes him similar to the gods; it is also a threat to them and reason for hope because the narrator invites Pompey and his readers to focus on a happier time when future generations will believe him immortal. At the beginning of book 9 the assertion comes true: Pompey reaches heaven on account of his innocence (9.1–18) and returns to earth in the breasts of Cato and Brutus to vindicate Caesar's crimes. Soon after at 9.603–7, on account of his *uirtus*, Cato too is hailed by the narrator as a god that future generations, restored to freedom, will honor.[69] The emancipatory potentials of these sublime apostrophes is unlocked when the narrator depicts for the reader the advent of new gods arising to fight the old ones in a sort of renewed theomachic cycle. In these invocations some optimism is produced, a cure to the disease of Caesar appears, and with it the hope programmatically invoked at 7.211 because "[b]y repeating the crucial act of human divinization, but at the same time altering the character and values of those divinized," the narrator wants to persuade the reader that the great error of the past can be rectified. [70] In this manner Lucan attempts to give power back to the self, threatened by an autocratic environment.

Some Conclusions

If, by common consent, epic expectations and Caesar erroneously habituated the Romans to perceive defeat as a disgrace and death as a stumbling block, philosophy teaches that "we have in ourselves (*in nostra postestate*) a remedy" (*Ad Marciam* 19.1). What we think and how we feel about something is up to us. This empowering aspect of Stoicism is highlighted by Michel Foucault when he describes Graeco-Roman "care of the self." Foucault's conceptualization of Stoic ethics provides a compelling interpretative framework for understanding Lucan's agenda in apostrophe. As we have seen, the idea of an educational process "that is capable of recovering rationally what a man, at first, non-rationally feels in himself" is characteristic of Stoicism and found in Seneca's writings.[71] For instance, Seneca describes the attentive scanning of one's action in a passage of his *De Ira* (3.36.1–3), which Foucault comments on in his *Care of the Self,* noting that the daily habit of self-scrutiny is portrayed through the verb *excutere* (3.36.2), entailing "shaking out" or "knocking so as to make the dust fall" and conducting an inquiry by which one locates the errors, wanting to remove them; self-scrutiny is also portrayed through the verb *remetiri* (3.36.3), which describes an inspection aimed at the "remeasuring" of the acts that were committed and the words that were spoken to see if they "measure up" to the standards the self has given to itself.[72] The purpose of this observation is not only "to liberate the subject, to make her independent of the power that her representations of objects have over her";[73] in this recollection "the fault is not reactivated in order to determine a culpability or stimulate a feeling of remorse, but in order to strengthen . . . the rational equipment that ensures a wise behaviour."[74]

So in Lucan's *Civil War* the long apostrophic movements that cut through the narration and redraw it empower the reader with a novel understanding of that same narration. Lucan realizes the determinative, institutional (that is Caesar-driven), coercive forces that bound every Roman and uses some of the discursive resources made available by Stoicism and poetry to find a way out of that prison. The operation indeed resembles Foucault's attempt to put the "subject" at the center by resorting to ancient "care of the self,"[75] which becomes a creation of the self and the only means the subject has to resist political power.[76] As Paul Allen Miller suggests, the turn toward the self "need not lead to indifference about the external world and, in fact, depends upon the relationship between self and external world. This, albeit implicitly, is a reply to the Hegelian caricature of Stoicism as an isolationist inner retreat."[77] Seneca's preoccupation with slavery of the soul (e.g., *De Ira* 3.14.1–2) is inherited by Lucan, whose apostrophes reveal an author intensely concerned with his readers and their psychological and political liberation. If the facts of the *Civil War*, bound to its immediate history, must represent the defeat of Pharsalus and the triumph of wicked men backed by oblivious and immoral gods, the narrator summons readers to think for themselves beyond the mere representation of those facts about new gods who care about morality and freedom.

Notes

1. For example, the four-element theory of physical philosophy emerges in Vergil's *Georgics*, cf. Ross 1987; the importance of self-control and self-knowledge are key elements in Persius's *Satires*, cf. Littlewood 2002.

2. Colish 1985, 252, and recently Garani and Konstan 2015.

3. Colish 1985, 252.

4. For example, Marti 1945; Dick 1967; Ahl 1976; George 1986; Radicke 2004.

5. For example, Due 1970; Narducci 1979, 2002; Bartsch 1997; D'Alessandro Behr 2007; Long 2007; Stover 2008; Lapidge 2010. For a review of approaches to Stoicism in *Civil War*, see Braund 2010, 1–13; Thorne 2010, 14–28; D'Alessandro Behr 2014, 217–24.

6. Henderson 1987; Johnson 1987; Masters 1992; Hardie 1993; Leigh 1997; Sklenář 1999; Hershkowitz 1998; Seo 2011; Tipping 2011.

7. Asmis 2009, 115, describing Seneca's morality.

8. Murnagham 1995, 758.

9. Martin 2005; Alexis 2011, 2–3.

10. Throughout this chapter my own translations of Lucan are used to illustrate most clearly the nuances I am emphasizing. Italics are mine unless noted otherwise.

11. On emotions and ethical health, Nussbaum 1994, 78–101.

12. Bartsch 1997, 85: for the narrator taking up of Pompey's banner.

13. Quoted in Murnagham 1995, 760–61, my italics. Bracketed ellipses indicate ellipses from original text. The arousal of emotions through the employment of words alone is highlighted at *Poet.*1453b1–6: "The plot should be so constructed that even without seeing the play anyone hearing of the incidents happening thrills with fear and pity as a result of what occurs" (trans. W. H. Fyfe).

14. Murnagham 1995, 765.

15. Day 2013, 90–92.

16. Staley 2010, 7.

17. Cf. *Inst.* 6.2.29 and Leigh 1997, 14, mentioning Longinus *Subl.* 15.2; D'Alessandro Behr 2007, 77–78. Rhetorical and Stoic conceptions of *phantasia* are different but related specializations of the same basic model and share the idea that "a mental impression of some kind is intimately bound up with the production of language," Webb 2009, 118.

18. Halliwell 2011, 327–36; Carrera 2016, 26.

19. Halliwell 2002, 93.

20. Halliwell 2011, 341, italics in original.

21. About Stoic ways of conceptualizing poetry and its effects on the readers, De Lacy 1958; Nussbaum 1993; Bartsch 2007.

22. Taylor 1989, 137: "The [Stoics'] singling out of . . . assent is one source of the developing notion of the will, and there is already an important change in moral outlook in making this the central human faculty. What is morally crucial about us is not just the universal nature or rational principle which we share with others, as with Plato and Aristotle, but now also this power of assent, which is essentially mine."

23. Bartsch 2009, 197: discussing Stoic cognitive theory.

24. De Jong 2005, 620–21.

25. This is a Stoic preoccupation, see Cato's linguistic concerns in Sallust (*Cat.* 52.11–12).

26. Lada 1998, 390. Among the techniques useful to the formation of a critical stance, Stoic texts recommend a running commentary on the action "that approximates to the criticism philosophy itself would offer," see Nussbaum 1993, 139. Martindale 1993, 31–32; Pucci 1998, 43–44.

27. Asso 2008, 163; originally this third element is the jury itself for which the strategy was ultimately conceived.

28. For a definition, De Jong 2004, glossary, xvi.

29. Kacandes 1994, 329.

30. For Regulus, Hor. *Carm.* 3.5; Cic. *Fin.* 2.65.

31. Fratantuono 2012, 171–73. Cf. Vergil's apostrophes to Euryalus, Nisus, and Lausus at *Aen.* 9.446–49 and 10.791–93.

32. Asso 2010, 285–93.

33. Asso 2010, 284.

34. Henderson Collins 2012, 162 quoting Woodruff 2008, 177.

35. Henderson Collins 2012, 162 quoting Woodruff 2008, 181.

36. Carson 2004. Cf. Halliwell 2011, 333, describing "*inter*subjectivity" as hallmark of the sublime.

37. Roche 2005, 70–72.

38. Rossi 2001, 320. Highlighting sarcasm against Caesar, Narducci 2002, 179–80.

39. Ormand 1994.

40. Cf. Day 2013, 985. For the mixing up of narrative planes and apostrophe as metalepsis, see De Moura 2010, 89.

41. Cf. Walde 2011; Day 2013, 182–88; Pendey 2014, 133.

42. Cavarero 2000, 90 (in Italian, translated by the author).

43. McHale 1987, 223–24.

44. Margolin 1990, 443.

45. Holland 1980, 363.

46. Iser 1988, 212.

47. Caterine 2015.

48. Caterine 2015, 359.

49. Bartsch 2012.

50. Roller 2015, 60, and Williams 2015. For Seneca's style, Mazzoli 1970; Traina 1974; Setaioli 2000, 111–217; Hadot 2014.

51. Lucan's style is so similar to that of Seneca that some ancient scholiasts (e.g., *Commenta Bernensia* 1.1 and *Life* in the MS Vossianus II) ascribed the first seven lines of the poem to him, see Conte 1966, 42.

52. Star 2012, 15; *Ep.* 113.29–30. Cf. Roller 2001, introduction.

53. Bartsch 2009 explores the importance of metaphors in the goal of shaping the soul.

54. Cf. *Ep.* 68.9 *non medicus sed aeger hic habitat* and *Ep.* 45.4, where Seneca affirms that he has not yet found the truth but he seeks it stubbornly (*uerum quaeram adhuc non scio, et contumaciter quaeram*).

55. Wilson 1987, 108.

56. Nussbaum 1994, 340.

57. Ahl 1993, 135–36. Virtue unaccompanied by practical result is also celebrated at 9.594–95.

58. Quint 1993, 46, and Roche 2005, 56–57.

59. Cf. *Ep.* 63 where Seneca consoles Lucilius for the death of Flaccus.

60. In the *Civil War*, the sage is able to preserve his composure; Cato is described as *securumque sui* (2.241), however the passage is rather complex.

61. The conflicting logic of *pietas* is well captured by Roller 2001, 33.

62. Cf. Ankersmit 2005.

63. Day 2013, 203.

64. Day 2013, 187.

65. Day 2013, 187.

66. Day 2013, 216.

67. Day 2013, 216.

68. Chaudhuri 2014, 185. For Pompey "in the sky," Narducci 2002, 335–53.

69. Narducci 2002, 339–45 and, highlighting a Stoic matrix, Brena 1999. For the titanism of the sage, La Penna 1979.

70. Chaudhuri 2014, 192. On hope, rightly linked to Cato, Thorne 2010, 33, 179–82.

71. Maso 2011, 3.

72. Foucault 1988, 61–62.

73. McGushin 2006, 143.

74. Foucault 1988, 62

75. Seitz 2012, 544.

76. Miller 1998, 205.

77. Sellars 2012, 538.

14

Lucan as Caesar's Epic Successor

LAUREN DONOVAN GINSBERG

He seems to have expected the reader either to be content with a vague impression or to recognize the allusions through familiarity with the history.

—Lintott 1971, 493

Put simply, Lucan's poem cannot replace his sources; it is parasitic on them.

—Masters 1994, 154

These works are alive in Lucan not just as "sources" for historical facts, but as intertexts.

—Ash and Sharrock 2001, 326

When Lucan came to write his epic *Civil War*, he had access to a rich literary-historical tradition created by his prose predecessors. Chief among them would have been Livy's *From the Founding of the City*, a work often assumed to have been *the* definitive account of the period's history, and Asinius Pollio's *Histories*, a work known for its firsthand account of events.[1] Unfortunately for the modern reader, the near total loss of both texts makes it impossible to say what use Lucan made of them or how he positioned his own rival narrative within and against their interpretations of history. And yet there does exist another work whose scope matches Lucan's almost exactly and whose author would surely have created a magnetic draw for our poet: the *Civil War* of Julius Caesar.

This chapter will offer a series of lenses through which the modern student or scholar can study the question of Lucan's relationship to his Caesarian predecessor. My goal throughout will be to view Caesar's *Civil War* not only as one of Lucan's sources for historical data but also as a rival literary model to which Lucan responds in manifold ways.[2] In doing so, I will examine Lucan's reception of Caesar from several interrelated perspectives: (1) Lucan's presentation of the historical actors, chiefly Caesar himself and the Pompeian soldiers, (2) his use of compression and expansion as complementary intertextual tools to shift the focus of Caesar's episode without contradicting Caesar directly, (3) his repurposing of Caesar's language and imagery to serve his own interpretive ends, and (4) his allusive response to the wider structural role that the Spanish campaign played in Caesar's *Civil War*.[3]

For ease of coherence, my primary focus will be the episode of fraternization between the Pompeian and Caesarian soldiers in Spain at and around Ilerda, part of a wider episode that occupies the second half of book 1 of Caesar (the longest unbroken narrative in his *Civil War*) and the first four hundred lines at the start of book 4 of Lucan. After some brief skirmishes and shifts in strategic advantage between the Caesarians (led by Caesar himself) and Pompeians (led jointly by Afranius and Petreius), the two armies set up camp outside Ilerda relatively close to each other. During this time the Pompeian commanders seize the opportunity of inspecting their fortifications at some distance away and so leave their camps unattended. This lucky confluence of absent commanders and locational proximity cause the two armies to intermingle and renew bonds of citizenship to such an extent they no longer seem to be enemies in civil war. Unfortunately for the soldiers, Petreius crashes back into the scene, destroys the peace, slaughters the enemy soldiers he finds, and sends the Caesarians scrambling back to their camp. The fighting renews, but Caesar is eventually victorious despite Pompeian attempts to prolong the violence of war. Caesar spares all of the opposing troops and does not force them to fight for his side.

This episode appears in all surviving accounts of the civil war including Caesar, the *periochae* of Livy, Velleius Paterculus, Lucan, Plutarch, Suetonius, Appian, Cassius Dio, and Florus.[4] The main take away from the episode in all these sources is Caesar's grandiose act of *clementia* ("forgiveness") and the reputational strategy behind it as Pompeians spread word to other Pompeians of Caesar's generosity. Particularly important to Caesar's account is the fraternization between opposing troops, a moment that for him becomes symbolic of how easily peace could have been obtained if it were not for Pompeian leadership. Nevertheless, in his focus on this otherwise strategically insignificant moment within the wider Spanish campaign, Caesar differs from most other surviving sources. In fact, Lucan's is the only other account to devote as much narrative space to the fraternization or to foreground its thematic importance.[5] This alone should suggest that we read the two texts alongside one another and explore the narrative tensions brought about through this process. But as we will see, Lucan also includes several unmistakable echoes of Caesar's text that signal an allusive relationship, that authorize his ideal reader to go hunting for further points of convergence or divergence.

Narrative and Characterization

Caesar's account of the fraternization is the lynchpin for his entire narrative.[6] It is his thesis, his argument:[7]

> quorum discessu liberam nacti milites colloquiorum facultatem uulgo procedunt, et quem quisque in castris notum aut municipem habebat conquirit atque euocat. 2. primum agunt gratias omnes omnibus quod sibi perterritis pridie pepercissent: eorum se beneficio uiuere. Deinde imperatoris fidem quaerunt rectene se illi sint commissuri, et quod non ab initio fecerint armaque quod cum hominibus necessariis et consanguineis contulerint queruntur. 3. his prouocati sermonibus fidem ab imperatore de Petrei atque Afrani uita petunt ne quod in se scelus concepisse neu suos prodidisse uideantur. quibus confirmatis rebus se statim signa translaturos confirmant legatosque de pace primorum ordinum centuriones ad Caesarem mittunt. 4. interim alii suos in castra inuitandi causa adducunt, alii ab suis abducuntur, adeo ut una castra iam facta ex binis uiderentur; . . . 7. erant plena laetitia et gratulatione omnia.
>
> (Caes. *BCiv.* 1.74.1–4, 7)

At their departure, the soldiers, having acquired free chance of open speech, came out in a crowd, and whoever had someone known in the other camp or a fellow townsman, inquired after them and called them out. 2. At first they all thanked everyone because they had spared the terrified men on the previous day: it was due to their good deed that they lived. Then they inquire about the *fides* of the general (sc. Caesar), whether they were right to entrust themselves to him, and they lament that they had not done this from the start and that they bore arms against friends and kinsman. 3. Moved by these conversations, they sought *fides* from the general concerning the lives of Petreius and Afranius, lest they seem to have plotted any

scelus or betrayed their own side. With such things confirmed they pledge that they will immediately transfer their standards and send centurions of the first order to Caesar as legates for peace talks.
4. Meanwhile some bring their acquaintances into the camps for the sake of entertaining, others are brought over by their friends, with the result that one came seemed to be made from two . . . 7. everything was full of happiness and thanksgiving.

Caesar uses this episode to show that once the Pompeian commanders are removed, their soldiers revert to friendly citizens who privilege social bonds, communitarian perspectives, and the virtue of sparing the enemy. Moreover, when free to act on these inclinations, the soldiers' trust in the loyalty (*fides*, Caes. 1.74.2–3) that Caesar shows to fellow Romans allows them to begin formal negotiations for a peace treaty, one which even makes provisions for the lives of their leaders (Caes. 1.74.3). For even when acting behind their generals' backs, the Pompeians are loathe to commit the sacrilege (*scelus*, Caes. 1.74.3) of treachery (*prodidisse*, Caes. 1.74.3). The successful beginnings to peace throughout this scene come only because Caesar had deliberately decided to find a peaceful, bloodless conclusion to the struggle, against the urging of his men by whom "Caesar's plan was not approved" (*hoc consilium Caesaris plerisque non probabatur*, Caes. 1.72.4). For this reason, he took the risk of putting his camps nearby the Pompeians, a choice emphasized by his artful juxtaposition of words punctuated with marked alliteration (*castris castra communit*, "[next to their] camp he fortified his camp," Caes. 1.72.5). If peace had found a way to break the passion of civil war at Ilerda, it would have been a Caesarian peace.

While Lucan's scene borrows many of Caesar's details and interpretive moves, several key differences emerge straight away:[8]

> mox, ut stimulis maioribus ardens
> rupit amor leges, audet transcendere uallum
> miles, in amplexus effusas tendere palmas.
> hospitis ille ciet nomen, uocat ille propinquum,
> admonet hunc studiis consors puerilibus aetas;
> nec Romanus erat, qui non agnouerat hostem.
> arma rigant lacrimis, singultibus oscula rumpunt
> . . . .
> pax erat, et castris miles permixtus utrisque
> errabat; duro concordes caespite mensas
> instituunt et permixto libamina Baccho;
> graminei luxere foci, iunctoque cubili

extrahit insomnis bellorum fabula noctes,
quo primum steterint campo, qua lancea dextra
exierit.

(4.174–80, 196–202)

       Soon, when burning love with its more powerful
spurs broke the rules, the soldiers dare to climb across
the rampart, to stretch their hands wide for embraces.
One calls out the name of his host, another shouts to his kinsman;
youth shared on boys' pursuits stirs this man's memory;
and he who had not recognized an enemy was not a Roman.
They drench with tears their weapons, with sobs they break their kisses . . .
. . . .
There was peace and the soldiers mingled and in both camps
freely wandered: on the hard ground they set up tables
of concord and made libations with mingled Bacchus;
the turf-built altars glowed and on couches side by side
talk of the wars prolongs the sleepless nights:
on which field they first stood, from which strong hand the lance
flew.

The most obvious difference is that Lucan's Caesar takes no part in the fraternization; he is entirely absent from the narrative during this pause in the fighting and only reappears after its dissolution when the Pompeians try to retreat at a later point.[9] In fact, Lucan attributes the camp's placement to the men generally (*castra locant* "they pitch their camp," 4.169), contrary to Caesar's emphasis on his own careful planning (*castra communit*, "he fortified his camp," Caes. 1.72.5).[10] At first, then, it seems Lucan has taken Caesar's insistence that the individual Pompeian men were ready to come to terms and has blended those details into a wider scene in which Rome's citizens on *both* sides are seen to default to peace when their *duces* ("generals") are not looking.[11]

But this is to miss what Lucan is up to, his reasons for keeping Caesar at bay. Lucan's aim throughout this scene is less to deny Caesar the credit for a successful battle strategy than to challenge Caesar's representation of the common soldier in the first place, especially the idea that the Pompeian soldiers were primed for peace. For this reason, the epic poet consistently has each side view the other as the enemy (e.g., *hostis* at 4.179, 208–9, 228–29) even amidst their reconciliation, as opposed to Caesar, who had abandoned the rhetoric of combat throughout this episode in order to describe both sides as citizens deserving of pity (e.g., *misericordia ciuium*, Caes. 1.72.3).[12] Lucan's soldiers, unlike those in Caesar's narrative, never stop being enemies, even as bonds of love are renewed. While Lucan lingers on the rituals of social reunification for a longer time than Caesar, allowing his men to embrace (4.176), to dine together (4.197), to converse (4.200–203), and to renew the bonds of hospitality, he stops short of what was the crucial moment in Caesar's account: the beginnings of capitulation and peace.

Within Caesar's text, as we have seen, once the men are assured of his trustworthiness, they promise to send their standards immediately along with legates for peace talks (Caes. 1.74.3). The negotiations go so well that some Pompeians even defect to Caesar's side (Caes. 1.74.5–6). Everything is full of joy and mutual congratulations (Caes. 1.74.7), and a formal peace seems at hand. Because Lucan's scene is driven by the men themselves and their passions (*rupit amor leges*, "love broke the rules," 4.175)[13] rather than by Caesar's plans, no formal negotiation takes place within the text. Thus his account never actually makes formal moves toward closure as Caesar's did but rather only creates a pause in the unstoppable forces of civil war.

It therefore comes as a surprise that when Lucan's Petreius comes back on the scene, he has heard of treaties with specific terms:[14]

> nam postquam foedera pacis
> cognita Petreio, seque et sua tradita uenum
> castra uidet, famulas scelerata ad proelia dextras
> excitat atque hostis turba stipatus inermis
> praecipitat castris iunctosque amplexibus ense
> separat et multo disturbat sanguine pacem.
>
> (4.205–10)

> For when Petreius learnt
> about the pact of peace and sees that he and his camp
> have been betrayed, he calls to wicked battle the sword-hands
> of his slaves and, screened by the throng, he hurls from the camp
> the unarmed enemy, with the sword parts men joined
> in embrace and shatters the peace with abundant blood.

Later as he speaks to the troops he accuses them of "forgetting their standards" (*signorum oblite tuorum*, 4.212) while preparing to raise the standards of Caesar. He also accuses them of further treachery because they made terms for their generals' lives:

> "ibitis ad dominum damnataque signa feretis,
> utque habeat famulos nullo discrimine Caesar
> exorandus erit? ducibus quoque uita petita est?
> numquam nostra salus pretium mercesque nefandae
> proditionis erit."
>
> (4.217–21)

"Will you go over to a master, will you bear his standards you once
    condemned,
will you have to plead with Caesar to treat his slaves
with no discrimination? And for your generals too has life been begged?
Never shall our safety be the price and the reward
of abominable betrayal."

But where is Lucan's Petreius getting his information from? The answer cannot be Lucan, who does not include any such details. So it seems that Petreius
has been reading his Caesar—and reading him carefully, as he imports Caesar's particular words and images into the new narrative (cf. *fidem ab impera-
tore de Petrei atque Afrani uita petunt . . . neu suos prodidisse uideantur . . . signa
translaturos*, "they begged for their general's promise concerning the life of
Petreius and Afranius . . . lest they seem to betray their own side . . . they would
transfer their standards," Caes. 1.74.3).[15]

Petreius's reactions also follow his Caesarian avatar's precisely:

armat familiam. cum hac et praetoria cohorte caetratorum
barbarisque equitibus paucis, beneficiariis suis quos suae custodiae
causa habere consuerat, improviso ad vallum advolat, colloquia
militum interrumpit, nostros repellit a castris. quos deprendit
interficit.

(Caes. BCiv. 1.75.2)

He armed slaves. With these and his Spanish praetorian cohort and a
few native cavalry for his own benefit whom he was accustomed to
have as bodyguards, he suddenly raced to the rampart, interrupted
the soldiers' talking, drove our men from the camp, and killed any
he caught.

In both accounts, Petreius uses armed slaves and foreigners as a tyrant waging
war against fellow Roman soldiers—his own and Caesar's—in an attempt to
restore order to his camp.[16] While this action was meant to be understood as
despicable in Caesar's narrative, it surely comes across even worse in Lucan's
given Petreius's total misreading of the situation.[17] For not only did Lucan's soldiers never talk of peace, but Lucan's removal of Caesar would make such
negotiation impossible. Petreius is, in effect, inserting violence where it need
not have been.

Thus, as Lucan uses Caesar's villainous Petreius to equally villainous ends,
he alludes to Caesar's presentation of history only to introduce an inconsistency
concerning the *foedera pacis* ("pact of peace," 4.205, cf. Caes. 1.74.3). This inconsistency, in turn, highlights the epic's deviations from the ethical world of

Caesar's *Civil War* and a crucial difference in the two presentations of the character of the common soldier.[18] In other words, I suggest that we are meant to ask about these treaties thrust upon us so suddenly and to compare and contrast the situations within Caesar's text that gave rise to formal peace negotiations and those within Lucan's text that deny such a possibility.

In doing so, we must not overlook that as Petreius imports these Caesarian details into his Lucanian scene, he also perverts their significance. Caesar's Pompeians received neither bribe nor monetary compensation; they sought assurance for their commanders' lives because it was the right thing to do. Lucan's Petreius turns these same soldiers into venal mercenaries (*sua tradita uenum | castra*, "his camp put up for sale," 4.206–7) willing to enslave themselves (*famulos*, 4.218) and betray their betters for material gain. For this reason, he later calls their loyalty "cheap" (*at uobis uilior hoc est | uestra fides*, 4.229–30), continuing the financial metaphor.[19] Thus as he imports Caesar's account of law and order into Lucan's lawless Spanish landscape, he simultaneously offers an alternative reading of Caesar's episode and the role of Pompey's soldiers in it, one which fits with Lucan's wider assessment of civilian behavior and motivation.

As we have seen from this brief glimpse into narrative and characterization, Lucan adheres both to the wider structures of Caesar's Spanish episode as well as to its key words and details. So too our cast of characters on the Pompeian side remains the same: a group of common soldiers susceptible to the temptations of fraternization against the will of their morally bankrupt commanders. It might even be argued that Lucan villainizes Petreius to a greater degree than Caesar had done. But within these wider points of narrative agreement, we have also seen Lucan shift the focus of these characterizations through his elimination of Caesar as a central, driving narrative force. Caesar's absence forces the Pompeian soldiers further into the spotlight as individual agents while denying them the ability to negotiate a formal (even if ineffective) end to fighting. As a result, Lucan is able to challenge Caesar's overarching arguments about the inherent goodness of common soldiers: in his view, Pompey's men are driven by passion (*amor*, 4.174, 242), not pursuit of peace. The significance of this shift in focus and characterization becomes clearer as we move further into the scene.

Suppression, Compression, and Expansion

Lucan's shifts in argumentation as mirrored in his shifts in the narration and characterization of the Pompeian soldiers appear even starker in the response of those soldiers to Petreius's intervention. In Caesar's text, after Petreius arms slaves and a bodyguard composed of foreign soldiers, he goes around to each soldier and makes them swear "that they will not again desert or betray their cause, nor will they undertake a plan for themselves as individuals separate from the rest" (*se exercitum ducesque non deserturos neque prodituros neque sibi separatim a reliquis consilium capturos*, Caes. 1.76.2). The soldiers dutifully swear, and Caesar indicates that this new oath (*noua religio iuris iurandi*, Caes. 1.76.5) combined with a fear (*terrore*, Caes. 1.76.5) of their commanders, "changed the soldiers' minds and returned the situation to the earlier mindset of war" (*mentesque militum conuertit et rem ad pristinam belli rationem redegit*, Caes. 1.76.5).

Lucan follows Caesar in his key details once more, though in a direct speech of much greater length (4.212–35). His Petreius harangues the soldiers for their betrayal, laments the harm done to absent Pompey (4.231–35), and chides them for ceasing the fight while blood still flowed in their veins (4.215–16). He also borrows the rhetorical strategy of Caesar's Petreius: while his soldiers swear no oath, he begins the speech by speaking to them with second-person singular verbs as individuals with diverse motivations (e.g., *potes* "can you," 4.213; *redeas* "that you return," 4.214; *ut uincare, potes* "you can be defeated," 4.215) and then, over the course of his speech, switches to collective second-person plural expressions (e.g., *feretis* "you will bear," 4.217; *uobis . . . uestra* "you, yours," 4.229–30). He thus actualizes the commands of Caesar's Petreius against soldiers hatching plans "as individuals" (*sibi separatim*, Caes. 1.76.5) by bringing his men back together as a collective syntactical unit ready for war. That his speech hits its mark becomes clear by Lucan's subsequent echo of Caesar (1.76.5, above): the words of Petreius "shook every mind and brought back their love of wickedness" (*omnis | concussit mentes scelerumque reduxit amorem*, 4.235–36).[20] But we should note that once more Lucan's account eschews the formality of oaths and treaties in order to foreground the workings of emotions on crowd psychology. No oath binds the Pompeian soldiers in Lucan's epic, only a passion that has shifted from a love of one's fellow citizens to a love for crime.

It is with this line that Lucan most dramatically diverges from Caesar, or rather diverges from the focus of Caesar's account. After the speech and the oath, Caesar's Petreius alongside Afranius "issue an edict that anyone who has a Caesarian solder in his tent must bring him forward" (*edicunt penes quem quisque sit Caesaris miles ut producat*, Caes. 1.76.4), and they "publicly execute those surrendered in front of headquarters" (*productos palam in praetorio interficiunt*, Caes. 1.76.4). According to Caesar, however, the Pompeians "who had taken men in conceal most of them" (*sed plerosque ii qui receperant celant*, Caes. 1.76.4) and "send them across the rampart under the cover of darkness" (*noctuque per uallum emittunt*, Caes. 1.76.4), hesitant even under oath to break renewed bonds of social reintegration. Caesar devotes twice as many words to the soldiers who were saved as to those who died, and this matters for his larger argument about the inherent goodness of the Pompeian troops. Moreover, Caesar rhetorically underplays the complicity of Pompey's men when he renders the surrender with a passive participle (*productos*, lit. "those brought forward," Caes. 1.76.4), which foregrounds the betrayed men while suppressing the agency of those who did the betraying.[21] He also delicately omits the subject of his verb of killing (*interficiunt*, Caes. 1.76.4), leaving ambiguous whether it refers to Petreius and Afranius or the soldiers who surrender their Caesarian friends. If some men died, so Caesar suggests, it was not really the soldiers' fault.

Lucan has no interest in the soldiers who helped their friends escape and suppresses this part of Caesar's narrative entirely.[22] Instead he takes Caesar's account of the few who were led out for slaughter and rhetorically expands this moment into the grand climax of his scene:

> itur in omne nefas, et, quae fortuna deorum
> inuidia caeca bellorum in nocte tulisset,
> fecit monstra fides. inter mensasque torosque
> quae modo conplexu fouerunt pectora caedunt;
> et quamuis primo ferrum strinxere gementes,
> ut dextrae iusti gladius dissuasor adhaesit,
> dum feriunt, odere suos, animosque labantis
> confirmant ictu. feruent iam castra tumultu,
> ac, uelut occultum pereat scelus, omnia monstra
> in facie posuere ducum: iuuat esse nocentis.
>
> (4.243–53)

They proceed to every guilt and their loyalty commits horrors
which if Fortune had inflicted them in battle's blind night
would have been to the gods' discredit. Among the tables, among beds
they slay the breasts which they had warmly hugged just now;
and though at first they unsheathed their weapons with a groan,
when the sword, discourager from justice, clings to their hands,
they hate their friends as they strike them and every blow reassures
their faltering spirits. Now the camp is seething in turmoil,
and as if a hidden crime would be wasted, all their horrors
they set before their leaders: they delight in their guilt.

Where Caesar had five words, Lucan gives us sixteen rich lines (4.237–53), complete with an epic simile (to which we shall return). But there is no ambiguity about Lucan's third person plural verbs of slaughter (e.g., *caedunt* "they slay,"

4.246; *feriunt* "they strike," 4.249; *confirmant* "they strike," 4.250): the epic poet's soldiers murder their friends in the middle of dinner, in the middle of embraces, in the middle of reunification.[23] And they do so under the compulsion of no renewed military oath; instead, the men turn on their Caesarian companions of their own accord.

And yet despite the absence of an edict or further intervention from their commanders, Lucan's Pompeians are even more eager for their generals' approval. Caesar's account noted briefly that those few men who died were killed in front of the camp's headquarters, presumably under the leaders' watchful eyes, and Caesar's artful alliteration (*productos palam in praetorio*, "those brought forward . . . openly at the headquarters," Caes. 1.76.4) drew attention to the shameful deeds. In Lucan's account, the soldiers worry that their great crime will go unnoticed if they keep it to themselves (*uelut occultum pereat scelus*, "as if a hidden crime would be wasted," 4.252), and so instead they make sure to "put every monstrosity before the face of their leaders" (*omnia monstra | in facie posuere ducum*, 4.252–53). This sentence receives pride of place at the end of Lucan's narrative of the fraternization, just before he turns to address Caesar directly. For this reason, I think it deserves closer scrutiny not only as an indicator of Lucan's focus on crowd psychology, but also as a metaliterary comment on the role of historical writing in shaping how the past is remembered.

Much ink has been spilt over the subsequent apostrophe to Caesar in which Lucan asserts that, though Caesar lost many men, he recognized his luck in being the leader of the better cause:[24]

> tu, Caesar, quamuis spoliatus milite multo,
> agnoscis superos; neque enim tibi maior in aruis
> Emathiis fortuna fuit nec Phocidos undis
> Massiliae, Phario nec tantum est aequore gestum,
> hoc siquidem solo ciuilis crimine belli
> dux causae melioris eris.
>
> (4.254–59)

> You, Caesar, recognize the favor of the gods, though robbed
> of many a soldier; since your fortune was not greater
> on Emathian fields or the waves of Phocian
> Massilia, nor was the exploit in the Pharian sea so great,
> seeing that thanks to this crime of civil war alone
> you will be the leader of the better cause.

I agree with those who read Lucan's future tense as a promise of literary immortality to Caesar-the-historical-actor, an immortality granted both by

Caesar's and Lucan's accounts, though in different ways.[25] I would posit, however, that it is equally an authorial address to Caesar-the-author, a nod to the general's own self-congratulatory account but one which highlights Lucan's adjustments to that narrative.[26] In particular, Lucan seems to be chiding the author Caesar for not taking rhetorical advantage of the slaughter of his men (*quamuis spoliatus milite multo*, "though robbed of many a soldier," 4.254) when he chose to highlight throughout how bloodless the entire episode had been.[27] To Lucan, the loss of men in civil war is an advantage to the general losing them because it puts the blame for killing Rome's citizens squarely on the opposing side.

It is within this context of authorial comment that I think we must understand the Pompeian soldiers' own desire for recognition. This desire too, I suggest, is as much literary as it is of the moment. In other words, Lucan seems to be chiding Caesar-the-author also for giving the Pompeian soldiers a moral pass, despite the complicity of some in the slaughter of men with whom they had just been talking peace.[28] It is Caesar's account that allows the crimes of those men to pass unnoticed (cf. *occultum pereat scelus*, Luc. 4.252). By highlighting and expanding the slaughter of Caesar's men rather than compressing / suppressing it as Caesar had done, Lucan aligns himself with the wishes of the civil warriors who want their perverse heroism recounted. At the same time, he also furthers Caesar's cause by showing the Pompeians as a whole (vs. simply their commanders) in an even worse light than Caesar's own text had done.[29]

Imagery and Metaphor

Thus far we have examined Lucan's shifts in narrative strategy and characterization as well as the ways in which his authorial choices to expand certain details and suppress others serve those wider ends. Now it is time to look to how Lucan responds to and repurposes the language and imagery found within Caesar's Spanish campaign, an aspect of Lucan's reception of Caesar that currently receives far too little critical attention.

After an extensive treatment of his military strategies through which he hoped to bring an end to the fighting and loss of Roman life (Caes. 1.78–84; Lucan condenses these skirmishes), Caesar highlights how he successfully cut the Pompeians off from water. Under the circumstances, the Pompeian generals are forced to seek terms of surrender. In his public speech, Afranius stresses the dehumanizing conditions to which he and his men have been subjected by their confinement:

> nunc uero paene ut feras circummunitos prohiberi aqua, prohiberi
> ingressu, neque corpore dolorem neque animo ignominiam ferre
> posse
>
> (Caes. BCiv. 1.84.4)

> Now, almost as though wild beasts, they were penned in, kept from
> water, and kept from moving, and their bodies could not stand the
> suffering nor their minds the disgrace.

Their physical and mental suffering have reached such a state that it is as if they are wild animals (*ut feras*) desperate in their thirst and deserving of compassion (*si qui locus misericordiae*, "if there is any room for pity," Caes. 1.84.5).[30] This is a rare moment of metaphor for Caesar's text designed to emphasize the thoroughly submissive tone (*subiectissime*, Caes. 1.84.5) of Afranius's groveling. Though his assimilation of Pompey's men to beasts is compressed and thus perhaps would not be labeled a full simile in an epic poem, its marked character seems to have caught Lucan's eye. In fact, I suggest that Lucan reduplicates his reception of this Caesarian simile and thereby refashions it to serve his own historical arguments.

The clearest point of contact between historian and epic poet occurs in Lucan's lengthy treatment of the dehumanizing depths to which the Pompeian soldiers sink in their search for water (4.292–318), including squeezing rotten muck into their parched mouths (4.308–13). When even this is not enough, they adopt the manner of beasts and suckle at the udders of herd animals so violently that they draw blood—and drink it.

> rituque ferarum
> distentas siccant pecudes, et lacte negato
> sordidus exhaust sorbetur ab ubere sanguis.
>
> (4.313–15)

> and like wild beasts
> they suck dry the swollen cattle and, when milk failed
> from the drained udder the dirty blood is sucked.

This twenty-seven line digression zooms in cinematically on Pompeian suffering but not in a way that arouses compassion. Rather, the hyperbole and paradoxes on display showcase the madness of the Pompeian soldiers and their increasingly desperate response to the blockade.[31] Caesar's *ut feras* ("as if wild beasts"), voiced by Afranius, is used to (attempt to) rouse Caesar's pity for the Pompeians who now surrender themselves into his power. Lucan's repurposing of it (*ritu ferarum*), however, makes a disgusting spectacle of Pompeian animalistic frenzy.[32]

But this is not the first time within this episode that Lucan has assimilated the Pompeians to *ferae* ("wild animals"). Lucan wrote an extensive simile less than a hundred lines earlier at the point in the narrative at which our previous section ended: the night-time slaughter of the Caesarians by their Pompeian friends. In between Petreius's speech and the ensuing scene of bloody devastation, Lucan inserted a bridge in the form of an epic simile:

> concussit mentes scelerumque reduxit amorem.
> sic, ubi desuetae siluis in carcere clauso
> mansueuere ferae et uultus posuere minaces
> atque hominem didicere pati, si torrida paruos
> uenit in ora cruor, redeunt rabiesque furorque
> admonitaeque tument gustato sanguine fauces;
> feruet et a trepido uix abstinet ira magistro.
> itur in omne nefas.

> (4.236–43)

He shook every mind and brought back their love of wickedness.
Just so the wild beasts unlearn the ways of the woods
and grow tame in the locked prison, dropping their threatening looks
and learning to submit to man, but if their parched mouths
find a little gore, their rabid frenzy returns
and their throats swell at the memory of the taste of blood;
their anger seethes, hardly sparing the trembling keeper.
They proceed to every guilt.

In Lucan's eyes, the Pompeian soldiers are like wild animals who have been constrained by the external domination of their masters and who thirst—in this case literally—for blood.[33] The connection between the two passages of Lucan are not only the comparison of Pompeian soldiers to wild beasts but also in their focus on thirst and the drinking of blood.[34] This earlier simile on its own would make the later image of violent suckling even more gruesome and foreboding, but the lengthy simile's connection to Afranius's speech in Caesar's *Civil War* is equally instructive.

The focus of both Caesar's and Lucan's simile is on the constraint imposed by external forces. Lucan's closed prison (*carcere clauso*, 4.237) responds to Afranius's description of animals walled in (*circummunitos*, Caes. 1.84.4). So too Lucan takes Afranius's emphasis on thirst due to lack of water (*prohiberi aqua*, Caes. 1.84.4) and uses imagery derived from that situation to refer to the beasts' dry mouth (*torrida . . . in ora*, 4.239–40) and the impact of a single drop of moisture. Thus Lucan responds both to the literal aspect of Caesar's Pompeian simile (*ferae*) and to its two most important descriptive details (constraint and thirst).

At the same time, Lucan's shift in the placement of the simile and in its finer details once more change its tenor. It is unclear, for example, in Caesar's text for how long the beasts have been constrained. This may seem an odd detail to bring out, but Lucan is quite clear that these are wild beasts who have, apparently, been tamed by becoming accustomed to a master over the course of a significant amount of time. Of course Lucan's point with this description of taming is to show the impossibility of wild beasts ever becoming habituated to the world of men. His beasts thirst not for water but for human blood (*cruor*, 4.240). If they even get so much as a drop of it in their parched mouths, their wild character returns and they turn on those who had foolishly thought them tame. And when similar behaviors appear in Lucan's own subsequent account of the soldiers' thirst and in his second bestial analogy (*ritu ferarum*), the animalistic threat that the Pompeians pose to peace seems ever present, never eradicated, even in a scene of capitulation.

If we accept that the origin of Lucan's two *ferae* similes may lie in Caesar's text, their repositioning and reworking deserve to be read as a comment on that text. Here once more we see Lucan allusively chiding Caesar for assuming that Pompey's civil warriors can be set free at the end of the Spanish episode, as if they are now tamed and harmless (Caes. 1.87.5). In Lucan's epic, it seems, these soldiers never give up their thirst for blood and civil war. For this reason, Lucan not only expands Caesar's metaphorical language to give it further significance within the wider narrative, he also doubles its role by activating the allusion in two separate yet interconnected moments in the surrounding narrative; in doing so he anticipates the context of Pompeian surrender in Caesar's text by putting the first instance at an earlier point in which those same Pompeians show their true stripes as killers who can never quench their thirst. When Lucan then repeats this image later in his own account of the suffering that leads to surrender (a moment closer to the original Caesarian context), the image of Pompeian *ferae* has been pre-infected with violent, murderous associations that their thirst only exacerbates. In other words, in Lucan's Spanish landscape, wild beast and Pompeian soldier are one and the same and cannot be trusted no matter how roundly defeated they seem.

Structure as Argument

Just as it is important to examine Lucan's debt to the particular details of Caesar's carefully written account, so too the reader must look to Lucan's reception of Caesar's wider narrative patterns. Scholars like Batstone and Damon have shown that Caesar's Ilerda episode programmatically falls at the end of his book and that this episode recycles many of the keywords, themes, and ideologies with which the *Civil War* began.[35] In particular, the scene of Petreius's interruption replays the events that catalyzed the war and the narrative of the war at the start of book 1 (Caes. 1.1–6), including the potential for peace, the Pompeian disruption of that potential, the violent removal of Caesarian agents, the terror, and the oaths.

Their analysis thus points to larger elements of Caesar's "structure as argument" through which book 1 of his *Civil War* seduces the reader into seeing Ilerda as the place where the *Civil War* could have and should have ended, thanks to Caesar and to the Pompeian soldiers' bravery. For this reason, Caesar here dramatically (and for the first time) breaks with his previous annalistic structure.[36] Instead, he interweaves his account of Massilia with the events in Spain in order to end on this triumphal note before the agents of discord force the war and the narrative of that war to continue in book 2.

I propose that Lucan does something similar, once more following Caesar's outlines but changing the structure along with the argument. On a most basic level, Lucan uses Ilerda to begin a book rather than end one. This choice means that the Caesarian victory in Spain is swiftly followed by and is narratively linked with two episodes of Caesarian defeat, each worse than the last.[37] In other words, Lucan positions the annihilation of some of Caesar's men in Spain as sowing the narrative seeds for the mutual slaughter of Vulteius's men in the next episode (4.402–581) and for the total disaster of Curio in Africa (4.581–824).[38] Thus not only does Lucan follow Caesarian victory with defeats, but he weaves into that very victory anticipations of those defeats, stripping from Spain any celebratory significance. Ilerda becomes not a culmination to the way civil wars should end but rather the first in a tricolon crescens of escalating horror driven by base passion.

But despite these changes to Ilerda's structural position within the narrative, Lucan follows Caesar's lead once more by weaving into his Ilerda a look back at the themes and rhetoric with which his epic began:

> Bella per Emathios plus quam ciuilia campos
> iusque datum sceleri canimus, populumque potentem
> in sua uictrici conuersum uiscera dextra
> cognatasque acies, et rupto foedere regni
> certatum totis concussi uiribus orbis
> in commune nefas, infestisque obuia signis
> signa, pares aquilas et pila minantia pilis.
>
> (1.1–7)

> Of wars across Emathian plains, worse than civil wars,
> and of legality conferred on crime we sing, and of a mighty people
> attacking its own guts with victorious sword-hand,

of kin facing kin, and, once the pact of tyranny was broken,
of conflict waged with all the forces of the shaken world
for universal guilt, and of standards ranged in enmity against
standards, of eagles marched and javelins threatening javelins.

As we see ties of hospitality and citizenship descend into bloodshed in Spain, we cannot help but remember the rhetoric of Lucan's proem in which a society turns into its own guts, battle lines are made up of friends and family, and there is a rush into communal depravity. Thus Lucan too chooses to use Ilerda to create ring composition with his narrative's opening, recycling keywords, themes, ideas, and narrative patterns. But he focuses not on an overarching narrative of the Pompeian leaders' depravity. Rather his target is both wider and lower: the individual citizens who fight civil war. Lucan refuses to allow the individual Pompeians to be remembered for their inherent goodness and drive toward peace; as he demands that individual nameless citizens be held accountable for their crimes, we might hear echoes of the poet's most insistent question: "What madness was this, o citizens? What this excessive freedom with the sword?" (*quis furor, o ciues, quae tanta licentia ferri?* 1.8). For Lucan's is an epic about individual madness and the individual choices that bring devastation in their wake. As Lucan borrows from Caesar the importance of Ilerda as a moment to reflect back on the origins of civil war, he finds in that reflection a different sort of truth.

Conclusion

There is, of course, much more one could say about Lucan's Ilerda and its response to Caesar, from its foregrounding of *fides* ("loyalty, duty") and *pudor* ("shame") to Lucan's compression and expansion of scenes like the summer storm or the behaviors of Caesar's own troops. But what I hope to have shown is the rich potential for a reading of Lucan that considers him a reader of Caesar, and a careful reader at that. Lucan responds not only to Caesar's interpretation of history but to the images, metaphors, language, structures, and characterization that narrativize that interpretation within Caesar's *Civil War*. These become some of the intertextual building blocks that form the foundation for Lucan's literary-historical project.

Nor does Lucan's reception of Caesar focus squarely on Caesar himself as historical actor or as apologetic author. Instead we have seen that Lucan is equally interested in the psychology and motivations of the common soldier, in their loyalties, and in the testing of those loyalties. This is a theme very much at the heart of Caesar's own *Civil War*, as has been well studied. In fact, once we divorce Lucan's response to Caesar-*actor* (Caesar the historical actor) as much as possible from his response to Caesar-*auctor* (Caesar the author of histories), it is possible to see a great subtly to Lucan's use of historical material—a trait for which the epic poet is not often credited. For Lucan was engaged in a project that was fundamentally historical in its outlook, and as we are increasingly coming to respect, intertextuality was just as important a tool in the historian's toolbox as it was in the poet's.[39]

Notes

1. Pichon 1912 argued for Livy's supremacy amongst Lucan's sources, and his opinion has long dominated scholarship (see, most recently, Rädicke 2004). Syndikus 1958 makes the most extensive argument that Asinius Pollio should be included, but this idea is widespread in scholarship. See also Lintott 1971, 488n6.

2. Owing to the influence of Pichon 1912, Caesar was rarely considered one of Lucan's chief sources for quite some time, but this has slowly changed over the past two decades. My study complements groundwork already laid esp. by Masters 1992, 1994, and Zissos 2013. See also Griset 1955; Haffter 1957; Rambaud 1960; Lintott 1971; Bachofen 1972; Lounsbury 1975; Ahl 1976, 190–230 (*passim*); and Henderson 1987. See also Roche (chapter 7) and Dinter in this volume.

3. Others have studied Lucan's response to Caesar in this episode, and I will occasionally tread familiar ground. See esp. Bachofen 1972, 17–22, 116–32; Ahl 1976, esp. 192–97; Masters 1992, 70–90; Leigh 1997, 50–54; Esposito 2009; Asso 2010.

4. Aside from Lucan and Caesar, our surviving sources for the Spanish campaign are: App. *BCiv.* 2.42–43; Dio 41.20–23; Flor. 2.13.26–28; Livy *Per.* 110; Plut. *Caes.* 36; Suet. *Iul.* 34.2, 75.2; Vell. Pat. 2.50.4. For a useful overview of Lucan's adherence to and deviations from the overarching historical tradition here, see Lintott 1971, 490–91.

5. On Caesar's and Lucan's foregrounding of the fraternization scene to a greater degree than other accounts, see also Lintott 1971, 491, and Masters 1992, 85. In Dio's full account, for example, the fraternization plays little to no role, and this may in turn reflect back on his sources.

6. See Batstone and Damon 2006, 75–84; Grillo 2012, 80–91, 160–64.

7. The text of Caesar used throughout is Damon 2015.

8. Book 4 is well served by two excellent recent commentaries, Esposito 2009 (in Italian) and Asso 2010 (in English).

9. His last appearance is when he "arrived ahead of the enemy making for the hills" (*ad montis tendentem praeuenit hostem*, 4.167). He reappears as a narrative character only after the slaughter when the military stratagems resume (4.264–65).

10. See also Ahl 1976, 193, and Esposito 2009, 121–22. Radicke (2004, 279) notes that the phrase *castra locare* is common in Livy, possibly suggesting his influence on Lucan's phrasing here in contrast to Caesar.

11. See, e.g., Leigh 1997, 51, on Lucan's portrayal of "mutual moves towards concord on both sides."

12. As Batstone and Damon (2006, 78) note, this is the first reference to citizens or to the Roman state since 1.32, making the return of the language of citizenship a notable aspect of Caesar's thematic argument throughout this episode. See also Grillo 2012, 81–82.

13. Thompson and Bruère (1970, 155–57) note that Lucan alludes to the breaking of the Italian truce in *Aeneid* 12, an intertextual model that complements Lucan's response to Caesar.

14. Note that Lucan uses the same language (*foedera pacis*, 4.365) to denote the Pompeians formal capitulation to Caesar at the end of the episode, marking it as a technical term for treaties rather than a vague description of fraternization.

15. Petreius's allusion to Caesar's *Civil War* has been the subject of several studies, although not all would make use of the language of allusion and/or intertext to describe the relationship. See esp. Ahl 1976,

194–95; Masters 1992, 79–81; and Leigh 1997, 51, though I disagree with Leigh's view that Caesar's account only enters from the perspective of Petreius. On the contrary, while Petreius's interpretation surely forces the reader to confront the differences between Caesar's and Lucan's account, Caesar influences Lucan throughout.

16. See Grillo 2012, 121, on how, in Caesar's *Civil War*, Caesar civilizes barbarian cruelty while the Pompeians merely succumb to its temptations.

17. I here differ from Ahl 1976, 194–95, who argues that our memory of Caesar's account legitimizes Petreius's reaction even as Lucan simultaneously tries to suppress that text here because Caesar comes across too well. Masters 1992, 79–81, sees this interpolation as part of a wider ideological split that does not allow his readers to commit to one side or the other. While I am sympathetic to such a reading of Lucan's epic as a whole, I see the intrusion of inconsistent details here as having a specific goal within its context.

18. On the role of inconsistency in flagging alternate versions of the story being told in Latin epic, see O'Hara 2007 *passim*, but see esp. the introduction on the phenomenon in earlier Greek literature, esp. 13–18, 24–32 (on Alexandrian poetry); for Lucan specifically, see 131–41.

19. As Coffee (2011, 430) notes, the fraternization itself represents a conflicting interpretation of *fides* as a social vs. military virtue.

20. On the precise parallels and shifts, especially in the verbs here, see also Bachofen 1972, 130.

21. Grillo (2012, 81) notes a similar sleight of hand earlier in the episode when Caesar laments the Pompeians who would be killed without indicating himself as the agent of that killing (*interficiendos*, Caes. 1.72.3)

22. Though he hints at a divided response when he describes how the slaughter firmed up their wavering minds (*animosque labantis*, 4.249).

23. Like Caesar, later accounts place the blame squarely on Petreius and Afranius, or leave the agents of slaughter to a generic "enemy" (cf. Appian 2.42–43; Dio 41.23; Suetonius *Iul.* 74.2). No surviving account highlights the agency of the Pompeian soldiers as Lucan does.

24. See also Dio 41.23.1 with Radicke 2004, 282

25. See esp. Leigh 1997, 53.

26. The literary immortality conferred upon Caesar by Lucan's epic and by Caesar's own *Civil War* is at the core of a more famous apostrophe in Book 9: "those to come will read me and you" (*uenturi me teque legent*, 9.985). While not all have seen this line as an allusion to Caesar the author as well as Caesar the actor, see the persuasive arguments of Bartsch 1997, 55–56; Rossi 2001, 323–25; Zissos 2013, 141–42.

27. This may also lie behind Lucan's earlier insistence that events will proceed "without much bloodshed" (*non multa caede*, 4.2), a fact he subsequently contradicts (*multo . . . sanguine*, 4.210).

28. On this reading, the episode becomes a prime example of what Henderson termed Lucan's agonistic rivalry with the *corpus Caesarianum* "as monuments to narration-*as*-success" (Henderson 1987, 133). For a reading of Lucan's frustration with those who blindly follow orders through the lens of *Aeneid* 4, see Casali 1999.

29. For expansion and compression—and the paradoxical blend of the two—as key features of Lucan's intertextual poetics, see Masters 1992, 29–31.

30. See Grillo 2012, 84–85, for an excellent discussion of Afranius's rhetoric. While Caesar's *ut feras* is a modern solution for a textual issue, it has been accepted by all modern editors and Lucan's potential double reception of it may speak further to its strength.

31. On paradox and hyperbole as important elements of Lucan's poetics of civil war, see Martindale 1976.

32. On similar lines, see Asso 2010, 172–73, 175–76 ("the picture of the soldier fighting his mates for a sip of muck is intentionally repulsive, but L. tastelessly insists on dehumanizing the soldiers"). See also Thompson and Bruère 1970, 159, who note that Lucan increases the "repulsiveness" of this scene through allusions to the "idyllic atmosphere of Virgil's *Eclogues*."

33. On this simile's thematic significance and echoes elsewhere in the epic, see Esposito 2009, 18–19, 145–48; Fantham 2010, 64; and Esposito in this volume. For its function as "testimony . . . to the warped mentality of those long exposed to civil war," see Leigh 1997, 52. For its origins in Vergil's Italian wars, see Thompson and Bruère 1970, 157. It will go on to influence Statius (*Theb.* 5.231–33 with Micozzi 1999, 354).

34. See Fratantuono 2012, 150.

35. See especially Caes. *BCiv.* 1.80–84. Batstone and Damon 2006, 75–84, and their appendix of thematic terms, 86–88. See also Raaflaub 2010; Grillo 2012, 80–91, 160–61.

36. Batstone and Damon 2006, 75. Radicke 2004, 264, hypothesizes that Livy, too, must have followed Caesar.

37. On Ilerda within the structure of book 4, see also Esposito 2009, 11–12, and Asso 2010, 15–17. See also Esposito in this volume.

38. Grillo (2012, 46–48) notes that Caesar, too, repeats motifs from the Spanish campaign in his account of Curio in Africa as part of his wider intertextual / structural nexus, though to a different end. For an alternative explanation of Lucan's decoupling of Massilia and Ilerda, see Masters 1992, 23–24.

39. See especially O'Gorman 2009 and Damon 2010.

15

Sex and Violence

Gender in the Civil War

Robert Cowan

Gender in Ancient Rome, as in the modern world, was not an innate quality but a cultural performance.[1] It was not enough to have been born biologically male or female to attain the socially constructed ideals of masculinity or femininity. Certain qualities were believed to be inborn in men and women respectively, but it was the successful performance of normative behaviors that made one truly masculine or feminine. Any failure to perform these behaviors, or any transgressive performance of non-normative behaviors, would lead to the accusation of effeminacy in men, while women might be considered either unnaturally masculine or "bad women." The values and practices associated with gender intersect with numerous other systems: ethnicity, social status, ethics, religion, politics. An "Oriental" (in the sense defined by Edward Said) might be considered effeminate while an undercivilized northern barbarian might be hyper- (and hence negatively) masculine.[2] An ethical transgression might compromise someone's masculinity, as might their being socially, politically, or militarily dominated by a rival. This relationship of gender to so many other fields of human society makes it particularly "good to think with" and fertile as a way of exploring multiple themes. Gender roles have a further significance in epic poetry, which was often characterized, and even characterized itself, as "all-male, all-war, all the time."[3] The intrusion of the feminine into epic, and the concomitant failure of the masculine, thus produces an additional means of dramatizing tensions between gender polarities and all the other polarities onto which they map. Lucan's depiction of gender roles is in many ways less radical than that of some other epicists, like Vergil, Ovid, and Statius.

Instead, he tends to manipulate normative conventions to explore the abnormal chaos that is the world of his poem.

Little Men: Masculinity and Its Discontents

Discussions of gender in classical literature, and in the ancient world more generally, tend to focus on women.[4] This in itself revealingly reflects tendencies in ancient society and modern scholarship to treat men and masculinity as normative, a default setting, so that the very notion of gender only comes into play when one diverges from that norm into the realms of the female and the feminine. Nevertheless, for all that masculinity is constructed as the norm, it is the maintenance of that norm and anxiety over falling short of it that is arguably Rome's, and especially Roman epic's, main preoccupation with respect to gender.[5] Roman epic is principally about men. The *Civil War* is no exception to this, as various characters succeed or fail to perform normative masculine behavior. On one level, the Roman masculine ideal is taken as a straightforward good, so that a character's failure to attain it diminishes him, while perversion of the gendered norm is yet another symptom of the societal breakdown caused by civil war. On another level, the very idea of masculinity is problematized and shown to be as unstable and potentially destructive as other conventionally positive values in the world of the poem.

The elements of the cultural construct that was Roman masculinity can largely be grouped under the heading of control.[6] A Roman male was expected to maintain control over his household, his body, and his emotions. The paterfamilias had immense legal power over all members of his household and even greater intangible authority, an authority that had to be maintained if his masculinity was not to be diminished.[7] He was expected to maintain bodily integrity and not allow himself to be penetrated, either sexually or in any other way, but rather to express his dominance by being the penetrator. Regulation of emotions and steadfastness (*constantia*) were part of the same complex of control mechanisms. In Rome's intensely competitive society—especially but not exclusively its elite levels—this necessity for control easily extended beyond the individual and his household to interactions with peers, with those of lower status, and beyond Rome's borders, with foreigners and provincials. Socially, politically, and militarily a man was expected to maintain control over his own status vis-à-vis that of other men and, in what easily devolved into a zero-sum game, that often meant asserting his masculinity at the expense of that of others. Any failure to exert control or to manifest the related qualities of courage and steadfastness could lead to accusations of effeminacy.

Perhaps the most obvious and explicit failure of masculinity in the poem is when Caesar, until now the poem's alpha male, is reduced to a state of "feminine" cowardice by Achillas's attack on him in Alexandria:

> quem non uiolasset Alanus,
> non Scytha, non fixo qui ludit in hospite Maurus,
> hic, cui Romani spatium non sufficit orbis,
> paruaque regna putet Tyriis cum Gadibus Indos,
> ceu puer imbellis uel captis femina muris,
> quaerit tuta domus.
>
> (10.454–59)

> The man whom the Alani would not have outraged
> nor the Scythian nor the Moor who ridicules the wounded stranger,
> this man for whom the Roman world's expanse is not enough
> and who would think the Indians with Tyrian Gades a tiny kingdom,
> like an unwarlike boy or a woman in a captured city,
> seeks the safety of a house.[8]

Caesar has been so emasculated and feminized by the sexual dominance of Cleopatra, the corrupting luxury of Alexandria, and the enervating "Oriental" environment of Egypt that he is no longer masculine. He is equated to the mature male's polar opposites, the male but physically and emotionally immature (and hence not properly masculine) boy and the mature but female woman. These inherently unmasculine figures are further diminished by being qualified as the passive, impotent victims of war, an "unwarlike" (*imbellis*) child and the stereotypical civilian object of martial and sexual violence beyond the battlefield. Both stand in antithesis to the embodiment of the masculine ideal who manifests his *uirtus*—his valor and his manliness—by actively inflicting rather than passively suffering military violence.

The comparison gains one final twist from its intra- and intertextual associations. The phrase "unwarlike boy" (*puer imbellis*) has been used twice already in book 10, its only occurrences anywhere in extant Latin, to describe and belittle Ptolemy XIII, but now the hypermasculine Caesar has been reduced to the same status. The image of a woman in a sacked city is a common one, but the comparison of an epic hero to one would evoke in most readers' minds the poignant moment in Homer's *Odyssey* in which the disguised Odysseus, hearing a song about his dead comrades in the Trojan war, is compared to a woman grieving for her dead husband before being dragged away to slavery by soldiers who have sacked her city (*Od.* 8.521–31). Yet where the Homeric simile is a sign of Odysseus's empathy with the victims of his own violence, a positive "feminization" of his emotional range, Lucan characteristically perverts the implications so that the solipsistic Caesar feels fear but no pity and is diminished but not enriched by his feminization. Outside the simile, the whole passage sets up a spatial antithesis that is also strongly gendered. The contrast between Caesar's erstwhile dominance of the entire known world and his present confinement to a single house works on several levels. One of the most important is the contrast between "outside" as masculine space through which men have the freedom to move around, and "inside," especially the domestic sphere, as the proper spatial, social, and ergonomic sphere of women. Caesar's sphere of influence has not only been drastically contracted in area, but it has been symbolically reduced to the feminine space of the household.

A more ambivalent depiction of the struggle to achieve and maintain an ideal of masculinity can be found in the death of Pompey on the shores of Egypt. Pompey's masculinity throughout the poem has been compromised by his passivity, his lack of control over himself and others, and his emotional vulnerability, particularly manifested in his devotion to his wife, Cornelia, and in his needy desire to be loved. As he willingly transfers from his own boat to that of the Egyptians, Lucan notes that "he was not now his own master" (Braund) or, more literally, "he had now lost jurisdiction / control over himself" (*perdiderat iam iura sui,* 8.612). This is a potent phrase. Control over one's own body and emotions is arguably the fundamental prerequisite for Roman masculinity. The loss of legal rights over his body rendered a man a slave while the loss of physical control over it rendered him a woman. After the military defeat at Pharsalus and the rhetorical defeat at Syhedra, where his plan to enlist the aid of Parthia had to yield to Lentulus's preference for Egypt, Pompey's external control over his party, his army, and even his own movements has been severely curtailed, constituting a concomitant curtailment of his masculinity. Surrendering himself to the control of the Egyptians and the renegade centurion Septimius in their tiny boat is the nadir of this process.

However, this external loss of masculine control is paradoxically bound up with an increase of internal control, or at least a desperate attempt to exert such control:

> ut uidit comminus ensis,
> inuoluit uultus atque indignatus apertum
> Fortunae praebere caput; tum lumina pressit
> continuitque animam, ne quas effundere uoces
> uellet et aeternam fletu corrumpere famam.

sed, postquam mucrone latus funestus Achillas
perfodit, nullo gemitu consensit ad ictum
respexitque nefas, seruatque immobile corpus,
seque probat moriens.

(8.613–21)

When he saw the swords close by,
he covered up his face and head, disdaining
to present them bare to Fortune; then he closed his eyes
and held his breath to stop himself from breaking
into speech and marring his eternal fame with tears.
But after murderous Achillas stabbed his side
with sword-point, with not a groan did he acknowledge
the blow and did not heed the crime, but keeps his body motionless,
and as he dies he tests himself.

There is a tension here between the inward and outward performance of masculinity. The stillness, impassivity, dry eyes, and silence that Pompey presents
to the audience (Roman and Egyptian soldiers, his wife and son, posterity), of
which he is acutely aware, all constitute the performance of self-control and
hence masculinity. Since Roman masculinity *was* constituted by social performance, perhaps Pompey here truly achieves it. Yet this outward performance
of masculinity is in exquisite tension with his inner anxiety about failing to
maintain that masculinity and thus ruining his reputation. If his natural inclination is toward "feminine" tears, screams, and thrashing about, is he truly
masculine, especially if his motivation is a pathetic desire for affection ("with
all the more endurance, pain of mine, I beg, suppress your groans; my son and
wife, if they admire me in death, love me," 8.633–35)? Or, to swing the pendulum back once more, perhaps his very ability to exert conscious self-control over
such involuntary weaknesses, to have *iura sui* ("control of oneself"), is itself the
ultimate act of masculinity.

Certainly, the partisan narrator asserts that Pompey died a noble and manly
death: "Such control of mind (*custodia . . . mentis*) had Magnus, he exercised this
power over his dying spirit" (8.635–36). Moreover, he asserts that, according to
those who saw Pompey's severed head, "the majestic beauty of his sacred features lasted, his expression reconciled with the gods; and utmost death changed
nothing of the hero's bearing and his face" (8.664–66). The crucial moment
comes when Septimius cuts off the head, "while features are alive and *singultus* of breath impel the mouth to murmur, while unclosed eyes are stiffening"
(8.682–83). The key word *singultus* has been translated (as Braund does) as
"sobs" and seen as an involuntary, nonverbal sign of Pompey's unmasculine

failure of self-control, despite his attempts to the contrary and the narrator's editorializing.[9] Yet *singultus* also means "the convulsive catching of breath of a dying person" (*OLD* 1b), which is arguably more appropriate to the context and the association with *anima*, "breath," and which would leave Pompey's outward performance of masculinity intact. Pompey's death is a performance enacted for internal and external audiences to view and interpret. Whether the reader interprets his *singultus* as sobs or convulsive catchings of breath may determine the success of that performance.

Caesar's failure of masculinity and Pompey's precarious attempt to maintain it are both predicated on its being fundamentally a good and desirable quality. However, such qualities are routinely perverted and problematized in the world of the *Civil War* and masculinity is no exception. The Latin word that most closely corresponds to the notion of socially performed masculinity is *uirtus*. This is an almost impossible word to translate, since it can mean, among other things, military valor, moral virtue, and abstract excellence in any field. Yet it rarely loses its association—one notably absent from its closest Greek equivalent ἀρετή ("excellence")—with its cognate *uir* and its root meaning of "manliness." *Virtus* in Lucan is a particularly problematic concept, for how can one be valorous when fighting civil war, virtuous when all morality has been confounded, excellent in any field when the whole cosmos is out of joint? Civil war produces a crisis of masculinity. One response is to redefine *uirtus* in a way that is less susceptible to the perversions of the world of civil war. Cato's austere, Stoic *uirtus*, with its emphasis on a very particular brand of self-mastery, can be seen as an alternative, superior form of masculinity. His manliness is twice called *durus*, "hard" or "enduring," during the Libyan expedition (9.445, 9.562).[10] This word is frequently associated with ideas of masculinity in contrast to the *mollis*, "soft," qualities of femininity and effeminacy, but very rarely applied to *uirtus* itself.[11] Lucan takes the conventional idea of the "hard man" and transforms it into the unconventionally tough and austere man, whose masculinity is manifested through endurance rather than performance. Yet, as ever with Cato, there is the possibility that his *uirtus*, like his other qualities, is excessive and even parodic, that his hardy manliness is not a positive adaptation of masculinity but another perversion.[12]

Certainly *uirtus* in the *Civil War* is most frequently either futile or destructive, or both.[13] The most overt act of hypermasculine martial valor opens book 6, when the centurion Scaeva performs a grotesquely hyperbolic version of the epic *aristeia*, the hero's achievement of a series of military feats. Scaeva effectively takes on the whole of Pompey's army single-handed and prevents their escape, thus, as the narrator scathingly enumerates, bringing about all the evils of the remainder of the civil war. Apostrophizing Scaeva himself, he underlines how the conventional scene of Scaeva being congratulated and carried off by his comrades would, in another war and in another epic, have been one of glory, commemorated by foreign spoils on temple walls. But this is civil war and the *Civil War*, and Lucan ends his apostrophe with the aphoristic *sententia*: "Unhappy man! with such enormous valor | masculinity you bought a master!" (*infelix, quanta dominum uirtute parasti!* 6.262) Not only has valor, which ought to be used to preserve Rome's freedom against foreign enemies, been perverted into ensuring her slavery, but Scaeva's enormous masculinity has bought not a slave but paradoxically a slave-owner who will emasculate him and remove his self-mastery.

While Scaeva's manliness is at best futile and at worst serves negative ends, it remains in itself an inherently positive quality, just one that cannot function positively in the world of the poem.[14] Sometimes Lucan also speaks about the perversion of not so much values themselves as of the language used to describe such values, as when the astrologer Figulus predicts that "impious crime shall bear the name of *uirtus*" (1.668). Elsewhere, however, Lucan suggests that *uirtus* itself has the potential to be a negative quality, in particular the excessive competitiveness of toxic masculinity that can be a spur to excellence but can also lead to ruthless pursuit of one's own ambitions at any cost. This idea is most clearly expressed in the extended proem when the narrator is recounting the causes of the war and describes how the death of Crassus removed a restraint on the other two triumvirs, so that "rivalry in excellence spurs them on" (*stimulos dedit aemula uirtus*, 1.120).[15] This is not the masculine ideal misdirected or its name misassigned. This is the inherent nature of Roman masculinity, the self-perpetuating impulse to compete against other males for status in a zero-sum game, taken to extremes and leading to civic and cosmic breakdown. As Lucan goes on to say, "Caesar cannot now bear anyone ahead nor Pompey any equal" (1.125–26). Masculinity is not simply out of place in civil war; it causes it.

Little Women: The Pervasive Femininity of the *Civil War*

The feminine ideal at Rome should not be oversimplified, since it varied with social status and changed over time. The oft-quoted tombstone describing the ideal wife, "She kept the household. She made wool" (*domum seruauit, lanam fecit, CIL* 1211.8), does not exhaustively sum up Roman femininity, but it does give a good sense of its fundamental features. Likewise, certain qualities and behaviors were considered feminine. In many ways, the feminine ideal is the complementary opposite of the masculine, stressing passivity, subservience, chastity, and domesticity. Some of these ideal feminine behaviors are natural extensions of what were considered innately female qualities, while some were meant to counteract and constrain the dangerous tendencies of such qualities. Thus, women were considered weak, passive, and lacking in agency, "natural" qualities that could be easily transferred into their cultural equivalents, thus eliding the fact that it was the culturally constructed qualities that were being naturalized and essentialized. At the same time, women were considered unable to control their bodies or their emotions (compare the complementary requirements for masculinity), in particular their sexual desires, and so subordination to rational male authority and a strict guard on chastity were required to regulate these "natural" tendencies. Lucan's female characters tend to manifest these expected qualities and either to observe or markedly transgress these ideal norms of behavior. As noted in the introduction, there is comparatively little of the radical problematization of gender boundaries that is found in Ovid, Catullus, the elegists, or even Vergil. Instead, Lucan manipulates these normative conventions to explore the abnormal chaos that is the world of his poem.

The role of women as daughters, wives, and mothers could, and in reality often did, forge links between men of different families, sometimes maintaining peace between rivals. This principle was enshrined in Rome's legendary early history by the story of the Sabine women, kidnapped by the first Romans but then interceding to prevent war between their fathers and their new husbands. Lucan draws an explicit connection between the Sabine women and Julia, the daughter of Caesar and wife of Pompey, whose death removed one of the obstacles to war:

> quod si tibi fata dedissent
> maiores in luce moras, tu sola furentem
> inde uirum poteras atque hinc retinere parentem
> armatasque manus excusso iungere ferro,
> ut generos soceris mediae iunxere Sabinae.
> morte tua discussa fides bellumque mouere
> permissum ducibus.
>
> (1.114–20)

> But if destiny had granted you
> a longer stay in the light, alone you could have
> here restrained your frenzied husband, here your frenzied father,
> thrown away their swords and joined their armed hands,
> as Sabine women in between joined fathers—with their sons-in-law.
> By your death the alliance was shattered and the leaders felt free
> to commence the war.

Here is a positive feminine role, but one that is only mentioned to be negated. In the world of the poem there are no Sabine women and no Julia to prevent civil war, and in fact, Julia is not merely removed but transformed from peacemaker to vengeful agent of civil war, pursuing Pompey in his dreams and enacting a sort of sexual civil war against his new wife, Cornelia. By contrast to the Sabines and the living Julia, the wives and mothers of the narrative present are impotent to avert the disastrous conflict. When soldiers depart for civil war, wives try in vain to dissuade them (1.504–6). The centurion Laelius swears that, if Caesar commands, he will plunge his sword into the belly of his pregnant wife (1.376–78). In his pre-battle speech to his army, Pompey even exhorts them: "Imagine that your mothers, leaning from Rome's highest city-walls with hair streaming, are urging you to battle" (7.369–70). Like wives, mothers are not only unable to thwart civil war but are enlisted to perpetuate it.

When women cannot prevent war, their other conventional response to it is to lament. This was an important role for women in the lived experience of Ancient Greece and Rome, but it took particular prominence in epic.[16] Homer's *Iliad* concludes with Andromache, Hecabe, and Helen mourning the death of Hector (*Il.* 24.710–75), while earlier Briseis and the other female captives in the Greek camp had mourned Patroclus (*Il.*19.282–302). In the *Aeneid*, the Trojan women repeatedly lament, for Polydorus and for Pallas, and the conventionality of this action is self-consciously marked as Vergil writes they loosened their hair "according to custom" (*de more, Aen.* 3.65, 11.35). Lament has multiple functions in epic. Its association with women genders it as the impotent gesture of the passive victims of war, whose agency is limited to responding to the actions of men. It offers a perspective on the cost of war, to be weighed against the glory it generates and the gains it achieves, a perspective that can also be gendered as feminine. Sometimes this (feminine) voice of lament goes further than balancing the (masculine) voice of triumph to challenge the very validity of war itself. This notion is dramatized in the *Aeneid* where the mother of the young warrior Euryalus laments his death and so demoralizes the Trojan army that she has to be silenced and confined to her tent (*Aen.* 9.473–502). At the same time, lament, in poetry as in real life, also served the function of perpetuating the memory of the slain and especially the sense of anger at their death, which would motivate (male) family and friends to avenge them. All of these functions of lament are at play in the *Civil War*.

Female lament is most prominently depicted at the opening of book 2 but with a typical Lucanian twist. In a vivid simile, the misery of the Roman people at the imminence of civil war is compared to a mother's reaction to the death of a son at the moment before shock gives way to grief (2.20–42). The parallelism between Rome and a household is a telling one, linking to images of civil war as fratricide and suicide and above all feminizing the act of lament as characteristic of a mother. Finely dressed *matronae* tear and dirty their clothes and beat their bodies, a conventional move but also one that symbolizes the degeneration of Rome into the ruinous state of civil war. However, all this conventional lamentation is a response not to deaths that have already occurred but, in a paradox characteristic of the poem, to the disastrous civil war that is about to begin. This is not merely a jarring reversal of chronological order but a reflection on the politics of the principate. For, as an unnamed *matrona* warns:

"nunc," ait "o miserae, contundite pectora, matres,
nunc laniate comas neue hunc differte dolorem
et summis seruate malis. nunc flere potestas
dum pendet fortuna ducum: cum uicerit alter,
gaudendum est."

(2.38–42)

"Now bruise your breasts, O miserable mothers,
now tear your locks; do not defer your grief
or save it for the last disaster. Now, while the leaders' destiny
is undecided, you may weep; once one of them has conquered,
you must rejoice."

Underlying the poem's horror of civil war is its sense, most explicitly articulated by Figulus (1.670), that the greater horror is the slavery of serving an emperor when the war is over. The *matrona*'s speech focuses particularly on how the start of the principate will bring the end to freedom of speech, as the people are no longer at liberty even to lament but must feign joy at the tyrant's command. This makes the connection between lament and dissidence almost explicit. Lament in the *Civil War* is not just about saying how terrible civil war is but about the freedom to say that, to speak against the triumphal voice of Caesarism. Like Euryalus's mother, the *matrona* speaks of war and the pity of war, and like her she is in danger of being silenced. Unlike the *Aeneid*, however, the dominant voice of the *Civil War* is the feminine one of lament and dissidence. Those who listen to it can share the numbing, enervating grief of Vergil's Trojan soldiers and Lucan's Roman citizens, but they can also be enflamed to take revenge, to avenge the dead republic. In particular, it is the voice of Cornelia, lamenting the death of Pompey, that urges her sons to continue the war and avenge their father (9.55–108, esp. 84–97).[17] The feminized voice of lament that is represented in the *Civil War* and which in many ways *is* the *Civil War* can reduce its audience to the torpor of grief or spur them to the action of resistance.

One female figure in the poem combines the roles of attempted peace-maker and lamenting *matrona* with another conventional feminine quality, the metaphorical association with the earth. When Caesar is about to cross the Rubicon, he is confronted by the personification of his Homeland (*Patria*) or Country:

> ut uentum est parui Rubiconis ad undas,
> ingens uisa duci patriae trepidantis imago
> clara per obscuram uultu maestissima noctem
> turrigero canos effundens uertice crines
> caesarie lacera nudisque astare lacertis
> et gemitu permixta loqui: "quo tenditis ultra?
> quo fertis mea signa, uiri? si iure uenitis,
> si ciues, huc usque licet."
>
> (1.185–92)

> When he reached the water of the little Rubicon,
> clearly to the leader through the murky night appeared
> a mighty image of his country in distress, grief in her face,
> her white hair streaming from her tower-crowned head;
> with tresses torn and shoulders bare she stood before him
> and sighing said: "Where further do you march?
> Where do you take my standards, warriors? If lawfully you come,
> if as citizens, this far only is allowed."

The personification of the Homeland—the only divinity to make a full appearance in the whole poem—fits into traditions that depict the earth as feminine, a mother who gives birth to and nurtures crops and men but also a passive entity that can be claimed and penetrated.[18] The description of *Patria* closely corresponds to those of other women in mourning (sad expression, hair and clothes in disarray), and she attempts to intercede and prevent the civil war, a Jocasta or a Veturia confronting her son as much as a Sabine woman.[19] The specificity of this description produces a slippage between *Patria* as metaphor for the land of Italy and *Patria* as representative of the real women of Italy who will be widowed, raped, or made homeless by the civil war. For Caesar rejects her intercession and his invasion is simultaneously an act of invasion, colonization, rape, and appropriation. Even the name with which he addresses her claims her as the imperial *Roma* rather than the republican *Patria*.[20] Feminist and ecofeminist critics differ as to whether the association of the land with the feminine serves to highlight the masculine abuse of both or whether it rather perpetuates a patriarchal construction of women as passive, inert matter to be acted upon by male agency.[21] Whether we read Lucan as pitying or objectifying her, or both, his gendering of *Patria* unquestionably enriches his depiction of Caesar's invasion.

Good Wives (and a Femme Fatale)

Each of the poem's three main characters has his "love interest": Marcia and Cornelia, the wives of Cato and Pompey, and Caesar's lover Cleopatra (his wife, Calpurnia, is notably absent). These women act in many ways as female counterparts of the men and show how gender can be used to develop the wider themes of the poem.

Marcia had been previously married to Cato but, when she had borne him what he considered the requisite number of children, he divorced her and gave her to his friend Hortensius so that she could bear him children as well.[22] In book 2, Lucan depicts her coming straight from Hortensius's funeral and asking to be remarried to Cato, in a sexless and even loveless marriage, so that she can die as his wife and have "Cato's Marcia" on her tombstone. In many ways, Marcia can be read as the essence of the idealized Roman *matrona*. She subordinates her will and her body to her husband and sees marriage as solely aimed at the production of children. In her strict and even extreme adherence to the most austere of Roman values, she is very much a female equivalent of Cato. In a world where such values are being confounded, this adherence to them can be taken as a final bastion of tradition. However, the depiction of their wedding ceremony is disturbing. Lucan extends an astonishing thirty-seven lines of narrative to describe, in a negative catalogue, all the traditional elements of a Roman wedding that were *absent* from this ceremony (2.354–80). This can be seen as a reflection of the disruption caused by civil war or of the austerity of Cato, but it inevitably raises the suggestion that something is *missing* from this ostensibly traditional scene as it is from the ostensibly traditional figures of Cato and Marcia. Torches, off-color jokes, flame-yellow veils, sex, all are an integral part of the Roman wedding, just as humanity is part of the role of the general that Cato signally fails to display in book 9. Marcia, like her husband, is so excessively idealized a wife as to go off the spectrum of normality and become as much of a perversion of wifehood as the decadent Cleopatra.

Probably the most appealing female character in the poem is Pompey's wife, Cornelia. The scenes of their parting in book 5 and their reunion after Pharsalus in book 8 offer a moving and attractive picture of a marriage founded on mutual affection and passion, far removed from the chilly chastity of Marcia or the cynical sensualism of Cleopatra.[23] Cornelia retains many features of the Roman feminine ideal and of the Roman feminine stereotype, and her loving relationship with Pompey, though reciprocal, is far from symmetrical. She subordinates her interests to his and blames herself for his misfortunes (8.88–97). She is unable to control her emotions and faints both when they are separated and when they are reunited (5.799–801, 8.58–61). She seems to have no interests or agency except those that relate to her husband. Pompey himself (although this says as much about his self-absorption as her self-abasement) sees her reputation as deriving entirely from her relationship with him: "You have an avenue to fame which will endure for centuries. In this your sex, the only means of praise is not respect for the laws nor warfare but an unhappy husband" (8.74–76). Even after Pompey's death, her final speech is a eulogy for him and her final determination is to die, not by suicide, but from grief (9.51–116). Lucan's portrayal of Cornelia is a relatively conventional one of an idealized Roman wife, tinged with a little more passionate eroticism than is often found in such depictions but offering a poignant image of how civil war destroys the personal as well as the political.

In many ways, it is Pompey rather than Cornelia whose gender is problematized in their scenes together. Excessive devotion to one's wife, uxoriousness, was considered a failure of masculinity, just like any other subordination of the male to the female.[24] Indeed, lovers in general tended to be vulnerable to the charge of effeminacy. While some modern, popular conceptions of gender classify the sexually promiscuous male—the stud or jack-the-lad—as hypermasculine, Greeks and Romans tended to see "ladies' men" such as Paris and Aegisthus as effeminate, in contrast to "real men" who concerned themselves with war rather than love. Catullus reasserted his masculinity in response to accusations that poems about kissing his girlfriend meant that he was effeminate (Catull. 16). Pompey's masculinity is thus doubly diminished by his erotically charged devotion to his wife, especially in contrast with the hypermasculine, war-focused Caesar. As we have seen, it is the latter's sexual capitulation to Cleopatra that leads to his own emasculation.

The loving relationship between Pompey and Cornelia is also an example of where gender and genre interact. The language used by and of them is strongly evocative of the erotic elegy written by Propertius, Tibullus, and Ovid.[25] This genre is frequently gendered as feminine—partly because of its foregrounding of women and love, partly for other literary-historical reasons—in antithesis with the obsessively masculine genre of epic. Any intrusion of elegiac motifs into epic tend to threaten not only its generic purity but its maintenance of masculine values.[26] The classic example is *Aeneid* 4, where Aeneas's love affair with Dido is simultaneously a threat that elegy will take over the epic narrative and that feminine concerns with the personal and erotic will overwhelm the masculine imperative toward colonization, empire, and public duty. So in the *Civil War*, Pompey's elegiac, feminized quality marks him out as insufficiently epic and insufficiently masculine and hence doomed to defeat. However, while most readers would agree that the dominant voice of the *Aeneid* is weighted in favor of war, epic, masculinity, and empire, a poem like the *Civil War*, where war is civil war, epic *nefas*, masculinity toxic, and empire tyranny, might be argued to hold a little more sympathy for the elegiac, feminine Pompey and Cornelia.

At the other end of the spectrum from the austere Marcia is the lecherous, opportunistic, Oriental femme fatale, Cleopatra. The depiction of Cleopatra in art, literature, and other discourses supportive of Octavian (later Augustus) and hostile to Mark Antony had long characterized her in very much this way, though more complex and nuanced portrayals are also to be found.[27] Lucan's depiction looks forward to her role in the Octavian–Antony civil war, curiously aligning himself with the Augustan discourse that framed it as an international war between Rome and Egypt:

> dedecus Aegypti, Latii feralis Erinys,
> Romano non casta malo, quantum impulit Argos
> Iliacasque domos facie Spartana nocenti,
> Hesperios auxit tantum Cleopatra furores.
> terruit illa suo, si fas, Capitolia sistro
> et Romana petit imbelli signa Canopo
> Caesare captiuo Pharios ductura triumphos;
> Leucadioque fuit dubius sub gurgite casus,
> an mundum ne nostra quidem matrona teneret.
>
> (10.59–67)

the disgrace of Egypt, deadly Erinys of Latium,
promiscuous to the harm of Rome. As much as the Spartan woman
with her harmful beauty knocked down Argos and the homes of Ilium,
so Cleopatra swelled the madness of Hesperia.
With her rattle she alarmed the Capitol, if such a thing can be,
and she attacked the Roman standards with unwarlike Canopus,
in her intent to lead a Pharian triumph with Caesar as a captive;
and doubtful was the outcome on the Leucadian flood:
would a woman—not even Roman—rule the world?

Cleopatra is set in the epic tradition of femmes fatales who cause terrible wars by comparing her with Helen ("the Spartan woman"), whose elopement with Paris sparked the Trojan War, immortalized in the *Iliad* and *Aeneid*. For Lucan, of course, Rome has already been possessed by the madness (*furor*) of civil war for nine books and almost two years, so even the femme fatale only "swelled" (*auxit*) that madness. The portrayal of Cleopatra is informed as much by ethnicity as by gender but above all by the nexus between the two. For Greeks and Romans, Eastern peoples, including Egyptians, were often depicted as effeminate, as can be seen in Lucan's references to the eunuch, Pothinus, and the unwarlike boy, Ptolemy. The negative connotations of universal femininity and Oriental effeminacy are blended in the figure of an Egyptian woman. At the same time, the East, and especially Egypt, was a place of inversions, where values and practices were the opposite of Greek and Roman norms.[28] The dominance of a woman is a symptom of this topsy-turviness, where the "proper" gender hierarchies do not apply. As she herself says to Caesar, "I shall not be the first woman to rule the Nile's cities: with no distinction of sex Pharos knows how to bear a queen" (10.90–92). This is not a radical advocation of the blurring of gender boundaries but rather an exploitation of their most rigid form so that their transgression can act as a symptom of the wider decadence of the Egyptian court.

Conclusion

Lucan's depiction of gender roles is complex but not especially radical. He does engage with the dangerous potential of *uirtus* to tip into the sort of toxic masculinity that contributed to the outbreak of the civil war and, likewise, with the possibility that the passive, "feminine" values of peace, devotion, and the valuation of loss may be preferable to the traditional, "masculine" ideals of martial valor. However, even these mild challenges to Rome's underlying gender ideology can be thought of as part of his wider construction of a poem and a world where *all* values and practices, including gender, are distorted and perverted. For it is the perversion—occasionally thrown into relief by small-scale normative performances—of gender roles that Lucan principally employs as a symptom, a cause, and a symbol of all that is wrong with the world of the *Civil War*. Gender remains important and "good to think with," but in Lucan, it is mainly good to think with about other themes.

Notes

1. On gender in the Graeco-Roman world, good starting points include Pomeroy 1995; McClure 2002; Holmes 2012; Foxhall 2013; Richlin 2014. On gender in Latin literature, see esp. Richlin 1992; Keith 2000; Dutsch 2008; Augoustakis 2010; Lovatt 2013; McCauley 2016; Panoussi 2019.

2. Orientalism: Said 1978. For effeminate Easterners, see the African king Iarbas on the Trojan Aeneas and his "half-man troupe" (*semiuiro comitatu*, Verg. *Aen.* 4.215). For (largely) positively masculine northerners, see Caesar on the Belgae, untouched by influences that "effeminize the mind" (*quae ad effeminandos animos pertinent*, *BGall.*1.1.3). In contrast, the Thracian king Tereus's barbaric (*barbarus*, Ov. *Met.* 6.515) hypermasculinity and native lustfulness (*innata libido*, *Met.* 6.458) drive him to rape and mutilate his sister-in-law, Philomela.

3. Hinds 2000, 226. On gender in Roman epic, see esp. Keith 2000; Augoustakis 2010.

4. This is true of all seven publications on gender in Latin literature cited in note 1.

5. Masculinity in epic: Graziosi and Haubold 1993; Hinds 2000; Barchiesi 2005; Masterson 2005; Ransom 2011; Augoustakis 2016.

6. On Roman masculinity, see esp. Gleason 1995; Walters 1997; Williams 1999; Gunderson 2000; McDonnell 2006; Olson 2017.

7. On the paterfamilias in life: Eyben 1996; in epic: Fowler 1996.

8. Lucan's Latin is slightly less emphatic than Braund's translation in underlining the gender polarities, since her "the man" and "this man" do not translate the noun *uir*, but only the masculine pronouns *quem* and *hic*.

9. Clark 2015, 152–56.

10. Braund translates, respectively, "hardy energy" and "strict excellence."

11. Only Cicero *de Amicitia* 48.9 and Tacitus *Germania* 31.5.

12. "Is excellence as 'harenivagrant' merely a mask for impotent fanaticism that mirrors elements of uncertainty and excess in the *sapiens* of *De bello ciuili* 2? . . . Is it a perversity insufficiently distinct from the corrupt valor of Caesar and Scaeva (an insanity that seeks to be seen as virtue)?" Tipping 2011, 235. For a survey of and compromise between conflicting views on Lucan's Cato: Caterine 2015

13. Fantham 1995.

14. As the narrator also says of Scaeva: "he did not know how great a crime is valour (*uirtus*) in a civil war," 6.148.

15. Cf. Caesar's "masculinity that does not know how to stand in one place" (*nescia uirtus* / *stare loco*, 1.144–45; Braund's succinct "never-resting energy" loses some of the phrase's nuance).

16. Life: Alexiou 1974; Treggiari 1991, 483–98; Richlin 2001; Erker 2009, 2011. Literature: Holst-Warhaft 1992; Dietrich 1999; Pagán 2000; Suter 2008; Panoussi 2009, 145–73, 2019, 85–113; Voigt 2016.

17. On Cornelia's call to vengeance, see esp. Keith 2008, 248–53.

18. On the motif: Dubois 1988; Dougherty 1993; Nugent 1994; Keith 2000.

19. In Greek myth, Jocasta vainly tried to persuade her son Polynices not to attack his native city of Thebes, while in semi-legendary early Roman history, Veturia (renamed Volumnia in Shakespeare) similarly, though successfully, interceded with Coriolanus.

20. Feeney 1991, 290–94.

21. "[E]cofeminism underlines the relation of men to culture and that of women to nature. . . . [W]omen and nature have been oppressed at the same time in the same way and thus it is a woman's duty to bring to an end male power over both." Kakkonen and Penjak 2015, 19. "The ramifications of this traditional assimilation become especially troubling when considering the faulty logic that confers upon both the unprivileged traits of passivity, materiality, and other markers of inferiority to justify domination of the ostensible analogues." Murphy 2019, 35.

22. On Marcia, see also Ambühl in this volume.

23. On the emotional dimension of Roman marriages, see Treggiari 1991, 229–61.

24. Sharrock 2013.

25. On Lucan and elegy: Caston 2011; Matthews 2011 (on Caesar); McCune 2013–2014; Littlewood 2016; Mulhern 2017.

26. Hinds 2000.

27. On Augustan Cleopatras: Wyke 2002, 195–243.

28. The most explicit articulation of this is Herodotus 2.35. On Herodotus and Egypt: Vasunia 2001, 75–135.

Glossary

The following brief definitions are intended solely to help the nonspecialist reader with some more technical terms or words and phrases used in a particular context or manner. For many of these entries, fuller definitions and more detailed information can be found in resources such as the *Oxford Classical Dictionary*, the *Princeton Encyclopedia of Poetry and Poetics*, the *Virgil Encyclopedia*, or the *Homer Encyclopedia*.

Alexandrian: used in literary criticism, it describes certain qualities and aesthetic principles—such as erudition, polish, and allusiveness—championed by a number of poet-scholars based in Alexandria from the early third century B.C.E., chiefly Callimachus, Theocritus, and Apollonius of Rhodes.

antiphrastic: opposed to something's proper or ordinary meaning. Lucan's antiphrastic engagement with Vergil's *Aeneid*, for example, may be seen in the manner in which he re-uses and reworks ostensibly positive scenes, characters, plots, and patterns in negative contexts.

apatheia: a Greek word (literally "freedom from passion") that refers to the Stoic concept that one should ideally be free from feelings that are based on mistaken beliefs, which may include emotions. See also *"ataraxia."*

Apollo: a god with many functions and associations. For readers of Lucan most relevant is Apollo's concern for poetry and poetic inspiration (Lucan forgoes the inspiration of Apollo and Bacchus at 1.63–66) and his association with prophecy and prophetic possession: Apollo possesses both the *matrona* at 1.673–95 and Phemonoe at Delphi during the visit of Appius Claudius Pulcher at 5.64–236. Nero took great pains to associate himself with Apollo.

apotheosis: an ascension into heaven or a transformation into a divinity, such as Lucan foresees for Nero at 1.43–59 or describes happening to Pompey at 9.1–18.

apostrophe: a direct poetic address. In Lucan the narrator very frequently apostrophizes his individual characters as well as groups and other entities, such as personified landscapes.

aristeia: a Greek word meaning "excellence" or "prowess." In epic poetry it describes a traditional set piece of narrative in which the poet recounts an individual warrior's moment of dominance on the battlefield. In Lucan see 6.118–262 for the *aristeia* of Caesar's soldier, Scaeva.

ataraxia: a state of imperturbability and freedom from anxiety; it was an ideal associated with both Stoic and Epicurean philosophy. See also "*apatheia*."

augur: official diviners, one of the four major colleges of priests. They were concerned with the auspices, the approval or disapproval of the gods of a planned or completed action through divinatory signs.

Berne scholiast: the author of the *Commenta Bernensia*.

cataclysm: one of the ways in which the Stoics believe that the universe would periodically consume itself in a universal destructive flood. See also "conflagration."

catalogue: a traditional element of epic poetry, consisting of a formal, elaborated list of names. The catalogue may describe contingents or leaders within an army, place names, or geographical elements. Lucan's *Civil War* contains many catalogues, including the Gallic tribes left unguarded by Caesar's army (1.392–465), the omens and prodigies of the civil war (1.522–83, 7.151–84), the mountains and rivers of Italy and Thessaly (2.392–438, 6.333–412), the contingents of Pompey's forces (3.162–297), the magical substances used by Erictho (6.685–718), and species of African snakes (9.700–733).

catasterism: a Greek word meaning "a placement among the stars." This term is often used to describe what happens to Pompey's soul at 9.1–18.

censor: one of two ex-consuls elected (in theory) every four years to hold office for eighteen months in order to form and maintain the census (the official list) of Roman citizens. The office was considered the summit of the senatorial career. In Lucan, Appius Claudius Pulcher is a censor.

Centuriate Assembly: one of four assemblies of the people in the Roman Republic, this gathering was envisioned as the Romans meeting as the army. It was responsible for electing officials with military power (praetors, consuls, censors), voting on war and peace, and hearing capital cases. The votes of the wealthy carried more weight than those of the poor in this assembly, as the rich were thought to have more at stake—that is, more they could physically lose—in the matters that this group considered.

clementia: a Latin word meaning "mercifulness" or "a disposition to spare or pardon." Caesar cultivated an association with this virtue by frequently pardoning his opponents in the civil war.

closure: a critical term used to describe the manner in which texts end or signal their own finality, resolution, or conclusion.

cognomen: the third element in the traditional "three names" of a freeborn male citizen at Rome: (1) praenomen, (2) nomen, (3) cognomen (e.g., (1) Marcus (2) Tullius

(3) Cicero). "Magnus" ("the Great") was an honorific epithet of Pompey that became his cognomen after 81 B.C.E.

Commenta Bernensia: "the Berne Commentary," an ancient set of notes on Lucan's *Civil War*, preserved in a ninth century manuscript (catalogued as "Bern 370").

conflagration: the Stoic concept (also known as "ekpyrosis") that over vast cycles of time the universe dissolves into fire and is regenerated again. See also "cataclysm."

consul: one of the two supreme magistrates annually elected at Rome.

council of the gods: a traditional set piece of epic poetry in which the poet narrates a meeting and deliberation of anthropomorphic gods.

diapeira (or "peira"): a Greek term (meaning "experiment") used to describe the moment in Homer's *Iliad* (2.110–41) when Agamemnon tests the Greek army by announcing that they should abandon the siege. The scene is one model for Pompey's failed attempt to stir his army to action at 2.526–609.

didaxis (adj. didactic): a Greek term (from *didaskein*, "to teach") describing a genre of epic poetry whose purpose is to instruct its readers.

divine apparatus (or divine machinery): a term used to describe the presence and intervention of anthropomorphic gods in the epic plot.

ekphrasis (pl. ekphrases; adj. ekphrastic): a Greek term (meaning "description") describing a verbal description of a visual image, such as a work of art or a location.

epitaph (adj. epitaphic): an inscription upon in a tomb; "epitaphic" describes expressions evoking such funerary inscriptions.

epos: a Greek term meaning "word" or "song"; also used to denote "heroic verse" and thus "epic poetry," for which it is a synonym.

etiology (adj. etiological): a Greek term (from *aetion*, "origin" or "cause") for an account of the origins or causes of, for example, names, places, or of cultural, civic, or religious phenomena and practices.

exemplarity: a term used to describe the moral and educational use made by Romans of examples (*exempla*; sing. *exemplum*) of figures from the past whom they celebrated and commemorated for performing great deeds in the service of their community; these exemplary figures became models to emulate.

focalization: a term used to describe the point of view or perspective from which a narrative is presented. An account, an event, or elements of either may be focalized through the perspective of a particular character within a story.

gigantomachy: an event in myth in which the earth-born ("chthonic") giants attacked the Olympian gods and were defeated and buried under volcanoes. Evocations of the myth in epic are often symbolic or suggestive of an assault on Jovian authority or cosmic order. In Lucan, the myth is a kind of mythic prequel to the civil war, and the two sides of the paradigm are often somewhat contaminated: Caesar, for example, is both the assailant and a representative of Jovian authority.

hyperbaton (pl. hyperbata): a term describing the emphatic disruption of word order.

hyperbole: a figure of speech characterized by exaggeration.

hypotaxis (adj. hypotactic): the arrangement of a complex sentence into subordinate and dominant clauses that shows the logical relationship of these clauses to each other. See too "parataxis."

in medias res: "into the middle of things," a famous phrase from Horace's *Ars Poetica* (148) to describe Homer's narrative strategy of beginning the *Odyssey* at an advanced point in its plot.

intertextuality: a term that broadly describes a text's relationship with other texts and how this relationship may generate meanings and nuances.

intratextuality: a term that describes the way different parts of the same text may have a relationship with each other that may generate meanings and nuances.

leitmotif: a theme that recurs throughout a work.

matrona **(pl.** *matronae***):** a Latin word for a married woman or matron. In Lucan, an unnamed *matrona* has a frenzied vision of the events of the civil war at 1.673–95.

metaliterary / metapoetic: terms that describe the way literary works or poems reflect on their own status or quality as literary works or poetry.

metaphor: a figure of speech in which something is said to be another thing or is called by another thing's name or is described in terms appropriate for another thing in order to evoke new meaning. In a metaphor, the "thing meant" is called the "tenor" and the "thing said" is called the "vehicle." Thus, when Lucan writes at 7.695–96 that Caesar and liberty are "that pair of rivals always with us," the Latin word translated as "pair of rivals" (*par*) makes clear that the metaphor presents Caesar's autocracy and Roman freedom (the tenor) as opposed gladiators fighting in the arena (the vehicle).

metonymy: the substitution of one word or phrase for another related word or phrase; the relationship may be material, causal, or conceptual. Examples may include using a god's name to describe the phenomena associated with that god ("Mars" for "war") or using a place name for the event that took place there ("Actium" for "the Battle of Actium").

mimēsis: a Greek word meaning "imitation." It is used to describe the representation or imitation of the real world in a work of art or literature.

mos maiorum: a Latin phrase meaning "inherited custom, tradition."

narratology: the study of the structure and function of narrative.

necromancy: the art of predicting the future by communication with the dead.

negative enumeration (or "negation antithesis"): a stylistic device favored by Lucan in which he enumerates things that the reader may expect to be present in a scene but are absent. A famous example is the wedding of Cato and Marcia at 2.354–71.

Neronia: a competitive festival comprising games, poetry, and theater established by Nero in 60 c.e. Lucan won a prize in the first Neronia for a poem in praise of Nero.

panegyric: a work or passage dedicated to praising a person, event, or thing. The most prominent example in Lucan is the praise of Nero at 1.33–66.

paradox: a statement that appears to be absurd or contradictory (or to contain contradictory elements) but upon reflection or explanation is revealed to be well founded or true.

parataxis (adj. paratactic): the arrangement of a compound sentence into clauses of equal grammatical importance by means of conjunctions that do not show the logical relationship of one clause to another ("It was raining and I took and umbrella" versus "Since it was raining, I took an umbrella"). Lucan's proem (1.1–7) is heavily paratactic, especially compared with the proem of Vergil's *Aeneid*. See too "hypotaxis."

peripeteia: a term from the criticism of Greek tragedy to describe an unexpected or abrupt reversal of fortune.

Phoebus: a cult title of Apollo.

Pisonian conspiracy: a widespread conspiracy against the emperor Nero that came to light in 65 C.E.; its aim was to assassinate Nero and make Gaius Calpurnius Piso emperor. The plot failed, and many conspirators, including Lucan, were forced to commit suicide in the aftermath of its failure.

proconsular governor: during the late republic, former consuls and praetors were given command of a territory that Rome controlled for one to two years. These proconsuls and propraetors—because they stood in "for" (*pro*) regular magistrates—maintained public order, decided capital cases, and defended the territory from external and internal threats.

proem: the lines that begin or introduce a longer poem. In Lucan these are the first 7 lines of book 1, which sit in a larger introductory section of 182 lines.

programmatic: an element of a literary work that establishes a norm or pattern for the rest of that work.

providence: the Stoics believed that everything happens in accordance with divine providence, which they also identified with fate.

Pythia, the: the title of the priestess of the Delphic Oracle. She was a Delphian woman who remained a virgin and served for life; her main religious role was to be possessed by Apollo and utter his prophecies. In Lucan, the Pythia is a woman called Phemonoe (5.64–236).

quaestor: the most junior of the regular, elected senatorial magistracies; it allowed its holder entry into the Roman senate. Vacca tells us that Lucan gave gladiatorial games with his colleagues when he held this office (in 60 or 61).

Quirites: a name given to the collected citizens of Rome in their peacetime functions.

res gestae: a Latin phrase, meaning "achievements." It can describe both an individual's account of his past achievements and the collective record of a people, in which sense the term is a synonym for "history."

second person: a grammatical term used to classify words that pertain to a person being addressed: "you," "your," "yours," "yourself," "yourselves."

sententia **(pl.** *sententiae***):** a concise, pointed, and moralizing expression; it may convey general truths or comment upon the context in which it is uttered.

simile: a figure of speech in which something is explicitly compared to, or said to be like, something else (in English words such as "like" or "(just) as" often mark similes). Formal similes extending over a number of lines of verse are a convention of epic poetry.

sphragis: a Greek word meaning "seal." It is a passage in which an author identifies himself or herself as the author of the work or makes other self-referential statements; it may contain reflections on the author's own fame or literary achievement. A sphragis can occur anywhere in a literary work, Lucan has one at 9.980–86. It commonly acts as a coda at the very end of the work, as at Verg. *G.* 4.563–66 or Ov. *Met.* 15.861–70.

sublime: a term of literary criticism that in antiquity described the quality and aspects of literary works that could delight, inspire, or overwhelm the reader.

synecdoche: a trope in which the part is substituted for the whole of something.

theodicy: a justification or explanation of why the gods permit evil on earth or human suffering.

topos (pl. topoi): a traditional or conventional motif in literary works.

trope: (1) a figure of speech, especially one in which words or phrases are used in a sense other than their literal or proper meaning. (2) A motif or a recurrent theme.

uirtus: a Latin word, related to the word for "man" (*uir*) and meaning "the qualities typical of a true man." It often encompasses the sense "manliness, courage, excellence."

Bibliography

Ahl, F. M. 1972. "Hercules and Curio: Some Comments on *Pharsalia* 4.581–824." *Latomus* 31: 997–1009.

———. 1976. *Lucan. An Introduction*. Ithaca.

———. 1993. "Form Empowered: Lucan's *Pharsalia*." In *Roman Epic,* ed. A. J. Boyle, 124–43. London.

———, trans. 2008. *Vergil, Aeneid*. Oxford.

Alexiou, M. 1974. *The Ritual Lament in the Greek Tradition*. Cambridge.

Alexis, F. 2011. "Lucan's *Bellum Ciuile* and the Epic Genre." Ph.D. diss., University of Tasmania.

Allendorf, T. S. 2013. "The Poetics of Uncertainty in Senecan Drama." *Materiali e discussioni per l'analisi dei testi classici* 71: 103–44.

Ambühl, A. 2010. "Lucan's 'Iliupersis'—Narrative Patterns from the Fall of Troy in book 2 of the *Bellum Civile*." In *Lucan's Bellum Civile: Between Epic Tradition and Aesthetic Innovation,* ed. N. Hömke and C. Reitz, 17–38. Berlin.

———. 2015. *Krieg und Bürgerkrieg bei Lucan und in der griechischen Literatur: Studien zur Rezeption der attischen Tragödie und der hellenistischen Dichtung im Bellum civile*. Berlin.

———. 2020. "Alternative Futures in Lucan's *Bellum Civile*: Imagining Aftermaths of Civil War." In *After the Crisis: Remembrance, Re-Anchoring and Recovery in Ancient Greece and Rome,* ed. J. Klooster and I. N. I. Kuin, 103–18. London.

Ando, C. 2008. *The Matter of the Gods: Religion and the Roman Empire*. Berkeley.

Ankersmit, F. 2005. *Sublime Historical Experience*. Stanford.

Ash, R. 2018. *Tacitus, Annals Book XV*. Cambridge.

Ash, R., and A. Sharrock. 2001. *Fifty Key Classical Authors*. London.

Asmis, E. 2009. "Seneca on Fortune and the Kingdom of God." In *Seneca and the Self,* ed. S. Bartsch and D. Wray, 115–39. Cambridge.

Asso, P. 2002. "The Function of the Fight: Hercules and Antaeus in Lucan." *Vichiana* 4: 57–72.

———. 2008. "The Intrusive Trope: Apostrophe in Lucan." *Materiali e discussioni per l'analisi dei testi classici* 61: 161–75.

———. 2010. *A Commentary on Lucan, De Bello Civili IV*. Berlin.

———., ed. 2011. *Brill's Companion to Lucan*. Leiden.

Augoustakis, A. 2006. "Cutting down the Grove in Lucan, Valerius Maximus and Dio Cassius." *Classical Quarterly* 56: 634–38.

———. 2010. *Motherhood and the Other: Fashioning Female Power in Flavian Epic*. Oxford.

———. 2016. "Achilles and the Poetics of Manhood: Re(de)fining Europe and Asia in Statius' *Achilleid*." *Classical World* 109: 195–219.

Avery, H. C. 1933. "A Lost Episode in Caesar's *Civil War*." *Hermes* 121: 452–69.

Aymard, J. 1951. *Quelques séries de comparaisons chez Lucain*. Montpellier.

Bachofen, A. 1972. *Cäsars und Lucans Bellum civile: Ein Inhaltsvergleich*. Zurich.

Backhaus, M. 2019. *Mord(s)bilder—Aufzählungen von Gewalt bei Seneca und Lucan*. Berlin.

Baier T., ed. 2012. *Götter und menschliche Willensfreiheit: Von Lukan bis Silius Italicus*. Munich.

Bailey C. 1935. *Religion in Vergil*. Oxford.

Barchiesi, A. 2005. "Masculinity in the 90s: The Education of Achilles in Statius and Quintilian." In *Roman and Greek Imperial Epic*, ed. M. Paschalis, 47–75. Rethymnon.

Barratt, P. 1979. *M. Annaei Lucani Belli Civilis liber V: A Commentary*. Amsterdam.

Barrenechea, F. 2010. "Didactic Aggressions in the Nile Excursus of Lucan's *Bellum Civile*." *Americn Journal of Philology* 131: 259–84.

Bartsch, S. 1997. *Ideology in Cold Blood: A Reading of Lucan's Civil War*. Cambridge, Mass.

———. 2007. "'Wait a Moment *Phantasia*': Ekphrastic Interference in Seneca and Epictetus." *Classical Philology* 102: 83–95.

———. 2009. "Senecan Metaphor and Stoic Self-Instruction." In *Seneca and the Self*, ed. S. Bartsch and D. Wray, 188–217. Cambridge.

———. 2012. "Ethical Judgment and Narratorial Apostrophe in Lucan's *Bellum Civile*." In *Götter und menschliche Willensfreiheit: Von Lucan bis Silius Italicus*, ed. T. Baier, 87–97. Munich.

Basore, J. W., ed. and trans. 1928–35. *Seneca. Moral Essays*. 3 vols. Cambridge, Mass.

Batinsky, E. 1992. "Lucan's Catalogue of Caesar's Troops: Paradox and Convention." *Classical Journal* 88: 19–24.

———. 1993. "Julia in Lucan's Tripartite Vision of the Dead Republic." In *Woman's Power, Man's Game: Essays on Classical Antiquity in Honor of Joy K. King*, ed. M. DeForest, 264–78. Wauconda, Ill.

Batstone, W. W., and C. Damon. 2006. *Caesar's Civil War*. Oxford.

Bergmann, M. 2013. "Portraits of an Emperor—Nero, the Sun, and Roman *Otium*." In *A Companion to the Neronian Age*, ed. E. Buckley and M. T Dinter, 332–62. Malden, Mass.

Bernstein, M. A. 1994. *Foregone Conclusions: Against Apocalyptic History*. Berkeley.

Bernstein, N. 2011. "The Dead and Their Ghosts in the *Bellum Civile:* Lucan's Visions of History." In *Brill's Companion to Lucan*, ed. P. Asso, 257–79. Leiden.

Bexley, E. 2010. "The Myth of the Republic: Medusa and Cato in Lucan, *Pharsalia 9*." In *Lucan's Bellum Civile: Between Epic Tradition and Aesthetic Innovation*, ed. N. Hömke and C. Reitz, 135–54. Berlin.

———. 2013. "Lucan's Catalogues and the Landscape of War." In *Geography, Topography, Landscape: Configurations of Space in Greek and Roman Epic*, ed. M. Skempis and I. Ziogas, 373–404. Berlin.

Blaschka, K. 2015. *Fiktion im Historischen. Die Bildsprache und die Konzeption der Charaktere in Lucans Bellum Civile*. Rahden.

Blisset, W. 1957. "Caesar and Satan." *Journal of the History of Ideas* 18: 221–32.

Bonner, S. F. 1966. "Lucan and the Declamation Schools." *American Journal of Philology* 87: 257–89.

Bosworth, A. B. 1988. *Conquest and Empire: The Reign of Alexander the Great*. Cambridge.

Bowie, A. 1990. "The Death of Priam: Allegory and History in the *Aeneid*." *Classical Quarterly* 40: 470–81.

Boyd, B. W. 1983. "*Cydonea Mala:* Vergilian Word-Play and Allusion." *Harvard Studies in Classical Philology* 87: 169–74.

Boyle, A., ed. 1993. *Roman Epic*. London.

Bramble, J. C. 1982. "Lucan." In *The Cambridge History of Classical Literature*. Vol. 2, *Latin Literature*, ed. E. J. Kenney and W. V. Clausen, 533–57. Cambridge.

Braund, S. H., trans. 1992. *Lucan. Civil War*. Oxford.

———. 2002. *Latin Literature*. London.

———. 2009. *A Lucan Reader: Selections from Civil War*. Mundelein, Ill.

———. 2010. "Introduction." In *Oxford Readings in Classical Studies: Lucan*, ed. C. Tesoriero, 1–13. Oxford.

Bremmer, J. N. 2003. *The Rise and Fall of the Afterlife*. London.

Brena, F. 1999. "Osservazioni al libro IX del *Bellum Civile*." In *Interpretare Lucano*, ed. P. Esposito and L. Nicastri, 275–301. Naples.

Carcopino, J. 1968. *Jules César*. Paris.

Carrera, A. 2016. "Rossellini's Holy Mountain. Cinema and the Aesthetics of the Sublime." In *Attraversamenti Culturali. Cinema, Letteratura, Musica, e Arti Visuali nell'Italia Contemporanea*, ed. F. Orsitto and S. Wright, 23–55. Florence.

Carson, A. 2004. "The Art of Poetry No. 88." Interview by Will Aitken, *Paris Review* 171 (Fall). https://www.theparisreview.org/interviews/5420/anne-carson-the-art -of-poetry-no-88-anne-carson.

Casali, S. 1999. "Mercurio a Ilerda: *Pharsalia 4* ed *Eneide 4*." In *Interpretare Lucano*, ed. P. Esposito and L. Nicastri, 223–36. Naples.

———. 2011. "The *Bellum Civile* as an Anti-*Aeneid*." In *Brill's Companion to Lucan*, ed. P. Asso, 81–109. Leiden.

Casamento, A. 2012. "Quando gli oracoli passano di moda: L'episodio di Appio e Femonoe nel quinto libro della *Pharsalia* di Lucano." In *Götter und menschliche Willensfreiheit: Von Lucan bis Silius Italicus*, ed. T. Baier, 141–57. Munich.

Caston, R. 2011. "Lucan's Elegiac Moments." In *Brill's Companion to Lucan*, ed. P. Asso, 133–52. Leiden.

Caterine, C. L. 2015. "*Si Credere Velis:* Lucan's Cato and the Reader of the *Bellum Civile*." *Arethusa* 48: 339–67.

Cavarero, A. 2000. *Relating Narratives. Storytelling and Selfhood.* London.

Celotto, G. 2018. "Alexander the Great in Seneca's Works and in Lucan's *Bellum Civile*." In *Brill's Companion to the Reception of Alexander the Great*, ed. K. R. Moore, 325–54. Leiden.

Champeaux J. 1988. *Fortuna. Recherches sur le culte de la Fortune à Rome et dans le monde romain des origines à la mort de César.* Vol. 2, *Les transformations de Fortuna sous la République.* Paris.

Chaudhuri, P. 2014. *The War with God: Theomachy in Roman Imperial Poetry.* Oxford.

Chiu, A. 2010. "The Importance of Being Julia: Civil War, Historical Revision and the Mutable Past in Lucan's *Pharsalia*." *Classical Journal* 105: 343–60.

Clark, C. A. "Masculinity, Nonverbal Behavior, and Pompey's Death in Lucan's *Bellum Civile*." In *Kinesis: The Ancient Depiction of Gesture, Motion, and Emotion*, ed. C. A. Clark, E. Foster, and J. P. Hallett, 143–59. Ann Arbor.

Clauss, M. 1999. *Kaiser und Gott: Herrscherkult im römischen Reich.* Stuttgart.

Coffee, M. 1996. "Generic Impropriety in the High Style: Satirical Themes in Seneca and Lucan." In *Satura Lanx: Festschrift für Werner A. Krenkel zum 70. Geburtstag*, ed. C. Klodt, 81–93. Hildesheim.

Coffee, N. 2011. "Social Relations in *Lucan's Bellum Civile*." In *Brill's Companion to Lucan*, ed. P. Asso, 417–32. Leiden.

Colish, M. 1985. *The Stoic Tradition from Antiquity to the Early Middle Ages.* Leiden.

Conte, G. B. 1966. "Il proemio della *Pharsalia*." *Maia* 18: 42–53. [Translated by L. Holford-Strevens and reprinted as "The Proem of *Pharsalia*." In *Oxford Readings in Classical Studies: Lucan*, ed. C. Tesoriero, 46–58. Oxford, 2010.]

———. 1968. "La guerra civile nella rievocazione del popolo: Lucano, II 67–233. Stile e forma della *Pharsalia*." *Maia* 20: 224–53.

———. 1988. *La Guerra Civile di Lucano. Studi e prove di commento.* Urbino.

———. 1992. "Proems in the Middle." *Yale Classical Studies* 29: 147–59.

Cornish, F. W., J. P. Postgate, and J. W. Mackail, eds. and trans. 1913. *Catullus. Tibullus. Pervigilium Veneris.* Cambridge, Mass.

Cornwell, H. 2017. *Pax and the Politics of Peace: Republic to Principate.* Oxford.

Courtney, E. 1993. *The Fragmentary Latin Poets. Edited with Commentary.* Oxford.

Cowan, R. 2010. "Virtual Epic: Counterfactuals, Sideshadowing, and the Poetics of Contingency in the *Punica*." In *Brill's Companion to Silius Italicus*, ed. A. Augoustakis, 323–51. Leiden.

———. 2014. "Fingering Cestos: Martial's Catullus' Callimachus." In *Flavian Poetry and Its Greek Past*, ed. Antony Augoustakis 345–71. Leiden.

———. 2018. "Sideshadowing Actium: Counterfactual History in Lollius' *Naumachia* (Horace, *Epistles* 1.18)." *Antichthon* 52: 90–116.

Currie, B. G. F. 2006. "Homer and the Early Epic Tradition." In *Epic Interactions: Perspectives on Homer, Vergil, and the Epic Tradition Presented to Jasper Griffin*, ed. M. J. Clarke, B. G. F. Currie, and R. O. A. M. Lyne, 1–46. Oxford.

D'Alessandro Behr, F. 2007. *Feeling History. Lucan, Stoicism, and the Poetics of Passion*. Columbus, Ohio.

———. 2014. "Consolation, Rebellion and Philosophy in Lucan's *Bellum Civile* book 8." In *The Philosophizing Muse: The Influence of Greek Philosophy on Roman Poetry*, ed. M. Garani and D. Konstan, 218–44. Newcastle upon Tyne.

———. 2020. "Sage, Soldier, Politician, and Benefactor: Cato in Seneca and Lucan." In *Lucan's Imperial World: The Bellum Civile in Its Contemporary Contexts*, ed. L. Zientek and M. Thorne, 151–70. London.

Damon, C. 2010. "Déjà vu or déjà lu? History as Intertext." *Papers of the Langford Latin Seminar* 14: 375–88.

———. 2015. *C. Iuli Caesaris Commentariorum Libri III De Bello Civili*. Oxford.

Dangel, J. 2010. "Les femmes et la violence dans le *Bellum Ciuile* de Lucain: Écriture symbolique des deviances de l'histoire." In *Lucain en débat: Rhétorique, poétique et histoire*, ed. O. Devillers and S. Franchet d'Espèrey, 91–104. Bordeaux.

Day, H. J. M. 2013. *Lucan and the Sublime: Power, Representation and Aesthetic Experience*. Cambridge.

Degl'Innocenti Pierini, R. 1990. *Tra Ovidio e Seneca*. Bologna.

De Jong, I. J. F. 2005. "Aristotle and the Homeric Narrator." *Classical Quarterly* 55: 616–21.

De Jong, I. J. F., R. Nunlist, and A. Bowie, eds. 2004. *Narrators, Narratees and Narrative in Ancient Greek Literature*. Leiden.

DeLacy, P. 1948. "Stoic Views of Poetry." *American Journal of Philology* 69: 241–71.

De Moura, R. 2010. "Lucan 7: Speeches at War." In *Lucan's Bellum Ciuile: Between Epic Tradition and Aesthetic Innovation*, ed. N. Hömke and C. Reitz, 71–90. Berlin.

Dewar, M. 1994. "Laying It on with a Trowel: The Proem to Lucan and Related Texts." *Classical Quarterly* 44: 199–211.

Dick, B. F. 1967. "Fatum and Fortuna in Lucan's *Bellum Civile*." *Classical Philology* 52: 235–42.

Dietrich, J. 1999. "*Thebaid*'s Feminine Ending." *Ramus* 28: 40–53.

Dilke, O. A. W. 1960. *M. Annaei Lucani De Bello Civili liber VII*. Cambridge.

———. 1972. "Lucan's Political Views and the Caesars." In *Neronians and Flavians: Silver Latin I*, ed. D. R. Dudley, 62–82. London.

Dinter, M. T. 2005. "Lucan's Epic Body." In *Lucan im 21. Jahrhundert*, ed. C. Walde, 295–312. Munich.

———. 2012. *Anatomizing Civil War: Studies in Lucan's Epic Technique*. Ann Arbor.

———. 2013. "Introduction: The Neronian (Literary) Renaissance." In *A Companion to the Neronian Age*, ed. E Buckley and M. Dinter, 1–14. Malden, Mass.

———. 2016. "Sententiousness in Roman Comedy—A Moralising Reading." In *Roman Drama and Its Contexts*, ed. G. Manuwald, S. Harrison, and S. Frangoulidis, 127–42. Berlin.

———. 2019. "Epigram in Epic and Greek Tragedy—Generic Interactions." In *A Companion to Ancient Epigram*, ed. C. Henriksen, 145–162. Malden, Mass.

Dougherty, C. 1993. *The Poetics of Colonization: From City to Text in Archaic Greece*. Oxford.

Dubois, P. 1988. *Sowing the Body: Psychoanalysis and Ancient Representations of Women*. Chicago.

Due, O. S. 1962. "An Essay on Lucan." *Classica et Mediaevalia* 23: 68–132.

———. 1970. "Lucain et la philosophie." In *Lucain: Sept exposés suivis de discussions*, ed. M. Durry, 203–32. Geneva.

Duff, J. D., ed. and trans. 1928. *Lucan. The Civil War*. Cambridge, Mass.

Durkheim, E. 1995. *The Elementary Forms of Religious Life*. Translated by K. E. Fields. New York.

Dutsch, D. M. *Feminine Discourse in Roman Comedy: On Echoes and Voices*. Oxford.

Dyck, A. R. 2013. *Cicero. Pro Marco Caelio*. Cambridge.

Dyson, S. L. 1970. "Caepio, Tacitus, and Lucan's Sacred Grove." *Classical Philology* 65: 36–8.

Eckert, A. 2016. "'There is nobody who does not hate Sulla': Emotion, Persuasion and Cultural Trauma." In *Emotion and Persuasion in Classical Antiquity*, ed. E. Sanders and M. Johncock, 133–45. Stuttgart.

Edmunds, L. 2001. *Intertextuality and the Reading of Roman Poetry*. Baltimore.

Edwards, C. 1993. *The Politics of Immorality in Ancient Rome*. Cambridge.

Eigler, U. 2012. "*Fama, fatum* und *fortuna*: Innere und äussere Motivation in der epischen Erzählung." In *Götter und menschliche Willensfreiheit: Von Lucan bis Silius Italicus*, ed. T Baier, 41–53. Munich.

Erker, D. S. 2009. "Women's Tears in Ancient Roman Ritual." In *Tears in the Graeco-Roman World*, ed. T. Fögen, 135–60. Berlin.

———. 2011. "Gender and Roman Funerary Ritual." In *Memory and Mourning: Studies on Roman Death*, ed. V. M. Hope and J. Huskinson, 40–60. Oxford.

———. 2013. "Religion." In *A Companion to the Neronian Age*, ed. E. Buckley and M. Dinter, 118–33. Malden, Mass.

Erler, M. 2012. "Der unwissende Erzähler und seine Götter: Erzählperspektive und Theologie bei Lukan und in Vergils *Aeneis*." In *Götter und menschliche Willensfreiheit: Von Lucan bis Silius Italicus*, ed. T. Baier, 127–40. Munich.

Esposito, P. 1987. *Il racconto della strage. Le battaglie nella Pharsalia*. Naples.

———. 1996. "Lucrezio come intertesto lucaneo." *Bollettino di studi latini* 26: 517–44.

———. 2004. "Lucano e la 'Negazione per antitesi.'" In *Lucano e la tradizione dell'epica latina*, ed. P. Esposito and E. M. Ariemma, 39–67. Naples.

———. 2009. *Marco Anneo Lucano, Bellum Civile (Pharsalia), Libro IV*. Naples.

———. 2012a. "Prima e dopo Lucano: dai modelli della *Pharsalia* alla *Pharsalia* come modello." In *Letteratura e civitas. Transizioni dalla Repubblica all'Impero*, ed. M. Citroni, 313–26. Pisa.

———. 2012b. "Su alcuni miti tragici in Lucano e nell'epica flavia." In *Götter und menschliche Willensfreiheit. Von Lucan bis Silius Italicus*, ed. T. Baier, 99–126. Munich.

Eyben, E. 1996. "Fathers and Sons." In *Marriage, Divorce, and Children in Ancient Rome*, ed. B. Rawson, 114–43. Oxford.

Faber, R. A. 2005. "The Adaptation of Apostrophe in Lucan's *Bellum Civile*." In *Studies in Latin Literature and Roman History* 12, ed. C. Deroux, 334–43. Brussels.

Fairclough, H. R., and G. P. Goold, eds. and trans. 2001. *Vergil. Eclogues, Georgics, Aeneid*. 2 vols. Cambridge, Mass.

Fantham, E. 1985. "Caesar and the Mutiny: Lucan's Reshaping of the Historical Tradition in *De bello civili* 5.237–373." *Classical Philology* 80: 119–31.

———. 1992a. *Lucan, De bello civili II*. Cambridge.

———. 1992b. "Lucan's Medusa-Excursus: Its Design and Purpose." *Materiali e discussioni per l'analisi dei testi classici* 29: 95–119.

———. 1995. "The Ambiguity of Virtus in Lucan's *Civil War* and Statius' *Thebaid*." *Arachnion* 3. https://www.telemachos.hu-berlin.de/arachne/num3/fantham .html.

———. 1996. "*Religio . . . dira loci*: Two Passages in Lucan, *De Bello Civili* 3 and Their Relation to Vergil's Rome and Latium." *Materiali e discussioni per l'analisi dei testi classici* 37: 137–53.

———. 2010. "Caesar's Voice and Caesarian Voices." In *Lucan's Bellum Ciuile: Between Epic Tradition and Aesthetic Innovation*, eds. N. Hömke and C. Reitz, 53–70. Berlin.

———. 2011. "A Controversial Life." In *Brill's Companion to Lucan*, ed. P. Asso, 3–20. Leiden.

Feeney, D. C. 1986. "*Stat Magni Nominis Umbra*: Lucan on the Greatness of Pompeius Magnus." *Classical Quarterly* 36: 239–43. [Reprinted in *Oxford Readings in Classical Studies: Lucan*, ed. C. Tesoriero, 346–54. Oxford, 2010.]

———. 1991. *The Gods in Epic: Poets and Critics of the Classical Tradition*. Oxford.

———. 1998. *Literature and Religion at Rome: Cultures, Contexts, and Beliefs*. Cambridge.

———. 2014. "First Similes in Epic." *Transactions of the American Philological Association* 144: 189–228.

Finiello, C. 2005. "Der Bürgerkrieg: Reine Männersache? Keine Männersache! Erictho und die Frauengestalten im *Bellum Civile* Lucans." In *Lucan im 21. Jahrhundert*, ed. C. Walde, 155–85. Munich.

Finkelberg, M. 1990. "A Creative Oral Poet and the Muse." *American Journal of Philology* 111: 293–303.

Flower, H. I. 2008. "Remembering and Forgetting Temple Destruction: The Destruction of the Temple of Jupiter Optimus Maximus in 83 B.C." In *Antiquity in Antiquity: Jewish and Christian Pasts in the Greco-Roman World*, ed. G Gardner and K. L. Osterloh, 74–92. Tübingen.

Fordyce, C. J. 1977. *P. Vergili Maronis* Aeneidos *Libri VII–VIII*. Oxford.

Foster, B. O., ed. and trans. 1919. *Livy. History of Rome, Books 1–2*. Cambridge, Mass.

Foucault, M. 1988. *The History of Sexuality*. Vol. 3, *The Care of the Self*. New York.

Fowler, D. P. 1996. "God the Father (Himself) in Virgil." *Proceedings of the Virgil Society* 22: 35–52.

———. 1997. "On the Shoulders of Giants: Intertextuality and Classical Studies." *Materiali e discussioni per l'analisi dei testi classici* 39: 13–34.

Foxhall, L. 2013. *Studying Gender in Classical Antiquity*. Cambridge.

Fox, M., trans. 2012. *Lucan: Civil War.* With introduction and notes by M. Fox and E. Adams. London.

Fratantuono, L. 2012. *Madness Triumphant: A Reading of Lucan's Pharsalia.* Lanham, Md.

Fratantuono, L., and R. A. Smith. *Virgil, Aeneid 8.* Leiden.

Friedrich, W. H. 1938. "Cato, Caesar und Fortuna bei Lucan." *Hermes* 73: 391–423.

Fucecchi, M. 2011. "Partisans in Civil War." In *Brill's Companion to Lucan,* ed. P. Asso, 237–56. Leiden.

Gall, D. 2005. "Masse, Heere und Feldherren in Lucans *Pharsalia.*" In *Lucan im 21. Jahrhundert,* ed. C. Walde, 89–110. Munich.

Galli Milić, L. 2016. "Manilius et l'éloge de Néron (Lucan. 1,33–66): Quelques considérations intertextuelles sur le *proemium* du *Bellum Civile.*" In *Lucan and Claudian: Context and Intertext,* ed. V. Berlincourt, L. Galli Milić, and D. P. Nelis, 107–25. Heidelberg.

Gallia, A. 2020. "The Roman Family as Institution and Metaphor after the Civil Wars." In *After the Crisis: Remembrance, Re-Anchoring and Recovery in Ancient Greece and Rome,* ed. J. Klooster and I. N. I. Kuin, 183–97. London.

Galtier, F. 2016a. "Le conflit entre Marius et Sylla: Un souvenir traumatique dans la *Pharsale.*" In *Présence de Lucain,* ed. F. Galtier and R. Poignault, 17–31. Clermont-Ferrand.

———. 2016b. "L'*imago* de Caton dans le livre 2 de la *Pharsale.*" In *Lucan and Claudian: Context and Intertext,* ed. V. Berlincourt, L. Galli Milić, and D. Nelis, 77–92. Heidelberg.

———. 2018. *L'empreinte des morts: Relations entre mort, mémoire et reconnaissance dans la Pharsale de Lucain.* Paris.

Garrison, D. 1992. "The '*Locus Inamoenus*': Another Part of the Forest." *Arion* 2: 98–114.

George, D. B. 1991. "Lucan's Cato and Stoic Attitudes to the Republic." *Classical Antiquity* 10: 237–58.

———. 1992. "The Meaning of the *Pharsalia* Revisited." In *Studies in Latin Literature and Roman History* 6, ed. C. Deroux, 362–89. Brussels.

Getty, R. J. 1940. *M. Annaei Lucani De Bello Civili liber I.* Cambridge.

Gleason, M. 1995. *Making Men: Sophists and Self-Fashioning in Ancient Rome.* Princeton.

Goold, G. P., ed. and trans. 1990. *Propertius. Elegies.* Cambridge, Mass.

Gordon, R. 1987. "Lucan's Erictho." In *Homo Viator. Classical Essays for John Bramble,* ed. M. Whitby, P. Hardie. and M. Whitby, 231–41. Bristol.

Gorman, V. B. 2001. "Lucan's Epic *Aristeia* and the Hero of the *Bellum Civile.*" *Classical Journal* 96: 263–90.

Gowing, A. M. 2002. "Pirates, Witches and Slaves: The Imperial Afterlife of Sextus Pompeius." In *Sextus Pompeius,* ed. A. Powell and K. Welch, 187–211. London.

———. 2005. *Empire and Memory: The Representation of the Roman Republic in Imperial Culture.* Cambridge.

Graver, M. 2011. "*De Bello Civili* 2.326–91: Cato Gets Married." In *Emotion, Genre and Gender in Classical Antiquity*, ed. D. L. Munteanu, 221–39. London.

Graziosi, B., and J. Haubold. 2013. "Homeric Masculinity: ἠνορέη and ἀγηνορίη." *Journal of Hellenic Studies* 123: 60–76.

Green, C. M. C. 1994. "The Necessary Murder: Myth, Ritual, and Civil War in Lucan, Book 3." *Classical Antiquity* 13: 203–33.

Grewing, F. F., B. Acosta-Hughes, and A. Kirichenko, eds. 2013. *The Door Ajar. False Closure in Greek and Roman Literature and Art*. Heidelberg.

Griffin, J. 1980. *Homer on Life and Death*. Oxford.

Griffin, M. T. 1984. *Nero: The End of a Dynasty*. London.

Grillo, L. 2012 *The Art of Caesar's Bellum Civile: Literature, Ideology, and Community*. Cambridge.

Grimal, P. 1949. "L'épisode D'Antée dans la *Pharsale*." *Latomus* 8: 55–61.

———. 1960. "L' éloge de Néron au début de la Pharsale: est-il ironique?" *Revue des études latines* 38: 296–305.

Griset, E. 1955. "Lucanea III: L'anticesarismo." *Rivista di Studi Classici* 3: 56–61.

Gross, G. 2013. *Plenus litteris Lucanus. Zur Rezeption der horazischen Oden und Epoden in Lucans Bellum Civile*. Rahden.

Grottanelli, C. 1993. "Evento e modello nella storia antica: due eroi cesariani." In *La cultura in Cesare*, ed. D. Poli, 427–44. Rome.

Guastella, G. 2017. *Word of Mouth: Fama and Its Personifications in Literature from Ancient Rome to the Middle Ages*. Oxford.

Gunderson, E. 2000. *Staging Masculinity: The Rhetoric of Performance in the Roman World*. Ann Arbor.

Hadot, I. 2014. *Sénèque: Direction spirituelle et pratique de la philosophie. Philosophie du present*. Paris.

Haffter, H. 1957. "Dem schwanken Zünglein lauschend wachte Cäsar dort." *Museum Helveticum* 14: 118–26.

Halliwell, S. 2002. *The Aesthetics of Mimesis: Ancient Text and Modern Problems*. Princeton.

———. 2011. *Between Ecstasy and Truth. Interpretations of Greek Poetics from Homer to Longinus*. Oxford.

Hardie, P. R. 1986. *Virgil's Aeneid: Cosmos and Imperium*. Oxford.

———. 1989. "Flavian Epicists on Virgil's Epic Technique." *Ramus* 18: 3–30.

———. 1993. *The Epic Successors of Virgil. A Study in the Dynamics of a Tradition*. Cambridge.

———. 2008. "Lucan's Song of the Earth." *Papers on Ancient Literatures: Greece, Rome and the Near East* 4: 305–30.

———. 2011. "Lucan in the English Renaissance." In *Brill's Companion to Lucan*, ed. P. Asso, 491–506. Leiden.

———. 2012. *Rumour and Renown: Representations of Fama in Western Literature*. Cambridge.

———. 2013. "Lucan's *Bellum Civile*." In *A Companion to the Neronian Age*, ed. E. Buckley and M. T. Dinter, 225–40. Malden, Mass.

Harman, G. 1997. *The Nature of Morality: An Introduction to Ethics*. Oxford.

Harrison, E. L. 1970. "Divine Action in *Aeneid* book 2." *Phoenix* 24: 320–32.

Harrison, S. 2017. *Horace. Odes, Book II*. Cambridge.

Haskins, C. E., ed. 1887. *M. Annaei Lucani Pharsalia*, Edited with English notes by C. E. Haskins; with an introduction by W. E. Heitland. London.

Heitland, W. E. 1887. "Introduction." In: *M. Annaei Lucani Pharsalia*. Edited with English notes by C. E. Haskins; with an introduction by W. E. Heitland, ix-cxxxi. London.

Helzle, M. 1993. "Die Beschreibung des Apennin in Lucans *De bello civili* II 392–438." *Würzburger Jahrbücher für die Altertumswissenschaft* 19: 161–72.

———. 2008. "*Indocilis privata loqui:* The Characterisation of Lucan's Caesar." *Symbolae Osloenses* 69: 121–36.

Henderson, J. 1998. *Fighting for Rome*. Cambridge.

———. 1987. "Lucan / The Word at War." *Ramus* 16: 122–64. [Reprinted in *Oxford Readings in Classical Studies: Lucan*, ed. C. Tesoriero, 433–91. Oxford, 2010.]

Henderson Collins, J. 2012. "Prompts for Participation in Early Philosophical Texts." In *Performance in the Ancient World*, ed. E. Minchin, 151–83. Leiden.

Hershkowitz, D. 1998. *The Madness of Epic. Reading Insanity from Homer to Statius*. Oxford.

Hill, D. E., ed. and trans. 1985. *Ovid Metamorphoses I–IV*. Oxford.

Hill, T. D. 2004. *Ambitiosa mors: Suicide and the Self in Roman Thought and Literature*. London.

Hinds, S. 1998. *Allusion and Intertext: Dynamics of Appropriation in Roman Poetry*. Cambridge.

———. 2000. "Essentialized Epic: Genre and Gender from Macer to Statius." In *Matrices of Genre: Authors, Canons, and Society*, ed. M. Depew and D. Obbink, 221–304. Cambridge, Mass.

Holland, N. 1986. *The Dynamics of Literary Response*. Oxford.

Hollis, A. S. 2007. *Fragments of Roman Poetry c. 60 B.C.–A.D. 20*. Edited with introduction, translation, and commentary. Oxford.

Holmes, B. 2012. *Gender: Antiquity and Its Legacy*. London.

Holst-Warhaft, G. 1992. *Dangerous Voices: Women's Laments and Greek Literature*. London.

Hömke, N. 2010. "Bit by Bit Towards Death—Lucan's Scaeva and the Aesthetisization of Dying, in Lucan's *Bellum Civile*." In *Lucan's Bellum Ciuile: Between Epic Tradition and Aesthetic Innovation*, ed. N. Hömke and C. Reitz, 91–104. Berlin.

Housman, A. E. 1926. *M. Annaei Lucani Belli Civilis Libri Decem*. Oxford.

Hunink, V. 1992. *M. Annaeus Lucanus, Bellum Civile, Book III. A Commentary*. Amsterdam.

Hutchinson, G. O. 2018. *Plutarch's Rhythmic Prose*. Oxford.

Inwood, B., ed. 2003. *The Cambridge Companion to Stoicism*. Cambridge.

Iser, W. 1988. "The Reading Process a Phenomenological Approach." In *Modern Criticism and Theory: A Reader*, ed. D. Lodge, 211–28. London.

Jal, P. 1962. "Les dieux et les guerres civiles dans la Rome de la fin de la République." *Revue des études latines* 40: 170–200.

Johnson, W. R. 1987. *Momentary Monsters: Lucan and His Heroes.* Ithaca.

Kacandes, I. 1994. "Narrative Apostrophe: Reading, Rhetoric, Resistance in Michel Butor's 'La modification' and Julio Cortazar's 'Graffiti.'" *Style* 28: 329–49.

Kakkonen, G. G., and A. Penjak. 2015. "The Nature of Gender: Are Juliet, Desdemona and Cordelia to Their Fathers as Nature Is to Culture?" *Critical Survey* 27 18–35.

Karakasis, E. 2016. *T. Calpurnius Siculus. A Pastoral Poet in Neronian Rome.* Berlin.

Kaster, R. A. 1995. *C. Suetonius Tranquillus: De Grammaticis et Rhetoribus.* Oxford.

Kaufman, D. H. 2020. "Lucan's Cato and Popular (Mis)Conceptions of Stoicism." In *Lucan's Imperial World: The Bellum Civile in its Contemporary Contexts*, ed. L. Zientek and M. Thorne, 133–50. London.

Keith, A. 2000. *Engendering Rome: Women in Latin Epic.* Cambridge.

———. 2008. "Lament in Lucan's *Bellum Ciuile*." In *Lament: Studies in the Ancient Mediterranean and Beyond*, ed. A. Suter, 233–57. Oxford.

———. 2011. "Ovid in Lucan: The Poetics of Instability." In *Brill's Companion to Lucan*, ed. P. Asso, 111–32. Leiden.

Kenney, E. J. 2014. *Lucretius: De Rerum Natura Book III.* 2nd ed. Cambridge.

Kersten, M. 2018. *Blut auf Pharsalischen Feldern. Lucans Bellum Civile und Vergils Georgica.* Göttingen.

Kessler, J. 2011. "The Irony of Assassination: On the Ideology of Lucan's Invocation to Nero." *Studi italiani di filologia classica* 9: 129–44.

Kimmerle, N. 2015. *Lucan und der Prinzipat: Inkonsistenz und unzuverlässiges Erzählen im Bellum Civile.* Berlin.

Korenjak, M. 1996. *Die Erichthoszene in Lukans Pharsalia.* Frankfurt.

Kubiak, D. 1990. "Cornelia and Dido (Lucan 9.174–9)." *Classical Quarterly* 40: 577–78.

Lada, I. 1998. "Hellenistic Aesthetic: Philosophers and Literary Critics." In *Encyclopedia of Aesthetics*, ed. M. Kelly, 389–91. Oxford.

Langlands, R. 2018. *Exemplary Ethics in Ancient Rome.* Cambridge.

Lanzarone, N. 2016. *M. Annaei Lucani Belli Civilis liber VII.* Florence.

La Penna, A. 1979–80. "Mezenzio: una tragedia della tirannide e del titanismo antico." *Maia* 32: 3–30.

———. 2000. "La campagna di Curione in Africa. La narrazione e l'interpretazione di Cesare." In *L'ultimo Cesare. Scritti, riforme, progetti, poteri, congiure*, ed. G. Urso, 175–210. Rome.

Lapidge, M. 1989. "Stoic Cosmology and Roman Literature, First to Third Centuries A.D." *Aufstieg und Niedergang der römischen Welt* 2.36.3: 1379–429.

———. 2010. "Lucan's Imagery of Cosmic Dissolution." *Hermes* 107: 344–70. [Reprinted in *Oxford Readings in Classical Studies: Lucan*, ed. C. Tesoriero, 289–323. Oxford 2010.]

Lausberg, M. 1985. "Lucan und Homer." *Aufstieg und Niedergang der römischen Welt* 2.32.3: 1565–622.

Le Bonniec, H. 1970. "Lucain et la religion." In *Lucain: Sept exposés suivis de discussions*, ed. M. Durry,159–200. Geneva.

Leeman, A. D. 1985. *Form und Sinn, Studien zur römischen Literatur (1954–1984).* Frankfurt.

Leigh, M. 1997. *Lucan. Spectacle and Engagement*. Oxford.

———. 2000. "Lucan and the Libyan Tale." *Journal of Roman Studies* 90: 95–109.

———. 2010a. "Lucan's Caesar and the Sacred Grove: Deforestation and Enlightenment in Antiquity." In *Oxford Readings in Classical Studies: Lucan*, ed. C. Tesoriero, 201–38. Oxford.

———. 2010b. "César coup de foudre. La signification d'un symbole chez Lucain." In *Lucain en débat: Rhétorique, poétique et histoire*, ed. O. Devillers and S. Franchet d'Espèrey, 159–65. Bordeaux.

Liebeschuetz, J. H. W. G. 1979. *Continuity and Change in Roman Religion*. Oxford.

Lintott, A. W. 1971. "Lucan and the History of the Civil War." *Classical Quarterly* 21: 488–505. [Reprinted in *Oxford Readings in Lucan*, ed. C. Tesoriero, 239–68. Oxford 2010.]

Littlewood, C. 2002 "*Integer ipse?* Self-knowledge and Self-representation in Persius' 'Satires 4.'" *Phoenix* 56: 56–83.

———. 2016. "Elegy and Epic in Lucan's *Bellum Ciuile*." In *Roman Literary Cultures: Domestic Politics, Revolutionary Poetics, Civic Spectacle*, ed. A. Keith and J. Edmondson, 159–84. Toronto.

Lobur, J. A. 2008. *Consensus, Concordia and the Formation of Roman Imperial Ideology*. London.

Long, A. 2007. "Lucan and Moral Luck." *Classical Quarterly* 57: 183–97.

Long, A. A., and D. N. Sedley 1987. *The Hellenistic Philosophers*. 2 vols. Cambridge.

Longi, E. 1955. "Tre episodi del poema di Lucano." In *Studi in onore di Gino Funaioli*, ed. A. Signorelli, 181–88. Rome.

Louden, B. 2005. "The Gods in Epic, or the Divine Economy." In *A Companion to Ancient Epic*, ed. J. M. Foley, 90–104. Malden, Mass.

Lounsbury, R. C. 1975. "The Death of Domitius in the *Pharsalia*." *Transactions of the American Philological Association* 105: 209–12.

Loupiac, A. 1988. *La poétique des éléments dans "La Pharsale" de Lucain*. Brussels.

Lovatt, H. 2013. *The Epic Gaze: Vision, Gender and Narrative in Ancient Epic*. Cambridge.

Luck, G., ed. and trans. 2009. *Lukan, De bello civili, Der Bürgerkrieg*. Stuttgart.

Lyne, R. O. A. M. 1987. *Further Voices in Vergil's Aeneid*. Oxford.

Macdonald, C., ed. and trans. 1976. *Cicero Orations. In Catilinam 1–4. Pro Murena. Pro Sulla. Pro Flacco*. Cambridge, Mass.

Maes, Y. 2009. "One but Not the Same? Cato and Alexander in Lucan's Pharsalia 9.493–618 (and Caesar too)." *Latomus* 68: 657–79.

Malamud, M. 2003. "Pompey's Head and Cato's Snakes." *Classical Philology* 98: 31–44.

Mannering, J. 2013. "Seneca's Philosophical Writings: *Naturales Quaestiones, Dialogi, Epistulae Morales*." In *A Companion to the Neronian Age*, ed. E. Buckley and M. T. Dinter, 188–203. Malden, Mass.

Margolin, U. "Narrative 'You' Revisited." *Language and Style* 23: 425–46.

Marks, R. 2010. "Silius and Lucan." In *Brill's Companion to Silius Italicus*, ed. A. Augoustakis, 127–53. Leiden.

Marti, B. M. 1945. "The Meaning of the *Pharsalia*." *American Journal of Philology* 66: 352–76.

———. 1966. "Cassius Scaeva and Lucan's *inventio.*" In *The Classical Tradition: Literary and Historical Studies in Honour of Harry Caplan*, ed. L. Wallach, 239–57. Ithaca.

———. 1970. "La structure de *la Pharsale.*" In *Lucain, sept exposés suivis de discussions*, ed. M. Durry, 1–50. Geneva.

Martin, R. 2005. "Epic as a Genre." In *A Companion to Ancient Epic*, ed. J. M. Foley, 9–20. Malden, Mass.

Martindale, C. 1976. "Paradox, Hyperbole and Literary Novelty in Lucan's *De Bello Civili.*" *Bulletin of the Institute of Classical Studies* 23: 45–54.

———. 1981. "Lucan's Hercules: Padding or Paradigm? A Note on *De Bello Civili* 4.589–660." *Symbolae Osloenses* 56: 71–80.

———. 1993. *Redeeming the Text. Latin Poetry and the Hermeneutics of Reception.* Cambridge.

Maso, S. 2011. "The Risk in the Educational Strategy of Seneca." *Journal of Ancient Philosophy* 5:1–20.

Masters, J. 1992. *Poetry and Civil War in Lucan's Bellum Civile.* Cambridge.

———. 1994. "Deceiving the Reader: The Political Mission of Lucan *Bellum Civile* 7." In *Reflections of Nero*, ed. J. Elsner and J. Masters, 151–77. Chapel Hill.

Masterson, M. 2005. "Statius' *Thebaid* and the Realization of Roman Manhood." *Phoenix* 59: 288–315.

Matthews, M. 2008. *Caesar and the Storm: A Commentary on Lucan, De Bello Civili, Book 5 Lines 476–721.* Bern.

———. 2011. "The Influence of Roman Love Poetry (and the Merging of Masculine and Feminine) in Lucan's Portrayal of Caesar in the *De Bello Civili* 5.476–497." *Materiali e discussioni per l'analisi dei testi classici* 66: 121–38.

Mayer, R. 1979. "*Pharsalica Damna.*" *Mnemosyne* 32: 338–59.

Mazzoli, G. 1970. *Seneca e la poesia.* Milan.

McCauley, M. 2016. *Reproducing Rome: Motherhood in Virgil, Ovid, Seneca, and Statius.* Oxford.

McClellan, A. M. 2019. *Abused Bodies in Roman Epic.* Cambridge.

McClure, L. K., ed. 2002. *Sexuality and Gender in the Classical World: Readings and Sources.* Malden, Mass.

McCune, B. C. 2013–2014. "Lucan's *Militia amoris*: Elegiac Expectations in the *Bellum Civile.*" *Classical Journal* 109: 171–98.

McDonnell, M. 2006. *Roman Manliness: Virtus and the Roman Republic.* Cambridge.

McGuire, D. T. 1997. *Acts of Silence. Civil War, Tyranny, and Suicide in the Flavian Epic.* Hildesheim.

McGushin, F. 2006. *Foucault's Askesis: An Introduction to the Philosophical Life.* Evanston, Ill.

McHale, B. 1987. *Postmodernist Fiction.* New York.

McKeown, J. C. 1987. *Ovid, Amores: Text, Prolegomena, and Commentary.* Liverpool.

Mebane, J. 2020. "Lucan and the Specter of Sulla in Julio-Claudian Rome." In *Lucan's Imperial World: The Bellum Civile in Its Contemporary Contexts*, ed. L. Zientek and M. Thorne, 173–90. London.

Merli, E. 2005. "Historische Erzählung und epische Technik in *Pharsalia* 4, 581–824." In *Lucan im 21. Jahrhundert*, ed. C. Walde, 111–29. Munich.

Micozzi, L. 1999. "Aspetti dell'influenza di Lucano nella *Tebaide*." In *Interpretare Lucano*, ed. P. Esposito and L. Nicastri, 343–87. Naples.

Middlebrook, L. 2009. *Imperial Lyric: New Poetry and New Subjects in Early Modern Spain*. University Park, Pa.

Miller, F. J., and G. Goold, ed. and trans. 1916. *Ovid. Metamorphoses*. 2 vols. Cambridge Mass.

Miller, J. F. 2014. "Virgil's Salian Hymn to Hercules." *Classical Journal* 109: 439–63.

Miller, P. A. 1998. "The Classical Roots of Poststructuralism: Lacan, Derrida, and Foucault." *International Journal of the Classical Tradition* 5: 204–25.

Moles, J. L. 1983. "Virgil, Pompey, and the Histories of Asinius Pollio." *Classical World* 76: 287–88.

Montgomery, G. F. 2004. *Noces pour femme seule: Le féminin et le sacré dans l'oeuvre d'Albert Camus*. Amsterdam.

Morford, M. P. O. 1967. *The Poet Lucan. Studies in Rhetorical Epic*. Oxford.

Morgan, L. 1998. "Assimilation and Civil War: Hercules and Cacus. *Aeneid* 8." In *Vergil's Aeneid: Augustan Epic and Political Context*, ed. H. P. Stahl, 175–98. London.

———. 2000. "The Autopsy of C. Asinius Pollio." *Journal of Roman Studies* 90: 51–69.

Moskalew, W. 1982. *Formular Language and Poetic Design in the Aeneid*. Leiden.

Most, G. W. 1989. "Cornutus and Stoic Allegoresis: A Preliminary Report." *Aufstieg und Niedergang der römischen Welt* 2.36.3: 2014–65.

———. 1992. "*Disiecti Membra Poetae*: The Rhetoric of Dismemberment in Neronian Poetry." In *Innovations of Antiquity*, ed. R. Hexter and D. Seldon, 391–419. New York.

Mulhern, E. V. 2017. "*Roma(na) Matrona*." *Classical Journal* 112: 432–59.

Murnagham, S. 1995. "Sucking the Juice without Biting the Rind: Aristotle and Tragic *Mimesis*." *New Literary History* 26: 755–73.

Murphy, P. 2019. *Reconceiving Nature: Ecofeminism in Late Victorian Women's Poetry*. Columbia, Mo.

Murray, J. 2011. "Shipwrecked 'Argonauticas.'" In *Brill's Companion to Lucan*, ed. P. Asso, 57–79. Leiden.

Murray, P. 1981. "Poetic Inspiration in Early Greece." *Journal of Hellenic Studies* 101: 87–100.

Narducci, E. 1973. "Il tronco di Pompeo (Troia e Roma nella *Pharsalia*)." *Maia* 25: 317–25.

———. 1979. *La Provvidenza crudele. Lucano e la distruzione dei miti Augustei*. Pisa.

———. 2002. *Lucano: Un'epica contro L'impero. Interpretazione della Pharsalia*. Bari.

Nelis, D. P. 2011. "Praising Nero (Lucan, *De bello civili* 1.33–66)." In *Dicere laudes: Elogio, comunicazione, creazione del consenso*, ed. G. Urso, 253–64. Pisa.

———. 2014. "Empedoclean Epic: How Far Can You Go?" *Dictynna* 11. https://journals.openedition.org/dictynna/1057.

Newlands, C. E. 2011. *Statius, Silvae II*. Cambridge.

Nill, H. P. 2018. *Gewalt und Unmaking in Lucans Bellum Civile: Textanalysen aus narratologischer, wirkungsästhetischer und gewaltsoziologischer Perspektive*. Leiden.

Nix, S. A. 2008. "Caesar as Jupiter in Lucan's *Bellum Civile*." *Classical Journal* 103: 281–94.

Norbrook, D. 1999. *Writing the English Republic: Poetry, Rhetoric and Politics, 1627–1660*. Cambridge.

Nugent, S. G. 1994. "Mater Matters: The Female in Lucretius's *De Rerum Natura*." *Colby Quarterly* 30: 179–205.

Nussbaum, M. 1993. "Poetry and the Passions: Two Stoic Views." In *Passions and Perceptions. Studies in Hellenistic Philosophies of Mind*, ed. J. Brunschwig and M. Nussbaum, 97–149. Cambridge.

———. 1994. *The Therapy of Desire: Theory and Practice in Hellenistic Ethics*. Princeton.

Ogden, D. 2001. *Greek and Roman Necromancy*. Princeton.

———. 2002. "Lucan's Sextus Pompeius Episode: Its Necromantic, Political and Literary Background." In *Sextus Pompeius*, ed. A. Powell and K. Welch, 249–71. London.

O'Gorman, E. 2009. "Intertextuality and Historiography." In *The Cambridge Companion to the Roman Historians*, ed. A. Feldherr, 231–42. Cambridge.

O'Hara, J. J. 2007. *Inconsistency in Roman Epic: Studies in Catullus, Lucretius, Vergil, Ovid and Lucan*. Cambridge.

———. 2018. *Vergil, Aeneid Book 8*. Indianapolis.

O'Higgins, D. 1988. "Lucan as *Vates*." *Classical Antiquity* 7: 208–26.

Olson, K. 2017. *Masculinity and Dress in Roman Antiquity*. London.

Opelt, I. 1957. "Die Seeschlacht vor Massilia bei Lucan." *Hermes* 85: 435–45.

Ormand, K. 1994. "Lucan's *Auctor Vix Fidelis*." *Classical Antiquity* 13: 38–55.

Owen Eldred, K. 2002. "The Ship of Fools: Epic Vision in Lucan's Vulteius Episode." In *The Roman Gaze. Vision, Power, and the Body*, ed. D. Fredrick, 57–85. Baltimore.

Ozanam, A. M. 1990. "Le Mystère et le sacré dans le stoïcisme romain à l'époque néronienne." *Bulletin de l'Association Guillaume Budé* 3: 275–88.

Pagán, V. E. 2000. "The Mourning after: Statius *Thebaid* 12." *American Journal of Philology* 121: 423–52.

———. 2002. "Actium and Teutoburg: Augustan Victory and Defeat in Vergil and Tacitus." In *Clio and the Poets: Augustan Poetry and the Traditions of Ancient Historiography*, ed. D. S. Levene, and D. P. Nelis, 45–59. Leiden.

Paleit, E. 2013. *War, Liberty, and Caesar: Responses to Lucan's 'Bellum Ciuile,' ca. 1580–1650*. Oxford.

Palla, R. 1983. "Appunti sul makarismòs e sulla fortuna di un verso Vergiliano." *Studi classici e orientali* 33: 171–92.

Pandey, N. B. 2014. "Dilemma as a Tragic Figure of Thought in Lucan's *Bellum Civile*." *Illinois Classical Studies* 39: 109–38.

Panoussi, V. 2003. "Vergil and Epic Topoi in Lucan's Massilia." In *Being There Together. Essays in Honor of Michael C. J. Putnam on the Occasion of His Seventieth Birthday*, ed. P. Thibodeau and H. Haskell, 222–39. Afton, Minn.

———. 2009. *Greek Tragedy in Virgil's Aeneid: Ritual, Empire, and Intertext.* Cambridge.

———. 2019. *Brides, Mourners, Bacchae: Women's Rituals in Roman Literature.* Baltimore.

Papaioannou, S. 2012. "Landscape architecture on pastoral topography in Lucan's *Bellum Civile*." In *Singing in the Shadow . . . : Pastoral Encounters in Post-Vergilian Poetry,* ed. E. Karakasis, 73–110. Berlin.

Paperno, I. 1997. *Suicide as a Cultural Institution in Dostoyevsky's Russia.* Ithaca.

Paratore, E. 1943. "Vergilio georgico e Lucano." *Annali della Scuola Normale Superiore di Pisa* 2: 40–69.

Perkell, C. 1999. "Editor's Introduction." In *Reading Vergil's* Aeneid: *An Interpretive Guide,* ed. C. Perkell, 1–28. Norman, Okla.

———. 2002. "The Golden Age and Its Contradictions in the Poetry of Vergil." *Vergilius* 48: 3–39.

Phillips, O. C. 1968. "Lucan's Grove." *Classical Philology* 63: 296–300.

Piacentini, U. 1963. *Osservazioni sulla tecnica epica di Lucano.* Berlin.

Pichon, R. 1912. *Les sources de Lucain.* Paris.

Pillinger, E. 2012. "'And the Gods Dread to Hear Another Poem': The Repetitive Poetics of Witchcraft from Vergil to Lucan." *Materiali e discussioni per l'analisi dei testi classici* 68: 103–43.

Pitcher, L. 2008. "A Perfect Storm? Caesar and His Audiences at Lucan 5.504–702." *Classical Quarterly* 58: 243–9.

Pocock, L. G. 1959. "What made Pompey fight in 49 b.c.?" *Greece and Rome* 6: 68–81.

Pogorzelski, R. L. 2011. "*Orbis Romanus:* Lucan and the Limits of the Roman World." *Transactions of the American Philological Association* 141: 143–70.

Pomeroy, S. B. 1995. *Goddesses, Whores, Wives, and Slaves: Women in Classical Antiquity,* 2nd ed. New York.

Pratt, N. T. 1983. *Seneca's Drama.* Chapel Hill.

Pucci, J. 1998. *The Full Knowing Reader: Allusion and the Power of the Reader in the Western Literary Tradition.* New Haven.

Pypłacz, J. 2015. *When Legends come alive. A reading of Lucan's Pharsalia.* Kraków.

Quint, D. 1993. *Epic and Empire: Politics and Generic Form from Vergil to Milton.* Princeton.

Raaflaub, K. 2010. "Creating a Grand Coalition of True Roman Citizens." In *Citizens of Discord,* ed. B. Breed, C. Damon and A. Rossi, 159–70. Oxford.

Radicke, J. 2004. *Lucans Poetische Technik. Studien zum historischen Epos.* Leiden.

Rambaud, M. 1960. "L'opposition de Lucain au *Bellum Civile* de César." *L'Information literaire* 12: 155–62.

Ransom, C. 2011. "Aspects of Effeminacy and Masculinity in the *Iliad*." *Antichthon* 45: 35–57.

Reed, J. "*Mora* in the *Aeneid*." In *Wordplay and Powerplay in Latin,* ed. P. Mitsis and I. Ziogas, 87–105. Berlin.

Reif, M. 2016. *De arte magorum: Erklärung und Deutung ausgewählter Hexenszenen bei Theokrit, Vergil, Horaz, Ovid, Seneca und Lucan unter Berücksichtigung des Ritualaufbaus unter der Relation zu den Zauberpapyri.* Göttingen.

Reitz, C. 1999. "Katalog." In *Der Neue Pauly*, vol. 6, ed. H. Cancik, H. Schneider, and M. Landfester, 334–36. Suttgart.

———. 2006. *Die Literatur im Zeitalter Neros*. Darmstadt.

———. 2013. "Does Mass Matter? The Epic Catalogue of Troops as Narrative and Metapoetic Device." In *Flavian Epic Interactions*, ed. G. Manuwald and A. Voigt, 229–43. Berlin.

———. 2017. "Das Unendliche beginnen und sein Ende finden—Strukturen des Aufzählens in epischer Dichtung." In *Anfänge und Enden. Narrative Potentiale des antiken und nachantiken Epos*, ed. C. Schmitz, A. Jöne, and J. Kortmann, 105–18. Heidelberg.

———. 2021. "Reliability and Evasiveness in Epic Catalogues." In *Lists and Catalogues in Ancient Literature and Beyond. Towards a Poetics of Enumeration*, ed. C. Scheidegger Lämmle, K. Wesselmann, and R. Lämmle. Berlin.

Reitz, C., and S. Finkmann. 2019. "Introduction." In *Structures of Epic Poetry*, vol. 1, ed. C. Reitz and S. Finkmann, 1–21. Berlin.

Reitz, C., C. Scheidegger Lämmle, and K. Wesselmann. 2019. "Catalogues." In *Structures of Epic Poetry*, vol. 1. ed. C. Reitz and S. Finkmann, 653–726. Berlin.

Richlin, A., ed. 1992. *Pornography and Representation in Greece and Rome*. Oxford.

———. 2001. "Emotional Work: Lamenting the Roman Dead." In *Essays in Honor of Gordon Williams: Twenty-Five Years at Yale*, ed. E. Tylawsky and C.Weiss, 229–48. New Haven.

———. 2014. *Arguments with Silence. Writing the History of Roman Women*. Ann Arbor.

Rimell, V. 2015. *The Closure of Space in Roman Poetics: Empire's Inward Turn*. Cambridge.

Rives, J. B. 2007. *Religion in the Roman Empire*. Malden, Mass.

Roberts, D. H., F. M. Dunn, and D. P. Fowler, eds. 1997. *Classical Closure: Reading the End in Greek and Latin Literature*. Princeton.

Roche, P. A. 2005. "Righting the Reader: Conflagration and Civil War in Lucan's *De Bello Civili*." *Scholia* 14: 52–71.

———. 2009. *Lucan: De Bello Ciuili. Book 1*. Oxford.

———. 2015. "Lucan's *Bellum Ciuile* in the *Thebaid*." In *Brill's Companion to Statius*, ed. W. J. Dominik, C. E. Newlands, and K. Gervais, 393–407. Leiden.

———. 2016. "Lucan in Claudian's *in Eutropium*: Rhetoric, Paradox, and Exemplarity." In *Lucan and Claudian: Context and Intertext*, ed. D. Nelis, L. Galli Milić, and V. Berlincourt, 227–42. Heidelberg.

———. 2019. *Lucan, De Bello Ciuili, Book VII*. Cambridge

Roller, M. B. 1996. "Ethical Contradiction and the Fractured Community in Lucan's *Bellum Civile*." *Classical Antiquity* 15: 319–47.

———. 2001. *Constructing Autocracy: Aristocrats and Emperors in Julio-Claudian Rome*. Princeton.

———. 2015. "The Dialogue in Seneca's Dialogues (and Other Moral Essays)." In *The Cambridge Companion to Seneca*, ed. S. Bartsch and A. Schiesaro, 54–67. Cambridge.

———. 2018. *Models from the Past in Roman Culture: A World of Exempla*. Cambridge.

Rosner-Siegel, J. A. 1983. "The Oak and the Lightning. Lucan: *Bellum Civile* 1.135–157."
    Athenaeum 61: 165–77. [Reprinted in *Oxford Readings in Classical Studies: Lucan*,
    ed. C. Tesoriero, 184–200. Oxford, 2010.]

Ross, D. O. 1987. *Vergil's Elements. Physics and Poetry in the Georgics.* Princeton.

Rossi, A. 2000. "The *Aeneid* Revisited: The Journey of Pompey in Lucan's *Pharsalia.*"
    American Journal of Philology 121: 571–91.

———. 2001. "Remapping the Past: Caesar's Tale of Troy." *Phoenix* 55: 1–15.

Ross Taylor, L. 1931. *The Divinity of the Roman Emperor.* Middletown, Conn.

Rostagni, A. 1944. *Suetonio De Poetis e biografi minori.* Turin.

Rowland, R. J. 1968. "The Significance of Massilia in Lucan." *Hermes* 97: 204–8.

Rudd, N., ed. and trans. 2004. *Horace. Odes and Epodes.* Cambridge, Mass.

Rüpke, J. 2007. *Religion of the Romans.* Translated by R. Gordon. Cambridge.

Rutz, W. 1960. "Amor mortis bei Lucan." *Hermes* 88: 462–75.

Said, E. 1978. *Orientalism.* London.

Sannicandro, L. 2007. "Per uno studio sulle donne della *Pharsalia: Marcia Catonis.*"
    Museum Helveticum 64: 83–99.

———. 2010. *I personaggi femminili del Bellum Civile di Lucano.* Rahden.

Santangelo, F. 2015. "Testing Boundaries: Divination and Prophecy in Lucan." *Greece
    and Rome* 62: 177–88.

Santini, C. 1999. "Lucan 3, 399–455: lucus horridus e codice etimologico in Lucano."
    In *Interpretare Lucano*, ed. P. Esposito and L. Nicastri, 207–22. Naples.

Saylor, C. F. 1978. "*Belli Spes Inproba*: The Theme of Walls in Lucan, *Pharsalia* VI."
    Transactions of the American Philological Association 108: 243–57.

———. 1982. "Curio and Antaeus: The African Episode of Lucan *Pharsalia* IV."
    Transactions of the American Philological Association 112: 169–77.

———. 1986. "Wine, Blood, and Water: The Imagery of Lucan *Pharsalia* IV.148–401."
    Eranos 84: 149–56.

———. 1990. "*Lux Extrema*: Lucan, *Pharsalia* 4.402–581." *Transactions of the
    American Philological Association* 120: 291–300.

———. 2003. "Open and Shut: The Battle for Massilia in Lucan, *Pharsalia* III."
    Latomus 62: 381–86.

Scheid, J. 2003. *An Introduction to Roman Religion.* Translated by J. Lloyd. Edinburgh.

———. 2016. *The Gods, the State, and the Individual: Reflections on Civic Religion in
    Rome.* Translated by C. Ando. Philadelphia.

Schein, S. L. 1984. *The Mortal Hero: An Introduction to Homer's Iliad.* Berkeley.

Schindler, C. 2000. "Fachwissenschaft und Lehrdichtung in den Gleichnissen
    Lucans." *Antike und Abendland* 46: 139–152.

Schmitt, A. W. 1995. *Die direkten Reden der Massen in Lucans Pharsalia.* Frankfurt.

Schotes, H. A. 1969. *Stoische Physik, Psychologie und Theologie bei Lucan.* Bonn.

Schrijvers, P. H. 1988. "Deuil, désespoir, destruction (Lucain, La *Pharsale* II 1–234)."
    Mnemosyne 41: 341–54.

Schröter, R. 1975. "Die Krise der römischen Republik im Epos Lukans über den
    Bürgerkrieg." In *Krisen in der Antike. Bewusstsein und Bewältigung*, ed. G. Alföldy,
    K. Fittschen, and H. Flashar, 99–111. Düsseldorf.

Seewald, M. 2008. *Studien zum 9. Buch von Lucans "Bellum Civile" mit einem Kommentar zu den Versen 1–733*. Berlin.

Seitz, B. 2012. "Foucault and the Subject of Stoic Existence." *Human Studies* 35: 539–54.

Sellars, J. 2012. "Marcus Aurelius in Contemporary Philosophy." In *Blackwell's Companion to Marcus Aurelius*, ed. M. Van Ackeren, 532–45. Malden, Mass.

———. 2014. *Stoicism*. London.

Seo, J. M. 2011. "Lucan's Cato and the Poetics of Exemplarity." In *Brill's Companion to Lucan*, ed. P. Asso, 199–221. Leiden.

———. 2013. *Exemplary Traits: Reading Characeriziation in Roman Poetry*. Oxford.

Setaioli, A. 2000. *Facundus Seneca. Aspetti della lingua e dell'ideologia senecana*. Bologna.

Shackleton Bailey, D. R., ed. 1997. *Lucanus, De Bello Civili*. Stuttgart.

———, ed. and trans. 2010. *Cicero. Philippics*. 2 vols. Cambridge, Mass.

Sharrock, A. 2013. "*Uxorius*: The Praise and Blame of Husbands." *European Network on Gender Studies in Antiquity* 3: 162–94.

Sklenář, R. 1999. "Nihilistic Cosmology and Catonian Ethics in Lucan's *Bellum Civile*." *American Journal of Philology* 120: 281–96.

———. 2003. *The Taste for Nothingness: A Study of Virtus and Related Themes in Lucan's Bellum Civile*. Ann Arbor.

Spencer, D. 2005. "Lucan's Follies: Memory and Ruin in a Civil-War Landscape." *Greece and Rome* 52: 46–69.

Spentzou, E. 2018. "Violence and Alienation in Lucan's *Pharsalia*." In *Texts and Violence in the Roman World*, ed. M. R. Gale and J. H. D. Scourfield, 246–68. Cambridge.

Staley, A. G. 2010. *Seneca and the Idea of Tragedy*. Oxford.

Star, C. 2012. *The Empire of the Self: Self-Command and Political Speech in Seneca and Petronius*. Baltimore.

Stover, T. 2008. "Cato and the Intended Scope of the *Bellum Civile*." *Classical Quarterly* 58: 571–80.

———. 2014. "Lucan and Valerius Flaccus: Rerouting the Vessel of Epic Song." In *Brill's Companion to Valerius Flaccus*, ed. M. Heerink and G Manuwald, 290–306. Leiden.

Suter, A. 2008. *Lament: Studies in the Ancient Mediterranean and Beyond*. Oxford.

Syndikus, H. P. 1958. "Lucans Gedicht vom Bürgerkrieg: Untersuchungen zur epischen Technik und zu den Grundlagen des Werkes." Ph.D. diss., University of Munich.

Tarrant, R. J. 2002. "Chaos in Ovid's *Metamorphoses* and its Neronian Influence." *Arethusa* 35: 349–60.

Tasler, W. 1972. *Die Reden in Lucans Pharsalia*. Bonn.

Taylor, C. 1989. *Sources of the Self*. Cambridge, Mass.

Tesoriero, C. 2002. "*Magno proles indigna parente*: The Role of Sextus Pompeius in Lucan's *Bellum civile*. In *Sextus Pompeius*, ed. A. Powell and K. Welch, 229–47. London.

———. 2005. "Trampling over Troy." In *Lucan im 21. Jahrhundert*, ed. C. Walde, 202–215. Munich.

Thomas, R. F. 1986. "Virgil's *Georgics* and the Art of Reference." *Harvard Studies in Classical Philology* 90: 171–98.

———. 1988a. "Tree Violation and Ambivalence in Vergil." *Transactions of the American Philological Association* 118: 261–73.

———. 1988b. *Vergil: Georgics*. 2 vols. Cambridge.

———. 2001. *Virgil and the Augustan Reception*. Cambridge.

Thompson, L., and R. T. Bruère. 1968. "Lucan's Use of Vergilian Reminiscence." *Classical Philology* 63: 1–21

———. 1970. "The Vergilian Background of Lucan's Fourth Book." *Classical Philology* 65: 152–72.

Thorne, M. A. 2010. "Lucan's Cato: The Defeat of Victory, the Triumph of Memory." Ph.D. diss., University of Iowa.

———. 2016. "Speaking the Unspeakable: Engaging Nefas in Lucan and Rwanda 1994." *Thersites* 4: 77–119.

Tipping, B. 2011. "Terrible Manliness?: Lucan's Cato." In *Brill's Companion to Lucan*, ed. P. Asso, 223–36. Leiden.

Tola, E. 2016. "Écrire l'histoire, redéfinir un genre." In *Présence de Lucain*, ed. F. Galtier and R. Poignault, 197–209. Clermont-Ferrand.

Tracy, J. 2011. "Internal Evidence for the Completeness of the *Bellum Civile*." In *Brill's Companion to Lucan*, ed. P. Asso, 33–53. Leiden.

———. 2014. *Lucan's Egyptian Civil War*. Cambridge.

Traina, A. 1974. *Lo stile 'drammatico' del filosofo Seneca*. Bologna.

Treggiari, S. 1991. *Roman Marriage: Iusti Coniuges from The Time of Cicero to The Time of Ulpian*. Oxford.

Tucker, R. A. 1975. "The Banquets of Dido and Cleopatra." *Classical Bulletin* 52: 17–20.

———. 1983. "Lucan and Phoebus." *Latomus* 42: 143–51.

Turner, A. J. 2010. "Lucan's Cleopatra." In *Private and Public Lies: The Discourse of Despotism and Deceit in the Graeco-Roman World*, ed. A. J. Turner, J. H. K. O. Chong-Gossard, and F. J. Vervaet, 195–209. Leiden.

Uhle, T. 2006. "Antaeus—Hannibal—Caesar. Beobachtungen zur Exkurstechnik Lucans." *Hermes* 134: 442–54.

Utard, R. 2016. "Le combat naval devant Marseille au livre III du *Bellum Civile* de Lucain: ecriture d'un scène entre tradition épique et innovation." In *Présence de Lucain*, ed. F. Galtier and R. Poignault, 179–95. Clermont-Ferrand.

Vasunia, P. 2001. *The Gift of the Nile: Hellenizing Egypt from Aeschylus to Alexander*. Berkeley.

Vessey, D. 1973. *Statius and the Thebaid*. Cambridge.

Vitelli Casella, M. 2017. "Gli eventi bellici della costa orientale dell'Adriatico nell'opera di Lucano." In *Présence de Lucain*, ed. F. Galtier and R. Poignault, 55–82. Clermont-Ferrand.

Voigt, A. 2016. "The Power of the Grieving Mind: Female Lament in Statius's *Thebaid*." *Illinois Classical Studies* 41: 59–84.

Von Albrecht, M. 1970. "Der Dichter Lucan und die epische Tradition." In *Lucain, sept exposés suivis de discussions*, ed. M. Durry, 267–308. Geneva.

Waddington, C. H. 1960. *The Ethical Animal*. London.

Walde, C. 2001. *Die Traumdarstellungen in der griechisch-römischen Literatur*. Munich.

———. 2007. "Eine poetische Hydrologie. Flüsse und Gewässer in Lucans *Bellum Civile*." *Antike Naturwissenschaft und ihre Rezeption* 17: 59–84.

———. 2011. "Lucan's *Bellum Civile*: A Specimen of a Roman 'Literature of Trauma.'" In *Brill's Companion to Lucan*, ed. P. Asso, 283–302. Leiden.

———. 2012. "Fortuna bei Lucan—Vor- und Nachgedanken." In *Götter und menschliche Willensfreiheit: Von Lucan bis Silius Italicus*, ed. T. Baier, 57–74. Munich.

Walters, J. 1997. "Invading the Roman Body: Manliness and Impenetrability in Roman Thought." In *Roman Sexualities*, ed. J. P. Hallett and M. Skinner, 29–43. Princeton.

Wanke, C. 1964. *Seneca, Lucan, Corneille: Studien zum Manierismus der römischen Kaiserzeit und der französischen Klassik*. Heidelberg.

Warren, J., ed. 2009. *The Cambridge Companion to Epicureanism*. Cambridge.

Warren, L. B. 1970. "Roman Triumphs and Etruscan Kings: The Changing Face of the Triumph." *Journal of Roman Studies* 60: 49–66.

Webb, R. 2009. *Ekphrasis, Imagination and Persuasion in Rhetorical Theory and Practice*. Surrey.

Weinstock, S. 1971. *Divus Iulius*. Oxford.

Welch, K. 2012. *Magnus Pius: Sextus Pompeius and the Transformation of the Roman Republic*. Swansea.

Wheeler, S. M. 2002. "Lucan's Reception of Ovid's *Metamorphoses*." *Arethusa* 35: 361–80

Wick, C. 2004. *M. Annaeus Lucanus, Bellum civile liber IX*. 2 vols. Munich.

Wildberger, J. 2005. "*Quanta sub nocte iaceret nostra dies* (Lucan. 9,13f.)—Stoizismen als Mittel der Verfremdung bei Lucan." In *Lucan im 21. Jahrhundert*, ed. C. Walde, 56–88. Munich.

Williams, C. A. *Roman Homosexuality*. Oxford.

Williams, G. 1978. *Change and decline*. Berkeley.

Williams, G. D. 2015 "Style and Form in Seneca's Writing." In *The Cambridge Companion to Seneca*, ed. S. Bartsch and A. Schiesaro, 135–49. Cambridge.

———. 2017. *Pietro Bembo on Etna: The Ascent of a Venetian Humanist*. Oxford.

Wills, J. 2011. *Repetition in Latin Poetry. Figures of Allusion*. Oxford.

Wilson, M. 1987. "Seneca's Epistles to Lucilius: A Revaluation." *Ramus* 16: 102–21.

Winterbottom, M., ed. and trans. 1974. *Seneca the Elder. Declamations*. 2 vols. Cambridge, Mass.

Woodruff, P. 2008. *The Necessity of Theater: The Art of Watching and Being Watched*. Oxford.

Woodworth, D. C. 1930. "The Function of the Gods in Vergil's *Aeneid*." *Classical Journal* 26: 112–26.

Wyke, M. 2002. *The Roman Mistress: Ancient and Modern Representations*. Oxford.

Zissos, A. 2013. "Lucan and Caesar: Epic and *Commentarius*." In *Generic Interfaces in Latin Literature*, ed. T. Papanghelis, S. Harrison, and S. Frangoulidis, 125–50. Berlin.

Zlobec, B. 1999. "L'Adriatico settentrionale nella Pharsalia di Lucano: tra scienza e mito." *Živa Antika* 49: 119–54.

Zwierlein, O. 1974. "Cäser und Kleopatra bei Lucan und in späterer Dichtung." *Antike und Abendland* 20: 54–73.

———. 2010. "Lucan's Caesar at Troy." In *Oxford Readings in Classical Studies: Lucan*, ed. C. Tesoriero, 411–32. Oxford.

Contributors

Annemarie Ambühl is Associate Professor in Classical Philology at the Johannes Gutenberg University, Mainz. Her research interests focus on Latin epic and tragedy as well as on Hellenistic poetry and its reception in Rome. She has published a monograph on war and civil war in Lucan that investigates the transformation of mythical and literary patterns from Greek tragedy and Hellenistic poetry (*Krieg und Bürgerkrieg bei Lucan und in der griechischen Literatur. Studien zur Rezeption der attischen Tragödie und der hellenistischen Dichtung im Bellum civile*, 2015), and she has several contributions to edited volumes on Lucan.

Konstantinos Arampapaslis holds a doctorate in Classical Philology from the University of Illinois at Urbana–Champaign. His work focuses on the depiction of magic and witchcraft in the literature of the Neronian period and especially its connections with the religious life of the first century c.e. His research interests include the topic of marginality in the setting of the Roman empire as well as stereotypes and prejudice in Neronian and Flavian literature.

Antony Augoustakis is Professor of Classics at the University of Illinois at Urbana–Champaign. He is the author of several books and edited volumes, most recently *Statius, Thebaid 8* (2016), *Fides in Flavian Literature* (2019), and *Campania in the Flavian Poetic Imagination* (2019). He is in the final stages of a commentary on Silius Italicus's *Punica 3*, coedited with Joy Littlewood. He serves as editor of the *Classical Journal*.

Christopher L. Caterine earned his doctorate in Classics from the University of Virginia in 2014. His research on rhetoric and its emotional impact on the reader of Lucan's *Bellum Ciuile* led him to a career as a communications strategist and writer. In addition to his scholarly publications, he is the author of *Leaving Academia: A Practical Guide* (2020). Chris currently lives in New Orleans with his wife, Mallory, their son, Caleb, and their cat, Li'l Easy.

Robert Cowan is Senior Lecturer in Classics at the University of Sydney, having previously held posts in Exeter, Bristol, and Oxford. His research interests range over much of Greek and Latin literature. He has published on Sophocles, Aristophanes, Plautus, Lucretius, Catullus, Cicero, Sallust, Cinna, Ticida, Varius, Virgil, Horace, Ovid, Columella, Seneca, Statius, Valerius Flaccus, Silius, Martial, Suetonius, and Juvenal, as well as on ancient graffiti, the politics of Graeco-Roman tragedy, and the operatic reception of Greek tragedy. His main specialisms are Roman epic and tragedy, and he is currently working on commentaries to Virgil *Aeneid* 4 and Statius *Thebaid* 10.

Francesca D'Alessandro Behr, a native of Italy, is Professor of Italian and Classical Studies at the University of Houston in Texas. Her interests cover ancient and renaissance epic poetry, classical reception, love poetry, gender studies, and translation studies. Her book on Lucan, *Feeling History: Lucan, Stoicism, and the Aesthetics of Passion*, appeared in 2007, and another focused on the classical reception, *Arms and the Woman: Classical Tradition and Women Writers in the Venetian Renaissance*, in 2018.

Michael Dewar is Professor of Classics at the University of Toronto. He is the author of the commentaries *Statius, Thebaid IX* (1991) and *Claudian, Panegyricus De Sexto Consulatu Honorii Augusti* (1996), and of *Leisured Resistance: Villas, Literature and Politics in the Roman World* (2014). He has also published numerous articles and book chapters on Virgil, Ovid, Lucan, Statius, Claudian, Sidonius Apollinaris, Venantius Fortunatus, and Corippus.

Martin T. Dinter is Senior Lecturer in Latin Literature and Language at King's College London. He is author of *Anatomizing Civil War: Studies in Lucan's Epic Technique* (2012), editor of the *Cambridge Companion to Roman Comedy* (2019), as well as coeditor of *A Companion to the Neronian Age* (2013). He has published articles on Virgil, Horace, Lucan, Seneca, Roman comedy, and Flavian epic and recently completed a book-length study on Cato the Elder. He has coedited three volumes on Roman declamation: *Ps-Quintilian* (2016), *Calpurnius Flaccus* (2017), and *Seneca the Elder* (2020), as well as a special issue of *Trends in Classics* on intermediality (2019).

Lauren Donovan Ginsberg is Associate Professor of Classical Studies at Duke University. Her research focuses on the drama, epic, and historiography of the early Roman empire. She is especially interested in cultural memory studies, intertextuality, and Roman literature's treatment of the theme of civil war. She is the author of *Staging Memory, Staging Strife: Empire and Civil War in the Octavia* (2017) and the coeditor of *After 69: Writing Civil War in Flavian Rome* (2018).

Paolo Esposito is Professor of Latin Language and Literature at the University of Salerno. He is the author of *Il racconto della strage* (1987), *La narrazione inverosimile* (1994), *Lucano, Bellum Civile libro IV* (2009), and many articles and chapters (mainly on Lucan but also on Catullus, Cicero, Virgil, Livy, Ovid, Seneca, Persius, Petronius, Calpurnius Siculus, Valerius Flaccus, Statius, Apuleius, and Claudian). He is also the editor of *Ovidio: da Roma all'Europa* (1998), *Interpretare Lucano* (1999), *Lucano e la tradizione dell'epica latina* (2004), *Gli scolii a Lucano ed altra scoliastiaca latina* (Pisa 2004), and *Letture e lettori di Lucano* (2015).

Lavinia Galli Milić is a lecturer in Latin at the University of Geneva and a Swiss National Science Foundation (SNSF) research associate. Her research focuses on first century c.e. epic poetry (Lucan, Valerius Flaccus, Statius) and late Latin (Dracontius, the *Anthologia Latina*, and Venantius Fortunatus). She is the author of *Blossii Aemilii Dracontii Romulea VI–VII* (2008), a critical edition and commentary, and coeditor of collective books on Lucan and on Flavian epic. She is currently collaborating on the project *Digital Statius: the Achilleid*, funded by the SNSF and led by Damien Nelis.

Markus Kersten studied Latin, Greek, and mathematics at the universities of Rostock and Groningen from 2006 until 2013. In 2017 he completed his doctorate at Rostock. Since 2019 he has held a postdoctoral position at the University of Basel. His main research areas are Roman epic, the appearance of classical poetry in bibliophile editions, and late Latin literature, especially Ausonius. In 2018 his thesis, *Blut auf Pharsalischen Feldern: Lucans Bellum Ciuile und Vergils Georgica*, won the Joachim Jungius-Preis and was published in the Hypomnemata series. Since 2020 Kersten is junior member of the Academy of Sciences and Literature (Mainz).

Damien Nelis has been Professor of Latin at the University of Geneva since 2005. Before that, from 1999 to 2005, he was Professor of Latin at Trinity College Dublin. He works mainly on Latin poetry, with a special interest in the epic tradition. He is currently writing a book on Vergil's *Georgics*.

Christiane Reitz is retired as Professor of Latin at Rostock University, where she worked from 1999 to 2019. She has published widely on ancient epic poetry, both Greek and Latin. Her latest project is *Structures of Epic Poetry*, a publication in four volumes, coedited with Simone Finkmann (2019). She is also interested in concepts of the preservation and transfer of knowledge—didactic poetry, technical writing, and epitomizing genres—and in the reception of the classical tradition, both in literature and art history.

Paul Roche is Associate Professor in Latin at the University of Sydney. He is the author of commentaries on two books of Lucan's *Civil War*, book 1 (2009) and book 7 (2019). He has edited volumes on politics in Latin literature (with W. J. Dominik and J. Garthwaite, 2009) and on Pliny's *Panegyricus* (2011). He is currently writing commentaries on book 10 of Lucan's *Civil War* and book 1 of Tacitus's *Annals*.

Andrew Zissos is Professor of Classics and Director of the Global Cultures program at the University of California–Irvine. He is the author of numerous articles on imperial Roman literature and its reception, along with a commentary on book 1 of Valerius Flaccus's *Argonautica* (2008); he is also editor of *A Companion to the Flavian Age of Imperial Rome* (2016) and coeditor, with Ingo Gildenhard, of *Transformative Change in Western Thought: A History of Metamorphosis from Homer to Hollywood* (2013). He is currently writing a commentary on book 6 of Lucan's *Civil War*.

Index of Passages Cited

General Index

CPSIA information can be obtained
at www.ICGtesting.com
Printed in the USA
LVHW112339280821
696353LV00020B/2546